Reflections on Intelligence

Also by R. V. Jones

Most Secret War
Future Conflict and New Technology
Some Thoughts on 'Star Wars'
Instruments and Experiences

REFLECTIONS ON INTELLIGENCE

R. V. JONES

HEINEMANN : LONDON

William Heinemann Ltd
Michelin House, 81 Fulham Road, London SW3 6RB
LONDON MELBOURNE AUCKLAND

First published 1989

British Library Cataloguing in Publication Data
Jones, R. V. (Reginald Victor) 1911–
Reflections on intelligence.
1. Intelligence operations
I. Title
327.1'2

ISBN 0 434 37724 4

Printed and bound in Great Britain
by Richard Clay Ltd, Bungay

Contents

Author's Acknowledgements

The first suggestion ever made to me that I could write a book based on my experiences in Intelligence came in 1945 from Mr A. J. W. Hill, then a Squadron Leader armaments officer in the Royal Air Force and later Managing Director of the Heinemann Group. It is therefore all the greater pleasure to acknowledge his help, more than 40 years later, in the publication of this book. I am most grateful, too, for the support and encouragement of Miss Helen Fraser, the present Publisher of William Heinemann.

I am especially grateful to Herr Peter Mayer for permission to describe how his father came to write the Oslo Report of 1939: the book will be, I hope, a testimony to its importance. The other main feature in the Oslo story was Harry Cobden Turner, and I gladly thank his son-in-law, Canon Maurice Ridgway, for comments on those chapters in which his part is described.

On the historical side, I have drawn on the generous help of Air Commodore Henry Probert of the Air Historical Branch of the Ministry of Defence, and of Herr Helmut Drubba and Professor Jürgen Rohwer and Herr Fritz Trenkle in Germany. M. Maurice Royaux, MBE, of the Belgian Resistance, gave me valuable enlightenment on the contributions of some of his colleagues, while M. Pierre Julitte of the French Resistance told me the inspiring story of endurance and sacrifice in the notorious 'Dora' concentration camp. Mr Stein Ulrich of the Norwegian Security Service has helped with some details of the Oslo story; and Dr Steven Dedijer, of the Department of Intelligence in the University of Lund in Sweden has, as ever, been a stimulating provider of little-known items of intelligence history.

Repeated encouragement has come from many authorities in

the United States: among them have been Dr Tony Cacioppo of the Foreign Technology Division, of USAF, Dr Michael Handel of the US Army War College, General Doyle Larson of Electronic Security Command USAF, the Hon. Amrom Katz of RDA, Dr John Roche of Tufts University, Dr O. G. Villard of Stanford Research Institute, and Dr Walter Pforzheimer, whose personal intelligence library is unrivalled. To all these gentlemen, and many more, I am much indebted.

Introduction

One of the features of the Second World War was the intense application of science and of scientific method to military technology and military logistics. It therefore became important, and sometimes vital, to find out what your opponent was likely to do in these fields. *Most Secret War*, published in 1978, gave an account of how scientific intelligence consequently evolved as a new branch of intelligence, and of my part in it. The task was to anticipate the new applications of science to warfare by the Germans, which included the radio-beams to guide the *Luftwaffe* to our cities in the Blitz, and radar to defend the Reich against our counter-offensive by Bomber Command and to protect the coast of France against surprise by Allied invasion forces, followed by the retaliation weapons, the V1 flying bomb and the V2 rocket.

From time to time, each of these episodes brought me into contact with the highest levels of command and most notably, of course, with Churchill himself. They also resulted in my meeting many of those who gained vital information for us and thereby learning something of their remarkable, and often heroic, exploits: the men and women of the Resistance movements, the airmen who flew the photographic and reconnaissance aircraft, the radio intercept operators who fed Bletchley, the cryptographers themselves, the interrogators of prisoners, and the examiners of captured equipment.

In *Most Secret War* I aimed to show how each of these sources contributed to the building up of our intelligence appreciations, and thus to some crucial decisions in the conduct of the war; and I attempted to draw some of the lessons I learned in the conduct of intelligence itself. Part One of the present book reflects on these lessons, supplemented by those arising from subsequent experiences in peace as well as war, and by what I have learnt from other authors with experience of work in intelligence and its kindred activities of security and deception. My aim has been to illuminate the philosophy and ethics of all these activities by following the precept of Thucydides that 'history is philosophy teaching through examples'.

An ethical approach to intelligence and security is all the more desirable in view of the much publicized scandals of the last forty years. These may well have given the impression that intelligence is invariably a dirty business; but although it has often to be shady, at least in the sense that intelligence can rarely be efficiently conducted in the full glare of public limelight, it need not be dirty. The same applies to a security service; but while there is a need for official secrecy, much will suffer if it is carried to paranoiac excess.

Such issues are discussed in Part One, along with two others that stemmed from my involvement in defence science. *Most Secret War* and other books of its period may have given the impression that scientific support for the armed services started with my own generation of scientists. In fact we could not have done nearly as much as we did, if the trail had not already been blazed for us by the immediately preceding generation, that of Lindemann and Tizard, through their efforts in World War I and the inter-war years. Space prevented *Most Secret War* from adequately making this point, and I have therefore taken the opportunity here to include a chapter on science in World War I in partial expiation. Moreover, since the help that science can give has at times been spurned and at others over-rated, Part One concludes with a chapter discussing both the value and the limitations of scientific method when applied to problems of defence and, by implication, of life generally.

Although *Most Secret War* with its 500-odd pages was so long, it was not long enough for at least one correspondent, who wrote:

> I have just finished reading your book 'Most Secret War'. I must say, how much I enjoyed it, and wished that there was Volume 2 still to come.

It transpired that the writer was at the time serving a sentence in a high security prison for burglary aggravated by violence. I trust that he is 'out' by now, and am only sorry that the present book could not be produced in time to lighten his sojourn 'inside'. His letter was one of many from both the Allied and the German sides which have added to my knowledge of wartime episodes; and I have drawn on such letters, and on some fresh experiences, to form Part Two of this book as a series of postscripts to *Most Secret War*.

The question most frequently raised by correspondents has been 'Who wrote the Oslo Report?' This report, which was anonymously sent to our Naval Attaché in Oslo in 1939, told us much about the forthcoming German applications of technology to warfare. The source was for many years a mystery; but in 1954 I learned his identity through a preposterous sequence of coincidences, which I was tempted to relate in *Most Secret War*. Even in 1978, though, disclosure might have embarrassed him; and since I had no secure way of ascertaining his wishes, I excluded any clues to his identity. Now, however, I am free to tell the story: it forms Part Three.

Part One

1

Personal Experiences in Intelligence Since 1946

'Nothing fails like success,' said Dean Inge, for success is apt to induce fatal complacency in the minds of those who have achieved it. At first sight this may be judged true of the fortunes of scientific intelligence in the years after 1945, but the basic reason was somewhat different. Up to 1940 there had been little interest in its possibilities, and even by 1943 neither the Admiralty nor the War Office had devoted even a single officer to it. But with the successive contributions it made in the Blitz, the Bomber Offensive, the U-boat War, the D-Day landings and the V-weapons campaign, its importance came to be realized: and its very success resulted in a scramble of too many bodies to take it over.

Its resulting misfortunes in the immediate post-war years have been outlined in *Most Secret War*;[1] and by 1952 these had reached the stage where Winston Churchill, now Prime Minister again, asked for my temporary release from Aberdeen to see what I could do to bring the organization of scientific intelligence back to its wartime efficiency. I was to be appointed as Director of Scientific Intelligence in the Ministry of Defence, and also as scientific adviser to GCHQ; and I was to have a seat on the Joint Intelligence Committee. Surely, all this should have been enough to give me the necessary power to put things right, especially with Churchill's backing – and so it might have been if we had been starting with clean slates and free from vested interests. But since these interests were those that had crippled scientific intelligence in 1945 and had in the meantime invested themselves still further, I was so far from sanguine that when my wife, Vera, commented that going back to Whitehall should 'make your reputation' I replied, 'I cannot make a reputation there, only lose one!' Even so, and even though it would entail seeing my family back in Aberdeen for only one weekend a month and halting the now promising build-up of research in my laboratory, to answer Churchill's call was evident duty.

Return to Intelligence, 1952

To sketch the situation that I expected to find, it is necessary to summarize what had happened after 1945. Besides matters of personal ambition, inter-service rivalry was still strong; moreover a climate of egalitarianism had set in, and so no one of the three Services was to have the major say in scientific intelligence, despite the obvious fact that the Air Staff had shown by far the greatest interest in what it could achieve. So air scientific intelligence was to be reduced in status while the other two Services created their own sections, largely with staff who had no experience of work in intelligence and not a great deal in science. The result was akin to that experienced in the contemporaneous socialization of Britain in the post-war years, where the mood was epitomized by J. K. Galbraith's 'If you can't comfort the afflicted, afflict the comfortable.' Then in a gesture towards inter-service co-operation the three scientific intelligence sections were to be separated from their service staffs and located together in some houses, long dilapidated by wartime use by American forces, in Bryanston Square. Co-ordination between the three service interests was to be effected by a committee of the heads of the three sections together with the heads of the technical intelligence sections of the three Services – and in the interests of egalitarianism, the chairmanship of the committee was to be rotated at three-monthly intervals between the six heads.

When, not surprisingly, this arrangement proved ineffectual, the rotating chairmanship was abandoned in favour of a full-time chairman, who was to be a scientist of standing, and Sir David Brunt was appointed. Again, he found the arrangements frustrating and he shortly resigned.

Then Dr B. K. Blount, who had been head of the scientific section of the Control Commission in Germany, came in; he succeeded in making several improvements, including getting the scientific intelligence sections back from Bryanston Square to the Whitehall area and the technical intelligence sections out of their service ministries into the same building. But, again, he encountered great frustrations and moved to be Deputy Secretary of the Department of Scientific Research. This was the point at which Churchill called me back in 1952.

Of the task to which I was now committed I knew that Sir David Brunt (later the Physical Secretary of the Royal Society) had written in his note of resignation, 'I am sure that if there is any one man in this country who will take on the job, knowing the true conditions, he must be unique, and either a saint or a fool.' It is for others to judge which of these two categories I fell into: in retrospect I find more comfort in an observation by the late Alexander Keith on the Menzies family in the fifteenth and sixteenth centuries: 'They were moreover never afraid to be on the losing side, a test of greatness that few families can pass.'[2]

So in September 1952 I moved to London to see what I could do. Fortunately I had recently been made a member of the Athenaeum and had been offered a bedroom in the Club, which was conveniently near my office on an upper floor of the building in Northumberland Avenue that had once been the Metropole Hotel. The building, which had for many years been occupied by a miscellaneous succession of lower-category government organizations, was in an advanced state of decrepitude with failing lifts, peeling paint, and rotting linoleum; and the scientific intelligence offices were in what were presumably once the servants' quarters on the top floor. Yet even these were better than the premises to which scientific intelligence had previously been exiled in Bryanston Square, north of Marble Arch.

As for a staff, there was a mixed assembly of men who had been posted to intelligence from the scientific research directorates connected with the armed services. Few had been selected by anyone with intelligence experience, and most had shown insufficient promise for their research directorates to be anxious to retain them. Fortunately I had inherited as Deputy Director Hugh Young, whom I had known in the early radar effort at Bawdsey and who was both a physics graduate and a Colonel in the Territorial Army. Added to a deep sense of service, he had such patience and tact as amply to compensate for all deficiencies in those qualities on my part.

As Director of Scientific Intelligence my primary task was to strengthen the Directorate so that it could effectively fulfil its function of anticipating the applications of science to warfare by potential opponents of British interests. In this function it needed to be able to direct the collection of intelligence by every available channel, and to form from the intelligence so collected appreciations of what potential opponents were likely to achieve regarding new weapons and techniques of warfare. To direct collection effectively, it would help the Directorate to know what lines were showing promise in our own research and development laboratories, for our opponents might be working on similar lines; and it would also be helpful to know where our own Services thought their own weapons and techniques were vulnerable, so that we could look particularly for any developments abroad that were particularly dangerous threats. Thus, we in scientific intelligence needed the closest possible contacts with the agencies collecting intelligence on the one hand, and with our Service and research directorates on the other. And in addition we needed a capacity for independent constructive thought, so as to conceive better or new ways in which intelligence might be gained, and to look for developments which our opponents might have made but which had not been invented or thought of by our own side.

To improve the staff in the Directorate, it was necessary to engage the interest of the research establishments and the chief scientists in the ministries who controlled them, so that they would understand that intelligence was a sufficiently vital function to justify the appointment to it of some of their best men, and would not use the intelligence organization as a convenient 'trash bin' for their misfits. And I quickly found that the close relationship between the scientific intelligence staff and the operational staffs in the Services which was – as *Most Secret War* described – so important in World War II, no longer existed. This was partly due to the isolation of scientific intelligence from the Services in the Blackett reorganization of 1946, emphasized by the interposition of the technical intelligence branches between scientific intelligence and the Services. Tizard himself had attributed the success of his famous pre-war committee on air defence mainly to the fact that this committee consisted 'of scientists and serving officers working together', and its brilliant progress exemplified his conclusion that 'This is the great lesson of the last war.'

That lesson, though, was being forgotten; and for this the creation of the Ministry of Defence was itself partly to blame. Personally I had supported its setting up, because I thought that the bringing together of all three service intelligence organizations into the one Ministry would improve inter-service relations on intelligence matters, particularly in those fields which were of interest to more than one service. In World War II, for example, German anti-aircraft guns were of the most vital interest to the Royal Air Force; but in Britain, the expertise with these guns resided in the Army, which also had a secondary interest in the German guns to find what could be learnt from them that might improve our own gunnery. Similarly, while the rocket-propelled glider bombs used by the *Luftwaffe* were primarily an intelligence responsibility of air intelligence, the Royal Navy was even more acutely interested in them because its ships were their intended targets. Since in such instances one service had the primary responsibility for intelligence of the greatest interest to one of its sister services, difficulties could occur through imperfect intercommunication. These difficulties would be lessened if intelligence for all three Services was carried out in a centralized Ministry of Defence.

This was what was gradually being aimed at, but I could see that there was a price to be paid. In such an arrangement we in scientific intelligence no longer had that direct contact with the 'sharp end' of the Air Force that had been so fruitful under the old arrangement – or, at the very least, we would have had to make strenuous efforts to keep the contact going. Reporting on the situation that I found, I described the post-war attenuation of relations:

> I regard this trend as unfortunate. The DSI staff were as much to blame as anybody, since it was the clearest foreseeable danger that they faced in going to the Ministry of Defence, and they should have made great efforts to maintain their contacts . . . No trouble would, of course, occur if officers in the service ministries could always see that the Ministry of Defence is not a foreign body, and that scientists in the Ministry are just as anxious to help the Services as they would be if they sat immediately in the service ministries. I felt, however, that even some of my former colleagues on the Air Staff regarded the Ministry of Defence not only as a foreign body but as a stage of degradation towards the nebulosities of NATO.[3]

The experience once again brought home to me the drawbacks of a large monolithic organization: the larger it is, the larger is also likely to be the number of links between those taking the decisions at the top of the organization and those at 'the sharp end' who actually have to carry out their orders, and the more difficult it is for the individual at the sharp end to identify himself with the aspirations and fortunes of the organization of which he is a part. Moreover, every further link introduced into a chain of command is likely to attenuate the acuity of experience of what is happening at the sharp end; and the bigger an organization is, the greater the demands – administrative, personal and physical – on the man at the top, and the fewer the individuals who can match up to them. Such factors tended to be overlooked in the enthusiasm for nationalization in the post-war years, and have justly contributed to the disillusion with the nationalized industries that has since occurred.

The three Services, with their intense internal loyalties, patently distrusted their subordination to the Ministry of Defence and their resultant loss of individual independence. To keep itself as strong as possible relative to the Ministry, a service would therefore try to hold its best officers on its own staff, and only release its second-best for posts in the Ministry. I tried to persuade my old colleagues on the Air Staff that this was a mistaken policy: the Service should post some of its best officers into the Ministry, so as to ensure that its interests would be represented as ably as possible at the centre where the key decisions would ultimately have to be made.

The drawbacks were compounded by the Ministry's own attitude, which appeared to me to be unduly timorous about exerting a co-ordinating leadership over the individual Services, the need for which had been the main reason for its creation. It seemed over-anxious to avoid following the precedent of the *Oberkommando der Wehrmacht*, whose creation in Germany in 1938 was held to have failed in its aims.

The Ministry was therefore not yet a strong base from which to work, and there were some difficult administrative problems to be solved. Of these, two were dominant: electronic intelligence and nuclear intelligence. Each of them had been inaugurated in World War II by my scientific intelligence unit on the Air Staff and had since 1945 been wrested away by other organizations.

Electronic Intelligence

With electronic intelligence the problem went back to at least 1939, for although the signals intelligence and cryptography of Room OB40 at the Admiralty in 1914–18 had been so brilliantly successful, as had Bletchley in 1939–45, the signals intelligence organization had shown almost no interest in radio signals other than those intended to convey messages. My very first survey of our intelligence organization, dated 7 December 1939, had reported:

> Enquiries have shown that there has been no systematic observation of evidence regarding German RDF [radar] transmissions . . . It is important that this matter be prosecuted vigorously.

Much of *Most Secret War* is concerned with the development of electronic intelligence in the war years following 1939, and so its progress will not be reiterated here. But we may fairly ask why the prospective interception of radar and radio-navigational signals had been so ignored by the signals intelligence organizations. The answer lies partly at least in the fact that, in the language of classical physics, the aether can be used in two quite different ways. The first is to transmit radio waves whose amplitude or frequency is modulated either in sympathy with sounds such as those of the human voice or musical instruments, or with signals such as the dots and dashes of the Morse code or the more complex characteristics of telemetry or remote control. In all these applications, intelligence is imposed on the radio signals as they are being transmitted, and can be extracted again, as they are duly processed upon interception. To such applications the classical signals intelligence organizations were impressively alert.

The second way in which radio waves and the aether can be exploited is quite different. Since the waves travel with a definite velocity they can be used to indicate distances between points, or how points are spatially related. Suppose a radio wave is sent out from one point and strikes an object, say an aircraft, at another point. If some of the wave is then reflected back to the first point, then the time that this echo takes to return provides a measure of the distance of the second point from the first: this is the principle of radar. Or we can send out similar waves at the same time from two points, and note the time interval between the two waves as they arrive at a third point. If, for example, they arrive simultaneously, they must have travelled equal distances from the two transmitting points, and therefore the third point must lie on the right bisector of the line joining the two transmitting points. This is the principle underlying the simplest system of radio-beam navigation. With more refinement we can measure the time interval between the waves arriving at any point not on the right bisector, and can therefore deduce how much further this point must lie from one of the transmitting points than from the other; and with three transmitting points this information can lead to a definite 'fix' of the receiving point. This principle underlies such navigational systems as the wartime 'GEE', and the modern Global Positioning System, where by also taking measurements of the Doppler effect the velocities of receiving points relative to the transmitting point can be determined.

Traditionally, classical signals intelligence was not alert to this second and more recondite way of using the aether, and during the war Bletchley advisedly left this form of intelligence to those better qualified to pursue it – my own unit, the research establishments and specially formed Service units. Even so, there were difficulties between us, mainly arising from the overlapping of terms of reference and responsibilities. For example, the head of signals intelligence on the Air Staff was responsible for the interception of radio signals from German sources, while I was responsible for elucidating new applications of science by the German armed forces. So, whenever the Germans applied new developments in science and technology to signals, whose was the responsibility to study, and if possible to anticipate, them? Given goodwill and understanding on both sides, such problems could usually be sorted out – but goodwill was not always present.

On the one side signals intelligence officers may have been over-anxious to take over responsibility for studying new German developments since this could attract kudos, while, on the other, my unit and I may have been reluctant to hand over responsibility just at the stage when our work had shown a new German development to be so interesting that we wanted to follow it right through into operation. The resultant tussle could sometimes lead to suspicion and bad feeling, as had happened towards the end of 1942. At its height, I happened to read in *The Times* of the engagement of the second-in-command of signals intelligence, Wing Commander Claude Daubeny. I called him on the telephone, and, without identifying myself, played the theme of the Mendelssohn wedding march on my mouth-organ. Months later he telephoned me and asked if he might come to see me. On arrival he told me that he had just been promoted to be head of signals intelligence. Now a Group Captain, he wanted to explain to me that as second-in-command he had served under the two previous heads. 'I have seen both of them do their damnedest to get you kicked out of your job. They haven't succeeded, and I want to tell you that I am not as clever as they are, and so I'm not going to try!' The telephonic serenade, whose origin he had traced, had led him to think that I was not such a bad chap as the previous heads had believed.

After such a generous approach we could only be the best of friends, and the friendship became life-long. Claude was a typical Cranwell officer of the early thirties – handsome, heavily moustached and of the same entry as Douglas Bader. His main relaxation towards the end of the war was in backing horses, at which he claimed considerable success: to my objection that the bookmakers would always win in the end he contended that what the clever punter did was not to bet *against* the bookmaker but against the less discerning public *through* the bookmaker. His manifest abilities as head of signals intelligence on the Air Staff led to his being offered the headship of signals intelligence for all three Services and the Foreign Office in the post-war reorganization. I saw him shortly after his interview by the appointing board. 'At the end they asked me whether I had any points I wished to make, and I told them that I must have plenty of time for meetings. They agreed – but of course I didn't tell them, Reggie, that I meant *race* meetings!'

Claude's preoccupation with racing had one remarkable legacy, for as head of post-war signals intelligence he had to look for a new site for the cryptographers who were vacating Bletchley. He deliberately chose Cheltenham, as he told me, so that he could combine visits from his London office to GCHQ with attendance at Cheltenham races.

Unfortunately, though, he did not stay long enough in his post to overlap with me on my return to the Ministry of Defence in 1952. In fact he had left some time before, and in the meantime old rivalries had acutely revived. In the post-war maelstrom signals intelligence had paid little, if any, attention to Russian radar, and almost the only interceptions that were being made came from the unit that I had established in 1946 under Eric Ackermann near Obernkirchen. So good was his work that our American colleagues told me that although this was almost the only British effort in the field, it made it well worthwhile for them to exchange information with us – and they were now flying excellently methodical 'Ferret' flights to plot Russian radar.

In the meantime GCHQ had prepared a new charter for itself and this charter included responsibility for intercepting all Russian signals, both communications and radar. Then, armed with this charter, for which they had obtained approval without my predecessor as Director of Scientific Intelligence having the chance to comment, they proposed to take Ackermann and his unit over. I was very much concerned to be presented with this *fait accompli* for I was sure that GCHQ, for all their ability in communications intelligence and cryptography (Comint), had neither the interest (as their record had shown) nor the expertise to study the technical transmissions associated with radar and radio-navigation (Elint). Moreover, there was a point of principle: Comint and Elint were basically two different sources of intelligence which happened to use the same medium, the aether. But so did photographic intelligence, for light waves are also, in classical language, transmitted through the aether. So if GCHQ were to be responsible for Elint, it would be only a short step to their taking over photographic intelligence as well, and since my Directorate was the co-ordinating centre which should be directing the intelligence attack, I thought that the Comint and Elint sources should each have the same relation to the centre as had photographic intelligence or the MI6 agencies.[4]

As a *quid pro quo* for my losing direct control of Ackermann's unit in Germany an uneasy compromise was reached in which I was to be scientific adviser to GCHQ. But when I advised the Director of GCHQ that Elint was so important that he ought to have a senior member of his staff with full-time responsibility for it he rejected that advice – despite the fact that he had no experience with Elint and I had been involved with it throughout the entire war. It augured badly for the future of Elint in GCHQ's hands. Moreover, it was difficult to be an effective adviser to GCHQ in Cheltenham from the distance of London. Ultimately it was agreed that I should have a full-time deputy appointed to Cheltenham, and this later bloomed into the post of Chief Scientist there. While I cannot comment on the subsequent history of the post, its importance has evidently been such as to merit the appointment of one of the ablest scientists in government service.

Atomic Energy Intelligence

The second of my major problems concerned the arrangements made over the collection and processing of information regarding the development of nuclear weapons abroad, and most notably in Russia. My own part in the wartime history of the arrangements was related in *Most Secret War*:[5] originally atomic intelligence was, as it should always have been, part of scientific intelligence; but, on the argument that special arrangements had been made for atomic intelligence in America and that it was therefore necessary that we should follow the American pattern, atomic intelligence was in effect removed from scientific intelligence and treated separately in a direct arrangement between the Foreign Office and the Tube Alloys (Atomic Energy) Directorate in the Ministry of Supply. It was also argued that atomic matters were too secret to be entrusted to the normal scientific intelligence organization, and that the Americans would only share their information with us if specially secret arrangements were made. By 1945 that argument was already hollow, for the

McMahon Act in America had all but severed exchanges with Britain in atomic matters. Senator McMahon is reported to have said that if he had known the terms of the Quebec Agreement between Churchill and Roosevelt in 1943 he would never have promoted his Act, but the fact was that he did.

Moreover, as for the argument that in excluding atomic intelligence from normal scientific intelligence we were conforming to the American pattern, I discovered that for some time before 1952 atomic intelligence in America was regarded as part of scientific intelligence, and was dealt with in the Office of Scientific Intelligence in the Central Intelligence Agency whose head, Dr H. M. Chadwell, was my American counterpart. So none of the arguments advanced for the separation of atomic energy intelligence from scientific intelligence was valid, and the true explanation was more likely to be found in the personal motives and ambitions of those who had jumped on the atomic bandwagon and who wanted to keep everybody else off. Maybe they thought that they alone were fit enough to be entrusted with the awesome responsibility of atomic developments or maybe they had less worthy motives. But how otherwise can it be explained that, for example, when Henry Tizard was brought back into the Ministry of Defence in 1948 as Chief Scientific Adviser, he was virtually excluded from atomic matters? Was he, with all his record of service, not to be trusted?

During my time as Director, one development actually showed how foolish it was to regard atomic intelligence as something apart. One of the problems at the time was, of course, the detection of Russian nuclear explosions, and one of my staff, Dr J. H. Lees, suggested that in a nuclear explosion there should be so much movement of charged ions that they might radiate appreciable amounts of radio energy, and that this could be detectable at long range. I coined the term 'radioflash' for the hypothetical pulse of radio energy which should accompany the brilliant visual flash of an atomic explosion, and we suggested that it should be looked for in our own atomic trials. Since radio interception was no longer the responsibility of my Directorate, we passed the suggestion to GCHQ, who informed us that our own nuclear experts were most discouraging. Fortunately, we also spoke to our American colleagues, who told us that they could confirm our guess. Ultimately our own nuclear people also confirmed it in their atomic bomb tests in Australia – as they informed us some months afterwards. The pulse of radio energy thus provided a method of detecting atomic explosions that those who had kept atomic intelligence to themselves had not thought of. In retrospect, it was amazing that the proposal had had to come from us who had been excluded, because once the phenomenon was examined it was found that the amounts of energy involved were enormous: it is now known as 'electromagnetic pulse' or 'e.m.p.' and its destructive effects on electronic equipment have become a major threat.

During my time as Director, relations with the Americans in atomic intelligence began to ease, and it happened that my visit to the Office of Scientific Intelligence in Washington in 1953 coincided with the first substantial exchange of atomic intelligence at a super-top-secret conference to which I was invited, the chief British delegates being John Cockcroft and William Penney. The codeword for the conference was 'Nomination', and on the very morning that the conference was to open we were horrified to learn that Chapman Pincher had announced in the *Daily Express* that an important conference between British and American scientists on atomic energy was about to take place in Washington under the code-name of 'Nomination'. It almost torpedoed our conference, and we could not have blamed the Americans if they had cancelled it forthwith, especially since the leakage seemed to justify the distrust in British security manifested by the McMahon Act. Generously, though, our American colleagues decided that the conference should go ahead, and it proved a turning point in the restoration of something approaching our close wartime relations.

Assiduous inquiries into the source of the leak were of course made in London, but without result. It was only twenty years later that I found the answer, when I met Chapman Pincher for the first time. This was at the high table in the Painted Hall at Greenwich, where he and I were successive lecturers to the Senior Officers' War Course. I told him how much embarrassment he had caused us in Washington in 1953, and asked him how he had come to learn about Nomination. Now that the culprit was dead, Chapman Pincher felt he could reveal his identity: he was Archibald Rowlands, the Permanent Secretary of the Ministry of Supply. Chapman Pincher has since recorded the details of the incident in *Inside Story*. As he says, it 'illustrates how insecure some senior civil servants can be and what damage others can cause by dishonest answers to Press inquiries'. For if he had not then been misled by official denials that such a conference was being contemplated he would not have published the story – 'the only potentially damaging security breach I ever made.'

Sidewinder

By coincidence I had had another and far less disturbing (at least, to me) experience with a code-name only a very few days before Nomination nearly shattered the Washington conference. In the previous week I had been in the Mojave desert in California visiting the Naval Ordnance Test Station at Inyokern, now known as China Lake. The visit was not of my own arrangement but had been 'fixed' by my hosts in the CIA who had kindly thought it up as an excuse for paying my fare to California to meet my wartime colleague, H. P. (Bob) Robertson, now a professor at the California Institute of Technology in Pasadena, where he was associated with the big telescopes at Mounts Wilson and Palomar. I was to spend the weekend with Bob and his wife Angela, and superb hosts they were. They introduced me to many of their friends, including Robert Oppenheimer, with whom I discussed what might be done to get the unfortunate McMahon Act repealed. His laconic answer was, 'You must shame us into virtue!'

After a particularly happy weekend, during which I was shown the 100- and 200-inch telescopes, there remained the penance of three days to be spent in the desert some hundred miles north of Pasadena. Bob drove me there, and on the way he told me that the CIA had told the Station at Inyokern that I was a British guided-missile expert and that they were to show me all that they were doing. I was much alarmed, because I was certainly no expert on missiles, and my ignorance would be evident within a few minutes. I was thoroughly wretched because on the one hand I did not want to let the CIA down by saying that they had heavily overshot their line, while on the other I wanted to apologize for the Test Station being misled and for my being an unwitting sham.

I was still unresolved when we reached Inyokern, and Bob had left me with the Commander of the Station and his chief executive officer and chief scientist. It was clear that they were going to 'come clean' about all they were doing, and that they were expecting from me genuine comments and advice on their work. Vaguely I recalled that as chairman of the Ministry of Supply's infra-red committee I had heard that our own missile experts at Malvern had wanted to know what their American counterparts had been doing but had had their requests to see the American work declined. Here I was, with *carte blanche* to see everything, but so unbriefed as not even to know the questions which our own experts would have liked answered. And when my American hosts found how bogus I was . . .

Before I had any chance to explain my unfortunate status, the Station Commander launched enthusiastically into their problems, and particularly those of a new missile they were developing, called 'Sidewinder'. Almost involuntarily I exclaimed, 'An infra-red homer!' The Commander and his colleagues were much surprised, and he at once asked, 'How do you know that? We thought it was a secret.' 'Well,' I explained, 'if you will give it such an obvious code-name, what would you expect?' The Commander then asked, 'What do you mean?' 'Well, look, a sidewinder is a small rattlesnake and all rattlesnakes belong to the family of pit-vipers, and these are so called not because they live in pits, which I once thought, but because they have two pits, one on either side of their heads, and these pits contain infra-red detectors which enable the snakes to detect and strike at warm objects in the dark!' The fact had fairly recently been discovered, and I had encountered it through an interest in the special senses of animals such as the homing of pigeons and the acoustic radar of bats.

The Commander and his colleagues were all but dumbfounded. 'Gee,' he said, 'we did not know that!' 'Then why,' I asked, 'did you call the missile "Sidewinder"?' 'That's simple', he answered. 'On this station our two biggest headaches are this missile, which won't work properly, and the sidewinders which come in from the desert at night and lie in the paths between our huts, and every now and again someone gets bitten. So when we had to choose a name for the missile we chose our other headache, sidewinder.'

Thanks to my fortunate zoological knowledge my credentials as a worthwhile visitor were established, and I had a marvellous three days in one of the best-run military (or other) establishments it has ever been my fortune to visit. The concept of Sidewinder was elegantly simple, and for all the difficulties its developers were experiencing I was sure that they were going to succeed. Now, thirty-five years later, it is still one of the best air-to-air missiles, and it has evolved through ever more effective stages such as the AIM.9L version used so successfully in the Falklands Campaign.

Scientific Aids to Intelligence

In memoranda as far back as 1939 and 1942 I had pointed out that scientists in intelligence had two functions, the first being the conduct of scientific intelligence itself and the second the provision of scientific aids for the collection of intelligence. The latter had already had a long history going back to secret inks, while even the microdot of World War II had been anticipated by Robert Hooke in his *Micrographia* of 1665: 'if this manner of small writing were made easy and practicable, it might be of very good use to convey Secret Intelligence without any danger of discovery or mistrusting'. So it was natural that as Director of Scientific Intelligence in 1952 I should look afresh at what science might do to provide new aids to intelligence. This brought me into particular contact with MI5, its head then being Percy Sillitoe, who proved one of the most human of my colleagues on the Joint Intelligence Committee. He told me how, when he was Chief Constable of Glasgow during the Blitz, he made a final effort to locate houses with no blackouts on their skylights by arranging to have an aerial survey by the RAF, whose observers would be aided in locating offending skylights in the dark by referring these to a network of markers provided by Sillitoe's police cars stationed at suitable pinpoints with their headlamps on and pointing vertically upwards. It happened that the night which he had picked for the operation was the same as that selected by the *Luftwaffe* for its first heavy raid on Glasgow, whose indignant inhabitants wondered whether the headlamps were the beacons that had attracted the bombing, and whether their Chief Constable was an arch member of the Fifth Column.

On another occasion when he and I were discussing our problems, he indicated to me some of the restrictive limits on his powers. I asked him whether he would like more power, for I would be ready to support him at the JIC. 'No!' he replied. 'If I had more power it would turn England into a police state. That would be the worst thing for England and' (banging his table) 'I say that as head of MI5!'

We set up the Committee for the Provision of Experimental Facilities for Intelligence of which the MI5 member was Malcolm Cumming who, after I had returned to Aberdeen, had recruited Peter Wright to work full-time in MI5. I had met Peter Wright's father, G. M. Wright, when the Deputy Chief Scientist of the Ministry of Defence, Fred Brundrett, had called me in to meet G.M. and hear him explain the working of the very clever clandestine microphone (of which our copy was called Satyr). The Russians had secreted it in the replica of the Great Seal of the United States which they had presented to the American Ambassador in Moscow, and which he unwittingly kept on his desk.

Incidentally, one result was that I recommended that all crucial offices in Whitehall should be checked once again for hidden microphones. I later heard that the search had been completely negative, with one exception: this was the Cabinet Room in 10 Downing Street, where a microphone and amplifier were found in Churchill's own chair. I have never confirmed the story, but the explanation given me was that Churchill had had the device installed himself privately by a Polish engineer, because his hearing was deteriorating, and he did not want an obvious deaf aid.

On resigning as Director, I reported on 1 June 1954 that I 'had come to acquire a general responsibility for advising the heads of other forms of intelligence, and particularly those of the collecting agencies, on the applications of science to their problems. This function is to a large extent independent from the first (that of anticipating the applications of science to warfare by potential opponents), and could if necessary be separated from it, except when problems arise of applying scientific aids to the collection of scientific intelligence.' This hardly suggested that I myself was 'making a play for the job' as stated by Peter Wright in *Spycatcher*.[6]

If Sillitoe's view of the function of MI5 was so gentlemanly as hardly to be credible today, I had a further example of the same attitude during my Washington visit of 1953. This was shortly before the Coronation when it was known that the Russians would be sending the new cruiser, *Sverdlovsk*, to the Coronation Review. We were of course by this time much aware of the electronic espionage by Russian 'trawlers' around our coasts; and so when, at a lunch they were giving me, the American Directors of Intelligence told me that they hoped we would have the *Sverdlovsk* 'covered' electronically and photographically, I told them they could be sure that our Director of Naval Intelligence would have made all suitable arrangements.

I was amazed on my return to find that no intelligence had been gathered. The DNI's arrangements had been cancelled because permission for an aerial reconnaissance had been sought from the Secretary of State for Air, the Lord De L'Isle and Dudley, a descendant of Sir Philip Sidney and holder of the Victoria Cross. He ruled that since the Russian cruiser was on a courtesy mission to honour our Queen, it would be a discourteous act to conduct any intelligence operations against her. And so we did nothing. What the Americans may have done is a matter for speculation.

The Director of Naval Intelligence, incidentally, was Rear Admiral Anthony Buzzard, an outstandingly forward-thinking officer, who caused some consternation by suggesting that it might be possible to put an atomic warhead on a rocket that could be fired from a submarine. The general opinion was that such a development would be 'unthinkable' – not so much, I suspected, due to the practical problems, but because of the difficulties of thinking of countermeasures should such a development take place.

The Joint Intelligence Committee

Further memorable experiences at Joint Intelligence Committee meetings, other than the deplorable treatment of Ian Colvin over 'The man who never was' that I related in *Most Secret War*,[7] were our interviews with Sir Gerald Templer and Sir Alvary Gascoigne. The General, who was then in Malaya countering the insurgents, had himself previously been a Director of Military Intelligence, and so his visit to the JIC to brief us while he was temporarily on leave in London was rather like an old boy's return to speak to his successors at school. The problems of the Malayan emergency were clearly telling on him, for I have never before or since seen a man under such manifest strain. He chain-smoked cigarettes incessantly with trembling hands the whole time he was speaking to us, and I wondered how long he could last. But he returned to Malaya and conducted a brilliant campaign, both military and administrative, which saved Malaya from the fate of Vietnam.

Sir Alvary was also a man under strain. He was just retiring as Ambassador in Moscow, and he was giving us his thoughts on developments in Russia. This was while Stalin was still alive, and diplomacy had proved a hopeless task. I recall Sir Alvary's concluding summary: 'Gentlemen, I went to Moscow in the hope of improving relations between my country and Russia. I've failed! I've failed! I've failed!' He was shortly to leave the Foreign Service, and I had the lasting impression of an English gentleman whose principles were too noble to match him to the chicanery of Stalin's Kremlin.

The Hydrogen Bomb

At about the same time the Russians firmly entered the thermonuclear arena. The Americans had made their first thermonuclear explosion in 1951 and now, on 12 August 1953, a Russian nuclear explosion took place, and within a few days our monitoring system (with the Americans) established that it had a thermonuclear component. The Russians were clearly catching up, and I can recall the feeling of relief that came over some of us when the new bomb was discussed at the JIC, for in a strange way we felt that the world might be somehow more secure. British policy since 1945 had consistently been to allay the fears of the Russians in the hope that as their country grew stronger they would come to realize that war would benefit neither side. The Russians might now feel less apprehensive, since they could shortly match the American potential, and it was less likely that the Americans would be tempted to resort to thermonuclear warfare. Moreover, once the Russians saw what awful damage such warfare might do, the more they themselves would be inclined to refrain from initiating it. This could be a dangerous assumption, but it partly anticipated the toast of Andrei Sakharov after witnessing in 1955 a successful Russian test of a hydrogen bomb that he himself had helped to develop: 'The evening after the test, at a private banquet attended only by the officials in charge of the test, I proposed a toast that "our handiwork would never explode over cities".'[8] He was reproved by the director of the tests and, later, by Khrushchev himself: but happily the hope of Churchill, which he expressed in Parliament after he had been informed of the Russian success, and of American progress, has so far held: 'Then it may be that we shall by a process of sublime irony have reached a stage in this story where safety will be the sturdy child of terror, and survival the twin brother of annihilation.'[9]

Russians and Robbins

One minor success that I had as Director of Scientific Intelligence was in the treatment of a Russian defector. From being a tractor driver at the age of fourteen he had benefited from the Russian educational system so much as to become a professor of aeronautics at the Soviet Air Force Academy and he had taken advantage of a posting to East Berlin to come across to us with his wife and daughter. Naturally, he was treated with the greatest interest in Whitehall so long as there seemed to be further information that he could provide, and then – as with most defectors – he was left to languish. Defectors are rarely trusted, however genuinely they want to help the country to which they have defected; and for an actively creative individual who has been involved in developments in, or fringeing upon, the defence field, he is likely to be utterly frustrated when he finds himself excluded from similar work in his new country. I saw this happen in World War II, when one of Heinkel's senior aerodynamicists came over to us, and all that he was ever allowed to do for us was to translate German documents.

With our Russian defector I ultimately succeeded in overcoming the understandable misgivings of MI5 by getting him a post at the Aeronautical College at Cranfield, from which he ultimately rose to a chair of aerodynamics at a British university. While he was in limbo we thought that we might learn something about the Russian educational system by inviting him to attend lectures at one of our universities, and asking him to compare the methods of instruction in Britain and Russia. He at once noted that in Britain neither students nor the lecturer greeted one another, whereas in Russia the lecturer would have said something like 'Greetings, comrades,' and the students responded by rising and saying, 'Greetings, Ivan Ivanovitch.' He criticized students for their noisiness, and particularly for stamping if the lecturer ran over time, while lecturers were sloppy, even sitting on the bench with hands in their pockets while lecturing, and paying very little attention either to their delivery or to the legibility of their writing and diagrams. Their technical knowledge, though, was good. And he found another comment with which he courteously tried to sweeten the sharpness of his criticism: 'The cleanliness in the lavatories is such as would be unheard of in any ordinary civilian Soviet higher educational establishment.'

From his insistence on the clarity and discipline of Russian lectures it was evident that the Russians had tackled the problem of teaching large numbers of students with the fewest possible staff. This confirmed many other pointers that we reported as indicating the large numbers of engineers and scientists that the Russians were producing, relative to our numbers in the West. Time after time we reported these prognostications, which agreed with those of others such as Lord Cherwell and Sir Francis Simon, but none of us succeeded in awakening our politicians – or indeed many of our scientists – until the scales were struck from their eyes by the launch of the Sputnik on 4 October 1957. We in intelligence were not surprised, because the German engineers and scientists who had been recruited after 1945 to work in Russia told us on their return that they suspected that there was a powerful Russian effort in rocketry quite independent of any help that the Germans might be able to give.

As so often happens, those who had previously been sceptical of Russian potential now swung to the other extreme, and the utmost priority was placed on catching up with the Russians: much money was accordingly thrown at any group of scientists or engineers who might be able to help. There is a happy story of this period concerning an international conference at which American and Russian scientists met, with the latter saying to the former, 'We hope that our Sputnik will be as much help to you as your atomic bomb was to us!'

In an effort to match the Russian output of scientists and engineers, frenzied efforts were made in education. In Britain the most dramatic – and disastrous – result was the Robbins Report on Higher Education of 1963, which sought to double the university output of graduates in science and engineering in three years. The intention was worthy enough, but even those of us who had been pressing for expansion in these subjects, ever since World War II had shown how vital they were to national survival, now felt it necessary to warn that to attempt such a rapid expansion would be futile.

We knew that, because of past neglect, talent could not be recruited at the required rate and that there would not be a sufficient flood of able students from the schools in the science subjects. Once again we were not heeded. Money and effort which were intended to go into science and engineering went instead, by default of adequate talent, into expansion in 'soft' subjects which demanded little of either staff or students. Buoyed up by the resultant increased number of students in so-called 'higher' education, Government and vice-chancellors for some years congratulated themselves on what they appeared to have achieved. But, to quote Dean Inge again, on the subject of the Gadarene Swine, 'No doubt they thought the going was good, for the first half of the way!' And the going began to harden in the early seventies, when the Government started to question whether the expansion was producing the intended results, and a reaction set in that has led to the present wretched situation in our universities. Frogs should ever be careful of inflating themselves to the size of bulls.

JIC Procedure

Apart from occasional highlights, such as the discussion on the hydrogen bomb and the meetings with Templer and Gascoigne, proceedings on the Joint Intelligence Committee were routinely dull. We met every Thursday morning, when one of the weekly reports submitted to us was the 'Perimeter Review', which surveyed incidents all round the Warsaw Pact perimeter to see whether there had been any movements which presaged an impending Russian thrust. The idea was worthy enough, but I felt that there was a danger that we could get so 'acclimatized by slow change' that we might fail to spot a stealthy build-up by the Russians in which there was no great change in any one week, but where the cumulative effect over a few months might be considerable. And our vigilance might tire through the boredom of a routine – until, as Bacon said, 'If a man watch too long 'tis odds he will fall asleep.'[10]

To emphasize the 'Joint' approach, JIC procedure was for the signatures of all directors to appear on all the important reports, even when some of the directors had not been personally concerned. There was even one instance when a report appeared over the signatures of three officers when none of the signatories had either seen the report or been consulted about it. Clearly the Whitehall organization had slipped far from its wartime tautness.

Only a minority of the members of the JIC had been selected on their past achievements as intelligence officers. Had they been, they might have realized that much of the time spent arguing around the table about the interpretation of evidence was due to there being too little information, so allowing for many hypotheses to explain it. Two members could therefore have two differing interpretations with neither being able to dispose effectively of the other. In such circumstances the remedy should have been to save time in argument and instead press for more intelligence.

I did my best to conform to the working of the JIC but I had to record that 'too much time and effort was dissipated in the JIC machine', with its 'dangerous system which may plunge a man with very little of the right background into a position of the highest responsibility in intelligence, and which will almost certainly remove him again as soon as he is beginning to learn his job'. As for the practice of joint reports, 'A joint report is only effective as far as common agreement will allow, and – so far as interpreting intelligence evidence goes – common agreement rarely goes far enough.'

All these criticisms and others, both negative and constructive, were made in my valedictory report on returning to Aberdeen in 1954. The report, dated 1 June 1954, may now be available in the Public Record Office. It certainly went into the Ministry's files, for twenty years later the Director General of Intelligence told me that he had just seen it, and he only wished that he could have read it when he took up office, because many of the faults recorded in the report were still present in the organization. Some of them concerning the ponderous nature of the JIC procedure showed up in the

Falklands affair. The Franks Committee inquiry into the amount of warning the JIC gave before the Argentinian invasion found[11] that the JIC organization 'was too passive in operation to respond quickly and critically to a rapidly changing situation which demanded urgent attention'. The Franks Report recommended that the chairmanship of the JIC should in future be a full-time post, with the chairman not being, as in the past, a Foreign Office official, but independently a member of the Cabinet Office. Such changes could only be for the good.

Such an improvement, though, lay thirty years into the future, and I had to consider how much I could achieve inside the organization as it was. There was always the thought of my students back in Aberdeen who, when I had told them that I would have to be leaving them for a year or so, stood up as a class of two hundred or more and sang 'Will ye no come back again?' and the balance in the conflict between duty to them on the one side, and what I might do further in the Ministry of Defence on the other, now definitely turned towards going back. Had I seen happier solutions to the problems of atomic and signals intelligence I would have been tempted to stay longer with the Ministry.

In retrospect, ought I to have risked drawing public attention to the situation in the hope of reforming the intelligence organization in the way that was much later realized to be necessary? I was presented with the opportunity to do so, because Chapman Pincher soon heard from his sources in the Ministry of Defence that I was returning to Aberdeen, and telephoned asking me the reason. Judging that publicity would at best be ambivalent in its effect, apart from any trouble with the Official Secrets Act, and the need for restraint in naming individuals, I told him nothing more than that I was keeping my commitment to return to Aberdeen.

It may well be wondered why, since I had been called back by Churchill, I could not have had more direct influence over the direction of events. I told him about my problems, and quoted his own words, from 'Painting as a Pastime' in *Thoughts and Adventures*, on his frustration after leaving the Admiralty in 1915 while still remaining a member of the Cabinet:

> Like a sea-beast fished up from the depths, or a diver too suddenly hoisted, my veins threatened to burst with the fall in pressure. I had great anxiety without means of relieving it; I had vehement convictions

> and small power to give effect to them. I had to watch the unhappy casting away of great opportunities, and the feeble execution of plans I had launched and in which I heartily believed.[12]

But, although moved, he was tired and all he could suggest was that I should discuss them with Lord Alexander, who was now Minister of Defence. I received the same advice from Norman Brook, the Secretary of the Cabinet, who always treated me warmly because he found that I had lived in the same rooms in Wadham as he himself had had as an undergraduate. Brook told me to request that 'the papers be laid before the Minister' because under civil service procedure the Minister must then interview me. I therefore did so.

'Alex'

The Field Marshal accordingly sent for me. It was the second time we had met, the first being a happier occasion a few months earlier, after he had read one of my reports describing a visit to Germany where I had been a guest of many of the German generals, including his old opponent Kesselring. 'Alex' told me how much he envied my freedom to talk to them, which protocol would not yet permit him to do, and how much he admired the Germans as soldiers. In particular he wanted to know what kind of man his old opponent was.

Now, though, the occasion was different. I had gone into his room to tell him how ineffective his Ministry was, and what he might do to improve it. Before I could start, though, he disarmed me by saying, 'I gather that you don't like this Ministry. Neither do I. I never wanted the job, and I was much happier as Governor General of Canada. But when Winston came through Ottawa on his first visit to Washington [as Prime Minister] he said: "I want you to come back as my Minister of Defence" – so what could I do?' He then began to tell me about his problems, and said that he felt out of his depth in dealing at the Cabinet table with, for example, 'The Prof' – Lord Cherwell. 'Alex' said, 'He will suddenly pull his slide-rule out of his pocket and calculate how much it is costing me to keep a soldier in the Canal zone, and I have no answer.' I told him that I could help him in such cases, especially since I myself distrusted glib figures. 'All you need do,' I said, 'is to quote George Canning's dictum that "if there's one thing more misleading than facts, it's figures".' 'Thank you very much,' said 'Alex'. 'Let me write that down.' And although I do not know whether he ever played it at the Cabinet, I later heard him quote it when he was chief guest at a dinner of the Institution of Electrical Engineers.

I then tried to make my own points, the first of which was the need for a clear ministerial policy. 'What is your policy?' I asked. 'Is the Ministry going to give a lead to the Service Ministries, or is it so afraid of the precedent of the OKW that it is going to continue falling over backwards to avoid upsetting them?' 'That is an important question!' replied 'Alex'. 'I haven't thought about it – but I must before I go!'

If that answer suggests a mismatch between 'Alex' and the task that he was asked to do, it is only fair to mention his genuine qualities, which had been lauded to me by Sir George Turner, the Permanent Under Secretary of State at the War Office. I had met Sir George a few months before at a dinner of the Saints and Sinners Club, where I was the guest of Claude Daubeny. As we sat down Claude said to me, 'See the chap who is sitting opposite you? Guess what he's been doing this afternoon.' I looked across to see a bespectacled man in his fifties, who might have been in any one of a dozen professions. It was hopeless to try to guess which, and so Claude said, 'He's been choosing the military music for the Coronation. He's Sir George Turner, the PUS at the War Office.' 'OK,' I replied, 'I can bat on that wicket,' and thereupon addressed myself to Sir George. 'I understand that you have been choosing the military music for the Coronation.' 'I have,' he replied laconically, which led me on to, 'Well what pipe tunes have you picked?' My question was based on genuine interest but I am not sure how it was taken, for to my amazement the senior civil servant at the War Office replied in a northern accent, 'Be fooked to the pipes.' As I reeled he added, 'Be fooked to the Scots, and the Irish. As for the Welsh, they're the bloody Foreign Legion.' Rebounding from this broadside I involuntarily exclaimed, 'You must have been a Grenadier.' 'I was,' he replied, and we were launched on an hilarious dinner as he recounted some of his experiences.

Entering the War Office at the age of fourteen as a messenger boy, he had been conscripted in the First World War and found himself in the Grenadiers. It says much both for him and for our supposedly stuffy Civil Service that, in his subsequent career in the War Office, he had risen through all the intermediate ranks to be its top civil servant. He enjoyed shocking people by emphasizing his northern accent, and told us that one of his first jobs as PUS was to inspect the Guards Depot at Caterham. Accompanied by a retinue of Guards officers, he kept himself in check until he reached the sergeants' mess, whereupon he burst out, 'Ehey, the last time I was in 'ere, I was peeling spuds.' And his greatest thrill, he told us, was to march up the steps of the War Office very morning while the Life Guard sentries across Whitehall came to the salute. 'If only they knew that all they were saluting was a private in the Grenadiers!'

More seriously, he then said to me, 'You work for a good chap.' 'Who?' I asked. 'Alex' he replied. 'I'll tell you what kind of a man Alex is! I have to go to meetings with the generals, and they look down their noses at me because they know I was only a private in the Grenadiers. The other day I said something they didn't like, and there was an awkward silence round the table. But Alex dealt with them. All he said was, "Gentlemen, Sir George and I fought in the same battle when all of you were little boys!"'

A Cataract of Ministers

Regarding the working of the Ministry of Defence, there was a major improvement in the late fifties and early sixties. With no less than eleven different individuals holding the post of Minister between 1946 and 1958, it was hardly surprising that policy had been almost incoherent. Ultimately the Ministry succeeded in welding itself together and in leading the three Services more in the way its early supporters had hoped. The improvement was obvious by 1963, when I was once again called back, this time to chair the working party on the needs for air defence in the decade 1975–85. So much so that I congratulated Lord Mountbatten who was now Chief of Defence Staff. I remarked that the Ministry now had a much more definite sense of purpose than it had had ten years before, and I knew that much of the credit for such a change must be due to the man at the top. 'Thank you very much,' he said. 'But I could not have done it if my wife had not died.' Seeing me reel at this unexpected comment he added, 'I suppose that sounds odd, so I'd better explain what I mean. You see, this is my second tour as CDS. I had already had three years and I was going to retire. But then she died, and I had little else to live for. So I asked to go on for another three years. And it is in this second time round, now that I have learnt the ropes, that I have been able to make the changes.'

Resignation

All that, though, lay ten years in the future in 1953, and I saw no route to making headway. Had the GCHQ and atomic intelligence situations showed any signs of being resolved favourably I would have offered to stay longer, but in their absence I could only hope that by making my points in a note of resignation I might make it easier for my successors to win support. I had left them some positive gains: both GCHQ and MI5 were to have full-time scientists, radioflash was a diagnostic tool in atomic intelligence, full-time officers were exchanged between the DSI and the CIA, and a fruitful watch on Russian rocketry was established. As for the future, all improvements would be 'dependent on there being a strong Ministry of Defence with a clear policy, and on that Ministry realizing that the first step towards the creation of a good intelligence system is to select the best possible man and then to give him both trust and support. He will certainly need them to an extent far greater than they were afforded to my predecessor and myself.' I am not sure of the extent to which this advice was heeded, but I have been glad to note that some of my successors have had distinguished careers in government service, both before and after their tour as Director of Scientific Intelligence.

One saddening legacy of resignation was that, since I could no longer speak of the current state of intelligence with that same confidence that I had had during the war, I felt it would be a hollow sham to continue lecturing at the RAF Staff College. I had spoken on scientific intelligence to every succeeding course from 1943 to 1954, which, I was told, was a record for a visiting lecturer, and I warmly enjoyed every occasion. Whenever, even now, I see a uniformed audience in front of me, my lecturing somehow changes gear, spurred by the invigorating memories of those wartime days of a hall packed with the most gallant, ablest and liveliest band of officers that any lecturer could be privileged to address, including men like Guy Gibson and every future Chief of Air Staff. But now those occasions could only be a memory, mocked by what had since happened to scientific intelligence, and although I pondered for three weeks after receiving the Commandant's invitation of 19 June 1954, I ultimately wrote to him:

Dear Air Vice-Marshal,

I am sorry to have been so long in answering your letter of 19 June, and your invitation to lecture again to the Staff College.

I hardly know how to write this letter, but the fact is that I do not feel that I can lecture again on Scientific Intelligence at the present time. As you may know, I went back in September 1952 to the Ministry of Defence for a temporary period to help Scientific Intelligence through a difficult time. I returned to my University last January because I could make almost no headway in trying to persuade the various authorities to straighten out the organisational muddle to the point where things could really be made to work.

What I found myself up against, fundamentally, was that without a war actually in operation, it is not easy to see who is right – and who is wrong – in Defence matters such as Intelligence. In these circumstances individuals and committees who have to take decisions tend to go for the easiest decision rather than for the right one, and if possible for no decision at all. I thus found my time being fruitlessly frittered away, and I could no longer justify my absence to my University.

I therefore feel that I cannot at the moment lecture with confidence about the present state of Scientific Intelligence, and to lecture about the past without reference to the present would be both out-of-date and misleading. I have the deepest regret in thus breaking my series of talks to you, for I have had the warmest attachment to the Staff College ever since I gave my first lecture in 1943. It was in fact at the Staff College that I learned how to lecture, and the enthusiasm of the successive courses has always been most gratifying. It has continually increased the respect which I have always had for the Royal Air Force.

Should the situation change, I would certainly be ready to lecture on Scientific Intelligence again. In the meantime, if there is any way in which I can help the Staff College, I shall be very glad to do so. Please accept my best wishes for the future, both for the College and for yourself.

Yours very sincerely,

R. V. JONES

After that my contact with Defence Intelligence – in Britain at least – was no more than fragmentary. Twenty-five years later my successor in the Ministry of Defence, the Director of Scientific and Technical Intelligence, asked me to give his Directorate a talk on my experiences. Afterwards he wrote to me:

May I thank you for the excellent talk you gave us during your recent visit to the Metropole. We were all most interested indeed especially as so many of the incidents you described have their parallels today – it is just a pity we cannot discuss these parallels further, as in some cases they are remarkably close.[13]

It is not surprising that problems of intelligence organization persist:

some are rooted in human nature, others in the need for secrecy, and yet more in the fact that while the input to intelligence has to be by source its output must be by subject, leading too often to tangles in organization.

2

Intelligence Ethics

When resources on a national scale can be applied in secrecy, as they have to be in intelligence, the power of public scrutiny cannot always be brought to bear against their prospective misuse. In the absence of such scrutiny, and particularly because of the opportunities for malpractice that intelligence offers, the only safeguard is a firm sense of ethics among its operators. This chapter therefore discusses some of the ethical problems that are involved.

Respect for Allies

Since intelligence often involves prying into another country's secrets, the question arises of the extent to which this can be justified. In my days in intelligence we observed a rule handed down to us that we should not spy on allies. The tradition was so strong that Churchill himself ordered that there should be no espionage against Russia once the German attack in 1941 had brought the Russians into alliance with us. And even after the alliance had dissolved in the Cold War, we have seen how Lord De L'Isle ruled that we should refrain from any reconnaissance against the *Sverdlovsk* at the Coronation Review of 1953.

Such a ruling, however, evidently had little effect at the later visit of the warship *Ordzhinikidze* which brought Khrushchev and Bulganin to Portsmouth in 1956, for it resulted in the affair in which Commander Crabb lost his life while attempting an underwater reconnaissance: and on the same visit the rooms to be occupied by Khrushchev and Bulganin were 'bugged', according to Peter Wright's account in *Spycatcher*.[1] It could, of course, be pleaded that this discourtesy was merely a reciprocation for the similar measures the Russians had long taken against us. But Peter Wright also relates how he and his colleagues 'bugged' the French Embassy between 1960 and 1963. It was clever work which resulted in our reading the French high-grade cipher coming in and out of the French Embassy in London. 'Every move made by the French during our abortive attempt to enter the Common Market was monitored.'[2] It is true that, as far as the Common Market was concerned, the French could no longer be regarded as our allies, and yet for me the episode jars.

The reason is that it brings back a memory of a very different episode in which we and the French were involved with ciphers. This was in 1945 when the British cryptographers at Bletchley were anxious to interrogate their German counterparts after the German surrender. We traced their flight from the wartime headquarters at Treuenbritzen and found that they were now in the relatively small zone of Germany that had been allocated for French control. After their wartime history the French were tending to re-establish their dignity whenever occasion arose, and this was one: they would not allow a mission of British and American cryptographers to enter their zone, and all representations, both military and diplomatic, had failed. I heard about the problem at Bletchley, and put it to my French colleague, Professor Yves Rocard, the Director of Research of the Free French Navy, whose contributions I described in *Most Secret War*.[3]

He said that he would see what could be done, and within a day he returned to my office to tell me that our cryptographers would now be welcome to go in, and to talk to the Germans. The French would not even ask to be present at the interrogations, and their only request was that if we discovered anything that affected the security of France, they would be grateful to know. Such a change had been brought about simply by the complete trust that the events of war had forged between Rocard and myself, and it shows how such a trust may prove much stronger than the wary relationships of diplomacy. With that memory, I for one could not have bugged the French Embassy.

Diplomatic Bags

A classic way of spying on embassies is, of course, the interception of diplomatic bags and the clandestine opening of the mail they contain. Much skill can be exerted in this process, as Peter Wright describes in *Spycatcher*, to avoid any sign that the contents have been read.[4] He also says that the simple application of Sellotape to the original sealing of the envelope makes it very difficult to open without giving the ultimate recipient any sign of tampering. During the war a colleague officer came to me with another simple suggestion for detecting whether our own confidential letters had been subject to unauthorized opening. This was simply to seal a letter in the ordinary way, and then to run it several times through a sewing machine. For if the letter were subsequently opened by cutting the thread it would be almost impossible to replace the enclosed sheets in such a way that all the holes would line up with those in the envelope so accurately that the ensemble could be re-stitched exactly as the original. He asked me whether I thought that it would work, and on receiving my encouragement he said he would send a stitched letter over to some of our security experts to see if they would agree. 'Just one more thing,' I suggested. 'Mark the cotton thread at intervals with a fluorescent dye, so that if they manage to replace the cotton we can identify that it is not what we used.' Here I banked on a human weakness that I had seen several times before (and many since) which beguiles clever minds to concentrate on the difficult parts of a challenge to such an extent that they overlook the simpler ones. After three days the envelope came back to us immaculately re-stitched with no visible sign of tampering, but including a complimentary card from our friends to show that they had opened it. They were furious when we told them that we were certain it had been opened, and that they had failed to spot the simple trick of fluorescent marking in concentrating, otherwise so successfully, on the very difficult task of re-stitching.

In such an instance the contest between the men trying to protect their country's secrets and the men who are trying to pry them open can be a battle of wits in which each side is aiming to be cleverer than the other, with all the thrust and parry of a mediaeval joust. And while such chivalry as Lord De L'Isle showed (see above, page 22) in the *Sverdlovsk* visit is rare, the contest tends to develop its own rules. Almost every power accepts that it is fair game to try and decrypt the signals of its potential opponents, even though there was the classic instance of the US Secretary of State, Henry Stimson, who in 1929 closed down the famous Black Chamber, the American cryptographic centre of World War I and afterwards, because, as he said, 'Gentlemen do not read each other's mail.' But while there may be something sneaky and furtive in reading a private letter, cryptography need have neither of these aspects and can be a highly intellectual exercise even though we may regret the diversion of so much intellect to such an uncreative end.

Open Skies

Much the same is true of both photographic and electronic reconnaissance. In pre-Sputnik days it could be argued that to fly a photographic aircraft over another country without its permission was an infringement of national sovereignty, and the Russians were prepared to shoot such aircraft down, as they showed in the U2 incident of 1960. This was after they had rejected President Eisenhower's offer of an 'open skies' policy in which the Americans and the Russians would have been free to fly photographic aircraft over one another's territory. In retrospect the Russian rejection looks all the more unreasonable because within a few years both sides were able to orbit reconnaissance satellites over each other's territory with impunity. What the Russian attitude would be if it should become readily possible to destroy or blind reconnaissance satellites is a matter for conjecture, especially in the face of the Strategic Defence Initiative. There was much to be said for Eisenhower's offer, if only because good intelligence can be a stabilizing influence in international affairs: it can contribute to both mutual deterrence and mutual reassurance.

The Espionage Convention

There was another noteworthy aspect of the U2 incident, for Eisenhower himself confirmed that he had authorized the U2 flights. He was criticized for making such an official acknowledgement, which was almost unprecedented in intelligence affairs, where the convention was that a government did not acknowledge its intelligence activities, and, for example, gave no support to any of its agents who had been caught in espionage. Notably, as William Colby records in *Honorable Men*,[5] it was Khrushchev's annoyance with Eisenhower's acceptance of responsibility for the U2 flight that led him to cancel the Paris Summit. But it was time that such a bogus convention was abandoned.

Curiously, although the pre-1914 era was the heyday of the convention, the European powers were surprisingly ready to make statements of their expenditure on their secret services. In 1912 the British Foreign Secretary, Edward Grey, easily obtained from his ambassadors the published expenditures in the countries to which they were respectively credited. The figures were published as a parliamentary paper[6] and they still make interesting reading:

Austria-Hungary	£62,500
France	£40,000
Germany	£80,387

Great Britain	£50,000
Italy	£120,800
Russia	£380,000 (+ £335,000 for secret police)

The preoccupation with secret service, both external and internal, is a Russian characteristic older than the 1917 Revolution. In fact in *The Craft of Intelligence*, Allen Dulles, who was Director of the Central Intelligence Agency from 1953 to 1961, traces the 'congenital suspicion' of the Russians at least as far back as the sixteenth century when, to resist the ravages of the Tartars and others, the inhabitants had to depend on the garrisons of walled stockades (kremlins) and cities in country that could easily be over-run. And since the Tartars sought to ascertain the strength of the defences in advance by sending agents in (as did Joshua at Jericho) the inhabitants developed a suspicion of strangers.

Secret Services

While there are relatively few problems of ethics in the operation of photographic, communications or electronic reconnaissance, it is otherwise with secret service. 'Oh, where hath our Intelligence been drunk, where hath it slept?' demanded King John, and knowing two of the traditional temptations – alcohol and sex – he might well ask. To these must be added money and disaffection with a native land, or greater affection for a foreign one. The problem for a secret service, or at least for one in a democracy which values decency, is how far the ends of national security can justify these means, nearly all of them disreputable, by which valuable information can sometimes be obtained.

The Russians, for example, have been ruthlessly unscrupulous in exploiting sexual weaknesses of both the hetero- and homo- varieties, not only by tempting employees of foreign powers to provide information in return for gratification but also by subsequent blackmail in threatening to bring such sexual indiscretions and treachery to the notice of an employee's superiors unless he (or she) continues to supply information. To any decent man such methods are thoroughly distasteful, even more so than the induction of an employee's treachery in return for money and material comforts; but the possibility that valuable information may thereby be obtained cannot be overlooked, although I for one would try to draw a borderline. This limit might be set at 'No sex, please, we're British!' or, rather shorter, at attempting to suborn an employee with money. I cannot conceive that a relation based upon mutual respect could be built up between the suborner and the suborned in such instances, and all my own experience of successes in intelligence has suggested that these have been based on some degree of mutual respect between the various elements in an intelligence chain.

But while I would have little respect for a man who attempted to sell his country's secrets for money, I would have to admit that information of value may be obtained in this way. For an example, the German cryptographic employee in 1932 to whom the French military intelligence gave the code-name 'Asche' (and whose real name may have been Hans-Thilo Schmidt) offered to sell them information connected with his employment in return for financial reward. When his offer was accepted, he provided among other items some operating instructions for the model of 'Enigma' machine then in use and tables of some current keys. These by themselves might not have been very helpful, but when the French gave them to the Polish cryptographers they greatly aided the latter's progress in solving the workings of Enigma. And, more recently, we saw the devastating Walker case in America. Not all such cases, though, end so brilliantly for either the accepter of the offer of treachery or its provider. Sometimes the offer is bogus, and ends in the accepter being duped; and sometimes the fear of being duped may lead the intended accepter to be suspicious and therefore to reject the offer, as appeared to be the case with Michael Bettany in 1983, whose treacherous overtures were treated so warily by the KGB that he was caught by his MI5 employers before his treachery could become effective.

The approach of Bettany to the KGB had some similarity to that of Oleg Penkovsky to the Americans in Moscow in 1960: to them his offer looked 'too good to be true', although it turned out to be for no personal reward but arose instead from a genuine disillusion with the Soviet system. Fortunately, although rejected by the Americans he established six months later a contact with the British, and a most valuable flow of information passed between him and his contact, Greville Wynn. Here mutual respect and friendship easily grew up between the two men.

That kind of respect was at its height of sublimity in World War II, among those of us in London who were working with agents in the many resistance networks in German-occupied territory. These agents were men and women who were risking themselves to help us and seeking no other reward than the liberation of their countries. On our side we were mainly amateurs who had been brought in to strengthen the previously slender organization, and one such was Jimmy Langley who so successfully headed the MI6 section responsible for helping our shot-down airmen and other service personnel to escape from the Continent. This effort was, of course, crucially dependent on specialized resistance chains whose sacrifices were such that Langley estimated that for each of the three thousand-odd men who were brought back one resistance worker had lost his or her life. No wonder, therefore, that some of us, including Langley, became completely committed to their support. In his book, *Fight Another Day*, he records the reaction of a 'professional' officer, Claude Dansey, the Vice-Chief of MI6, upon Langley's outburst at the directive that nothing could be done to help some workers in the famous Comet line who had been caught and condemned to death. 'Your trouble is, Jimmy,' said Dansey, 'that you love your agents.'[7] That cynical verdict would have applied to most of us.

Can Agents (and Others) Be Expendable?

Certainly we would not have countenanced any suggestion that one or more of our agents should be intentionally betrayed by another agent whom we aimed to ingratiate with the Germans as a double agent whose sympathies lay with them, and through whom we would subsequently feed false information about, for example, the coming landings in France. We were therefore concerned when the publication of Anthony Cave Brown's *Bodyguard of Lies* gave the impression in France that we had been prepared to do just that. One of the most gallant of French Resistance workers, the Vicomtesse de Clarens, wrote to me in 1981: '*Bodyguard of Lies* has stirred reactions and emotions, as you can well imagine, among those who have been led to think by Cave Brown that their lives and fates were considered of little value indeed when balanced with the dire necessity of avoiding the Germans finding out their Enigma was no longer secure.' Appealing to me to write to one of the Resistance journals, she continued: 'You will no doubt put things in their proper perspective, and publication in *Voix et Visages* could help to soothe some rather peeved feelings.' Faced with so much trust I took every possible step with old colleagues throughout the wartime intelligence organizations to check whether anyone could recall an instance where an agent had been intentionally betrayed, or which might be so interpreted. In reporting to *Voix et Visages* the firmly negative result, I could only console the French Resistance with the fact that the same author had said that Churchill himself had sacrificed both Coventry in 1940, to preserve the Ultra secret of our breaking Enigma, and also Bomber Command on the Nuremberg raid in 1944. He argued that the bogus agent who delivered such accurate information would be so entirely convincing that the Germans would believe the false information that he would subsequently provide about the coming D-Day landings. Neither the Coventry nor the Nuremberg claim has, to my knowledge, the slightest element of substance.

The Coventry story, though, for all its falsity has a widespread appeal because of the ethical problems that it illustrates for an operational commander and his intelligence officer. Let us suppose that the intelligence organization has established a source that can reveal the enemy's intentions, and so give notice of an impending attack in such detail that it can be parried by suitable preparation. The danger that then has to be faced is that this preparation may be so specific as to indicate to the enemy, either before or after his attack has been defeated, that information has been leaked, and that it has probably been leaked by a particular channel, for example, an insecure cipher or an agent in a key position. The enemy can then block the leak, and so valuable information on some future operation, or operations, will have been lost. Not only this, but the agent – if a human one – may have been caught and executed: an ungrateful reward for his work. Apart from this problem in ethics there are also the relative values to be assessed in the short-term advantage of acting on the information about an imminent threat and the long-term loss of information about later and possibly greater threats should the secret source be sacrificed.

Had Churchill in fact been faced with the Coventry dilemma, for example, a successful defence might have saved five hundred deaths in Coventry. But as the argument goes, if the necessary preparations could have led the Germans to realize that we were reading Enigma, and had they then changed the machine, some tens, or even hundreds, of thousands more lives might have been lost in the subsequent battles (the Atlantic, the Desert, and France) in which Enigma played a part. So Churchill must inevitably have had to decide on the sacrifice of Coventry. Actually, though, such decisions are rarely so clearcut: even in the hypothetical case of Coventry, for example, the Germans might have preferred to suspect that we had divined their intentions by some method other than breaking Enigma, such as observing the settings of their radio-beams as they were lined up in the afternoon prior to the bombing. Indeed, this is what they actually did when, later in the Blitz, they realized that we were somehow anticipating their nightly targets. Similarly, in the Battle of the Atlantic, where the Enigma information was invaluable, we were able to lead the Germans to think (as we had also done in 1914–18) that the information about U-boat positions came not from cryptography but from accurate direction-finding on the signals transmitted by the U-boats. The possibility of creating such an alibi may therefore ease the discomfort of making a painful decision; but it will always be a matter of judgment, and sometimes this judgment will have to be stern.

'Block 26'

As for whether it is ethical to risk sacrificing an agent as a result of using information he or she has provided, I am grateful never to have been confronted with the problem. But an instance has come to my notice where the agent himself took the decision for us, and it deserves to be placed on record. Pierre Julitte was an officer on the staff of General de Gaulle in London who volunteered to be parachuted back into France on intelligence missions. Captured on his third mission by the Gestapo in March 1943, he spent the next twenty-five months in prisons and concentration camps, including Buchenwald and Nordhausen (Dora). At the former, in early 1944 he and his fellow inmates of Block 26 were living in terrible conditions when they were set to work in a nearby factory making and assembling electronic components, gyroscopes and control equipment. With their knowledge of engineering they considered ways in which they might subtly sabotage the components so that whatever these were to be used for would fail in operation. Gradually they realized that the 'whatever' must be something new and important, and Julitte deduced that this could be 'a self-propelled projectile, navigating in space, subject to vibration and remote-controlled by radio'. A colleague returning from a stint in the works where the V2 (A4) rockets were being assembled confirmed Julitte's guess. And when they learned from the German radio that the V1 campaign had opened on 13 June 1944, they decided to try to warn the British and American Air Forces about the production of the V2.

One of Julitte's colleagues was to attempt to escape with a message to Julitte's sister in Paris and his cousin in Neuilly. The message gave instructions that the information be forwarded to London with the advice that their factory should be bombed – even though Julitte and his colleagues might be killed if this advice were acted upon. When I wrote *Most Secret War* I was quite ignorant of this heroic episode; but Julitte himself then sent me a copy of his own book *Block 26* in which he had recounted his story, though with all the personal names changed. This gave the book the atmosphere of a novel; but so many of the details rang true that I was convinced. Later I was able to meet M. Julitte and ask him why he had falsified the names. His characteristic reply was that some of his colleagues had not shown up so well, and that if he had changed only their names and given credit to those to whom it was truly due, a reader might deduce those who had behaved badly, and so he decided to falsify all names.

The one remaining item in his story that puzzled me was his precise statement that the factory had been heavily bombed in daylight on 24 August 1944. The factory had been destroyed and five hundred of his co-workers had been killed, as he himself might have been. I could, though, find no mention of such a raid in the Official Histories of either Bomber Command or the Air Defence of Great Britain, although other raids to inhibit the development of the V-weapons had been faithfully listed. Ultimately the Air Historical Section found the answer for me: the factory had indeed been attacked by 128 Flying Fortresses on 24 August 1944, but the target had merely been described in the records as 'an armaments factory at Weimar (Buchenwald)' and so the historians had failed to connect the factory with V2 production.[8] The air intelligence summary described the results of the subsequent photographic reconnaissance: 'Smoke from extensive fires obscures the greater part of the armaments factory but in the southern and eastern parts which are visible it can be seen that the USAAF attack on 24 August has caused severe damage to almost every building. The radio factory to the north has been completely gutted and some barrack huts in the concentration camp have been severely damaged.'[9] Through the lost production of V2s the lives of many must thereby have been saved in London and Antwerp who never knew what they owed to Julitte and his colleagues. Can anyone wonder that Langley and I 'loved our agents'? Their sacrifice stands in sublime contrast to the hideous conditions under which they made it.

Torture (and Reprisals)

The German treatment of captured agents raises the question of how far a captor is entitled to go in forcing a prisoner to disclose information, and in discouraging intelligence activities in occupied territory by reprisals on the civilian population. The German treatment of prisoners-of-war was, with some exceptions, correct: but their attitude towards civilians was harsh and, often, brutal. They followed the doctrine of Clausewitz, that terror was justified as a way to shorten war. They had employed it after Sedan in 1870, and again in 1914 in Belgium. Barbara Tuchman in *August 1914* gives the examples of 211 civilians shot at Andenne, 50 at Seilles, 400 at Tamines, 612 at Dinant, and uncounted numbers at Louvain.[10] In World War II they again used terrorism as a policy; the massacres at Oradour and Lidice were among the appalling results. While it may not be entirely fair to cite these examples as inhumanity specifically to intelligence agents, they do indicate the utter harshness of the German viewpoint during both wars. And the harshness undoubtedly had its effect on intelligence agents; of which there are two examples in *Most Secret War*. One was of the outstanding agent, Georges Lamarque, who gave himself up to the Germans when they surrounded the village from which they had detected his radio transmissions, sacrificing himself to protect the villagers who might otherwise have suffered the fate of those at Oradour. The other was of the agent Yves le Bitoux, who surrendered to the Gestapo at Tréguier in 1944 because he feared that the Germans would savage the town if he had succeeded in escaping. He later died in a concentration camp.[11]

Apart from the questions of the morality of reprisals and also of the extent to which they may be counterproductive by stimulating resistance rather than cowing it, we need to consider the morality of torture as a means of forcing a captive to reveal information. We in Britain eschewed it. From the interrogators whom I knew personally I am sure that this was on the grounds of humanity, although it was also doctrine with them that torture could produce misleading results because a person under torture is likely to tell his torturers what he thinks they would like to hear rather than what he truly knows. But we would have to admit that the Germans did achieve some successes by torturing captives; and we would also have to admit that the sadism from which we so firmly refrained has sometimes been exhibited in Britain.

I am personally grateful never to have been confronted with a problem of this type: suppose you have captured a terrorist who has planted a bomb which has not yet exploded but which you have reason to think he has left in some place where its explosion will cause casualties and damage. In an extreme case it might be an atomic bomb. He refuses to tell you its location. To what limits are you justified in going to make him talk?

I would hate to resort to torture, all the more so if he has shown himself to be a brave man; but the same fundamental respect for human life and dignity that makes torture so repulsive would also justify driving him to the point of death if you could thereby save the many more lives that would perish if the bomb exploded. And then, if you admit the argument for torture in such an instance, where do you draw the line? A rationalist answer might be: at the point where you are reasonably certain that the total of human suffering will be less if the torture succeeds in extracting the information required. But while this argument may have been valid for the overall saving of human lives by the atomic bomb on Hiroshima, it also underlies Clausewitz's justification of terror tactics, and we have seen the depths into which it can so easily slide.

If we admit that torture might in some circumstances be justified, we have to return to the responsibility of an intelligence service towards its agents in the field who risk capture and torture by the opposing security service. They may also risk death. My own experience was almost entirely in the circumstances of war, where such considerations were much simpler. In peace, there are not only agents at risk but also foreign relations if an operation goes wrong. Such problems have been described by Admiral Stansfield Turner, who was Director of the CIA from 1977 to 1980, in *Secrecy and Democracy*.[12] Coming into intelligence after a distinguished career in the US Navy, the Admiral looked afresh at all such problems, and his conclusions have much in common with those that I myself formed in wartime. This might be partly due to the fact that even in peacetime an intelligence service is in effect engaged in a war with its opposing security service. One difference, though, that makes peacetime working more difficult is that intelligence operations are then regarded far less sympathetically by the public, and there is much more time for post-mortems and recrimination if mistakes have been made.

Covert Action

This last factor has dogged the CIA over the last thirty years, all the more so because the agency has been involved not only with intelligence but with the more aggressive forms of covert action. In Britain in World War II there was originally a section in MI6 concerned with sabotage, but in 1940 this was hived off into a completely new organization, the Special Operations Executive. On the whole this was beneficial to both activities, since the intelligence organization – if it had an agent placed in a good position to gather information – aimed to keep him there, even sometimes to the extent of not using his information if this might lead to his being discovered, and therefore to his inability to provide more valuable information in the future, whereas SOE tended to regard its sabotage agents more as elements in an active army where casualties were to be expected, and where the results of their work would be much more immediately obvious to the enemy. Again, sabotage usually required greater numbers of personnel, and the organization had therefore to be larger: and so, although the same conflict between short- and long-term operations could arise in sabotage as well as in intelligence, there was much merit in separating the two activities as far as possible. They also attracted rather different types of officer – some who would be repelled by actions of the 'dirty tricks' variety would have less hesitation in working for intelligence.

Admiral Turner, though, takes a differing view. While accepting that separating covert action from intelligence might solve some problems, he argues that it would create others: 'The CIA's intelligence agents overseas are often the same people needed for covert action. It would be confusing, and at times dangerous, to have two agencies giving them orders and managing their activities. And if one agency did only covert action, what would it do during periods of slack demand?' This last consideration did not apply to us in war because there were continuous demands for both activities; but we certainly encountered problems in rivalries between the two types of organization operating in the same territory.

A further complication arises from the fact that an intelligence organization – if it is doing its job – will often be the first to realize, from its unique viewpoint, the vulnerability of an opponent, actual or potential. Therefore intelligence will know where and how the enemy can best be hindered by deception, sabotage, or – in war – overt military action. For example, I myself was sometimes in this position in World War II, as in the cases of 'Window' (or 'Chaff') and countermeasures to German radio bombing techniques: but it was clear that once I had made a technical or tactical suggestion for action the responsibility for its implementation belonged to the operational staff. Obviously action is facilitated if both intelligence and operations can be controlled under one organization; but an offsetting merit of separation is that an intelligence unit is more likely to be impartial in its assessment of the success of operations if it is independent of any attempt by the operational side to interpret the evidence regarding success or failure too favourably. For all these reasons I continue to stand for the independence of intelligence from operations, both covert and overt, to the highest possible level in government organization, although of course recognizing the need for the greatest possible understanding between intelligence and operational staffs.

Returning then to America, it can be seen how the responsibility of the CIA for both intelligence and covert operations has created many problems for the Agency. Its involvement in, and part responsibility for, the Bay of Pigs disaster in 1961, which attempted to overthrow Castro, led to the resignation of the Director, Allen Dulles. Richard Helms, who had been Director from 1966, was fired by President Nixon in 1973 because, according to his biographer Thomas Powers, he refused to provide a CIA cover-up for Nixon in the Watergate affair.[13] These grounds would have been quite implausible if the CIA had always kept itself apart from covert operations concerned with internal security. William Colby, who became Director in 1973, was in his turn dismissed in 1975 by President Ford largely because of public outcry at the CIA's involvement in assassinations, over which Colby himself had been scrupulously honest – too honest, many of his staff thought – in exposing the Agency's past mistakes. His departure was finally precipitated by Press and public indignation over his revelation to a Senate Committee of the existence of a dart gun and small quantities of virulent poisons that had come to light in an obscure store-room which had been overlooked in his previous survey, conscientious though this had been. Colby welcomed me in his office shortly after his dismissal. When I expressed my regret he nobly told me that he did not mind how much he himself suffered from the episode if by 'taking the rap' he could leave the Agency in a healthy condition. Finally, this story of the fates of CIA Directors might have had a further melancholy chapter over the arms for Iran affair, had not the death of William Casey early in 1987 intervened before the official inquiries into the affair could be completed – although Casey himself was convinced that he and the Agency would be vindicated.

Assassination

Helms himself observed that 'war corrupts and secret war corrupts secretly'.[14] So it is easy to slip towards the acceptance of assassination as one of its techniques. In 1940 there was a suggestion that there should be a special British clandestine operation to attack the aircrews of the German pathfinders who were causing us so much trouble in the Blitz. They were to be ambushed while being ferried by bus between their billets and the airfield at Vannes before taking off for an attack. This was vetoed by Sir Charles Portal, the Chief of Air Staff; but as the war progressed, feelings became less delicate. Later, at the time of the Suez crisis in 1956, there was even talk – it appears – of attempting to assassinate President Nasser.[15] In America, Allen Dulles, aware of the danger of the CIA slipping towards an acceptance of assassination, specifically forbade it when he was Director, and an embargo was included in presidential directives on three occasions. Nevertheless it was sometimes attempted, with disastrous results for the CIA when it came to light.

Torture and Duress

Torture, too, was officially barred – at least to the extent of a rule being formulated by Helms in 1955 under Dulles's directorship: 'You may not use electrical, chemical, or physical duress,' it read, although, as Powers then went on to point out, 'psychological duress was okay'.[16] We, in World War II, certainly tried to bluff prisoners-of-war into thinking we knew much more than we did in the hope that this would mislead them into giving away things about which we knew little or nothing. And it seemed not too unfair to 'fence' psychologically with a prisoner and thus to trap him into saying more than he had originally intended. But there had to be a limit such as, for example, not playing on a man's emotions by encouraging him to worry about the safety of his family. I take it that no such restraint is likely to be widely observed today.

'Character Assassination'

Short of killing a key individual on the opposing side, his value to them may be destroyed if his colleagues or countrymen can be misled into suspecting that he is a secret agent for your own side, or has some other motive for working against his side's interests. This mischievous technique is only likely to succeed when the individual in question is working in an organization prone to mutual suspicion; but in so far as it exploits a moral weakness in that organization, so 'hoisting the engineer with his own petard', it may be less repugnant than other measures.

Intervention

In parallel with the ethical problem of the humane limits of conduct towards individuals, there is the problem of the extent to which any one state can be justified in attempting to interfere in the internal affairs of another. The 'Irangate' affair and the clandestine mining of Nicaraguan harbours under CIA auspices are cases in point. In discussing such questions Stansfield Turner in *Secrecy and Democracy*[17] quotes John Stuart Mill's *A few words on non-intervention* (1859):

> The doctrine of non-intervention, to be a legitimate principle of morality, must be accepted by all governments. The despot must consent to be bound by it as well as the free state. Unless they do, the profession comes to this miserable issue – that the wrong side may help the wrong, but the right must not help the right.

Thus a Gresham's Law will tend to operate in international affairs, especially in any field of covert action where the operators think that their actions will be free from public scrutiny. All the more reason, therefore, to endorse Turner's specification for CIA personnel selection: 'The CIA needs people not only with skills, but with high moral standards, with the confidence to be independent, and with the desire to be innovative.'[18] He also stated that 'there is one overall test of the ethics of human intelligence activities. That is whether those approving them feel they could defend their decisions before the public if the actions became public. This guideline does not say that the overseers should approve actions only if the public would approve them if they knew of them. Rather it says that the overseers should be so convinced of the importance of the actions that they would accept any criticism that might develop if the covert actions did become public, and could construct a convincing defense of their decisions.'[19]

Internal Intelligence

Besides the ethical questions concerning how a nation and its officials and agents should restrain their activities in gaining information about another nation's secrets, or in attempting to interfere in its internal affairs, there are other questions that will arise when a nation's officials have to seek out activities within its own borders that could jeopardize its security. In Britain these are the province of MI5, while MI6 covers intelligence about other nations. Although this is a neat division of functions, MI5 and MI6 at times have joint interests. For example, when foreign agents operating outside Britain attempt to organize sub-agents for espionage, sabotage, terrorism, or whatever inside it, the agents abroad are, strictly, targets for MI6 and the sub-agents in Britain for MI5. For such problems, liaison between MI5 and MI6 has to be very close: in 1939–45 this was largely effected by having a special section inside MI6 – ironically its head was Kim Philby.

In America a rather similar separation of functions is made between the Central Intelligence Agency and the Federal Bureau of Investigation, although the separation there is now more on a territorial basis; the CIA being responsible for all intelligence and counter-intelligence activities abroad, and the FBI for all inside the United States. Much the same problems arise in America as in Britain respecting individual privacy; for example, in opening private correspondence, tapping telephone conversations, or breaking into private premises. According to Colby in *Honorable Men*,[20] the CIA in 1952 started a programme of opening selected letters in the mail between the United States and Russia in the hope of detecting undesirable activity. This was 'a direct violation of a criminal statute' and the practice was shelved in 1973. Admiral Turner records that the tapping of telephones and other forms of electronic communication in the United States have since 1978 been governed by the Foreign Intelligence Surveillance Act, which stipulates that if it has to be done it should be carried out using the least obtrusive technique that will do the job; every such operation should be certified as necessary before the Attorney General and reviewed by a special court of senior judges. Breaks into private premises presumably now require similar authorization, since the Watergate and Ellsberg (1971) cases brought such break-ins so embarrassingly to public notice.

Following disclosures by former MI5 officers about break-ins by MI5 in Britain, the Government has introduced a Bill to put such operations – hitherto illegal – on a legitimate basis and subject to the safeguard that each operation must be authorized by the Home Secretary and 'only when he was satisfied that the information was likely to be of substantial value and assistance to [the Security Service] . . . and . . . could not reasonably be obtained by other means'.[21] An independent commissioner would be appointed to review the issuing of warrants and to make an annual report to the Prime Minister. There appear to be few reasonable alternatives to these proposals in a democratic society.

Privacy

While any decent individual instinctively reacts against break-ins and less violent infringements of privacy, a state legitimately requests some details about each of its individual citizens for a wide range of social purposes such as taxation, educational planning, transport facilities, and potential for military and other forms of public service. It might therefore be asked why we set so much store by a right to privacy. Apart from the nightmare of a 'Big Brother' state, there is an instinctive dislike of surveillance, even parental surveillance; and there may well be an apprehension based deeply back in the evolutionary process arising from a feeling of vulnerability while executing bodily functions or in sickness, and of latent trouble from a stalking predator whose staring eyes betray his intentions. More rationally, I for one would have little objection to any authority having any information it wished about my actions – or even my thoughts – provided that I could be sure that it would not misinterpret the information to come to false conclusions about me.

Just as technology is tending to modify concepts of sovereignty (from a three-mile limit for territorial waters based on the range of a gun to a limit of 200 miles today, and the free movement of satellites over the territories of other nations, for example) so also it is tending to change the balance between the rights of individuals and the states of which they are members. The complex organization of a modern state needs to know more about its individuals for optimum functioning, and this is all the easier to achieve because of the technical advances in handling and storing information; and, unfortunately, it will be only too easy for zeal to replace judgment in the process.

Oversight

Some of the problems of internal intelligence, both in the United

States and in Britain, have arisen from excessive zeal. Thirty years ago Percy Sillitoe's determination as head of MI5 to stop Britain from becoming a police state (see above, page 21) was all the safeguard that was needed; but today with the various exposures regarding both MI5 and the greater surveillance needed to protect against penetration, it is difficult to be so sure. The attempted remedy in America is 'oversight', where the activities of the intelligence and security services are overseen by committees, one from the Senate and the other from the House of Representatives. Much obviously depends on the selection of members for these committees, but on balance Admiral Turner, in whose time as Director of the CIA they first became effective, records a favourable impression. On the negative side, he found them restrictive: 'We tend to apply our new enthusiasm for oversight of the ethics of intelligence to micromanagement by the Congress of the development of new intelligence technologies . . . Another false economy that congressional oversight has fostered is the frugality in stockpiling intelligence collection systems . . . One other dangerous hindrance is that the CIA's research branch is gradually losing out to the large and clever military bureaucracy at the Pentagon . . . The espionage people also deserve better protection from the Congress and the White House.'[22] But on the positive side, he wrote, 'oversight, especially by Congress, can give helpful guidance to the CIA as to what is and what is not acceptable conduct in the pursuit of secrets . . . the better the oversight process is, the less concern there need be about concentrating too much authority in the hands of the DCI . . . If we want good intelligence in the long run, our only option is to make oversight work.'[23] At the same time Admiral Turner would fuse the Senate and Congressional oversight committees into one with a membership limited to reduce the possibility of leaks.[24]

While, though, Admiral Turner so firmly supports oversight, the record in Washington since it was introduced has not been one of unqualified success. It is now generally agreed that the CIA-sponsored mining of Nicaraguan harbours in 1983 was a mistake, and it was allowed to go ahead despite nominal oversight by both the Senate Intelligence Committee under Barry Goldwater and the Congressional Intelligence Committee under Edward Boland. The latter had been so disturbed by earlier developments that in August 1982 he had succeeded in moving that the CIA and the Defense Department should be prohibited from furnishing military equipment, training or support to anyone 'for the purpose of overthrowing the Government of Nicaragua'.[25] Robert Woodward, who with Carl Bernstein exposed the Watergate affair, has described this episode at length in *Veil: The Secret Wars of the CIA 1981–7*.[26] Formally, the members of the oversight committee were in a difficult position. The law which established them stipulates that they must be informed of major intelligence activities, but appears not to have given them a right of veto: moreover, the individual members had been sworn to secrecy, and so they could be in trouble if they made a public disclosure.

It is not easy to see a way out of this difficulty. No intelligence organization can surrender its executive responsibility to an oversight committee, no matter how able, experienced and responsible the individual members of the committee may be. Two reasons preclude any such procedure. The first is that an intelligence organization is constantly waging a war, and any operations in that war need a commander with full responsibility for their planning and execution. At times risks have to be taken, and a committee approach is likely to be inhibiting. Clive of India said that he had held a council of war but once, and had he heeded the advice of the council rather than his own judgment the British would never have been masters of India.

The second reason against the committee approach is allied to the first; it arises from the way in which intelligence appreciations have to be formed from the information that has been gained. Despite Napoleon's worry about the danger of 'making a picture of the enemy', this is what an intelligence organization has to do in presenting its conclusions for assimilation by those who have then to undertake executive action. Just as an artist has to present as faithful an impression as possible, according to his lights, with the economy of detail of a painted portrait as contrasted with a photograph, so an intelligence officer has to convey a portrait of the opponent constructed to give the truest possible impression from the limited amount of detailed information that will be available even to a good intelligence service. An intelligence report therefore has much in common with a work of art; and my experiences on the Joint Intelligence Committee (see above, page 28) suggest that committees are hardly more likely to produce good intelligence reports than they would be to paint good pictures. When information is sparse it permits a multitude of explanations, and committees can lose much time over indecisive argument as to which is the correct one.

This was also the experience of General Eugene Tighe, head of the Defense Intelligence Agency in the Pentagon from 1977 to 1979. In thirty-six years of intelligence work, 'he had seen administrations, Secretaries of Defense, and DCIs come and go, and the shape and tone of intelligence work change. But the real squabbles arose when they didn't have enough information. When US intelligence had a lot of good data, there was rarely a fight.'[27]

While not wishing to under-rate the second of the foregoing reasons, I believe the first is decisive in determining that an intelligence service must have freedom to act as it thinks best, and to that extent oversight must have limits. The example of the mining of Nicaraguan harbours may suggest that these limits were too loosely drawn, or that an enterprising DCI could too easily find a way round them. The same example may also suggest that it is dangerous for an intelligence organization to have such autonomy, even though nominally subject to oversight. But, once again, intelligence is waging a war and risks sometimes have to be run. Churchill's delighted soldiers in the Royal Scots Fusiliers in 1916 told how he, as their commanding officer, was visited in the front line by a general from some rear headquarters. 'If you would care, sir,' said Churchill, 'to step over the parapet, we could go for a walk in no-man's land.' 'Wouldn't that be dangerous?' asked the general. Churchill replied, 'Sir, this is a dangerous war!' And that will always be true of war fought by intelligence agencies too, where the lines may be covertly drawn.

As for whether we in Britain should adopt oversight of the intelligence services on the American pattern I would have said in the days of men like Percy Sillitoe that there was little need for it – at least as regards the danger of the services overstepping the limits of reasonable conduct. The oversight that was needed then was more in looking for inefficiencies in the system such as were all too evident in 1939 and, more recently, were the subject of the Franks inquiry over the Falklands. But moral standards have fallen from the days when an Englishman's word was his bond, as we have seen in other walks of public life, such as the City. It cannot be guaranteed that this is never likely to affect the conduct of intelligence affairs, with all the temptations that they may afford. Some measure of oversight is therefore desirable, if only to assure Parliament and the public that intelligence is being wisely and scrupulously conducted.

Successive prime ministers have strongly discouraged the discussion of intelligence affairs in Parliament, where obvious dangers could arise from disclosure. But, while it was easy to protect the intelligence services from scrutiny when these were small, it is less easy today when organizations like GCHQ are much larger. Besides the problems that thereby arise from trades unions, increases in numbers give rise to increased chances for treachery and for leaks that will sooner or later come to public notice and so lead to discussion in Parliament. There appears to be a body inside government itself that could provide oversight, the Ministerial Steering Committee on Intelligence. But whether this is the best body for the purpose, or whether a small inter-party body of senior politicians (and perhaps others of experience, discretion and judgment) might be better, would itself be a fitting matter for Parliamentary discussion.

Minimum Trespass

Two final points on ethics are worth making. The first is that, despite all the opportunities – and temptations – that it offers for malpractice, intelligence can be an honourable pursuit. Indeed, by improving the assessment by one nation of another it can, on occasion, contribute to international stability. On less happy occasions, of course, the children of light will be at a disadvantage unless they know enough of the ways of the world to forestall or counter any unworthy exploitation of those ways by the children of this world. There need be absolutely no dishonour in trying to ascertain what a potential or actual opponent is likely to attempt, be it by external armed threat or by internal subversion. The risk of disrepute will depend on the extent to which the individual intelligence officer or his organization departs from the norms of morality in uncovering an opponent's activities.

The second point follows from the first. One of the canons governing military or police action is the doctrine of minimum force, and a parallel canon should govern intelligence: it should be conducted with the minimum trespass against national and individual human rights. This canon applies to all forms of intelligence, both external and internal, that a civilized state may find it necessary to undertake.

3

Official Secrecy

'Concerning Government,' wrote Francis Bacon in *The Advancement of Learning* in 1605, 'it is a part of knowledge secret and retired, in both these respects in which things are deemed secret; for some things are secret because they are hard to know, and some because they are not fit to utter. We see all governments are obscure and invisible . . .' Bacon's observations will strike resonances in the minds of many who have encountered official secrets either from inside government organizations or from outside. Since official secrecy has become increasingly a matter of public concern, thanks largely to the impact of technology on intelligence, it may be helpful if I attempt to distil some points of lasting value from my own experiences, gained alternately from inside and outside officialdom.

Bacon's 'hard to know' category might fairly be applied to such secrets as those encountered in defence or in industry, where some technique or process may have been developed as a result of a painstaking study or a lucky discovery, and where the discoverer has a reasonable claim to keep the essential details secret to give him a defence or a commercial advantage. But what of the other category of secrets, covering things which 'are not fit to utter'? Much depends here on how we interpret 'fit'. If, for the moment, we substitute 'proper' or 'right', then we can agree that – for example – it would not have been proper or right to publish the success of Bletchley in breaking the Enigma ciphers in World War II, for this would have lost us a great military advantage. Such secrets, together with those of the 'hard to know' kind of military technology, are a legitimate concern of official safeguards.

Granted the need for official secrecy in such instances, we can also agree that it has to be extended to the non-military sphere where, for example, leakages of budget secrets or of plans for a wide variety of social developments could enable individuals and organizations to take unfair social or financial advantage.

The fundamental dilemma then confronting official secrecy is how to prevent the disclosure of any clues which could enable an undesired recipient to take action, either military or social, harmful to the well-being of the state without this secrecy imposing so many restrictions that the workings of the state are themselves thereby hindered. Once again, this second horn of the dilemma had been grasped by Bacon: 'But, contrariwise, in the governors towards the governed, all things ought, as far as the frailty of man permitteth, to be manifest and revealed.'

Secrecy to Excess

The most obvious danger of excessive security is that it may prevent information reaching people who have a genuine and legitimate need for it in work which they are doing in the interests of the state. The research and development effort towards the atomic bomb in America in 1943 was, for example, highly compartmentalized in the interest of security so that any one worker had minimal knowledge of what progress was being made outside the limited field in which he had been directed to work. In Britain, the leadership of men like Tizard – and the emergency in which we found ourselves – had led us as far as possible to break down barriers, for example between scientists and serving officers and between scientists of differing disciplines and seniority. So when a British physicist was visiting the American atomic effort, and naturally moved around the various compartments, he found that in one of them progress was held up for lack of data about some particular nuclear characteristics that he knew had already been measured in one of the other compartments that he had previously visited in the same laboratory. Admiral Turner, in *Secrecy and Democracy*,[1] gives another example concerning a presidential request in the late seventies for some aerial photographs to show what was happening in a minor war between two third world countries. It took him weeks to acquire the photographs – only afterwards did he learn that suitable photographs already existed in another part of the intelligence community in Washington, the Defense Intelligence Agency. 'I didn't know till months later that while I was frantically looking for photos, the DIA had them right in Washington.'

A classic example of the benefit to be gained from breaking down unnecessary security was given by Lord Mountbatten who, as Chief of Combined Operations in 1943, had among the scientists on his staff the eminent physicist J. D. Bernal, and who contributed this telling anecdote to the Biographical Memoir of Bernal in the Records of the Royal Society. It refers to the planning of the landings in Normandy in 1944.

> The particular problems which I assigned to Bernal related to the initial landing across the beaches. He worked with my Director of Experiments and Staff Requirements, Captain T. A. Hussey, Royal Navy, and made significant contributions to techniques for dealing with under-water obstacles and defences on the beaches, with the assessment of the gradients of beaches, and the consistency of their bearing surface, and with runnels and sand banks.
>
> Soon after the arrival of the scientists, I told my staff that they were not to be asked just to answer questions posed by the uniformed staff but to be fully brought in to the framing of the questions for whose solutions their help was wanted. Curiously this went rather badly at first with the uniformed staff. But then fate played into my hands. A young naval officer went to Bernal and asked him what he thought the chances were of making a very small light portable echo-sounder to measure very small depths accurately. Bernal asked, 'Why?' The officer replied that the matter was too secret to explain, and it was up to Bernal to answer the question. To this Bernal replied, 'No' and that I had given an instruction that the scientists were to participate in the formulation of the problems to be investigated. He therefore wished to know more.
>
> Rather reluctantly the young officer then told him that what was wanted was a way of finding out, without the Germans knowing what we were doing, how to measure beach gradients, the runnels, as well as the consistency of the kind of beaches which we might assault. His own idea was to put a light echo-sounder on a board and push it in at night from a submarine with a swimmer who would try to obtain this information.
>
> Bernal's reply was 'You've asked the wrong question, you should have said "How do we measure the beach gradients and runnels without the Germans knowing?"' His own answer was that PR Photography should be used, taking vertical photographs of the desired beaches at various stages of the tide and directions of the wind, and that the coverage should extend beyond the desired beaches so as to disguise from the Germans what we were up to.
>
> This incident has been quoted before but I mention it here because it shows how strongly Bernal resisted the attempt by uniformed staff to put him into a position of merely answering questions which they were putting. He insisted on participating in the formulation of problems. This was a very great pioneer service which he performed.

Lord Mountbatten's faith in Bernal, amply justified by subsequent events, was all the more noteworthy because Bernal's untidy appear ance was not such as to inspire confidence in the conventional serving officer. I myself had a sidelight on this when I was visiting the Central Interpretation Unit for aerial photographs at Medmenham. Over a drink before lunch, one of the officers inquired whether I knew a Professor Bernal. Following my reply that I did, I was asked what kind of man he was. Guardedly I replied that he was a very good physicist, and in return I asked why the Unit was interested in him. It transpired that in the previous week Bernal had visited the Unit because of a common interest in the assessment of bomb damage on German targets from air photographs. Having explained this, my host continued: 'We thought he was a bit "off". After all, we are a regular air force station, and we thought that he might have put on a decent suit to come to visit us. However, during the afternoon he seemed quite a decent chap, and just as he was leaving he invited us to go across to see his work. We went yesterday, and as soon as we saw him in his establishment we realized that we had done him an injustice. He *had* put on his best suit to come to see us.'

Zeal and Ridicule

The foregoing examples, illustrating the hindrance that security can create and the advantages that can result when it is reasonably relaxed, could be multiplied profusely from the memories of many who have been concerned with security. In addition, an excessive zeal for security can give rise to a further danger, for it can sometimes produce results so ridiculous that they bring security and those responsible for it into public disrespect; and this will make it less likely that measures genuinely needed and promulgated in the interests of security will then be willingly observed.

To the many examples given by David Hooper in *Official Secrets* a host more could be added where misplaced zeal has brought security into ridicule. Some of these have incidentally been painful to men who have served their country with distinction and outstanding loyalty. David Hooper records[2] that Admiral Lord Lewin, the Chief of Defence Staff, was investigated with a view to prosecution for revealing the use of towed sonar arrays in the Falklands; and it is certainly true that the head of the Admiralty cryptographic effort in the famous Room OB40 in World War I, Sir Alfred Ewing, was threatened with prosecution years later for giving a lecture describing his experiences, even though in general terms. Since the incident has echoes today, it may be worth briefly recounting.

Room 40's most important feat was the decrypting of the Zimmermann telegram of 1917 which showed that Germany was inviting Mexico into a military alliance. The telegram proposed that, in the event of the United States coming into the war, the States of Texas, New Mexico and Arizona would be ceded to Mexico if the alliance were successful. The contents of the telegram were made known to the Americans through their Ambassador in London, Walter Page, and the outcome was their declaration of war on Germany. The decrypting of the telegram was of course a matter of the highest secrecy, but in order for the Americans to be convinced that it was genuine, full details had to be shown to their own experts. The secret was loyally kept by those concerned; but in 1918 Page died, and his papers came into the hands of biographers who in 1925 published some of the details in an American magazine. The effect was rather like it would have been if the 'Ultra' secret of Bletchley's successes in World War II had been published in 1952 rather than in 1974. Still, no one on the British side 'broke ranks' in writing of the achievement or in naming those responsible, until November 1925 when Stanley Baldwin, then Prime Minister, was being entertained at a civic lunch in Edinburgh where one of the speakers was Lord Balfour, then Chancellor of the University, who had been First Lord of the Admiralty at the time the Zimmermann telegram was broken. Perhaps seeking to impress upon the Prime Minister the contributions of universities to national life, Balfour referred to the topical matter of the telegram and its importance, and went on to reveal that the man who had set up the great organization responsible for its decryption was none other than Sir Alfred Ewing, now the Principal of the University.

Balfour's revelation naturally aroused the interest of the Press, and Ewing was thereafter under much pressure to tell his story. He resisted for two years, and then agreed to give a public lecture in the Assembly Hall of the University, which he did on 13 December 1927. It was a splendid lecture, with an audience of nearly 1,500; but despite all his discretion it aroused the retribution of the security authorities of the day, as Ewing's successor at Room 40, Admiral Sir William James, described many years later in 1964 at a talk he himself gave in Edinburgh.

> I hope I will not be arrested tomorrow. The last person who told the story of Room 40 in Edinburgh, Sir Alfred Ewing, narrowly escaped arrest. I was Naval Assistant to the First Sea Lord when I heard that

> prosecution of Ewing under the Official Secrets Act was being considered.
>
> Officers and officials then at the Admiralty knew that Room 40 had been a secret but little else. In its early days it had been a carefully guarded secret, but the veil of secrecy soon wore thin when we established a close liaison with the French Room 40 and the Russian Room 40 (up to the Revolution) and sent out cryptographers to found an Italian Room 40.
>
> When a war lasts long enough it is always possible to detect the efficiency of the enemy's Intelligence service, and the Germans from time to time knew we were reading their messages and we knew that the German cryptographers were very skilled. It was impossible to write the history of the war without quoting the intercepted signals, and though the diplomatic intercepts were kept secret during the war, ambassadors and statesmen could not give a faithful account of their stewardship without quoting them, and all the important intercepts were published in Dr Page's letters, Robert Lansing's Memoirs, Amos Peaslee's book on the hunting down of the German saboteurs, and Colonel House's letters.
>
> The Admiralty would have looked extremely foolish if they had prosecuted Ewing. I explained all this to the First Sea Lord and the stupid project was dropped.[3]

Nevertheless, the security authorities insisted that Ewing must not be allowed to publish the text of the lecture, and thereafter it survived only as a typescript in his personal papers. Ewing himself was 'certain that the narrative had enough historical value to justify its appearance in print'. He commented that 'it would be nice for the grandchildren to have later'.[4]

In 1978, following the publication of *Most Secret War*, Ewing's great-grandson, Mr D. J. Wills, wrote to me saying that the book reminded him of his great-grandfather's work in intelligence, and enclosed a copy of the typescript. It was fascinating to see how many of our problems in World War II had earlier been encountered in World War I, and the lecture even contained the phrase 'ultra secret'. Cryptographers to whom I showed it were anxious that it should at last appear in print, and this I was able to arrange because Ewing was a distinguished Fellow of the Royal Society, and its *Notes and Records*, of which I was editor, was therefore a most suitable venue.

Naturally, I wrote to Mr Wills telling him of the interest in the lecture, and asking his permission for its publication. He replied that the family would be delighted to see it at last in print, provided that this time I could assure them that there would be no trouble over security. It seemed to me that there could now be no possible security objection, for the events Ewing described had all happened more than sixty years before. They had since been treated in detail in several books, such as the biography of Ewing written by his son (who had in fact drawn on the lecture for some of his material), or Barbara Tuchman's *The Zimmermann Telegram* or William James's biography of Reginald Hall, the famous Director of Naval Intelligence. Again, Admiral James had not only himself been head of Room OB40 but had also worked from Hall's papers, which contained the whole story and included many of the actual decrypts. However, to reassure the family it was easy enough to play the matter 'straight down the middle' and so I sent in the lecture to the Cabinet Office for, as I thought, formal clearance in 1978.

Six weeks passed before I received the official reply. It would now be permissible to publish the lecture, but three sentences would still have to be deleted. At first I was inclined to accept, but on further thought I concluded that if I, as editor, could not say that this was the full text, then readers would wonder what was still being held back, and publication would therefore lose some of its value. The sentences in question seemed trivial to what I would claim to be my professional eye, in view of the fact that their import was thoroughly well known. When I showed them to the cryptographic historian, David Kahn, his verdict was 'these facts have long been known and you may rest assured that you are in no way shaking the foundations of British security if you now reprint them for what must now be the tenth or twentieth time.'

Even so, I informed the authorities that I would consider withholding the three sentences if I could be told why they might be objectionable. Remembering my earlier past as scientific adviser to GCHQ and my wartime associations, I hoped that the objections could be explained to me, at least in confidence, for I certainly had no thought of embarrassing the working of an organization for whose wartime achievements I had the profoundest respect. I was then told by telephone that such information was too secret to be sent by post. I replied that my office had for years been 'cleared' by security officers to accept not only secret but also top secret material, which reached me from government offices by registered post; if that were not safe enough, I was frequently in London and would be content to hear a verbal explanation.

After a further six weeks, any form of explanation was still refused, and so I informed the security authorities that I could only conclude that they had no explanation that would bear even a sympathetic scrutiny, and so I intended to publish the text with the three sentences intact. In this, I had the agreement of the Ewing family and publication finally took place in July 1979. Incidentally, I subsequently met the security officer who had had to present the official view to me, and I suspect that he had thought the GCHQ objections no more reasonable than I had done myself.

As for why GCHQ was so unforthcoming, I was inclined to speculate that memories of our 1952–4 differences over electronic intelligence outweighed the cordial ones of 1939–45, and this speculation seems to be confirmed by what then happened on a visit to the RAF Station at Wyton in 1984 where the Commanding Officer had asked me to write about the part played by the Station in the hunt for the German radio-beams in 1940; the article was to be printed in the commemorative brochure for the Station's Open Day to raise funds for RAF charities. As further publicity the Station was going to duplicate the listening flight on the anniversary of the day, 21 June, on which the *Knickebein* beams were first detected. I was asked to talk about the flight and its significance as part of a filmed programme for subsequent showing.

It happened that history had turned full circle, for one of the squadrons based at the station had as its main task a reconnaissance function that made it the descendant of Nos 109 and 192 Squadrons, the specialized wartime reconnaissance squadrons, with whose formation in 1940 and 1943 respectively I had been associated. Modern aircraft had of course now replaced the Ansons and Wellingtons of those days, and in gratitude for the trouble and expense of my travelling from Aberdeen, the Station Commander said that he would like me to be shown over one of the latest successors to the wartime aircraft which had served us so well. I would have gone anyway, because I have hardly if ever declined to answer a call from any unit of our armed services, but the invitation to look over the current equipment was a happy bonus.

When after a night's travel I arrived at the base, I found an indignant Station Commander. He had assumed that with all my association with the Royal Air Force and with specialized reconnaissance from its earliest days, there could be no possible objection to letting me see the modern equipment. But at the last moment he had received a telephoned instruction that I was not to be allowed inside the aircraft. He pointed to a published book on his shelves, Gunston's *Spy Planes*, which I already had, and said, 'There is more in that book than I am allowed to tell you.' Referring to whoever it was who had imposed the ban (and I was led believe that it came from GCHQ) he said, 'They just don't know their history!' If the rebuff did come from GCHQ, it was neither the first nor the most serious by far that I was to experience from an organization which had failed to detect Geoffrey Prime until his treachery came to light through criminal propensities in another direction. In retrospect I am half sorry that in the interests of not aggravating an uneasy relationship I did not yield to the temptation of sending the Director of GCHQ a record of Maurice Chevalier's 'Thank Heaven For Little Girls'.

'Positive' Vetting

Presumably Prime, Bettany and others had all survived the process of 'positive vetting' before they were admitted into the intelligence services. This must give cause to question how effective the procedure is; and if it can sometimes err in letting undesirables in, can it also err in keeping desirables out? An individual who is thus rejected by the procedure has no means of knowing the reasons for his rejection (and if he asks for them, the authorities will refuse to tell him), and therefore has no opportunity of refuting any false information that may have been gathered by the vetting officers. Even the notorious Star Chamber of Henry VII was governed by the *Pro Stella Camerata* Act of 1487, which enjoined the Chamber and its associated Council to call offenders for examination before deciding whether they had in fact offended – a right which is not today afforded to an individual rejected by positive vetting. He can then only echo the final cry of anguish of the much tormented Job:

> Let the Almighty state his case against me.
> If my accuser had written out his indictment
> I would not keep silence and remain indoors . . .
> I would plead the whole record of my life
> and present that in court as my defence.[5]

Although it is to be hoped that such instances as the wartime 'blacking' of Barnes Wallis (see below, page 70) are rare, there is little in the current procedure to prevent them.

Paranoia

My own encounters with GCHQ's zeal for security are not unique. In *The Times* of 1 July 1983, the late Professor G. C. McVittie told of his experience in 1982 when he had been invited by *Meteorological Magazine* to outline the contribution of Bletchley Park to the production of weather charts covering enemy-held Europe, in which he himself had been involved. He was told that his article had been banned by GCHQ on the grounds that it revealed the methods of breaking the German weather reporting ciphers. In fact, not only had the weather charts themselves been previously released to the Public Record Office, but also with them many of Professor McVittie's wartime reports which included brief accounts of the cipher-breaking procedures, where anyone could read them.

A more painful example of the attitude of the present authorities in GCHQ towards its wartime predecessors, to whom GCHQ owes much of its present strength, concerns two of the most vital contributors to the wartime success – Gordon Welchman and Stuart Milner-Barry. Welchman was the first head of Hut Six, where the German Army and Air Force Enigma signals were broken; and, when he left to liaise with the Americans, Milner-Barry succeeded him. In 1982 Welchman published *The Hut Six Story* describing in convincing detail how Enigma was broken. Whether or not he thereby breached any reasonable security restrictions is questionable, because the fact that Enigma was broken had been released with Government acquiescence since 1974, and it was blazoned in the *Official History of Intelligence*, whose first volume appeared in 1979. Moreover, when I learned in 1974 of the Government's decision to allow Bletchley's success in breaking Enigma to be published in Winterbotham's *The Ultra Secret*, and I expressed much surprise, the official responsible for clearing it, himself a former head of GCHQ, told me that there was no longer any basic objection because no foreign powers were still using machines of the Enigma type.

Welchman's book was of course authoritative as regards the work at Bletchley, and many of us are grateful that it was written. Welchman himself was troubled when he found that he had not done justice to the earlier work of the Polish cryptographers, on whose efforts Bletchley had been able to build, and in the journal *Intelligence and National Security* for January 1986 he published a corrective addendum. This invoked a letter to him from the Director of GCHQ, Sir Peter Marychurch, reproving him for both the article and the book, and accusing him – according to the *Guardian*[6] – of causing 'direct damage to security', and setting 'a disastrous example to others'. The text of the letter can be found in *Intelligence and National Security*, May 1986,[7] along with Sir Stuart Milner-Barry's consequent letter to the *Guardian* of 29 November 1985, part of which runs:

> Even had there been substance to Sir Peter's complaint, he might, I should have thought, have refrained from writing to a man of Welchman's distinction, 20 years his senior, in terms more appropriate to the rebuke of an erring subordinate.
>
> But in fact, the complaint is, as Dr Christopher Andrew has pointed out, a prime example of the lengths to which GCHQ's paranoia about the preservation of ancient secrets will carry them.

I can only add my whole-hearted support for Sir Stuart's strictures, further grounds for which can be found both in *Intelligence and National Security* and in David Hooper's *Official Secrets*. If any further example is needed of the paranoia to which he refers, I could add that the author Ronald Lewin told me that when he submitted one of his books (either *Ultra Goes to War* or *The Other Ultra*) he was asked to omit mentioning that 'C', the Chief of the Secret Service and Director General of GCHQ in World War II, was Sir Stewart Menzies – ten years after *The Times*' obituary columns for 31 May 1968 had been headed 'Sir Stewart Menzies former Head of the Secret Intelligence Service'.

The Security of Ultra

The foregoing examples show the ridiculous limits to which a zeal for security can be carried. They stand in remarkable contrast to the tremendous security feat of the GCHQ wartime and pre-war organization in maintaining the Ultra Secret for more than thirty years, even though some thousands of staff had been involved. I am sometimes asked how this was achieved. Part of the credit must undoubtedly go to F. W. Winterbotham and his American counterparts who were responsible for 'indoctrinating' new recruits as they joined the effort and were brought into the secret; but part of my answer runs deeper. Those of us who were most closely concerned knew that however much any of us had contributed (and in cases such as Welchman, Milner-Barry and Turing it was an enormous amount) it was only a fraction of the total effort, and it would be invidious for any one of us to tell the story, with the risk of acquiring in the process credit that was really due to others. I doubt whether the fact that it might have brought us into trouble with the Official Secrets Act weighed with us to anything approaching the same extent. It was much more a matter of not 'breaking ranks' or 'letting the side down'. Moreover, we knew that a history of the wartime effort was being written at Bletchley with the hope that this should constitute an impartial record that might be published at some future date: until then none of us should speak.

There were in fact occasional breaches, but these were few, and not at the privileged level to which the preceding paragraph refers – apart, of course, from Philby and his associates. The one instance that I myself encountered arose when the author David Irving was writing his book on the German V2 effort and our attempts to frustrate it, *The Mare's Nest*. By talking to a former NCO who had been at Bletchley, Irving discovered that the reason why we knew the works numbers of the spent V2s that were being returned to Peenemünde from Poland was that we had broken the line of Enigma traffic in which these numbers were reported. When GCHQ learned of the leak, two of its officers called on me and told me that it would be difficult for them to proceed against Irving if he insisted on publishing the text. They had come to me because they believed that he respected me, and they thought that there might be a chance that if I were to talk to him he might accept my persuasion not to publish. And so his book appeared without the vital disclosure. Years afterwards GCHQ told me that they could not have risked the publicity caused by a prosecution that would have blown the very secret of Ultra that they were still trying to keep, and that this was why they had sought my help.

Unfortunately I did not see much of Irving for many years following that episode because shortly afterwards he adopted the theory of Hockuth, that Churchill had organized the murder of the Polish leader, General Sikorski. However, in about 1980 we met accidentally when he saw me trying to find a taxi in South Audley Street to take me to Heathrow. He was driving a Rolls Royce and promptly offered to take me the whole way. The drive was memorable for two things.

The first was Irving's driving technique, which reminded me of Lord Wavell's advice on handling an army:

> The relation between a general and his troops is very like that between a rider and his horse. The horse must be controlled and disciplined: he should be 'cared for in the stable as though he were worth £500, and ridden in the field as though he were not worth half-a-crown.'[8]

Irving evidently regarded his Rolls in the same light; 'Everyone gives way to a Rolls,' he commented as we charged headlong from Mount Street transversely into the dense traffic in Park Lane.

On the way I asked him, 'What stopped you publishing the fact that we had broken Enigma when I asked you?' His terse reply was 'Patriotism!' I tell the story because Irving has at times provoked many of us; but when it is remembered what a 'scoop' he sacrificed, surely one of the biggest ever, he has a lasting right to our respect alongside Governor Dewey, who in 1944 and in similar circumstances sacrificed his chance of becoming President of the United States.

I encountered one other instance where the Ultra secret was 'blown' if anyone was alert enough to recognize it. It was in Air Vice-Marshal Peter Wykeham's book *Fighter Command*, published in 1960. In describing the *Knickebein* episode he wrote, 'By a stroke of luck, Intelligence came up with an intercepted code message otherwise unintelligible, which read "*Knickebein Kleves* is at 53 24 N, 1 W".' Now, although I myself had recounted the story many times I had been careful never to indicate that this vital message was a decrypted intercept, although, of course, this fact was known both at Bletchley and in the headquarters of the RAF Signals Intelligence Service. Somehow and somewhere the security classification must have been degraded, because the Air Vice-Marshal had no idea that it should have been of 'Ultra' quality, and neither did those security authorities to whom he submitted the text for clearance. They appear to have been no more discriminating than their successors who in 1972 authorized the transfer of a set of wartime reports to the Public Record Office without consulting me as to whether they might contain matter of 'Ultra' significance or which might, for example, point to the identities of wartime agents who might still prefer to remain unrecognized. I make this observation not from petulance at not being consulted, but to make the point that security can only be as good as the current generation of security officers, and their inadequate knowledge of the past – and indeed sometimes of the present – may lead them to misjudgments.

They indeed have a difficult job in deciding what would and what would not be helpful to a potential opponent. Who would have thought, for example, that a 1935 fixture list for the football team of one of the ICI factories would have been useful to German intelligence? Yet we found that our opponents had depended on it for locating the entire layout of ICI factories in England, for each factory team played home and away matches with its counterparts in the other factories, and thus German intelligence was able to target several ICI plants of whose existence it was not previously aware.

'Star Chambers' in Security

It is understandable that any security officer who had attempted to ban the publication of the fixture list would have been subject to ridicule of the 'reds-under-the-bed' type, and could in time have developed a 'persecution complex'. Two Directors of the CIA, William Colby and Stansfield Turner, came to this conclusion about one of their outstanding counter-intelligence officers, James Angleton. The former described him as having developed a 'super-secretive style'[9] and removed him from his post in 1974. The latter, in discussing a 1978 incident in which the chief of one of the CIA's overseas stations was unjustly suspected of being a 'mole', wrote, 'if Angleton had been around he would have secretly blackballed the man from future assignments with access to secret information. That would have played it safe for the country but would have ruined the man's career without him knowing why.'[10]

Whether or not Angleton would have so acted, we were near to having a similar situation in wartime Britain, which I encountered in 1941 or 1942 when Lord Cherwell's office showed me a list of inventors whom he had been warned against by an inter-service security body because the inventors were suspected of being German agents. There were some thirty to forty names on the list, including one who had been my personal mechanic in Oxford, and of whom I was certain that he was no German agent. And there were several who were well known, of whom the most astonishing was Barnes Wallis. However could such a patriot's name appear in such a list! Naturally I inquired how it had come to be compiled: the reasoning behind it was that the Germans would naturally be trying to find out what new weapons and techniques of warfare we had under development. It was therefore supposed that they had conceived a way of testing our intentions, in which they provided the 'agents' with bogus inventions which were plausible enough to merit serious consideration but which were unlikely to work. The agents were then to offer these to scientific branches of the service ministries, and from their reactions clues might be gained about what those branches were actually doing. This preposterous theory was pursued enthusiastically enough for the list to be compiled; I inquired who had been responsible for the individual nominations. It turned out that eighty per cent or so had been nominated by one officer, and it is hardly a caricature to say that if in a patriotic spirit you submitted an invention that might help his Ministry, you were in much danger of being put on the blacklist. And since you could not know of the list's existence, you had no chance of refuting the suspicion against you. I heard no more of the list after I made this analysis, and I have never mentioned its existence before, because Barnes Wallis, with his sensitive patriotism, might have been deeply hurt by the thought that even a madman could have suspected him of working against Britain.

Leaks and Indiscretions

While such instances call for judgment and observation in a security service, the efforts of even an excellent service can be ruined by indiscretion on the part of others. I have already recounted (see above, page 18) how the renewed co-operation between America and Britain in atomic intelligence in 1953 was nearly wrecked by the indiscretion of the Permanent Secretary of the Ministry of Supply by giving the codeword for the vital conference to Chapman Pincher. And this was one of a pattern in my experience where the leak occurred at the very top level, where the most responsible behaviour would normally be expected. An earlier example was when the Prime Minister, Stanley Baldwin, publicly if unintentionally revealed in Parliament in 1927 that we were decrypting the messagess sent to the Russian Trade Delegation in London, which traded as a firm under the Arcos name, and whose premises had been raided by the police because the content of the messages suggested that it was a cover for subversive activities. Naturally, the Government was attacked by the Socialist opposition, which stung Baldwin into justifying the police action by actually reading out in Parliament the exact decrypts. As I heard the story from the Bletchley cryptographers, he even read out their standard phrase 'group mutilated' wherever some word had proved unintelligible, but Hansard[11] merely records at such points 'there is one word missing'. According to my cryptographic colleagues, the Russians changed their codes shortly after this revelation, and they were not broken again before our wartime alliance. And this damage was done by a Prime Minister who had achieved a reputation for discretion with his standard parry of 'my lips are sealed' when he did not wish to reveal compromising facts.

To take a more recent example of how difficult it is not to give something away at the highest level, an alert intelligence officer would have concluded that signals intelligence contributed substantially to British success in the Falklands campaign, and perhaps directly to the sinking of the *Belgrano*. One of his clues would have been Mrs Thatcher's reply to Mrs Diane Gould in a pre-election question session on television on 24 May 1983. When the latter insisted, correctly, that a course of 270° (due westwards) meant that the *Belgrano* was sailing away from the British force when she was sunk, the former implied that the Government had knowledge that her intentions were still offensive as would be shown when the facts known to the Government could be revealed. Such a very positive attitude by the Prime Minister suggested the sharpness of information that could only have come from a decrypt. And if there were any residual doubts about the contribution of signals intelligence these would have been dispelled by her victory dinner of 11 October 1982, where the published photograph showed the Director of GCHQ among the rejoicing company assembled in 10 Downing Street.

It is indeed difficult for those at the summits of power to avoid giving away details from time to time to a hostile intelligence officer. Thus, in 1942, when Bomber Command HQ thought the German AA guns were preponderantly responsible for their losses, and were therefore concentrating their tactics against the guns rather than nightfighters, Goering announced his new defensive measures, which were to increase the numbers of nightfighters without mentioning any increase in guns. I was able to point to this as confirming that the bulk of our losses was due to nightfighters, as we in intelligence had already concluded.

All three preceding instances of evidence being given away at the very top have one factor in common: Baldwin, Mrs Thatcher and Goering were all speaking in the face of pressure. But much is also given away when there is no greater pressure than self-importance. In *Inside Story*, Chapman Pincher gives several examples besides that of Archibald Rowlands, whom we have already mentioned.[12]

Moreover, since self-importance is a human failing, it is not confined to Britain. Admiral Turner, writing in *Secrecy and Democracy* of his experiences as Director of the CIA, says, 'it was my experience that the most dangerous leaks about intelligence came from the White House . . . Sometimes the President's staff were so anxious that it would help his political position, they "forgot" where it came from. Sometimes this was innocent; most of the time it was not.'[13] And Thomas

Powers, in his biography of Richard Helms, *The Man Who Kept the Secrets*, told of Helms's reaction as Director of the CIA when a leak was reported to him: '"I always call the White House first", meaning that's where most of the leaks come from, and he never began a hunt for a culprit until he was sure that it wasn't some high official.'[14]

The Official Secrets Act

Such leaks occurring at the ministerial level are difficult to deal with by Official Secrets Acts, as James Callaghan indicated to the Franks Committee, which reported in 1982: 'I suppose in the case of a minister in charge of a department it would be difficult to find a circumstance in which he could not authorize himself to release the information and therefore under the Act it would be very difficult to catch a minister.'[15] But it should be difficult for a minister so to excuse himself if he reveals information that has been gained by any department other than his own.

In addition to those instances where a politician intentionally gives something away to relieve himself from pressure, or where he or a senior civil servant gives something to the Press, sometimes to show his personal importance, or more often to keep the reporter 'sweet', there are other instances where the give-away is innocently made because the giver has no experience of working at the intelligence front-line, and therefore does not realize the significance of clues that he may unwittingly provide. Again, such instances are difficult to cover either by the present Official Secrets Acts or by any future successor.

Cover-ups

While it is difficult to control the conduct of either ministers or officials fully by legislation, they themselves can employ the Official Secrets Acts to protect items that they wish to hide from public knowledge. Sometimes their reasons are good, but at others they aim to cover scandals that may come into one of Bacon's 'not fit to utter' categories. Somewhere between might be placed Baldwin's suppression in the mid-thirties of the knowledge that Germany was rearming. On 12 November 1936 he attempted to justify himself in Parliament in the face of Churchill's reproaches: 'Supposing that I had gone to the country and said that Germany was rearming, and that we must rearm, does anyone think that this pacific democracy would have rallied to that cry at that moment. I cannot think of anything that would have made the loss of the election from my point of view more certain.'[16]

Baldwin could doubtless plead that, in an atmosphere where the Socialist London County Council in 1937 could abolish the Cadet Corps in the schools under its control, Britain would have been even less prepared for World War II under a Socialist government than it was under a Conservative, and that it was therefore a matter of patriotism to keep the Conservatives in power. But if Baldwin's line of reasoning is hard to follow, even uneasier may be that of the Socialist Government of the late seventies, when a senior member of our intelligence organization told me that the Directors of Intelligence were so concerned by the evidence of a Russian build-up that they wished to make a public statement but this was vetoed by the Government who ostensibly argued that this would disturb the public too much.

A further example was the action of Harold Macmillan in having some of the details of the 1957 nuclear accident at Windscale suppressed. His reasons are said to have been a fear that a full statement might have shaken American opinion regarding the discretion of the British Government in maintaining nuclear secrets, coupled with a fear that a frank statement might have encouraged public doubts regarding the technical competence of the Atomic Energy Authority.[17]

Clearly there is a genuine difficulty: if the democratic process succeeds in selecting some of its most able citizens to govern, then because of their outstanding foresight, combined with their access to special sources of information, situations can arise where their conclusions regarding the best future policy are different from those of the man-in-the street, perhaps diametrically so. And it is conceivable that the Government could not disclose the key information on which its views are based without sacrificing some of its sources. Obviously the Government should educate the electorate by providing as much information as possible but decisions may have to be taken before the educative process can become effective. And when the public later discovers that it has not been fully informed by the Government the latter may be accused of a 'cover-up'.

Unfortunately, while such reticence may be justified on occasion, the acceptance of the practice may tempt a government to extend it to situations where the issue is not merely one where in the fullness of time the public would have approved the government action had it been able to appreciate all the facts, but one where disclosure would reveal that government actions had been wrong. Such a suppression may justly be described as a 'cover-up', about which the General Secretary of the Association of First Division Civil Servants has recently in *The Times*, 14 January 1988, given the Association's view: 'We have come to the conclusion that there is only one way to remove the unnecessary barriers of secrecy which ministers of all political persuasions will be tempted to retain in order to prevent the release of politically embarrassing information. This is through a freedom of information Act.' When the professional body of senior civil servants expresses such a firm view, the case for an Act must be seriously considered, even though its terms and implications require the greatest care in working out, and we must bear in mind that neither a freedom of information Act nor oversight was able to prevent the Irangate intrigue in Washington.

Loyalties

In the absence of an Act, problems arise for any member of a government organization who becomes aware of a cover-up: should he expose it or not? Technically, if he adopts the former course he may contravene the Official Secrets Act and he may well be charged with disloyalty to his minister, if not to the Government. According to *The Times* of 29 December 1987, Sir Robert Armstrong as Head of the Civil Service told his officials after the Ponting affair, 'You must serve ministers unquestioningly and with the utmost energy no matter what your own views. There was no mystic higher authority called the Crown to which civil servants could owe allegiance.' Sir Robert appeared to be following the precept of the philosopher David Hume who, in his *History of England* of 1754, wrote:

> All speculative reasoners ought to observe the same cautious silence which the laws, in every species of government, have ever prescribed to themselves. Government is instituted in order to restrain the fury and injustice of the people; and always being founded on opinion, not on force, it is dangerous to weaken, by these speculations, the reverence which the multitude owe to authority, and to instruct them beforehand that the case can ever happen when they may be freed from their duty of allegiance. Or should it be found impossible to restrain the license of human disquisitions, it must be acknowledged, that the doctrine of obedience ought alone to be *inculcated*; and that the exceptions, which are rare, ought seldom or never to be mentioned in popular reasonings and discourses.

Assuming that Sir Robert was correctly reported, and accepting that loyalty to ministers must be the general rule, an honourable civil servant will have to consider his courses of action if he is called on to acquiesce in a cover-up, or to obey seemingly dishonourable instructions. Ever since the Nuremberg trials, obedience to dishonourable instructions may no longer be taken as a satisfactory defence for any officer obeying them. And well before Nuremberg we had the examples of such officers as Desmond Morton, Ralph Wigram, Lachlan MacLean and others who 'leaked' secret information to Churchill in the thirties when he was not in the Government[18] so that he could criticize policy with which they did not agree. All had broken confidentiality – but, in retrospect, were they wrong? A recent, and welcome, pronouncement on behalf of the Attorney General in *The Times* on 19 January 1988 allows that such actions might be justified: 'We have always recognized that there can be situations where there is just cause or excuse for breaking confidence.'

Loyalty is an admirable quality – but should it always be paramount? Military history teems with examples such as Thermopylae or the Alamo or Bir Hacheim where unquestioning obedience to orders and loyalty unto death have changed the course of a campaign. But there are other examples where initiative has proved better than blind obedience, and disobedience wiser than routine loyalty. Reviewing Jellicoe's dispatch after Jutland, Admiral 'Jackie' Fisher is said to have commented, 'That man has all Nelson's qualities but one – he doesn't know when to disobey!' The old Austrian Empire had a special decoration, the Order of Maria Theresa, which could be awarded to an officer who had disobeyed higher orders in battle if his disobedience proved subsequently to have been justified: if not, he was shot.

I have sometimes wondered what I would have done had I been an American naval pilot taking part in the low-level torpedo attack on the Japanese fleet at the Battle of Midway in 1942. The 15 aircraft in the first wave were all shot down; of the 14 in the second wave, 10 were destroyed; and 8 of the 12 in the third wave – in total 33 out of 41, without a single torpedo striking home.[19] To any pilot in the later waves it must have seemed criminal to waste the lives of his crew and himself against such odds and to such a fruitless end. And yet, in a flash, the sacrifice proved justified, for to follow up the low-level attack the American admiral had sent over his high-level and dive bombers. These found the Japanese carriers with their defending aircraft all at low level and unable to intercept the new waves of bombers which then destroyed three of the four Japanese carriers within six minutes, permanently changing the balance of power in the Pacific.

Such a salutary example should always be borne in mind by any officer contemplating disobedience: he must be sure that he has a sufficiently comprehensive view of the situation before he acts otherwise than in accordance with instructions. Just once have I myself been in such a situation, as I recounted at length in *Most Secret War*. This was in the summer of 1944 and it concerned our policy in supplying misleading information to the Germans about the points of impact of their V1 flying bombs; the War Cabinet had ruled that we should make no attempt to mislead our opponents, and I was so convinced that this instruction was ill-founded that I decided that I could not obey it. As a result I was able subsequently to show that disobedience had helped to save the lives of between 2,500 and 3,000 Londoners and serious injuries to around 8,000 others.[20]

In the V1 instance my action was certainly not prompted by a sense of grievance, and it did not involve the public disclosure of any information such as Peter Wright has made in *Spycatcher*. In what little defence can be conceived for his action, grounds might be sought in the inadequate pension he was offered, and the lack of any financial reward for those of his original contributions to intelligence technology that might have been deemed 'beyond the call of duty'. If instead of being in MI5 he had made an important invention as a government scientist in a normal research establishment he might have qualified for a special award. So clearly was this recognized after World War II that a Royal Commission on special awards to inventors was set up, to grant financial rewards to inventors, both inside and outside government service. Besides a host of other inventors, Frank Whittle for the jet-engine and Robert Watson-Watt for radar received financial rewards. The appearance of the latter before the Commission was made memorable by the breadth of his claims, which included the training of women as radar-plotters, drawing from the Chairman of the Commission the inquiry, 'Are we to understand, Sir Robert, that you claim to have invented women?'

Today such concepts as the jet-engine and radar would in themselves be recognized as 'intellectual property', and lawyers might have to be called in to assess the ownership rights between the inventor and the organization to which he belonged. And new concepts in intelligence techniques might equally come into the category of intellectual property; but I know of no awards in World War II for any such contributions to parallel the awards for inventions of the more material type, and yet when we consider the example of some of the techniques invented at Bletchley, these were equally deserving of recognition by awards. If the same discrimination against contributions to intelligence technology still holds today, a sense of grievance by such as Peter Wright could be understandable.

Ombudsmen

The possibility of such a grievance arising is one of the matters which call for the appointment of an ombudsman for the intelligence services, although this type of grievance is likely to be less common than unease by a member of one of the services about the morality of the actions which he or she may be asked to undertake. Another type of disquiet can occur where a member suspects that some other member may be a traitor, and yet another where a member finds that he is being barred from confidential work because of unfavourable allegations against him whose nature is not disclosed to him and whose import he therefore has no chance to refute. The recent appointment of an ombudsman for the security services, largely as a result of the Wright, Ponting and Massiter cases, is therefore warmly to be welcomed.

If the ombudsman is successful in dealing with grievances and misgivings among members of the security services, and a similar office is created for the intelligence services, this would make it easier to accept the proposal in the White Paper[21] presented to Parliament in June 1988 that a plea of 'public interest' should not be a valid defence for an individual who decides to make public what he or she believes to be facts that show misconduct or incompetence in the intelligence and security services or in the Government itself, and which are being ignored or condoned by his superiors.

More generally, the same problem arising from the proscription of a public interest defence has troubled four former Civil Service heads – Lord Croham, Sir Frank Cooper, Sir Patrick Nairne and Sir Douglas Wass – who in a letter to *The Times* on 25 January 1989 have written: 'We believe that there could be circumstances in which consideration of public interest would be of great importance . . . it does not seem wholly unimaginable that a government might perpetrate some serious impropriety in circumstances in which the Head of the Civil Service might be unable to respond effectively to representations about it from within the Service . . . we believe that it should be open to a Civil Servant who had exhausted the existing internal procedures to refer the matter to a responsible authority independent of the Government.' Pointing out that such a procedure already exists in the financial field, where the Comptroller and Auditor General acts as referee, Lord Croham and his colleagues suggest that its extension to other fields would 'remove all possible justification on public interest grounds for the leaking of information by a member of the Civil Service'.

It might well require the appointment of more than one ombudsman to cover all the fields in which public interest problems might arise, for each field requires specialist experience; but that is not an argument for rejecting the idea, even though it may require integrity and judgment of a superhuman calibre in an ombudsman if he is to resolve all the problems that may be put to him without some individual sooner or later deciding that an issue is so nationally vital that the public interest will only be served by disclosure, even though this involves breaking the law.

Unions and GCHQ

As an aside at this point it may be worth noting that another conflict of loyalties could occur if a member of either the intelligence or security services is a member of a trades union, which was the issue at GCHQ. If his union orders him to withdraw his labour, what should he do? While trades union leaders may say that they would never ask their members to strike against national interests, and so the conflict could not arise, the fact is that this forbearance has not always been observed: in 1978 a naval dockyard strike paralysed the movement of Her Majesty's ships, and it became a question of whether one of the Polaris submarines could leave port and relieve one of her sisters on the nuclear patrol. At last the Government plucked up courage, which the BBC news bulletin of 26 July 1978 announced as: 'The Government has ordered HMS *Revenge* to sea *in defiance* of the dockyard workers.' So there can be no guarantee that unions will not on occasion attempt to disrupt the workings of defence establishments; and while it is reasonable for workers in any one of these establishments to have some internal union for representing their interests, it is entirely understandable that the Government should insist that any such union should have no external affiliation that could oblige it ever to threaten the performance of the establishment in its prescribed duty.

Confidentiality, Memoirs and History

The Wright case is the latest to bring into question the propriety of persons who have been in confidential positions later publishing their memoirs. The practice became common after the cataclysm of the First World War, where many individuals went through experiences that moved them to publish books 'mainly autobiographical and justificatory',[22] and the Second World War stimulated a further outcrop. The Government realized that even if it wished to do so, it could not in many cases use the Official Secrets Act to prevent publication, since much confidential information had been made available to the United States during the war, where it had been since released by the American Government. For example, RAF secret reports compiled from the interrogation of *Luftwaffe* prisoners, while still kept secret in London, could be openly purchased from a US Government office in Washington.

While, therefore, having to acquiesce in such instances, the official attitude was to bring the Official Secrets Act to bear wherever possible or, failing that, the civil law of confidence whereby an offender can be legally liable if he communicates confidential information in breach of an obligation. Even Lord Hankey, who had been Secretary to the Cabinet from 1916 to 1938, and a member of the War Cabinet from 1939 to 1942, was repeatedly threatened by Section 2 of the Official Secrets Act when he wanted to publish his own memoirs.[23] Hankey could with justification point to the fact that the publication of Lord Alanbrooke's diaries had been permitted, for these must have been of equal confidentiality to his own; and Alanbrooke had in effect kept a diary through the war in contravention of an instruction issued to all in official posts. Indeed, it would be hard to disagree with David Hooper's comment that 'It is at times difficult to discern any consistent principle in the attitude taken by the government towards the use of the law of confidence to restrain the publication of potentially secret material.'

The publication of the diaries of Richard Crossman in 1975 brought about the setting-up of the Committee of Privy Councillors under Lord Radcliffe to lay down the lines of a consistent policy. Their considerations primarily concerned memoirs written by ministers, to whom they were prepared to grant privileges that would not necessarily be extended to officials in government service. Their report concluded that 'legislation is not the right solution . . . [since] the reasons that confidentiality is a value that it is important to maintain in this special field of governmental relations do not lead us to think that a Judge is likely to be so equipped as to make him the best arbiter of the issues involved.'[24] Having laid down the principles governing confidentiality, they firmly concluded that the referee in ministerial cases should be the cabinet secretary, and that if his recommendation is disputed then the final reference must be to the prime minister. The Committee went on to extend their conclusions to publications by all former members of the public services:

> . . . the obligations which we have suggested should rest upon them [ex-Ministers], and the periods for which these obligations should be maintained should all be reflected in the rules governing the publication of memoirs and other works relating to their official experience by former members of the public services[25]

In anticipating the implementation of their recommendations the Committee expressed a caveat: 'We should be somewhat conscience-stricken if we thought that what we have recommended was calculated to impoverish or distort the sources of history.'[26] They balanced this, however, by saying that 'Government is not to be conducted in the interests of history. That is an obvious proposition. But if that is so, the historian cannot have as of right a smooth highway constructed for him through the intricate paths of public administration and statecraft. He must make the most of his sources as he can find them . . .'

This brings us to the possible value of memoirs as contributions to history. Here the Radcliffe Committee clearly recognized two points: (1) history is important, and (2) memoirs can provide valuable raw material for historians. So anyone attempting to justify the writing of memoirs in general would be beating against an open door; but this is not the case for memoirs concerning intelligence and security, and the new Official Secrets Bill (1988) aimed to discourage their publication even further. So what can be said in their favour? In the first place, intelligence and security are essential components in the conduct of government; and therefore no historian of that conduct who is constrained to ignore them is likely to write with a sufficiently deep understanding of policies, actions and events.

In the second place, even though this gap can be partly filled by Official Histories, the writers have to give overwhelming weight to what has appeared in official records, and these frequently give only part of the story. Lord Slim in his delightful *Unofficial History* showed how inadequate and unilluminating (and at times misleading) were the accounts in Official Histories of actions in the two World Wars and in India in which he himself had been involved, and on which he could throw much greater light from his first-hand experiences. And here I may mention that one of the first requests that I should write a book on my work in World War II came from the Air Historical Branch of the Air Ministry in 1954 because it would enable historians to piece together sequences of events where documents provided only fragmentary knowledge.

In the third place comes a point eloquently made by Mr Julian Amery in Parliament on 21 December 1988 in the debate on the Bill to replace Section 2 of the Official Secrets Act 1911, where he emphasized the need for good sense rather than doctrinaire zeal in applying whatever form the wording of a new Act may ultimately be given:

> The obligation of lifelong confidentiality is, of course, right. Those who join the service must take a Trappist vow, but it must be interpreted with some flexibility. There is a human aspect to it. A man – or, in these modern times, a woman – who joins the service has, perhaps, a lifelong career, but must never explain to his friends, his wife, or his children what he is doing. Nobody knows when he goes to the office in the morning what it is about. He can never talk about it when he comes home. Nobody knows whether he has been a success or whether he has been promoted in rank.
>
> Therefore, it is not unreasonable that, when he retires after a lifelong career – he may only have been in part-time service or loosely connected with it, as I have been – he would want to write something about it. So long as what he writes is not prejudicial to the safety of other members of the service, the reputation of the service or the national interest, he should be allowed to do so.[27]

Speaking from personal experience, Mr Amery said that this point and others were formerly recognized by the secret service, and that there had been a reasonable procedure whereby an author could submit his intended book for official clearance before publication. Mr Amery had sought confirmation from the Home Secretary that this recognition would not be withdrawn if the new Bill becomes law. The Home Secretary had replied, saying,

> I am happy to confirm . . . that it is and will remain possible for members and former members of those services to publish with authority, without contravening the criminal law. Applications for authority will continue to be received and carefully considered.[28]

Although this reply was at first sight reassuring, Mr Amery pointed to two recent cases where books had been stopped 'on a narrow interpretation of the lifelong obligation to confidentiality', and these led him to question whether the Home Secretary's statement was reassuring enough. Later in the debate the Minister of State at the Home Office stated, 'I can give my Right Honourable Friend the necessary assurances that he sought. I listened carefully, as he enjoined me to do, to everything he said . . . So the sole criterion for authorizing publication is whether publication will jeopardize national security directly or indirectly. It is a judgment about considerations that are relevant today, not about past history or former embarrassments.'

Although differences could still arise regarding the interpretation of 'indirectly' and 'relevant' this ready commitment by the Government should help to allay fears about the draconian application of the new Act; but in the further debate of 24 January 1989, Members from both sides of the House still feared that governments might tend to approve memoirs showing their past actions in a favourable light while banning others more critical.

The fourth place in the arguments for allowing, and even on occasion for encouraging, the writing of memoirs is the need for the intelligence service to enjoy a degree of esteem, if not among the populace in general then at least in those sections of it from which recruits are likely to come. As Mr Amery said,

> The British secret services have been held in high esteem all over the world by those who are interested in such matters. How do we maintain that esteem? Of course, partly by secrecy, but partly by allowing the different successes to be known after an appropriate time.
>
> New recruits to the service must also be considered. As a young member of one of those services, I profited a great deal from the memoirs of Paul Dukes and Compton Mackenzie and others, who had been through the mill. What they had to say taught me a lot and in a sense was an inspiration.[29]

Moreover, since money has to be provided by Parliament on behalf of the people for the services, then both Parliament and the electorate need reassurance that the money has been wisely spent. Therefore, wherever possible without prejudice to future operations and the safety of individuals, both successes and failures in intelligence and security should be placed on public record with no more delay than is necessary to avoid that prejudice.

Finally, if one purpose of traditional history was 'to rescue the acts of brave men from oblivion'[30] then that, too, is a worthwhile aspect of the history of, for example, the resistance movements and the RAF reconnaissance crews of World War II, for these can inspire succeeding generations. For the same reasons it has been good to record, alongside bravery, the intellectual achievements of the cryptographers both in pre-war Poland and at Bletchley, and of the MI5 Double Cross operation and the Fortitude deception before D-Day. These form a refreshing contrast with the darker side of intelligence and security which, while it must not be ignored, must not be so exclusively portrayed as to exemplify Gibbon's assessment of history as 'indeed little more than the crimes, follies, and misfortunes of mankind'. And since in recent years there have been many books presenting the darker side and failures in British intelligence and security, it is all the more important that, while discretion will always be necessary, no Official Secrecy should obstinately prevent public knowledge of their successes when no true sacrifice of security is involved.

4

Intelligence and Security

The military purpose of a security service is to prevent a hostile intelligence service from gaining clues from which it might infer the state of your weapons and techniques and how you would use them. Security is thus counter-intelligence, and it will best be effectively conducted if its staff understand the principles of intelligence and the techniques that they will have to encounter. Let us therefore consider how an intelligence service functions, and what can be done by security and deception to frustrate its operations.

Channels of Intelligence

An apposite example of an intelligence system is the human head. Its eyes, ears and nose are its main sensory channels for gathering information. Its brain correlates the incoming signals from these channels and interprets them in the light of previous experience stored in its memory, and then directs its senses to gather further information to confirm, refine, or refute the interpretations that it has so far built up from the signals already received.

The smell of smoke, for example, will generate a subconscious alarm which will cause an individual to start a visual search for a fire, or the crack of a dry twig will alert the hearer to turn his eyes to look for the intruder who caused it, and to assess from his visual appearance whether his intentions are hostile. The brain has available other sensors, too, including not only touch but also the semi-circular canals which signal when the head is being accelerated, whereby the first clue that a vehicle is moving may come from an initial jerk which will then cause a passenger to look outside the vehicle to confirm that it is now in motion.

In this gathering and interpretation of information coming in through several different channels, human senses are by no means unique. Animals have these same channels, too, which are in some instances developed well beyond those possessed by man. A German shepherd dog, for example, has a nose some millions of times more sensitive than that of man. Other animals possess senses that we do not have – bees can detect polarized light in the sky, and rattlesnakes infra-red radiation, while bats have sonic radar. But the same principles govern their operation: signals received by any one of their sensing channels cause animal brains to direct their other channels to search for other information about the cause that gave rise to the primary signal.

If, though, human senses are in some respects inferior to those elsewhere in the animal kingdom (as, for example, we readily acknowledge in the use of dogs to detect drugs and explosives) we have one overwhelming advantage without which human progress would hardly have been possible. A human brain has available not only the primary information coming in through its sensors but also that arising from the development of human communication and of storage systems. Speech, writing, books and audio and visual recording systems all result in a vast amount of human experience gained by others, both past and present, being available to any single human brain that cares to use them. This may help the individual brain to interpret the signals acquired by its own sensors; and may sensitize it to signals from them that it might otherwise ignore; and also may lead it to direct them to look for signs that they have not hitherto discovered. This is probably what Pasteur had in mind when he said: 'In the field of observation chance favours only the trained observer.'

So a human head serves as a model for an intelligence system both by its use and control of sensors and by the interpretation of their signals in the light of not only its own memory but also the corporate memory of human experience. Confidence builds up if consistent signals are received in successive channels: if the signals are inconsistent something is wrong. An intelligence service should aim at observing the object of its attention through as many channels as possible: the aim of a security service protecting that object should be to discover and block as many of these channels as possible; and the aim of a deception service should then be to provide consistent and misleading clues in these channels which will lead the opposing intelligence service to build up a false picture of the object.

The nature of the exchange between intelligence and deception may be illustrated by a biblical example – that of Jacob and Esau. Isaac, their father, lay dying, and his intention was to give his blessing to Esau as his elder son. He asked Esau first to go hunting for a deer and from it to prepare a dish of venison for Isaac to enjoy before bestowing the blessing, and Esau complied. In the meantime Isaac's wife, Rebecca, conceived a plan whereby Isaac might be deceived into blessing Jacob, the younger brother and her favourite, instead. She told Jacob to kill two goat kids, which she would then cook in a savoury dish where, presumably, the herbs would mask any difference in flavour from venison: thus she would simulate the correct signal for venison in one of the sensory channels – taste – available to Isaac. Jacob was then to wear Esau's best clothes, which would have the smell of the open country and thus give the correct signals in the olfactory channel. And she also placed goatskins on Jacob's hands and neck to simulate Esau's hairiness so that signals in the tactile channel would also seem correct. There was no need to simulate Esau's visual appearance for Isaac was blind.

Jacob, thus camouflaged, took in the savoury dish to Isaac, who was at first puzzled. Jacob had failed to disguise his voice, and so the auditory channel was signalling that there was something wrong. Moreover, Rebecca had slipped up on the temporal channel, because the 'venison' had appeared in a much shorter time than it would have taken Esau to hunt it in the country. Isaac therefore asked Jacob how he had found it so quickly, and here Jacob improvised brilliantly. The reason was, he said, 'Because the Lord thy God brought it to me.' The implied flattery of Isaac, that God himself had helped satisfy his wish, made the explanation all the more acceptable – a point not to be lost on would-be deceivers, for that 'filthy vice of flattery', as King James VI/I put it, has been one of their most potent weapons. It helped to lead Isaac to reject the evidence of his ears, 'The voice is Jacob's voice,' in favour of 'the hands are the hands of Esau' and so Jacob got the blessing. Biblical retribution, however, to some extent ensued, for in his turn Jacob was himself deceived by Laban, who purported to give him his daughter Rachel as the reward of seven years of unpaid labour: but when the agreement came to be honoured Laban substituted his less attractive daughter, Leah, in the dark of the marital tent, so that when Jacob awoke in the morning he found that he had committed himself to the wrong sister.

Occam's Razor

The problem of deciding between mutually contradictory indications coming through his several channels of intelligence is one that often confronts the intelligence officer. And he may also have the opposite challenge of insufficient information from which to draw his intelligence picture. Both these problems call for the exercise of judgment and in both I found that the best guide was Occam's Razor: hypotheses are not to be multiplied without necessity; you should seek the simplest hypothesis that is consistent with the information coming through your various channels of intelligence. This will not necessarily be the correct explanation, but it will usually provide the best basis to work on, while of course you seek further information to check its validity. *Most Secret War* gave several working examples, including a rare one where Occam's Razor led to an incorrect conclusion.[1]

If the intelligence officer is so unfortunate as to be obliged to submit his raw information for a committee to mull over, he may be bewildered to find on it individuals who so far from adhering to Occam's Razor will instead indulge in flights of fancy, and propose complex hypotheses that are consistent enough with the reported facts as not to be readily disproved. And he may even find individuals who subconsciously reject Occam's Razor in favour of what may be termed Crabtree's Bludgeon: 'No set of mutually inconsistent observations can exist for which some human intellect cannot conceive a coherent explanation, however complicated.' In such circumstances, all the intelligence officer can do is to stand by Occam.

New Channels

Pursuing the concept of intelligence collection as the attempt to observe an objective through as many different channels as possible, let us now survey the channels which are available. Up to World War I these had hardly changed through the ages, for they were the eyes and ears of spies, and the acquisition of documents (including the interception of messages) and material by theft, bribery, blackmail or torture. The inventions of photography, telegraphic and radio communication, the microphone and the aeroplane made possible the new channels of intelligence[2] that began to be exploited in World War I and which were greatly expanded in World War II.

Since 1945 the establishment of nuclear factories and the explosion of nuclear weapons has resulted in abnormal nuclei appearing in the atmosphere, which can therefore be monitored to provide a channel for obtaining nuclear intelligence. The need to locate and assess nuclear explosions has resulted in seismic and acoustic intelligence, which may be regarded as the successors to the sound-ranging of 1914–18 and the attempts by the Peenemünde scientists to use seismology to locate the fall of V2 rockets by the minor earthquakes that they created on impact. Also in the last thirty years thermal reconnaissance by infra-red systems has opened yet a further channel. Moreover the development of satellites as platforms for thermal and electronic as well as visual reconnaissance of an opponent's activities has added much to the armoury of intelligence technique.

The need to detect submarines not only encouraged the application of underwater acoustics to detect them, either by sonar or by the noises they emit, but also the application of powerful chemical methods to detect unusual molecules that are emitted into the atmosphere by diesel engines or by the waste material that may be excreted into the ocean (such methods can be so sensitive, it is claimed, that analysis of a submarine's wake may detect whether the crew's diet includes butter rather than margarine).

Another important channel that was in fact present in classical intelligence but whose function and importance hardly emerged until World War II is that of expert knowledge in those fields of science and technology relevant to the development of new weapons. The experts in these fields on his own side are in effect the intelligence officer's spies on the laws of nature and on the current state of technological achievement. The second law of thermodynamics, for example, would rule out any interpretation of intelligence evidence that might suggest that the enemy had developed a weapon dependent on perpetual motion. Contrariwise, if his side's experts had succeeded in making centimetric radio waves or a device that would make possible vision at night, the intelligence officer would know that he should be looking for similar developments by the enemy. So the intelligence officer may fairly regard such experts as an arm of his espionage effort. Usually their information will be highly reliable, but he must keep in mind that it can sometimes be crucially wrong: this is when they too easily assume that because they have developed something new the enemy must have done so too, or more dangerously they may conclude that because they have failed in a particular development it will also have proved beyond the capability of the enemy. Episodes can be found in *Most Secret War* to exemplify all these points.[3]

Intelligence Channels in World War II

As an introduction to the way in which the foregoing techniques can be operated together in a multiply-probed intelligence attack, it may be helpful to look back on how they were jointly brought to bear on some of the problems of World War II, for that experience has been the basis for many of the developments that have occurred since. Signalling by radio was, of course, well established before World War II – in fact there were Marconi operators with the British forces in South Africa even before 1900;[4] and electronic warfare appears to have started, surprisingly, in the civil field in September 1901 when one of the news companies reporting the America's Cup races by radio succeeded in jamming its rivals.[5] Jamming was tried in exercises by the Royal Navy in 1902, and its first use in warfare was by the Japanese at Port Arthur in 1904. The important part played by the decrypting of German naval signals of 1914–18 particularly by Room OB40 in the Admiralty is justly famous in the history of intelligence; and the great expansion in the use of radio in the mobile warfare of 1939–45 offered new opportunities for cryptography that Bletchley and its American counterpart exploited with such brilliance.

In the naval field, the Battle of the Atlantic was fought predominantly, from the British side, on the intelligence provided by the Bletchley decrypts of German naval signals, aided by 'fixes' on transmissions from the U-boats.[6] The interplay involved in the location of our convoys and the setting up of U-boat screens by the Germans, who were frequently able to decrypt signals to and from the convoys, and the location of the screens by the British side and the consequent efforts to re-route convoys around the screens is one of the most absorbing exchanges in the history of warfare.

Even so, the prodigious use of radio communication was not the sole cause of the vast growth of intelligence in World War II. Warfare itself was becoming more technological, and some of the new techniques were more vulnerable to attack by intelligence. Radar, whether employed defensively or offensively, inevitably gave rise to transmissions which could be intercepted and studied by an opposing intelligence service, which could find the features that might be vulnerable to counter-measures; and the same was true of radio aids to navigation and bombing. Moreover, while the invention of the aeroplane had led to the development of photographic reconnaissance in World War I, its contribution there was minor compared with its effect in World War II, where aircraft of Photographic Reconnaissance Units could photograph any required target in Germany, with improving resolution as lenses and photographic emulsions advanced in performance.

Thus new channels were opened by which we might gather intelligence, and in addition we had the older ones of human observation – thanks largely to the resistance movements in occupied territories – and of interrogating prisoners-of-war and examining captured documents and equipment. *Most Secret War* gave accounts of episodes in which I myself was involved, a feature of those episodes being our increasing ability to conduct intelligence attacks on specific objectives, using every one of the several channels of intelligence in the way it was most likely to be effective, rather as an army commander might use his various arms in a balanced attack with artillery, tanks and infantry. The specific objective to be attacked might be suggested by what we knew was being developed by our own side, and which therefore might also be under development by the enemy, radar and atomic bombs being two such examples. Or the objective might be proposed from what we guessed the enemy might try to develop in order to exploit one of our own vulnerable features, such as our cities at night or our bombers over Germany. And a third stimulus might come from one of our intelligence channels alerting us to a German development that we had otherwise failed to foresee.

One example of the last class of objective was the V2 rocket, where our incentive to pursue it came neither from knowledge of what we ourselves were developing nor from a concern about weak points in our defences but instead from clues picked up by our intelligence channels with little previous briefing. The most vital of these clues were a conversation overheard by a Danish chemical engineer in Berlin, another overheard conversation between two German generals who were prisoners-of-war in Britain, and reports coming mainly through Luxembourg from workers who had been drafted to work at Peenemünde. These, as it were, constituted the cracking of dry twigs that then caused us to focus all our available senses in the direction of Peenemünde and rockets, and so plan a co-ordinated intelligence attack. Most of the possible thrusts in that attack were obvious: Peenemünde could be photographed by reconnaissance aircraft, further contacts with the conscripted workers at Peenemünde should be pursued, prisoner interrogators could be encouraged to seek further clues, and indeed all available channels could be alerted – for example, the French Resistance to look for constructions possibly connected with launching sites in north France.

We did, of course, brief Bletchley, although it was relatively unlikely that the Germans would at that stage, early 1943, have much cause to send radio signals by Enigma, since Peenemünde would be adequately served by landline. But in visualizing the problems of following the trajectories of rockets in trials, I wondered whether the Peenemünde staff might call for assistance from radar plotters – and I knew from previous Enigma signals that the most skilled radar operators in Germany were in two companies of the Air Signals Experimental Regiment. It was a long shot, particularly since Peenemünde was a German Army establishment, but it was a lucky one, for Enigma shortly told us that one of the two companies had been moved up to the Baltic Coast, and we intercepted its transmissions which were in a low-grade cipher and which proved to be the plots of its radar units as they followed the flights of the weapons being launched from Peenemünde. The full story is told in *Most Secret War*,[7] and it is only cited here as an example of the wide range of channels that could be brought to bear on an intelligence task in the later years of World War II. In the end, Enigma, low-grade ciphers, photographic reconnaissance, prisoner interrogation, resistance reports from Luxembourg, Poland, Denmark and France, and from factories in Germany – and also the 'casual' source of the Oslo Report – all played their parts.

Peacetime Channels

Regarding the operation of intelligence in peacetime, some of the wartime channels are not available: there is no captured equipment or documentation to be examined and there are no prisoners to interrogate. But, while equipment cannot be captured it can sometimes be acquired – for example, a defecting pilot may bring his aircraft with him, or equipment ostensibly bought by a third country may in fact have been bought on behalf of one of the two superpowers anxious to discern the state of the other's technology. And instead of prisoners there will be an occasional defector, and documents and plans may sometimes be acquired by subversion or espionage. All these channels, though, are fitful; and the need for secrecy in their operation may result in that secrecy being used as a cover for various, more general enterprises of a morality doubtful enough to result in criticism and distrust if they come to light.

In general, signals intelligence is free from questions of legality if not invariably of morality, since it can usually be conducted without infringement of an opponent's or a neutral's territory, or from satellites. All other channels of intelligence, such as photographic or thermal, are similarly immune when conducted through satellites – at least, for the time being. This fact, coupled with the seemingly 'hard' nature of the intelligence thereby obtained, has resulted in these channels being developed to the utmost since 1945. The National Security Agency in Washington, for example, which is responsible for signals and electronic intelligence, has so expanded its activities that there are said to be more rooms in its headquarters at Fort Meade than there are in the Pentagon, the headquarters of all three armed services. Much may be read about its activities in James Bamford's *The Puzzle Palace*, more in fact than the NSA would like to have been revealed. In a rather similar vein, though with less inside knowledge, William E. Burrows has published *Deep Black* describing the development of photographic reconnaissance in America by both aircraft and satellite, and some aspects of electronic reconnaissance from satellites.

Computer 'Hacking'

Over the past decade or so there have been widespread developments of telephonic and other networks whereby an individual user may communicate with the central computer and data store of his organization, or one computer can communicate directly with others on a worldwide basis. Since much of the stored data is confidential, access to any one store needs to be limited to those subscribers whose interests have been approved by the operators of the store. Such subscribers are therefore given coded identifications which can be recognized by electronic devices guarding access to the store; and further security may be gained by encoding the data in a way that can only be decoded by a subscriber with the appropriate decoding equipment.

Although a high degree of security can in principle be achieved, there have already been many cases where ingenious 'hackers' with suitable electronic and cryptographic ability have gained embarrassing and entirely unauthorized access to some key-data stores. *The Times* for 4 March 1989 reported that Herr Friedrich Zimmermann, the West German Interior Minister, announced that a 'ring' of West German computer hackers aged between 25 and 35 had broken into hundreds of most secret data banks and that their illegal entry had created 'an extremely dangerous new problem. Governments and businesses must therefore become extremely vigilant. The hackers had gained knowledge of many defence secrets, including the layout of new electronic microchips, and had been selling them to the Russians.' Hacking thus provides a new peacetime channel of intelligence (and sabotage) which will doubtless be exploited both in international and in commercial relations, and therefore offers new scope for the interplay between intelligence and security.

These are also treated, along with the other channels of intelligence in the public domain, in an admirably illustrated and enlightening book, *The Intelligence War* introduced by Ray S. Cline, formerly a Deputy Director of the CIA, and with chapters contributed by authors drawn internationally from the intelligence world.

Satellites

The technical achievements involved in satellites are marvellous and their applications ingenious. A photograph from an American KH11 satellite of the Soviet Union's first nuclear-powered aircraft-carrier from a slant range of 504 miles shows detail with a resolution of about one foot. (If these figures are correct, they suggest that the satellite optics have a diameter of at least one metre, and that a camera looking vertically down from a height of 100 miles would be able to resolve detail of about two inches, that is to say, to distinguish between two golf balls lying an inch or so apart.) These figures are consistent with Burrows's observation that the US Air Force has surplus 1.8-metre mirrors that it has donated to civil astronomical observatories. Burrows also states that photographic emulsions have been superseded in the KH11 satellites by arrays of charge-coupled devices (CCDs) that result in pictures of 800-line television quality, or perhaps better, with a sensitivity a hundred times greater than standard photographic emulsions. And the pictures recorded by CCDs are in an electronic form that can readily be encrypted as television signals and transmitted to receiving points on the ground. And since CCDs can be devised which will record infra-red, or thermal, radiation, satellites can provide thermal as well as visual pictures.

Besides carrying electronic cameras for optical and infra-red surveillance, satellites can of course carry radio-listening receivers and complete radar installations. Here there is a premium on deploying the largest possible antenna from a satellite, both to collect and concentrate weak signals and to sharpen the resolution. Thanks to the ingenuity of designers, such an antenna may be self-erecting, so that, like an umbrella, it can be packed into a relatively small space in a launching vehicle such as a space shuttle and then opened up automatically and aimed once the satellite is in orbit. Although the antenna has to be of light, even flimsy, construction, this is far less of a drawback than it would be in a ground-based antenna because the entire satellite is in free fall. Designs exist for antennae up to 100 metres in diameter.

While satellites have to orbit at low altitudes (a hundred or two miles) to obtain detailed pictures, and thus normally move on trajectories which take them round the earth in ninety or so minutes, they can therefore be over any one point on the earth's surface only for a very short time; but other satellites can be sent into an orbit some 22,500 miles above the equator, when they will orbit at such a speed that they will stay exactly over some pre-determined point (geostationary) on the equator. They can thus keep a permanent, though necessarily distant, watch on some region on the earth's surface. The daily weather maps displayed on television are obtained in this way, while much more refined detail can be achieved by satellites watching for missile launching, as would be required for the Strategic Defense Initiative.

An ingenious application of geostationary satellites was conceived as a means of intercepting the sharply beamed signals in the point-to-point microwave communication links which had previously been regarded as immune from interception because microwaves hardly bend round the earth, giving a system that had been considered as secure as the telephone wires that would previously have been used. But the line-of-shoot of a microwave link in many instances will continue past the intended receiving point out into space, and it may cross the geostationary orbit above the equator at some point where a satellite equipped with a receiver of adequate sensitivity may therefore be able to intercept it. This was one of the intentions behind the 'Rhyolite' satellites first put into orbit by the Americans in 1973, who were thereby able to eavesdrop on Russian microwave links, as well as on telemetric signals concerned with missile tests that the Russians had thought secure. Treachery in a manufacturing firm resulted in the Russians being alerted to the capability of Rhyolite in 1977. Even so, the advantages of observation from geostationary orbits were enough to encourage the Americans to follow Rhyolite by further satellites, Chalet in 1978 and Magnum in 1985. Presumably these were even more advanced, the last costing 300 million dollars, according to the USAF's Director of Public Affairs, General Abel. Presumably a similar purpose lay behind the intended British satellite, Zircon, about which there was so much initial publicity early in 1987, and in which GCHQ had – to say the least – an interest. It was to be positioned over the equator at 53° East (roughly over the Seychelles) which would have been a good vantage point for intercepting Russian transmissions. Its position was to have been a secret but was inadvertently revealed by the contractors, British Aerospace, and it would soon have been obvious to the Russians once it was in orbit. If its cost is 400–500 million pounds, as reported in the *New Statesman* for 23 January 1987, it may be even more sophisticated than its American counterparts.

To control and direct satellites in orbit, and to receive the intelligence that they collect, ground stations are needed. For any particular satellite in geostationary orbit and so positioned as to 'look' at a specified region of the earth's surface, its associated ground station must be so placed as to have a direct line of sight to it. This condition, along with the need for the ground station to be in friendly territory, limits the choice of sites; and among those chosen by the Americans are Menwith Hill in Yorkshire and Pine Gap south-west of Alice Springs in Australia. Desmond Ball, of the Australian National University, has painstakingly assembled an impressive account of the latter station in his book *Pine Gap*, which gives much insight into its development and activities.

Acoustics and Seismology

The optical, thermal, and radio channels for surveillance of the activities of an opponent, actual or potential, all depend on the propagation of electromagnetic waves, and the major powers have large organizations for observing activities in these channels. Further, channels can be devised using the fact that land, sea and air will all transmit mechanical waves; these are exploited for two main purposes, the detection of nuclear explosions and the location of submarines. Great efforts have gone into the development of seismological instruments and techniques for detecting and pin-pointing underground nuclear explosions, so that by the early 1970s it was possible from outside the USSR to locate any underground explosion greater than a kiloton equivalent within its territory and to distinguish it from an earthquake. Nuclear explosions in or somewhat above the atmosphere could be detected by the microbarographic distances they create, the waves from the big Russian explosion of 1961, for example, still being detectable after they had travelled twice round the earth. Such explosions can also be detected by the electromagnetic pulses that they generate, and their constituents deduced by sampling the air in their downwind plumes and analysing the fission and other products that it may contain.

The other sources of acoustic waves that are of prime military interest are submarines where noises from their engines and propellers may be propagated through the oceans for thousands of miles. The problems in locating submarines through this acoustic channel lie in distinguishing the true noise of a submarine from the great background of noises arising from wave action and from other vessels (and even shrimps) and in the vagaries of the oceans as transmitting media. Just as temperature conditions in the atmosphere can result in optical mirages, so they can operate in the ocean to create acoustic mirages. It generally requires highly sophisticated analysis of the observations from several different stations to locate and follow a particular submarine, but this is of such paramount importance that great efforts have been spent in developing the appropriate techniques. Great arrays of hydrophones are used, for example, in the US Sound Surveillance Underwater Systems (SOSUS) that were reported in 1979 to be capable of detecting Russian submarines at 3,000 miles range. Since then, though, the Russians have acquired the necessary knowledge and techniques to reshape their propellers to American and British standards which give less noise, and so the detection range of SOSUS may have been reduced, unless detection sensitivity has advanced in the meantime. According to Burrows in *Deep Black*, SOSUS arrays stretch for hundreds of miles across the Atlantic and Pacific Oceans, and signals from their hydrophones are transmitted by satellites for correlation at shore bases, where the acoustic 'fingerprints' may enable individual submarines to be identified and their positions to be located within about 25 miles, at ranges of some thousands of miles.[8]

On the more intimate scale of eavesdropping devices, techniques have correspondingly advanced; just as with SOSUS on the large scale, an individual submarine being recognized through the welter of stray oceanic noises, so can an individual human voice be sorted out from stray noises in a room, so that the old trick of 'deafening' a microphone with the noise of running bath-taps would no longer work. It may even be unnecessary to place a microphone in the premises under surveillance, if the vibrations of a surface inside the premises, 'driven' by the sounds of nearby voices, are recorded by invisible radiation from a distant laser being reflected or scattered back by the vibrating surface.

The Growth of Instrumental Intelligence

For all its superficiality, the foregoing outline of the principal current sensors for intelligence purposes may serve to convey an impression of their vastly expanded use since 1945, while the advances in sensor technology have been matched, and indeed enhanced, by advances in the processing and storage of information by computers and memory banks. And, since inanimate sensory methods can frequently be operated without infringement of foreign sovereignty and without the penalties that could be encountered by human spies, it has become increasingly attractive to depend more and more on these sensors and less on traditional espionage. Moreover, much of the intelligence gained by inanimate sensors is immediate and therefore of paramount value in a crisis, with photographic intelligence carrying the greatest conviction of all.

It was therefore realistic for Admiral Stansfield Turner to conclude, when he came to the CIA as Director in 1977, that 'human espionage has become a complement to technical systems.'[9] Indeed, this was becoming true from 1939 onwards: far more manpower and effort went into GC & CS (the forerunner of GCHQ) and photographic intelligence than into MI6 and prisoner interrogation. If we include the tremendous efforts of the resistance agents in occupied Europe, the balance of effort may then still have been on the side of gathering intelligence by human observation, but these agents, of course, disappeared from the balance after 1945.

The best use of human intelligence in the changed circumstances is to employ it for tasks that inanimate intelligence cannot do. In a review of *Deep Black*, in *Commentary* for May 1987, Angelo Codevilla made the point that for all their brilliant resolution, the US satellites 'have never *seen* an SS-18 missile' and that it is not positively known whether the silos are loaded or not. A simple calculation will show the difficulty facing the photographers if they had to cover the whole of Russian territory without aid from other forms of intelligence, and they had only their high resolution cameras available. Since each picture has 800 x 800 elements, and at the highest resolution each element could cover only a 2-inch square, the area of the ground covered by a single photograph would be 800 x 2 inches, or about 40 metres, square. Since the area of Russia is about 22 million square kilometres, it would take more than ten thousand million photographs to cover the entire Russian territory at high resolution once. Of course, no sensible operator would dream of attempting such a task. He would first cover the territory at much lower resolution, and only use high resolution cameras to examine areas that these might suggest to be interesting – but even with cameras giving no better resolution than a hundred metres, more than two thousand pictures would be required.

Photographic reconnaissance has generally to be selective to reduce the magnitude of its task, with its attention directed to particular areas by other channels such as signals intelligence. This is in fact what usually happened in World War II, the main exception occurring before the V-weapons bombardment of 1944, where official concern was so great that every conceivable region on the Continent was repeatedly covered in the search for launching points, whether or not constructional activity had been reported in it by resistance agents. The point to be made here is that, marvellous though they are, the inanimate sensory methods require discriminating control in their application. It would be far too expensive, if not impossible, to expand them to cover all of an opponent's activities – and even if it were possible they would produce so much information that this would super-saturate the organization that was trying to interpret it – the collation cat would be choked by cream and drowned in whey.

Human Intelligence Still Essential

Further, inanimate sensors can throw little light on some of the most important of intelligence problems – the failure to anticipate the upheaval in Iran that deposed the Shah, for example. That incident led me to recall another in World War II, when my colleague, Group Captain Peter Stewart, who was in charge of photographic intelligence, was frequently exasperated by the diffuse requests he had for information, the particular one in this instance was for 'all available intelligence' about some country – I forget whether it was Germany, Italy, or even France. 'Certainly,' he minuted back, 'if you will first tell me what kind of intelligence you require – naval, military, air or ecclesiastical.' Facetiously as this was intended,[10] it is possible that if someone had been paying attention to ecclesiastical intelligence in the mid-seventies, he might have noticed the Islamic ground-swell that overturned Iran in 1978. Indeed, an historian of nineteenth-century Islam, writing in 1972, did:

> Despite all the inroads of the modern age, the Iranian national consciousness still remains wedded to Shi'i Islam, and when the integrity of the nation is held to be threatened by internal autocracy and foreign hegemony, protests in religious terms will continue to be voiced, and the appeals of men such as the Ayatullah Khumayni to be widely heeded.[11]

Incidentally, the Iranian Revolution occurred at a time of which

Admiral Turner later wrote, with justice beyond question, that the CIA's inanimate surveillance methods were so good that 'in 1978 we were easily able to detect Cuban mercenaries massing with Ethiopian forces against Somalia in the Ogaden desert. We had forewarning when the Soviets prepared to invade Afghanistan in 1979, when the Chinese lined up against Viet Nam in the same year . . .'[12] But if the Iranian Revolution is not a sufficient example of how important the human side of intelligence still is, the fact is that a good human agent, be he spy or defector, can throw light on an opponent's intentions and policies ahead of their manifestations that may only later be detectable by technical means, when they result in the movements of forces or the trials of new weapons. Admiral Turner of course recognizes this, and although one of his early steps as Director was to cut the strength of the espionage branch of the CIA by 820 posts,[13] his doctrine for espionage is that it 'either reaches out into voids where technical systems cannot probe or double-checks the results of technical collection. In short, human intelligence today is employed to do what technical systems cannot do . . . [and] no matter how much we rely on technology, there will always be a need for human spies.'[14]

If human effort still has a place as a means of gathering information, by personal contact and on-the-spot observation, it remains essential both to the direction of technical collection, which, as we have seen, would otherwise be a task of impossible proportions, and also in the collation of the manifold results of collection into the assessments about the capabilities and intentions of potential opponents and about other developments which might threaten national or international well-being. Admiral Turner gave a telling example[15] of the danger of inadequate collation, and the importance of remembering past events, when in 1979 the National Security Agency concluded from its own signals intelligence, combined with photographic and espionage evidence, that the Russians had a 'combat brigade' in Cuba. This aroused much alarm in the White House, and even threatened the SALT II talks – until it transpired that the brigade was no more than the brigade that President Kennedy agreed could remain in Cuba as part of the settlement of the 1962 crisis. The incident also provided an example of the danger of allowing any one of the collection agencies, however competent, to take over the role of ultimate collation that should belong to a central organization able to take into account and balance the evidence from all the collecting agencies and from past experience.

This reflected my own worry about the wisdom of allowing GCHQ to become responsible for both communications and electronic intelligence (see above, pp. 15–16).

Admiral Turner rightly makes the point that 'accurately reported information can be misinterpreted . . . a completely accurate copy of someone's telegram or a transcript of his telephone conversation can be accepted too readily as an indication of what he is going to do . . . Often only a person who has watched over a scene for a very long time can place an event in true perspective.'[16] I myself all but fell into a trap of interpretation early in 1945, when a routine photographic reconnaissance that I had requested of the village of Hechingen in southern Germany showed frantic constructional activity at several sites in the surrounding terrain. My reason for the reconnaissance was purely precautionary because Hechingen had been reported to us as the place to which Heisenberg and his nuclear physics colleagues had evacuated from Berlin. Could it be that the new sites were frantic efforts to set up atomic piles or separation plants? Otherwise, what coincidence could account for all the new activity precisely around the temporary headquarters of German nuclear physics? Fortunately, I was saved from creating a scare by a knowledgeable photographic interpreter, who discovered from geological maps that all the sites were on a seam of shale – their activity was certainly frantic, but was in an effort to extract oil from shale because fuel was running so short. In contrast with Admiral Turner's example of the Soviet brigade in Cuba, in the Hechingen scare the dispelling expertise lay in the collecting organization, and not on my collating side, but it shows the same need for collectors and collators to pool their experiences.

East–West Asymmetry in Intelligence Collection

The purpose of the foregoing brief survey, of the change in balance between intelligence methods as technical systems have developed, is to provide a background for a task that is complementary to intelligence: security. For the object of security is to frustrate the operations of a hostile intelligence system by blocking all the channels through which that system might gain information. So each channel has to be considered in turn to find ways in which it might be blocked, or at least constricted. As a first approximation, the opposing intelligence system may be assumed to have at its disposal all the same kinds of channels of observation that you have yourself; the second step is to take into account any factors that might lead the opponent to favour a different balance of effort between the various channels from that which you yourself have found optimum; and a third step is to add in any further factor which may offer him some other channel that is not available to you.

It is reasonable, for example, for the Americans to assume in the first place that the Russians are able to exploit the same inanimate sensors – satellite, aerial and ground-based reconnaissance by photographic, signals intelligence and electronic techniques, together with atmospheric monitors, seismographs, microphones and acoustic sensors for submarines – as they have themselves. They also might attempt to assess how good the Russians might be in these channels, having regard to how the state of Russian instruments and computational technology compares with their own. Their assessment would probably be that, despite such Russian ingenuity as was exemplified in the clever microphone in the US Moscow Embassy in 1952, the Russians are not so advanced in sensor technology generally. The parallel comparison between Russian and American successes in espionage would probably give a large advantage to the Russians, partly because in the open societies of the West espionage is so much easier and because, as we have seen (page 39) the Russians have long devoted abnormal expense and effort to it. In addition, while its faults remained unexposed, the professed doctrine of communism had a strong appeal to individuals in the West that led some into treachery.

The open societies of the West, especially in the United States, are much more generous in the release of technical and social information in the Press. Here it is instructive to recall a letter that I received from former Hauptmann Albrecht H. Zetsche who, having been one of the *Kampfgruppe* 100 pilots using the X-beams against us in the Blitz, then served in the air intelligence department of the *Luftwaffe*. In 1980 he wrote telling me what he found to be the most fruitful channels of intelligence in his wartime experience:

> We established a pretty reliable knowledge of your actions based mainly,
>
> 1 on the efficient Signal Intelligence of the German Air Force, and to a lesser extent of the German Navy;
> 2 on interrogations (of prisoners-of-war) in Oberursel;
> 3 on American newspapers and magazines – you won't believe what we found as to production, technical and military items;

4 on close connections with 'Fremde Heere West'[17] under the outstanding Freiherrn von Roenne.

If so much intelligence could be obtained from publications in war, there is little reason to suppose that they are any less valuable sources in peacetime.

Aims of Security

With so many channels through which information may be gained, it might be a counsel of perfection to suggest that a security service must block all the available channels. In a lecture to the Royal Signals Institution in 1979 I suggested that a security service in war must aim at preventing the enemy from deducing at least one of the following:

Where you are, and/or where he is.
What forces and weapons you have at your disposal.
What you intend to do.
When you intend to do it.
How you intend to do it.
Your knowledge of the enemy's intentions and technique.
How successful his operations are.

Sometimes the enemy could be at a disadvantage if one of these is unknown to him, but it would clearly be good to deny him knowledge of as many of them as possible. And there should be some additions to the list, including: Where you believe your own most vulnerable points to be.

In peacetime, the list for a defensively minded nation would still be much the same, with emphasis on intentions and capabilities, and the effects of new technology. Those channels which a security service would be unable to block out completely are:

Photo and thermal reconnaissance by satellite, but this cannot divine much of what is being done under cover and inside buildings.
Signals intelligence, where the sources of transmissions are difficult to conceal but where communications may be made secure by encryption.
Electronic intelligence, where much information can be gained about navigational and detection methods such as radar, at least when they are brought into service.

Defection.
Treachery, although this may be discouraged by severe penalties, and loyalty encouraged by a high national ethos.
Espionage.
Publications, although voluntary censorship can help.
Technology transfer, as civil technology tends to permeate national frontiers, although key technological advances may be temporarily contained by restriction.
New discoveries in science which may have been published before their applications are realized, and where intervention by a security service is more likely to be harmful than beneficial.

Composing an intelligence appreciation has more in common with painting a picture which omits unnecessary, and often obscuring, detail rather than with taking a photograph. If this renders intelligence an art, then so is security, or counter-intelligence, also an art. In a modern, open state there are so many channels of observation available to an outside body, and so many aspects of national activity to be observed, that it would be impossible for a security service to cover them all. As with the intelligence officer, his security counterpart must select out of all the features of national activity those which it is most important to protect, and concentrate his efforts on them. Those which he selects, and how he aims to protect them, are responsibilities which can only be detailed in the particular circumstances in which he finds himself.

'Dynamic' Security

There is a temporal aspect that may sometimes ease the task of the security organization protecting a particular development or intention: protection may be necessary only up to some specific time, for example, a D-Day or a commercial launch. And in the latter stages of World War II there were occasions when I judged that we could run risks in exploiting our knowledge of the enemy in operations, even if this might alert him to the extent of that knowledge, because we had so many new devices coming along and he was being increasingly hard put to counter them. Again, despite all the difficulties of the Americans in maintaining technical security over the years of the Cold War, provided that they could create and introduce new technology at a rate greater than the Russians could learn about and counter it, the Americans could maintain an advantage. If the flow into the bucket of technological advantage is large enough and if the leaks are not too great, the bucket can be kept full. These are, of course, important 'ifs' and they should be no encouragement to lax security; but it may help to bear in mind that security has often to deal with situations that are not static but dynamic, and that something less than perfect static security will suffice.

Aims of Deception

Good security is an art in itself: it is also a prerequisite for successful deception. If the aim of deception is to beguile the opponent into a false appreciation, then the first step must be to block any clues going into those channels of intelligence by which he might divine your true situation and intentions. Your next step, assuming that you have decided what impression you want to create in the opponent's mind, is to devise a set of false clues to feed into all the appropriate channels that will lead him towards that impression. So while security is a negative activity, in that you are trying to stop the flow of clues to an opponent, deception is its positive counterpart. And corresponding to a list of security objectives (such as that on page 103), a corresponding list of deception objectives may be compiled, from which you hope by suitable clues to lead the opponent to one or more of the following conclusions:

> You are somewhere different from where you actually are.
> He is somewhere different from where he actually is.
> Your weapons and forces are different (e.g. in location, character, equipment, numbers, readiness and morale) from those which you actually have.
> You will do something different (e.g. in place, time, scale of effort and weapon technology) from what you actually intend.
> Your knowledge of the enemy is either greater or less than it actually is.
> His operations are either more or less successful than they are.

And if intelligence and security are arts, deception is even more so, as the following chapter will show. As an introductory thought, I recall Sir Walter Scott's lines in *Marmion*:

> O, what a tangled web we weave,
> When first we practise to deceive!

I learned those lines at the age of thirteen from a schoolmaster who stressed the significance of 'first', with its intriguing implication that practice might make perfect.

A Note on Casual Sources

In surveying the regular channels of intelligence available in peace and war, this chapter has not mentioned casual sources. These are difficult to include in any intelligence plan, because they occur fitfully and are outside the control of the planner of an intelligence campaign.

They tend to arise at times of national emergency, when some private individual thinks that he may have information of interest to the intelligence authorities, and is moved by the sense of emergency to bring it to their notice. Although most of the items so produced are trivial in content, and some can be mischievously misleading, the possible value of information from casual sources is not to be underrated: the Oslo report, which is the subject of Part III (pages 265–337) is the outstanding example.

Although no intelligence officer can create casual sources, a wise one will be careful not to reject any such source out of hand, but to exploit his good fortune if he finds its information sheds new light.

5

Intelligence and Deception

Deception in Nature

Deception was a common phenomenon in the world of animals and plants long before the appearance of man. Various flowers simulate the appearance of insects and thus attract the attention of other insects of the opposite sex; and passion-flower plants produce growths that look like the eggs of passion-flower butterflies, and thus deceive the butterflies into moving elsewhere to lay their eggs. And there are many instances of harmless animals that mimic the appearance of dangerous ones, and thus bluff predators into refraining from attacks; for example the Sonora shovel-nosed snake of Arizona which mimics very closely the highly coloured banding of the true Sonora coral-snake.[1] By contrast, there are other snakes, and indeed many other animals, that have markings which, instead of standing out, blend into the background and so tend to deceive predators and/or potential victims as the camouflage enables an animal to remain unnoticed.

Nor is visual disguise the only means of deception. The tanagar shrikes and the ant shrikes of the Amazon are fly-catching birds which operate in flocks guarded by sentinels whose function is to give alarm calls at the onset of danger. But some sentinels have been found to sound alarms when there are no predators about, apparently with the object of 'grounding' the flock so that they themselves have an easier chance to catch flies.[2]

Deception is also a means used by predators for luring victims into traps. The angler fish employs a double deception of which the first part is its camouflage as a rock, and the second a slender extension in front of its mouth which ends in a flag-like member which it waves to simulate the appearance of a small, possibly wounded, fish to attract would-be predators who are then snapped up by the angler fish when they come within range.[3]

Sex is an even better bait than food, as observational zoologists have discovered. The flashing of fireflies is a means of attracting and responding to potential mates, the female of each species having its own characteristic sequence of flashes to which males of that species can respond and home. But the females of one species, *Photuris versicolor*, can imitate the flashing of females of other kinds of firefly and so attract males of those species which arrive expectantly only to be devoured by the larger females of the rogue species.[4] While this deception occurs between one species and another, deception between members of the same species can sometimes be equally profitable. The male of the scorpion fly, *Hylobittacus Apicalis*, normally attracts females by first catching a smaller insect such as a blowfly which he then holds out as a succulent offering, hanging himself upside down for the purpose from a convenient leaf or twig. At the same time he emits a female-attracting scent, and when an optimistic female arrives he offers her his prey, and takes the opportunity for copulation while she is feeding on it. Some males, however, save themselves the trouble of catching prey by adopting a transvestite role, and mimicking attracted females who allow themselves to be manipulated into the copulatory position, only to snatch the offered prey and fly off with it just as this is achieved. Such males then revert to normal behaviour and in turn set themselves up to offer the prey to attracted females according to the convention of their species.[5]

Scent plays a key part in the deception used by the bolas spider to catch the fall army worm moth. Instead of weaving a web, the spider spins most of its thread into a sticky ball, which it suspends by the remaining thread after the manner of a fishing bait. The ball is also impregnated with a scent which imitates that emitted by a female moth. A male moth which picks up the scent as it is wafted downwind, may therefore home on to it. Just as the spider detects his approach it swings the ball to hit the moth (hence, somewhat incorrectly, 'bolas') which sticks to the ball and is then hauled up to be consumed.

The functioning of sexual attracting scents, or pheromones, such as the bolas spider exploits, may be more complex than has so far been thought, to judge by some recent research by C. E. Linn, M. G. Campbell and W. L. Roelofs.[6] Previously it seemed that females attracted males by emitting a scent that had a molecular composition that was unique to the species, and to which the antennae of the males were specially sensitive. This explanation still holds, but it appears that there are several different molecular components in the scent emitted by any one species, and while the males home from some distance on a synthetic pheromone made from the major component in the natural scent, they can home from greater distances if the minor components are blended in. It is as though the simultaneous signals received in the multiple scent channels are more convincing than the signal in the major channel if the others are not present.

Classic Military Deception

With deception so prevalent as an aid to survival in the natural world, it is hardly to be expected that humanity would be free from it, with the extra factor that whereas natural deception involves no thought on the part of the deceiver, either animal or plant, human deception usually has a component of intellectual effort. Sarah, for example, had to think out the steps necessary to convince Isaac that Jacob was Esau; and a military commander has to plan the steps by which he may lead his opponent to a false appreciation of his strength and intentions. So, while it is easy enough to understand how unhappy experiences could have led Clausewitz to write that 'A great part of the information obtained in war is contradictory, a still greater part is false, and by far the greatest part is of a doubtful character,' it is not so easy to accept his verdict on the value of craft and cunning in misleading an opponent: 'these qualities do not figure predominantly in the history of war. Rarely do they stand out amid the welter of events and circumstances.'

For once Clausewitz's conclusion flies in the face of much historical evidence. Perhaps he was taking a blinkered view confined to those epochs of history where 'the heroic ethic and battle as a display of military virtues were dominant'.[7] That there were such epochs, Goldhamer demonstrates by citing the Battle of Maldon in AD 991, where the Vikings requested permission to cross a ford unmolested in order then to attack their English opponents, and their request was granted by the English commander. He could also have cited Alexander before the battle of Gaugamela, when his advisers 'besought him to attack Darius by night, that the darkness might conceal the danger of the ensuing battle'. To this he gave the celebrated answer: 'I will not steal a victory', and waited until daylight.[8] Similarly, deception might have had little place in the chivalrous warfare between medieval knights, or at Fontenoy in 1745 where in a confrontation between British and French Guards each side invited the other to fire first, while in the nineteenth-century wars of Maori resistance to British settlers there is said to have been an occasion when the besieging Maoris sent supplies to a beleaguered British garrison so that it might put up a better fight.

In *The Radar War* David Pritchard recounts an episode in the introduction of airborne radar into an elite nightfighting unit of the *Luftwaffe*, which was staffed by officers who were mainly from the highest ranks of German society and in the Richthofen tradition. According to General Martini, the director general of Signals, they refused to use the radar since they considered it an unsportsmanlike aid; and when one of their comrades from a working-class background began to shoot down our bombers with its help, the commanding officer had him 'grounded' because his victories would shortly have earned him the Iron Cross, First Class, well before any of the more aristocratic and 'sporting' pilots in the unit.[9]

Perhaps in the same theme we find Pericles conducting the Peloponnesian War in a similar spirit, for in his famous funeral speech he said of his Athenians, 'We rely not on management or trickery but upon our own hearts and hands.'[10] But this was in stark contrast to the approach expected by the Spartan general Brasidas, who held that 'the greatest reputation is gained by those stratagems in which a man deceives his enemies most completely, and does his friends most service.'[11] Ominously for Clausewitz, Athens lost the war.

We may also note that in Ancient China, the scope for military deception was appreciated by Sun Tzu, who wrote, in c. 500 BC, 'War is based on deception . . . Lay on many deceptive operations . . . The crux of military operations lies in the pretence of accommodating oneself to the design of the enemy.'[12]

Three hundred years after Sun Tzu, Rome and Carthage were locked in the Punic Wars, with deceptive stratagems being employed by both sides, a favoured one being to vacate a camp while leaving it to appear to the enemy as still occupied.[13] Hannibal employed this stratagem at least twice, once successfully and the second time less so, while on a third occasion he was the victim of a similar stratagem by the Consul, Gaius Claudius Nero. The latter detached himself with an elite group of his force from Canusium, some 200 miles south-east of Rome, where it had been confronting Hannibal, leaving a strong enough force in the camp to create enough activity to make Hannibal think that he was still there. He then force-marched 250 miles in seven days to Sena to strengthen the defences of his fellow Consul, Livius, who was confronting Hannibal's nephew, Hasdrubal, near the river Metaurus, some 140 miles north of Rome. He took pains to conceal his arrival from Hasdrubal, with his soldiers crowding into the tents with those of Livius, so as to show no change of appearance. One point, though, he overlooked: Hasdrubal heard two trumpets sounding in the camp, which suggested that there were now two consuls present, and not one as before. But he was too late in grasping the unsuppressed clue and, outnumbered, was forced to fight the battle of the Metaurus in 207 BC, with the loss of his own life and 57,000 of his soldiers; and after that defeat Hannibal was never again strong enough to threaten Rome. It is a classic tale of deception and stealth leading to a decisive surprise, although it was nearly frustrated by the overlooked clue of the two trumpets.

With examples such as this, Thomas Hobbes had good grounds when in 1651 he wrote, 'Force, and Fraud, are in warre the two Cardinall virtues.'[14] In 1704 Marlborough furnished yet another example, which closely resembles that of Nero and the Metaurus. Marlborough was in command of the Anglo-Dutch forces in Holland and, finding himself confined to relative inaction because of the caution of his Dutch allies, he conceived a plan to march his army five hundred miles south-eastwards to join Prince Eugene in the hope that their combined forces could then inflict a severe defeat on the French. First he had to deceive the Hollanders, who would naturally be apprehensive of a French attack in his absence. He told them that he was only going as far as the Moselle in order to proceed up that river to attack France, and so would not be far away if Holland came under threat. But when he reached the river he turned left instead of right, and made his own way down it until it joined the Rhine, which he crossed at Coblenz by a bridge of boats. He then marched up the right bank of the Rhine, and led the French to believe that this was an outflanking movement from which he would re-cross the Rhine at Philippsburg, 120 miles up-river from Coblenz, to invade Alsace. To add conviction to this picture of his intentions he had a bridge of boats built at Philippsburg in advance of his arrival. The French commander, Tallard, therefore poised his army in Alsace to withstand the impending attack. But instead of re-crossing the Rhine, Marlborough turned eastward to the Danube, leaving Tallard behind and joining Prince Eugene unmolested. The result was the victory at Blenheim, and of this whole venture Winston Churchill wrote, 'The annals of the British Army contain no more heroic episode than this march from the North Sea to the Danube. The strategy which conceived, the secrecy and skill which performed, and the superb victory which crowned the enterprise have always ranked among the finest examples of the art of war.'

The bridge of boats at Philippsburg is an outstanding example of technical spoof to back up verbal spoof in classical warfare. Many commanders had, of course, used technical spoof in the sense of mounting feint attacks to get their opponents to concentrate their forces in the wrong places, but few went to the trouble of building bridges so as to cause a whole army to be misplaced. An even greater stratagem was employed by Marlborough in his forcing of the Ne Plus Ultra Line guarding northern France in 1711. He decided that a good point to penetrate it was at Arleux, some fifteen miles east of Vimy Ridge, which stood on a firm causeway through country that on both sides was marshy and difficult: but Arleux was fortified. If he attacked it, he would betray his intentions, and so he conceived a plan to lead the French to destroy it themselves. So he did in fact attack it, and proceeded to strengthen its fortifications – but not enough to make it impregnable to a French attack to recover it, which they then did, at the sacrifice of his garrison. The French, concluding that somehow Arleux must be essential to Marlborough's plan, then destroyed it themselves – and he, once again by feigning an attack some twenty miles to the west and with a forced march by night, caught the French off balance, and took both Arleux and the causeway it covered without opposition. 'This feint of the duke's on the enemy's left and the sudden march to force the right of his lines, may be considered as one of the best examples of strategy ever carried out in presence of so large a force of the enemy. He was much congratulated by ministers at home, who said that, without losing a man, he had gained an advantage that would have been reckoned as cheaply bought at the expense of several thousands.'[15]

George Washington

British forces have not always fared so well, as they were to find in the American War of Independence, where they were repeatedly misled by a master of deception – George Washington. He had the advantage of fighting on home territory with a friendly population and in familiar conditions of terrain. The fact that both sides were of a common stock and a common language made espionage easier for both, so here the balance of advantage was neutral. But numerically, and in equipment, the advantage was generally and heavily with the British – so Washington repeatedly used deception to offset it. In 1777, for example, the British commander, Howe, had 27,000 troops and Washington 4,000; but by scattered raids and by preparing false returns of his strength which he allowed to leak to the British, Washington led them to believe that his strength was 12,000.[16]

In the winter of 1777–8 Washington's strength was up to 10,000 but in the bitter conditions of Valley Forge 2,500 died. To prevent his opponents realizing his weakness Washington had the dead buried in unmarked graves (anticipating 1944 London under the V1 bombardment, where Lord Cherwell had the addresses suppressed in the death columns of newspapers, to prevent the Germans gaining evidence of where the V1s were falling). Only twenty miles away from Valley Forge, the British had 24,000 men under Howe in Philadelphia; but Washington so bluffed Howe with leaked papers that, so far from attacking Valley Forge, Howe actually asked for another 10,000 men, and the British even considered falling back to Nova Scotia because in addition they felt the need to divert troops for the defence of the West Indies which were under threat from the French.

Again, in 1780 Washington succeeded in averting a threat to Rhode Island by getting the British invading force recalled to New York by allowing false plans to be discovered by the British which gave details of a fictitious plan by which Washington would attempt to invade New York City with 12,000 men. Finally, in the prelude to Yorktown in 1781, he completely misled the British commander, Clinton, into thinking that his intention was to attack Staten Island, when actually he was going to march south to Virginia:

> Much trouble was taken, and finance used, to misguide and bewilder Sir Henry Clinton, in regard as to the real object, by fictitious communications as well as by making a deceptive provision of ovens, forage, and boats, in his neighbourhood . . . Nor, was less pains taken to deceive our own army; for, I have always conceived, when the imposition does not completely take place at home, it would never sufficiently succeed abroad.[17]

The deception enabled Washington to concentrate a force of 9,000 Americans and 8,000 French against Cornwallis, who had garrisoned the small seaport of Yorktown with 6,000 men. Clinton, realizing that he had been misled, sent 5,000 to reinforce Cornwallis, but they were too late. Cornwallis, who may not have appreciated the strength of Washington's forces, had been confident that he could hold out and had even abandoned his outer defences. Yorktown was lost, and the war was effectively over.

In passing, we may note that the American Revolutionaries were also supported by the talent for deception of another of their heroic figures – Benjamin Franklin, who employed it in both peace and war. In peace he could write, in 1765, to the *Public Advertiser* in London happily ribbing its readers for their ignorance of life in their American colonies, telling them, for example, that 'The grand leap of the whale in that chase up the Fall of Niagara is esteemed by all who have seen it, as one of the finest spectacles in nature!' But he could also turn his skill in hoaxing to black propaganda, as in 1782 when he was American Ambassador in Paris and he caused to be circulated a bogus and macabre letter to the *Boston Independent Chronicle* purportedly coming from a New England captain of militia who had intercepted a package of scalps of American colonists – men, women and children – who had been murdered by Red Indians who were sending the scalps to Governor Haldimand in Canada to be forwarded to King George as a token of their support for the British cause. The paper was reprinted with some effect in both France and England, but Horace Walpole pronounced it a hoax, too good not to be by Franklin.[18]

Besides being an adept hoaxer, Franklin was also an effective intelligence operator; he ran a covert service in England from his Paris office throughout the war. Washington, too, had an even greater dual propensity for deception and intelligence. So highly did he rank the importance of intelligence that he wrote in July 1777 to Elias Dayton:

> The necessity of procuring good intelligence is apparent, and need not be further urged. All that remains for me to add, is, that you keep the whole matter as secret as possible. For upon Secrecy Success depends in most Enterprises of the kind, and for want of it, they are generally defeated, however well planned and promising a favourable issue.[19]

In addition to all his other duties as Commander-in-Chief, Washington acted as head of his intelligence service, whose success along with his own triumphs in deception, did so much to win the war.

British Military Deception 1914–18

Hall and Meinertzhagen

With the two examples of Washington and Franklin, even a lay observer might begin to wonder whether abilities in intelligence and deception are linked. And if these examples are not sufficient to convince him, then that of Admiral Reginald Hall, the British Director of Naval Intelligence in the First World War, almost certainly would. Becoming DNI in November 1914, after successfully commanding the battle-cruiser *Queen Mary* at the battle of Heligoland Bight, Hall found that he already had one great advantage: the cryptographic unit OB40, which Alfred Ewing had started. Hall proceeded to build up all the available means of intelligence to create a remarkably effective service covering not only naval but political intelligence as well. One of his breaks with tradition was to bring in men and women from the academic, legal, library and business worlds where he thought that their talents would help, and not confine his staff exclusively to naval officers. Unfortunately although he wrote five chapters of an autobiography after the war, he did not continue with it; whether or not he would have been allowed to publish it, in view of the treatment by officialdom of Alfred Ewing's solitary lecture, is at most doubtful.

Fortunately, though, the main outlines of his successful deceptions have survived. One of his early efforts was to mislead the Germans regarding the extent of the damage to the battle-cruiser HMS *Lion* after the Battle of the Dogger Bank in January 1915. She had been brought back to Britain, and was laid up for repair in a dockyard on the Tyne. She could be repaired in a fortnight, but she had been trailed there by a U-boat, and it seemed that another U-boat had been posted to lie in wait if she steamed into the open sea. Hall hit on the idea of persuading the Germans that she was so badly damaged that she would take months to repair, and so it would be a waste of effort to keep a U-boat on station until repairs were nearing completion. Using photographs of a damaged Russian warship, suitably faked to make her resemble the *Lion*, Hall arranged for these to be sent to Germany with a letter which he had forged and which purported to come from one of their best agents, who in fact had been quietly arrested in England. The letter explained that these photographs had been purloined from the Admiralty and must therefore be promptly returned so that they could be replaced before their loss could be noticed, and that in view of their importance a good sum of money should be remitted. The photographs were duly returned, the money was paid, and the U-boats were taken off watch.

One of the brightest of Hall's deceptions concerned the way in which the text of the famous Zimmermann telegram came into British hands. Actually, of course, it had been obtained by cryptography from the coded messages which the German Foreign Office had sent by wireless and cable to their Ambassador in Mexico City. When the decrypt was brought to him, Hall realized that with its offer of Texas, New Mexico and Arizona as an inducement to Mexico to join Germany – if unrestricted U-boat warfare (which the Germans intended to introduce) were to lead the United States to declare war – the contents might by themselves be sufficient to lead the United States to declare war. Hall's problem, as he saw it, was how to bring this about in such a way that the American Government could be convinced that the telegram was genuine, and not a British contrivance, with the inevitable result that its contents would then be published by the American Government to justify its consequent action, without giving the Germans any clue that their code had been broken, and without letting the Americans know that the first intercepts of the telegram had been made on an American link.

First, he obtained a copy of the encoded telegram in Mexico, which he could reveal to the Americans without embarrassment. Then he convinced the American Ambassador in London, Walter Page, that the telegram was genuine and told him the whole story, but gave him the impression that the British had acquired the German code-book by stealth rather than cryptography. Then he invited the Americans to decode the telegram for themselves, working on the coded text which they could independently obtain because it had been relayed to Mexico by the German Embassy in Washington. Now convinced that it was genuine, the Americans entered the war.

In the meantime Hall had put into circulation various stories of how the clear text of the telegram had been betrayed, hinting that the Swedish Minister in Washington might have been involved. Decrypts of further telegrams showed that the Germans originally suspected treachery in their Mexican Embassy, but that they later concluded that the insecurity must somehow have occurred in Washington, where in their Embassy the clear text of the telegram would have been known. So Hall achieved his object of convincing the Americans without the Germans deducing the truth that would have led them to change their code.

Of the many deceptions planned by Hall, the one that showed his talents at their best started with his inventing a Secret Emergency War Code which he hoped to foist on his German opponents so that when they were convinced that it was genuine he could use it to hoax them into erroneous action. The first step was to get the code-book suitably printed, bound and weighted, and the second was to get the Germans to steal it. This he did by sending an envoy to the Consulate in

Rotterdam on Whit Saturday 1915, who travelled with special priority and an official dispatch-case which contained a copy of the new code-book. The envoy was to stay at a hotel frequently used by British visitors, and therefore under constant watch by German agents, among them the hall-porter; whenever any visitors who might appear official arrived a blonde lady would take a room in the hotel next day, and she duly appeared on this occasion. Because it was the Whit weekend, the Consulate was closed, and the envoy was therefore apparently at a loose end. He consulted the hall-porter about suitable places of entertainment in which an unattached gentleman might find diversion and, having learnt of a promising address, ostensibly set out in the evening from the hotel in pursuit of pleasure. Actually, he had found a hiding place among some barrels on the quayside from which he could watch his room, where he had left his dispatch-case unlocked, but hidden under a suit of clothes. Half an hour later he saw the light come on in his room and shadows moving about. He continued to watch for three hours or more, on the assumption that the intruders would be thinking that his pleasures would occupy him long enough for them to remove the book to be photographed and to replace it without his knowledge. And indeed at about 1 a.m. the light in his room briefly came on again. Half an hour later he himself returned to the hotel, apparently very drunk after failing to locate the address given him by the hall-porter but having enjoyed himself all the same. The hall-porter kindly helped him upstairs and put him to bed.

Hall was now sure that the Germans had a copy of the code; as a further touch he succeeded in selling them a copy of an appendix issued a year later for £500. In the meantime he arranged for wireless messages to be transmitted from time to time in the code which contained genuine but non-vital information, to convince the Germans of its authenticity while giving the impression that it would only come into serious use in some important emergency. Artist that he was, he was making his paint for pictures whose subjects he had yet to choose.

His great occasion arrived in the autumn of 1916, when he was asked if he could do anything to relieve our hard-pressed army in France and Belgium. He conceived the idea of persuading the Germans that we were planning a large-scale landing behind the German lines in north Belgium by means of an expeditionary force from England conveyed in flat-bottomed boats – *The Riddle of the Sands* reciprocated.

First, he started to spread rumours in the London clubs, and began to send signals in the Secret Emergency War Code which built up the impression that the expedition was being assembled with monitors and tugs in three groups, at Harwich, in the mouth of the Thames, and at Dover. Then, as the master stroke, he had a special edition of the *Daily Mail* printed on 12 September which ran to no more than twenty-four copies before it was ostensibly stopped by the censor. Of these copies, six had a particular paragraph blacked out, and these with a few others with the paragraph intact were allowed to escape the censor and to be sent over to Holland. The paragraph was headed 'EAST COAST READY. GREAT MILITARY PREPARATIONS. Flat-bottomed boats', and described how a special correspondent had witnessed a large assembly of boats and troops, with all leave stopped, at an undeclared base on the east coast, and hinting at both Harwich and Dover. The next edition of the *Daily Mail* appeared with a blank where the paragraph had been removed, to be followed by another in which the blank had been filled with other matter.

The ruse succeeded admirably – but too well. So convinced were the Germans that they indeed diverted troops from their own lines to man the Belgian coast; but then British agents began to report the German movements, which were in turn misinterpreted in London as a massing for an invasion of our east coast. England thereupon experienced its worst invasion scare of the war – trenches were hurriedly manned, and orders to evacuate coastal populations were prepared for issue. And Hall had to sit apprehensively through it all, for while he thought that the German movement was very probably the result of his work, he could not absolutely disprove the possibility that by some unhappy coincidence the Germans had in fact planned to invade, since they were as stalemated on the Continent as we were.

Hall's fictitious army in East Anglia was to have a successor in 1944 – 'FUSAG', the First US Army Group (see below, page 124). Another famous deception in 1917, not by Hall but by another master of intelligence and deception, Richard Meinertzhagen, was to be the precedent for the 1942 deception of 'The man who never was', Operation Mincemeat (see below, page 123). In the course of a widely varied career Meinertzhagen had become intelligence officer to Allenby in his move northwards from Egypt into Palestine. Across Allenby's path lay the strongholds of Gaza and Beersheba, separated by about thirty miles of difficult country running south-eastwards from Gaza. Allenby had to take one of these strongholds. He chose Beersheba, and so Meinertzhagen aimed to get the defending Turks to concentrate their strength at Gaza. He first concocted a bogus plan which had Gaza as its main objective, with merely an armed reconnaissance towards Beersheba, and then put papers giving the principal details into a haversack purportedly belonging to a staff officer, with other documents including an agenda for a meeting with Allenby, some rough notes about a cipher, money, and a telegram asking for a reconnaissance of Beersheba. As a final touch Meinertzhagen had his sister write a highly personal letter to the staff officer supposedly from his wife, and that went into the haversack too.

Meinertzhagen contrived to make a reconnaissance in front of Beersheba, where he encountered – as he had hoped – a Turkish cavalry patrol which chased and fired at him. Feigning the shock of being hit, he galloped away, having dropped the haversack (suitably spattered with fresh blood) and his rifle, field glasses and waterbottle. These were recovered by the patrol, and after some doubts, were accepted by the Turks as genuine – a conclusion that seemed confirmed when a few weeks later Allenby opened up a heavy bombardment on Gaza. This was in accordance with tactics Allenby had used on the Western Front when he softened up an objective before sending in his infantry, as the Germans supporting the Turks might well know. Having now caught the opposition off balance, Allenby took the weakened Beersheba and could then concentrate on Gaza, which fell as well. It is pleasing to record that sixteen years later when Meinertzhagen was visiting Turkey he was identified by some Turkish officers who feted him handsomely.[20]

Self-Deception

The deceptions practised by Hall and Meinertzhagen had the specific objective of beguiling the enemy into ill-advised action (or inaction). There was a deception of a rather different kind initiated by the British Admiralty early in World War I which had the different aims of boosting home morale, depressing the enemy, and encouraging the neutrals to believe that it was safe to come to British ports. The aims had been all but forgotten by 1917, when the question was hotly debated as to whether the convoy system ought to be adopted for merchant shipping. Most of the senior admirals were against the change, which was ultimately forced on them by Lloyd George and Winston Churchill, who later wrote in *The U-boat Crisis*:

> No story of the Great War is more remarkable or more full of guidance

> for the future than this . . . The politicians were right upon a technical, professional question ostensibly quite outside their sphere, and the Admiralty authorities were wrong upon what was, after all, the heart and centre of their own peculiar job. A second fact is not less noteworthy. The politicians, representing civil powers at bay and fighting for the life of the State, overcame and pierced the mountains of prejudice which the Admiralty raised and backed with the highest naval authority. In no other country could such a thing have happened . . . In the naval service the discipline of opinion was so severe that had not the channel, or safety-valve, of the Committee of Imperial Defence been in existence, these opinions [of junior officers] could never have borne fruit or even come to light. The firmly-inculcated doctrine that an admiral's opinion was more likely to be right than a captain's, and a captain's than a commander's, did not hold good when questions entirely novel in character, requiring keen and bold minds unhampered by long routine, were under debate.

The episode is of extraordinary importance on two counts. The first is Churchill's point that those senior officers who have to take key decisions must keep themselves alive to the actual conditions of battle 'at the sharp end', and that almost the only way they can do this is to talk directly to the officers, necessarily younger, who are there. This is what Lloyd George and Churchill did, and what the latter continued to do afterwards. 'It is no use being intolerant of young men,' he wrote to the Chief Whip of the Conservative Party in the twenties, and one of the refreshing experiences to us who were his juniors in the Second War was to find him eager to learn what we had to tell him. Thus he overcame the problem of what I have termed 'the hierarchic attenuation of front-line experience', which so often happens as it is reported upwards through service lines in a chain of command.

The second point concerns why the admirals were so wrong, which is all the more surprising since admirals were often more in contact with sharp-end conditions than their army counterparts, because many of them did go regularly to sea (although more usually in battle fleets rather than in the destroyers that were fighting the U-boat war). Moreover, tradition could point to the Napoleonic Wars, where the chance of a merchant ship being lost in convoy was one-tenth of what it was in sailing independently.[21] The admirals, however, had plenty of figures which appeared to support them: there were far too many ships that would have to be escorted in convoys, and in any case the number of ships that were sunk by U-boats was but a small proportion of all those that sailed to and from British ports.

How had these figures been derived? Statistics showed that about 5,000 ships entered or left British ports in a typical week.[22] Even if these were put into convoys of forty, some hundreds of escorts would be needed, and such numbers could never be available. A monthly loss of 300,000 tons, or perhaps 100 ships, was serious, but not critically so – 25 out of 2,500 entering per week. But when a relatively junior officer in the Admiralty, Commander R. G. Henderson, went over the figures he found that they included the movements of all ships over 300 tons. These therefore included all coasters and cross-Channel ferries making several movements each week. When he removed these from the reckoning by counting only ships over 1,600 tons, which were carrying the overseas trade, the weekly figures fell from 5,000 to around 250. At once it emerged that there were far fewer ships that it would be necessary to escort and so the convoy system would be entirely practicable; moreover, so far from the losses to U-boats being sustainable, they were a large fraction of the ocean-going merchantmen, whose declining numbers could bring Britain to starvation.

Why had the misleading figures not been challenged before? It transpired that early in the war the Admiralty had deliberately counted in all the smaller ships so as to play down the proportionate magnitude of the U-boat successes, and to make the neutrals think that they would be reasonably safe in using British ports. As the war went on, it seemed that the Admiralty had forgotten how it had biased the figures, and had become the dupe of its own propaganda, achieving a feat beyond the wit of even the Cambridge philosopher, F. M. Cornford, who once defined propaganda as 'that branch of the art of lying which consists in very nearly deceiving your friends without quite deceiving your enemies'.[23]

The Road to Endor

While Hall and Meinertzhagen left my generation with their magnificent examples of deception on the strategic scale, E. H. Jones did the same on the more intimate scale of a prisoner-of-war camp in Turkey in 1917, later describing his experiences in *The Road to Endor*. Jones was marvellously ingenious in faking conversations with spirits through the medium of the Ouija board, and completely deceived both his fellow prisoners and his Turkish guards. Having thereby demonstrated to himself how it is possible to play so convincingly upon human gullibility through spiritualism, he wrote:

> If this book saves one widow from lightly trusting the exponents of a creed that is crass and vulgar and in truth nothing better than a confused materialism, or one bereaved mother from preferring the unwholesome excitement of the seance and the trivial babble of a hired trickster to the healing power of moral and religious reflexion on the truths that give to human life its stability and worth – then the miseries and sufferings through which we passed in our struggle for freedom will indeed have a most ample reward.

1919–39

So *The Road to Endor* and the exploits of Hall and Meinertzhagen became an inspiration for us to emulate in World War II. But in the meantime, there were twenty years of uneasy peace where deception was concerned with threats rather than operations, ourselves in Britain being one of the main targets. Germany had made clandestine preparations to rearm before 1933; after this date, with the Nazis in power, Hitler began to vaunt his military strength, and especially that of his air force. He so cowed the British and French that he was allowed, in his own words regarding Czechoslovakia,

> to take possession of fortifications representing a front of almost 2,000 kilometres long without firing a single shot. Gentlemen, this time, by means of propaganda in the service of an idea, we have obtained ten million human beings with a hundred thousand square kilometres of land.[24]

An analysis of Hitler's programme of deception has been given by Michael Mihalke in a report, N.1557–NA, published by the Rand Corporation under Secretary of Defense sponsorship in 1980.

After Munich Hitler could well have claimed that he had emulated Sun Tzu's good general, who 'does not contend against powerful combinations nor does he foster the power of other states. He relies for the attainment of his aims on his ability to overawe his opponents.' Once again, though, deception was to have ambivalent results. The same apprehension that resulted in the Chamberlain policy of appeasement and British acquiescence in the reoccupation of the Ruhr, the annexation of Austria and the taking of the Sudetenland, also resulted in the bringing together of officers from the Royal Air Force with the scientists and engineers whose co-operation would ultimately turn the tide when war broke out.

Military Deception 1939–45

World War II gave further scope for operational deception. Of the senior British commanders, Wavell was the first to employ it successfully, having created 'A Force' under Brigadier Dudley Clarke in the Western Desert in 1940.[25] Clarke's men used a plethora of trickery, including lorries that looked like tanks, tanks that looked like lorries, devices to produce false tracks in the sand, and so forth. It was now not enough to send false espionage reports, or even fake radio messages, for air reconnaissance had become a powerful channel of intelligence in which genuine activity needed to be concealed and bogus activity to be simulated. 'A Force' had its culminating success at El Alamein in 1942, where a full spectrum of deceptive measures was undertaken, including building some twenty-five kilometres of dummy pipeline to lead Rommel to expect that the main thrust would be against his southern flank, and not against his other flank thirty to forty kilometres to the north, where El Alamein would be fought. The operations also displayed another facet of deception, for on the southern flank dummy guns had been massed, and these were identified as such by the Afrika Korps in the early stages of the battle. They were then replaced by genuine artillery which was later brought into action to support a subsidiary attack.

While all this was happening in the eastern Mediterranean theatre, the famous Mincemeat deception was being executed in the Western. The story has been so often and so well told that it need not be recounted here – Ewen Montagu's *The Man Who Never Was* gives the details, which are reminiscent of, and were even more meticulous than, Meinertzhagen's ruse with the lost haversack. A body, ostensibly that of a Royal Marine major lost in an air crash as a courier of secret instructions to General Alexander, was washed up on the coast of Spain. All conceivable physiological, personal and sartorial details had been suitably simulated, with papers and dog-eared tickets in the pockets of the clothing to suggest that the bearer had been recently in London, and to indicate his family background, while those in the dispatch-case revealed that the next thrust would be against Sardinia or Greece rather than Sicily where it was genuinely to take place. While the success of Mincemeat has recently been questioned in Germany, Sir David Hunt has shown that it was complete. Hitler himself accepted the evidence from the corpse and so did General Jodl, and their dispositions were made accordingly.[26]

The second great British deception in World War II was Operation Fortitude, which was a project to mislead the German forces defending the continental coast in 1944 into thinking that the Allied landings would be anywhere but the Normandy beaches where they were in fact planned to be made. In particular, it was aimed to give the impression that the main landings would be in the Pas de Calais, with subsidiary actions as far north as Norway. The former deception received the cover-name Fortitude South, the latter Fortitude North. In general conception Fortitude South in particular resembled Hall's 1917 exploit in creating the fictitious army in East Anglia, but with the important difference that whereas Hall's was more or less an individual effort, the Fortitude deceptions were part of a co-ordinated plan with the full knowledge and agreement of the operational staff involved in planning the landings. There was to be no chance of deceivers and operators getting at cross purposes as had resulted in the reciprocated invasion scare of 1917, for Dudley Clarke – who had proved to be a master of deception in North Africa – laid it down that 'Deception is essentially a matter for the "Operations" Branch of the staff and *not* the "Intelligence".'[27] This is a sound principle but, as we have seen, it needs a mind with a penchant for intelligence to devise the steps by which an opposing intelligence service, and therefore its operational commander, is most likely to be misled.

After ensuring the strictest possible security regarding the true landing place, the Fortitude planners then used every means they could imagine to induce the impressions that they hoped to create in the minds of the German commanders: dummy tanks, aircraft, landing-craft and paratroops, lighting schemes for fake activity, false noise generators, and meticulously simulated radio activity to suggest the presence of an entire US Army Group. Features which could not be concealed, such as the Mulberry Harbours, were verbally camouflaged as 'boom defence units'. In addition the planners had the powerful channel of deception provided by MI5's success in rounding up virtually all the German agents in Britain, and in 'turning' some of these to send false or misleading information. This channel was directed by Roger Fleetwood Hesketh who subsequently reported his experiences in 'Fortitude: a History of Strategic Deception in Western Europe April 1943 to May 1945' – a document which has not been published but which has been drawn upon by other writers.[28] The 'Double Cross' aspect is, of course, treated in J. C. Masterman's *The Double-Cross System*. The deception so well succeeded in making the German commanders think that the main attack would come in the Pas de Calais that, even on 25 June 1944, von Rundstedt was still keeping forces there to oppose the landing of 'FUSAG' (First US Army Group) in the belief that all the activity in Normandy from 6 June onwards was a mere diversion. And had he instead reinforced his troops in Normandy from the Pas de Calais, he might have changed the outcome – certainly Allied losses would have been much greater.

This is a fitting place to remark the extraordinary achievement of MI5 and its associates in rounding up German agents and then 'turning' some of them so successfully that they could be employed in deceptions against their German masters. It was an exemplary campaign marked not only by imagination and painstaking consistency in deception but also by the thoroughness with which the agents were detected and captured: had some of them remained undetected and free to report objectively, the falsity of reports sent back by 'turned' agents might have become apparent. As it was, MI5 succeeded brilliantly; at a time when, fifty years later, there has been much criticism of the security services, the wartime work of MI5 should be remembered with admiration and gratitude.

We had the advantage that Britain was an island. Without the firm frontier control that this permitted, the tasks of security and deception would have been more difficult. For a German security service trying to achieve the same feat in reverse, this must have been even more difficult because it had to operate in occupied territories where the populations were inclined to hostility. Nevertheless one German security officer, Oberstleutnant H. J. Giskes, successfully deceived London for many months from February 1942 onwards into sending courageous Dutch agents into Holland, thinking that they were joining resistance networks when in fact they were being captured by his men as soon as they landed. Giskes published an account of his work in *London calling North Pole*. The deception only came to an end in December 1943 when Dutch agents who had been captured and interrogated by Giskes succeeded in escaping back to London. For nearly two years he had manipulated the deception with superb artistry, and was even credited on one occasion with hoodwinking London into dropping a consignment of tennis balls, as well as arms supposedly for the Dutch Resistance, on the pretext that some of the agents were in touch with the King of the Belgians, whose sport was suffering from wartime shortages, and the balls would act as *douceurs* to engage his co-operation.

Another instance of German deception that troubled us was directly due to Hitler himself. Thanks particularly to the French Resistance and to photographic reconnaissance, we had been able in early 1944 to locate the prospective launching sites for the V1 and V2 missiles that would be fired at us later in the year. We therefore mounted a massive bombing campaign against them, and this – though expensive – was successful. The sites that were especially challenging were huge concrete covered bunkers such as those at Watten and Wizernes in the Pas de Calais, the latter having a million tons of concrete in its protective shield. Thanks to Allied bombing, and particularly to 617 Squadron's attacks with Barnes Wallis's big bombs, the sites became unusable, either because of direct hits or because the surrounding terrain was so drenched with craters that it was impassable for heavy equipment. The Germans therefore switched to mobile sites for V2 and easily erectable sites for V1. But on Hitler's orders, they kept construction and repair teams constantly at work on the large sites even though there seemed no hope of using them, so that we would be misled into continuing to bomb them and so waste much effort and bombs which would have been much more useful elsewhere. Even if we had seen through the deception, and I am not sure that we did, we should nevertheless have been forced to continue to some extent with the bombing – for had we stopped and henceforth disregarded the sites, then the Germans could have re-started work on them, just as they themselves came to disregard the dummy artillery. This variant type of deception is particularly appealing, since the bogus plan which is foisted on the opponent is so plausible as to be entirely feasible, so that you can switch to it if he discovers it as bogus and henceforth discounts it.

With their innately suspicious nature, and with the tradition of the Potemkin villages, it could be expected that the Russians would be adept at military deception. Instead, for the first months of the 1941 German invasion, the Russians were themselves deceived despite British warnings; but once engaged in war, they developed impressive deception techniques, under the general and appropriate title of Maskirovka (masquerade). Their first big success was in 1942 at Stalingrad, where they led the Germans to believe that they were planning only for defence, while they managed to assemble, in secret, enough forces – 300,000 men, 1,000 tanks, 5,000 guns – for Stalingrad to be encircled and captured. In 1944 they misled the Germans into thinking that their next major offensive would be in south-eastern Poland, so getting the Germans to concentrate all available armour and mechanized forces there, and thus weaken their Army Group in Belorussia, where the real attack was to be made. The Germans estimated that the Russians had no more than 1,100 tanks in Belorussia, when there were actually 5,000,[29] for the Russians had moved in more than 400,000 men, 3,000 tanks and 10,000 guns. Thus Maskirovka had become an important factor in Soviet success.

Technical Deception

Nearly all the deception techniques we have so far discussed have been aimed directly at deceiving human senses, particularly eyes and ears, although latterly through photography and radio transmission as well as by the more traditional channels. But while the associated techniques of deception continued to apply through World War II up to the present day and will continue into the future, the growing reliance on inanimate means of gaining information by such techniques as radar, radio-navigational aids, infra-red, nuclear and seismic detection, has meant that from 1939 onwards it has not been enough to rely solely on traditional techniques of deception. You must now prevent an opponent from gaining through the new channels a true picture of your activities and intentions, or at least enough correct information to unmask any deceptions that you may be attempting in the traditional channels. But while this adds to your difficulties it also adds to your opportunities, for many inanimate systems have weak points through which they may be fooled.

An example of a highly sophisticated system that could be misled by the simplest means was the 'sniffing' detector for human body odours that the American army used in Vietnam alongside seismic and other detectors to provide automatic warning of the proximity or the trail of the Vietcong. Since it has to be very sensitive to detect the minute concentrations of the particular organic molecules involved, the instrument is necessarily sophisticated but its value was neutralized by the Vietcong who simply hung bags of urine from trees in the jungle, so giving rise to many false trails.[30] An elegantly simple measure to deceive a U-boat commander into thinking that an aircraft, which he knew by listening to its radar might have been searching for him, was nevertheless flying away from him was devised by the future Nobel prizewinner, Luis Alvarez. Since the strength of a radar echo varies inversely with the fourth power (i.e. the square-squared) of the distance to the target, once the echo from a U-boat has been detected and the aircraft flies towards it its strength will increase at a very rapid rate, for example sixteen times when the range is halved. In that case the aircraft transmitter could reduce its power to one-eighth and the echo at half-range would still be twice as strong as it was when first detected. But because the inverse-square law, and not inverse-fourth, holds for the strength at which the U-boat hears the aircraft, the strength at half-range appears to be only a half[31] what it was when the aircraft was at full-range. Thus, although it is now easier for the aircraft to detect the U-boat, and it is in fact now much closer, the U-boat will conclude that the aircraft is flying away and so any threat is receding. So if the aircraft radar can be adapted to reduce its power at a suitable rate while closing range, it can get much closer to the U-boat before its visible presence will warn the U-boat of its danger.

The first opportunities offering the possibility of technical deception came early in World War II, when German bombers were expected to be seeking their targets in Britain. Apart from navigating by the stars and dead reckoning, they could establish their positions relative to known radio beacons by taking bearings on these beacons, which would generally be radio transmitters erected at positions in German-held territory. In principle we could listen ourselves to these beacons and with transmitters of our own could imitate their recognition signals – usually a letter in Morse – on their correct wavelengths. An aircraft trying to take a bearing on a genuine German beacon would therefore hear at the same time a similar signal coming from the British masking-beacon (or 'meacon' – after 'macon', the name under which imitation bacon made from mutton rather than pork was marketed early in the war) which would generally be in quite a different direction. At the least, we hoped that the navigating officer would therefore be confused, and indeed meaconing proved successful.

To cope with the more advanced methods of radio-navigation developed for the *Luftwaffe*, meaconing would not be nearly enough. These methods, known as '*Knickebein*', and the X- and Y-systems, involved radio-beams directed from German territory so that one beam would point directly on a target, and bombers could therefore fly along the beam in the knowledge that if they then released their bombs at the correct point they should hit the target. That point might be defined by other beams that were set to cross the director beam, or by range measurements along it from its point of origin. Our countermeasures were to send false signals which would obliterate or, better, seem to distort the beams or spoil the range measurements. An account of the cut-and-thrust of the consequent 'Battle of the Beams' can be found in *Most Secret War*.[32] Many German bombers still hit our cities, but many more missed, and the only point I wish to discuss here is what a German pilot could do in principle if he were in danger of being deceived by our countermeasures into thinking that he was still on his beam when in fact his beam-indicating instruments were leading him astray because of the counterfeit signals they were receiving. He could, of course, use his compass, which should tell him that he was in fact deviating from the true direction of the beam: in principle, he would then be using a second channel of information – the magnetic – in parallel with the radio channel. More subtly, he could even use the radio channel itself, because however artfully we might simulate the beam signals a careful experiment could show him that there were differences between our signals and those we were trying to imitate. For example, our signals were emanating from a point in England, usually either ahead or abeam of the aircraft, while the genuine signals were coming from behind. As a result of the Doppler effect the frequency of the genuine signal would appear to be slightly lower than that of our counterfeit, which could thereby in principle be unmasked.

In practice, though, the counterfeit often succeeded because in the heat of operations the bomber crew would not have the time or the equipment to detect the differences. But the example will serve as a first illustration of the principles by which a deception may be unmasked: checking by the compass is a means of bringing in a second channel of intelligence, while listening for the slight changes of frequency is a means of exploring information at a greater depth in the radio channel in which deceiving signals are being counterfeited.

'Spoof' and 'Chaff'

If this is difficult to follow it should become clearer if we consider the second example of technical deception with which I became concerned, 'Window' or 'Chaff'. I had started to think about it in 1937 when considering the comparative weaknesses of radar and infra-red as methods of detecting aircraft. The advantages at that time lay heavily with radar, but a foreseeable weakness was its very sensitivity in that a very small weight of metal wires or strips cut to the right length to resonate to the radio waves from the radar would give as big an echo as an entire aircraft. The story of the subsequent struggles to get this idea adopted and into use can be found in *Most Secret War*.[33] Eighteen months before it came into operation on 24/25 July 1943, I wrote a report that included a philosophical section on 'the theory of Spoof'.[34]

To confound the enemy radar system: 'This may be done in two ways: by persuading that you are either (a) where you are not, or (b) not where you are.' The second of these alternatives was not available in 1942, because it required means of suppressing your own echo. Although we had considered this possibility, which is gradually becoming feasible through 'Stealth' techniques, it could never have been applied to World War II aircraft, and so we would be forced towards alternative (a). Since a bomber must give rise to a positive echo, the report continued,

> It is therefore almost impossible to avoid giving to the enemy the necessary evidence from which he can deduce your true position. The art of Spoof lies in so colouring his appreciation of this evidence that he comes to a false conclusion. The only method philosophically possible, when you are bound to give him a positive indication of your position, is to provide him with a requisite number of imitation positive indications. No imitation can be perfect without being the real thing, but it is surprising what can be done by dexterous suggestion.

One old adage is worth remembering here: a good way to hide a pebble is to put it on a beach. Window or Chaff can provide the radar beach on which the echo from a bomber can be hidden. To use another analogy, clouds of Chaff provided a radar smoke-screen, which could be made to appear much the same whether a few or many aircraft were concealed in it. Window became one of the successes in technical deception[35] and it remains useful today. It is now more sophisticated than the form in which we first used it, but the Falklands campaign showed how it could act as a decoy for Exocet missiles.

To Unmask Deception

There now emerges an important point in the theory of deception and of how to unmask. What can the opposing observer do to check whether the echo on his screen is coming from a packet of Chaff or from a real aircraft? Probably his first step would be to change the frequency of his radar so that the bogus strips would no longer resonate to it, and so give a much smaller echo. The counter-step for the deceiver is to find this new frequency and to use strips of the appropriate length, as well as of the resonating length to the first frequency; and if the defending observer goes on to complicate his radar by using several different frequencies the deceiver must use strips of suitable length for every one of these frequencies. This is in fact what is done in modern Chaff, which is packed into rockets or shells after having been cut to the appropriate lengths to give strong echoes on all the frequencies an opponent is known to employ.

There is a second difference between the echoes coming back from a cloud of Chaff and an aircraft, since the latter is usually moving at a speed of some hundreds of miles an hour, while the former is drifting with the wind. The frequencies of the aircraft echoes will thus be shifted by the Doppler effect markedly more than those from the Chaff, which can in principle be filtered out if the radar is sophisticated enough. So if you want to counterfeit all the radar symptoms to an omniscient observer, you have to make the body giving rise to the counterfeit echoes (1) reflect strongly enough over the entire range of frequencies that he can use, and (2) make it move with the speed of an aircraft. Otherwise, the small differences detectable by a sophisticated observer will provide him with clues that your counterfeit is not genuine. To reflect strongly enough at all frequencies entails the use of more and more metal in your Chaff, and it may then be sensible to make it into the shape of an aircraft, which you can then arrange to glide with a speed approaching that of an aircraft.

What can the opposing observer do next, after you have matched his sophistication in the selected intelligence channel provided by radar? He can bring in the alternative channel of infra-red: your glider may reflect like an aircraft, and move like an aircraft – but it has no engines, and so it will radiate very little heat compared with the hot engines and exhaust plumes of an aircraft. So if you want to fool his infra-red sensors too, you must put hot devices on your gliders that will simulate aircraft on infra-red. What can he do next? A hot glider will make far less noise than an aircraft, and so if he brings in sound-locators you will have to add devices to your glider to sound like aircraft engines.

If you pursue this process to the end, you come to the conclusion that by the time you have made the glider hot and noisy, and have found some way of preventing it losing height, you will have gone to as much trouble as you would to build another entire aircraft, which would serve your purposes better, anyway. It was this consideration that led me to write in 1942 that 'No imitation can be perfect without being the real thing' while warning 'It is easy to fall into the trap of thinking that the enemy is omniscient and panoptic, and hence of believing that no spoof could fool him. German RDF [radar] personnel are only human, and even relatively modest spoof might succeed.'

In practice, much of our spoof did succeed; but the point to be made here is that which the episode demonstrates regarding the principles by which deception can be unmasked: (1) in any channel of intelligence through which you may be deceived, arrange to work down to a greater level of sophistication than your opponent has expected you to adopt, and (2) bring all other possible channels of intelligence to bear on the problem, to see whether the evidence that they can provide is consistent with the evidence in the channel through which you suspect you are being deceived.

Technical Deception for D-Day, 1944

Besides providing a defence for our bombers against radar, Window had another application in 1944, when we used it in support of the Fortitude South deception on the night preceding the Normandy landings. The idea was to create on the German radar screen all the symptoms of two large convoys crossing the English Channel, one to land near Fécamp and the other in the Pas de Calais, where the Germans would be expecting the invasion to strike if the main deception, so painstakingly built up, had succeeded. Nos 218 and 617 Squadrons RAF were to create great clouds of Window that would advance towards the French coast at the speed of surface convoys, while underneath these clouds would be motor gun-boats containing equipment that would respond to German radar signals by amplifying and repeating their pulses so that a single gun-boat would give all the symptoms of many large ships. This device was known as 'Moonshine' and, having tried it out in 1942, we now brought it into a major operation.

The Germans had so many radar stations that it would be difficult to deceive all of them. Moreover, those covering the Normandy coast should be able to detect the approach of our genuine invasion forces. We therefore decided to make direct attacks on as many radar stations as possible in the hope of knocking them out, both within and without the invasion area. The fewer that survived in this area the better, and we had to give the others the same treatment so as not to betray our intention to land in Normandy; so for every one attack in the area, we made two outside it. Also, of those radar stations that survived, the more that were shaken the better; those inside the invasion area because their operators might be so disconcerted as to misinterpret genuine radar echoes, and those outside because they might for the same reason more easily accept our bogus echoes as genuine. Overall, the deception worked remarkably well: 'extraordinarily successful' was the verdict of the Allied Expeditionary Air Force's Commander, Sir Trafford Leigh Mallory, in his Official Despatch of 2 January 1947, while of the attacks on radar and signals stations he reported, 'These attacks saved the lives of countless soldiers, sailors, and airmen on D-Day.' Some details of the episode can be found in *Most Secret War*.[36]

Deception Against V1, 1944

Only a week after D-Day we encountered an entirely different problem in deception, for the V1 bombardment started and the Germans asked their supposedly free agents in London to report where the missiles fell. This presented MI5 with a dilemma: if the agents sent back false reports the deception might be detected by photographic reconnaissance which would show the Germans that there was no damage where the agents had said that there was. In that event, the whole 'Double Cross' system would be unmasked, and we might still have important uses for it. On the other hand, if the agents reported correctly, then Double Cross would be preserved, but at the cost of giving the Germans valuable intelligence. One of the MI5 officers concerned, Charles Cholmondley, consulted me about the problem, and fortunately I saw a solution that might preserve Double Cross but at the same time help to deceive the enemy. I might never have thought of it had I not been able to watch the trials of the V1 weapon at Peenemünde, where a curious feature was the persistent tendency of the missiles to fall short of their intended targets: lo! this same tendency was evident within the first few days of the bombardment, where the mean point of impact was in south-east London, around Dulwich, some four miles short of Central London.

One other fact I also knew from experience: agents usually reported locations accurately, but could be badly wrong about times (and in interpreting any activity they might observe). Therefore, if we arranged for an agent to report correctly that a missile had fallen at a particular point, but gave a not-too-erroneous time, his German masters would probably excuse the timing error and the location would be seemingly confirmed by photographic reconnaissance. But, better than that, could we encourage them to think that their bombardment was truly centred on London, without so many falling harmlessly short? If we arranged for the agents to report accurately the points of impact, with a tendency to report more of those that had fallen on Central London or to the north-west of it, and associate every impact with the time of one that had fallen short, then we might bemuse our tormentors into thinking that even those that they might have other reasons to suspect of falling short were in fact tending to overshoot. They might then even try to shorten rather than lengthen their range.

So MI5 decided to take my advice. And while the German commander, Colonel Max Wachtel, never shortened his range he never lengthened it as he should have done. When we later captured his battle map, it showed the fall of shot as reported by the agents which gave the reassuring impression that he was strafing London squarely. Also on the map, though, was something that I had not allowed for: he had another channel of intelligence. In a few of the bombs there were radio transmitters, so that they could be tracked by direction-finding stations in France; these showed that the sample bombs were falling badly short. Which of Wachtel's two channels was telling him the truth?

He had a third channel, the photographic reconnaissance that we had anticipated, and here we had fantastic luck. As it turned out, he had no photographic cover available until the campaign was nearly over, for it seems that there had been no reconnaissance of London after 10 January 1941. Wachtel had therefore to choose to believe either the agents' reports or the radio fixes on the sample bombs. At that stage of the radio art, advanced though it was, fixes were notoriously inaccurate; but if that were so, the fixes should have been scattered north of London as well as south of it. However, the agents' reports were much more numerous, and so effective had been MI5's build-up of German confidence in the reliability of the agents that Wachtel decided to accept them and to discard the evidence of the radio fixes. In his conclusion he may have been subconsciously biased by a natural preference for evidence that suggested that he was doing well, fatally disregarding Crow's Law: do not believe what you want to believe until you know what you ought to know.

When ultimately, on 10 September 1944, the Germans at last succeeded in getting aerial photographs of London we had further luck: there were clouds over much of the area south of the Thames, and these obscured much of the damage that had been done there. The photographs showed heavy damage north of the river, and although this had in fact been done in the later stages of the Blitz, it had of course never been seen on photographs, and so it was readily claimed to be the result of the V1 bombardment, seemingly confirming what the agents had so bogusly reported. Further details of the episode can be found in *Most Secret War*.[37] Had the Germans received information which would have enabled them to correct their aim, the extra casualties which they would then have inflicted might well have been as many as 2,750 killed and 8,000 seriously injured, making the bombardment half as much worse again as it actually was. The success of the deception, or at least its effect in leading the Germans not to lengthen their range, led MI5 to attempt to apply the same technique to the V2 bombardment: but so many V2s were falling short without our persuasion, and in any event were being fired at their maximum range, that I doubt whether we could claim any credit for their continuing to fall short, as we could fairly do for the V1s.

The episode had forced a choice on me personally, for my mother and father lived in Herne Hill very near the mean point of impact of the flying bombs. By trying to persuade Wachtel to keep it there, I knew that I was increasing the risk to them; but I also knew that they would never have wanted me to do otherwise, and so the deception went ahead. Only since writing *Most Secret War* have I learnt that Wachtel himself had to take an even harder personal decision: before the V1 bombardment he had fallen in love with a Belgian nurse, Mlle Isabella de Goy, who was at a hospital in Antwerp. After Wachtel's Flak Regiment 155(W) had to retreat from its launching sites in north France, it re-formed; with London now out of range Wachtel was given his new target – Antwerp. He had to obey, but should he try to warn his fiancée? His military duty would forbid it, but if he did not warn her he might become the agent of her death. Duty gave him no choice, but happily, despite Antwerp being bombed much more intensely than London, she survived and they were married and lived in Hamburg, where he became manager of the airport. It was odd that he and I, so much involved on our respective sides, should have found that the inhumanity of war had faced us with human issues so similar in character.

The 'JAY' Deception, 1941

The episode that gave me personally the greatest scope for deception started in August 1941 when Bomber Command had made the classic mistake of trying out a prototype weapon in actual operations to reassure itself that the large-scale adoption of the weapon would be justified. The danger in this otherwise reasonable procedure is that you may thereby expose it to the enemy in such detail that he is able to devise countermeasures that will be ready by the time that you are able to employ the weapon on a large scale. The weapon in this instance was the GEE system of radio-navigation which consisted of transmitting radio pulses simultaneously from their stations in England which could be detected by a bomber over the Continent, and from the differences between the times that the pulses arrived at the bomber its navigator could quickly determine where he was. Up to the summer of 1941, Bomber Command had no such aid – indeed for long it believed that astro-navigation and dead reckoning were all that would be necessary, and only when we found how few of our bombers were hitting their targets did the Command reluctantly accept scientific help, of which the GEE System was the first fruit. Contrary to orders, the Command surreptitiously tried the system out in three aircraft of No. 115 Squadron, whose navigation was so much improved that the Command was converted. In its new born enthusiasm it started to use these aircraft as pathfinders for its main force. Inevitably, within a short time one of them was lost, presumably crashing in German-occupied territory where intelligence officers would very probably examine the wreckage, and might therefore be able to divine the purpose of the new equipment. Since this could not be produced for full-scale use before March 1942, the Germans could then have seven months' clear warning in which to develop countermeasures, which were relatively easy.

Like everyone else on the Air Staff I had no knowledge of any of this when I received a telephone call from Sir Henry Tizard late one day asking me to be at the Air Council Room at eleven o'clock the following morning. I arrived to find that he had called a meeting of the officers concerned to discuss what should now be done. He had brought me in because he knew that a year before, in trying to forestall the use by the Germans of radio-beams to bomb us in Britain, I had myself been confronted with very similar problems to those which would now face the German intelligence officers trying to work out the purpose and functioning of our GEE equipment.

Before answering, I asked where the lost aircraft had been stationed, and, on being told that it was Marham, I then asked how many aircraft and aircrew had been lost from that airbase between the time that the GEE equipment had been installed and the night it had been lost. The answer was seventy-eight aircrew, from which I estimated that about a third might have survived and become prisoners-of-war. The point of these questions was to find whether German intelligence officers were likely to have been sensitized to the coming introduction of GEE by chance remarks by prisoners which they may have overheard, as we had been alerted to the *X-Gerät* in 1940. Aircrew always had a lively interest in any new equipment or gadget that might come into use, and we had to assume that perhaps all aircrew at Marham had heard something about the new system, particularly since it would be so vital to them.

From our experience in 1940, I believed that if we had had twenty prisoners who knew about *Knickebein* or the *X-Gerät* they would almost certainly, even though unintentionally, have given us clues about forthcoming equipment. So we had to assume that our German opposite numbers would have been on the look-out for reports of any crashed bombers from the base at Marham, and even more specifically from the squadron carrying out the GEE trials. Technical officers would then have been sent to make a special search of the wreckage, and they might well have found enough for them to devise countermeasures, which they would have seven months to develop and deploy. Our prospects looked black.

In the gloom that had settled on the meeting Tizard asked me whether there was any chance of our misleading the Germans about the purpose of the equipment. The chance seemed slim, but I offered to try, at which Tizard said that I could call on any facilities that might be needed, so important would be the outcome.

Before the meeting ended I learned an awkward fact which might undo even a convincing hoax, for it appeared that, long before GEE came into operational use, all new aircraft coming from production lines into squadrons would have to be fitted with hooks to accommodate the equipment, and the fittings would have to be labelled. Labels had already been printed, and these would indicate that the equipment to be installed at some future date would have the designation 'R' followed by a number in the '3000' series. Not only would the hooks alert German intelligence to expect new equipment and to ask shot-down aircrew about its purpose, but also the 'R' would tell them that it would be a receiver, and the number would suggest something of the pulse type, for radar equipment had systematically been numbered in the '3000' or '5000' series. So here was an awkward problem to be dealt with but, happily, it could be turned to our advantage. Since the hooks must be labelled, we let new labels be printed for what would seem to be normal communications equipment, by designating it 'TR 1335'. The 'TR' indicated a transmitter-receiver combination, and '1335' was the next number that would have been given to such equipment in the normal course of evolution. So GEE now became TR 1335.

We had also to expect that German interrogators would have heard our prisoners talking about GEE, and would then have asked other prisoners about it. Henceforth, I advised, 'GEE' must be dropped, and 'JAY' used instead. In fact, talk about JAY should be discreetly encouraged. I hoped that if then the Germans heard our prisoners talking about JAY they would be led to conclude either that they had misheard the word in their earlier recordings, or that the previous aircrew had been similarly misled into calling the equipment 'GEE' instead of 'JAY'.

The fictitious JAY had now to be given a physical reality sufficiently different from GEE as to demand entirely different countermeasures so that nothing that the Germans might devise against JAY could be turned to use against GEE. How about flattering the Germans into thinking that what we were going to do was copy them by developing a system of intersecting beams such as they had used against us? So the JAY beams were conceived, but the word had still to be made flesh. This was fairly easy, because I knew that No. 80 Wing had in fact made a beam that had been used in an attempt to bomb the German battle-cruisers in Brest. So we duplicated this equipment, and set up some JAY beam stations on the east coast; they worked on frequencies of about 30 megahertz, the same as *Knickebein*.

I had also to consider all the other channels of intelligence by which our German opponents might receive information, and to make as sure as possible that these channels would provide no clues that could still reveal the existence and mode of functioning of GEE; instead, where convenient, they would contain clues that were consistent with the notion that the new system would be JAY. The GEE transmitters were sending out pulses regularly for continued trials over England; to an electronic intelligence listener they would sound very much like ordinary radar pulses, but they differed in that the pulses from all three stations were precisely synchronized. I therefore asked that the synchronization should be broken except when the system was in actual use (and it later proved possible to run the pulses out of step if the user was given prior knowledge of how much). The Germans could also send over photographic reconnaissance aircraft, so we had to disguise any feature about the GEE stations that was different from normal radar; the most obvious was that the latter had four towers, the former only three. So extra masts should be erected at the GEE stations. By such steps we hoped to suppress all possible clues regarding the genuine nature of GEE.

What extra could we do to provide information in channels that we had not so far considered but which might offer further means of misleading our opponents? The outstanding channel was espionage, and here we had the tremendous advantage of MI5's control over the German agents in Britain. One of these had been built up as having made various RAF acquaintances from whom he gleaned useful items from time to time. He accordingly reported back to his German masters that a Professor Ekkerley had been giving special lectures to RAF units in which he described the new 'Jerry' system of radio-navigation using Lorenz-type beams. I hoped that 'Ekkerley' would be recognized as a verbal corruption of 'Eckersley', since T. L. Eckersley of the Marconi Company was well known to the Germans for his work on radio propagation, and that 'Jerry' was a verbal expansion of 'JAY', all the more appropriate because JAY had been copied from the German techniques. In any event, I wanted to introduce some errors into the account, such as were likely to occur in a genuine report by an agent who was not well acquainted with technical matters – especially since an intelligence officer tends to set more store by items in whose clarification he has taken some part.

I also arranged for it to seem that another agent supposedly free in London had overheard a conversation between two 'browned off' RAF officers in the Savoy Hotel on the evening of New Year's Day 1942, when they were discussing the Honours List. Why were so many honours given to men who had done nothing of consequence, and so few to those doing really good jobs? they griped. One of them cited Sir Frank Smith, who was in charge of radio production in the Ministry of Aircraft Production and who had been awarded a GCB in the List – had he done anything to deserve it? All he had done was to copy the German beams, and a year late at that. In any case, it wasn't he but the chaps under him who had done the work. 'But,' said his companion, 'you must admit that we now have the JAY beams to get us to our targets; they worked okay in Brest, and we shall soon have them over Germany.' He then demonstrated the system by placing a salt-cellar as one beam transmitter and a pepper-pot as the other and impressing the lines of the beams on the table cloth with a fork.

These reports from the agents appeared to be much appreciated by the *Abwehr*, for we had the satisfaction of witnessing through the Enigma decrypts the special arrangements made for their most urgent forwarding to Berlin. Even so, we did not know whether the deception would succeed. For a long time, all we could point to was the fact that the Germans set up a special organization to monitor the JAY beams; this information came from Enigma, from which we had the satisfaction of learning that some of the signals personnel involved were our old opponents of the Blitz with our mutual roles now reversed. Even more satisfying was the fact that there was no jamming whatever of GEE until five months after its first large-scale use, when our most optimistic estimate for any equipment of which the Germans had no prior warning had been three months. So it seemed that not only had the hoax succeeded, but GEE had thereby been kept free from jamming for nearly twice the time that we estimated might be possible even in the most favourable circumstances.

Prisoners were still being questioned about the JAY beams as late as August 1942, even though a conference in Berlin on 26 May showed that at last the Germans had established the separate identity and purpose of GEE. The officer in charge of the investigation, Engineer Colonel Schwenke, told the conference:

> We have also carried out a systematic interrogation of prisoners. The following facts have come to light. As a result of the extensive use by us of the *Knickebein* and *X-* and *Y-Gerät* systems these devices fell into British hands; this was because we did not fit demolition charges.
>
> In mid-1940 orders were given for the immediate construction of copies of the *Knickebein* and a year later, in August or September 1941, these were ready for service. The British found it comparatively simple to copy the German set, as the airborne *Knickebein* uses the installation for (Lorenz) blind beam (airfield approach) receivers, and the British had obtained the licence for the Lorenz set before the war . . . From the interrogation of prisoners, we know that this system was used under the designation 'Julius'.[38]

He went on to tell how captured GEE sets now indicated that we had also developed another system, and then gave an accurate account of the GEE principle. He added that the Director General of Air Signals, General Martini, was going to call a conference on the jamming of GEE, and so it seems that even after it had been in full-scale use for more than two months, jammers were not yet even designed.

Finally, when the Germans ultimately dismissed JAY as a major threat, and left it unjammed, our bombers were able to use the JAY beams as aids in setting out to, and returning from, their targets, exemplifying the value of a deceptive measure that can be turned to positive use when the enemy thinks that he has unmasked it.

An Infra-red Deception, 1943

Another technical deception in which I was involved arose when the Naval Intelligence Division asked me whether I might be able to put the Germans off the scent of the new centimetric radar that we were introducing into our aircraft for locating U-boats. The latter were now well aware of our earlier radar, to which they could listen and so dive to safety before the aircraft came near. The new radar, on wavelengths for which they had no receiver, should enable the aircraft to approach and bomb without warning. Once this began to happen, they would come to realize that we had new detection equipment and of the various possibilities easily the most likely to occur to them would be a maritime version of the H_2S equipment which we were using in our bombers, samples of which they would have already acquired from crashed bombers. Indeed this was what the new U-boat detector was, and once they knew its wavelength they could quickly make receivers which would again enable U-boats to detect the approach of danger.

All that I could hope to do was to lead our opponents to think that the new detector was something entirely different, and so I thought of infra-red. On pre-war infra-red photographs, for example, stretches of water looked darker than they did in ordinary light, and so ships painted grey to match the normal background of the sea might show up better on the darker background of an infra-red photograph. Alternatively another type of infra-red detector might be able to register the difference between heat-radiation coming from a U-boat and that from its background.

As for channels through which we might feed misleading clues, there was only one conveniently available – the MI5 controllees. So one of them, who was purportedly on familiar terms with some RAF personnel, reported that he was 'on to' talk of some new equipment that they were talking about called 'Cat's Whiskers', and which he had gathered was to be for use in Coastal Command. I hoped that the name might indicate something very special, perhaps tinged with the ability of cats to see in the dark. Later, one of the RAF men supposedly revealed to him after a few drinks something which he could hardly believe, but would report for what it was worth: this was that whatever the device was it would somehow make the sea look black.

Here I was employing what I termed the 'Herodotus technique' after Herodotus IV Chapter 42, in which he reported the Phoenician claim to have sailed round southern Africa: 'On their return they declared – I for my part do not believe it but others may – that in sailing round Libya [i.e. Africa] they had the sun on their right hand.' This cryptic passage suggests a reversed orientation such as would be experienced when following the east coast of Africa northwards after following the west coast southwards or perhaps the track of the sun across the sky as seen from south of the Equator. In either case, historians have held it to be convincing evidence both of the honesty of Herodotus in reporting things against his own belief, and of the Phoenician achievement. I hoped that our controllee's German masters would credit him in a similar way; certainly they thanked him, and we could only wait and see.

Part of what transpired can be found in *Aircraft versus Submarines* by Alfred Price. Bomber Command lost its first H_2S-equipped aircraft near Rotterdam on 2 February 1943; by 23 February the Germans had unravelled most of its mode of functioning, and had appreciated that it could be applied to U-boat detection, and that new warning receivers would have to be developed for U-boats. However, owing to difficulties in their development it was only towards the end of 1943 that suitable receivers became available. It is impossible to tell whether or not any of the delay was due to a nagging suspicion besetting the Germans that our aircraft might be depending more on something quite different from radar. For this they certainly entertained at least two possibilities; infra-red, or radiation coming from the U-boats' older receiver for longer-wavelength radar. The Germans had been led to look into the latter possibility by the statement of an RAF prisoner-of-war that we were somehow homing on the U-boats' own receivers. When their experts looked into the story, they found that the 'Metox' receivers did radiate from their local oscillators, and urgent measures were taken to suppress them. Incidentally, many years later Peter Wright appears to have reinvented the technique foreshadowed by our imaginative prisoner; whoever he was, he deserves a high place in the record of solo efforts in deception.

As for infra-red, we knew from Enigma a year or so later that it must have been taken seriously, for the Germans developed an ingenious paint (using the Christiansen-filter effect) to make a U-boat appear grey in visible light but black by infra-red, simulating the reflexion characteristics of the sea-surface and rendering the U-boat less detectable. And Peter Cramer, a U-boat commander, in his book *U333*, wrote: 'At that time we could not explain how the enemy more and more frequently located us on the surface without our improved

Naxos set giving any warning of radar impulses . . . we looked for plausible explanations and finally decided to credit the enemy with infra-red procedures.' So the infra-red herring had worked.

The episode is also referred to in Volume 3 of *British Intelligence in the Second World War*, where the official historians state: 'The Germans wasted precious time not only in developing a non-radiating search receiver but also in devising means against detection by infra-red. The Allies knew of this preoccupation with infra-red from naval Enigma and played on it by spreading reports through double agents that they were in fact achieving success by this technique.'[39] Actually the deception deserves more credit than that because we started it as a cover for the new radar quite independently of whether we might later learn anything from Enigma. It was, of course, of much satisfaction to learn from Enigma that our ruse was working, and we *then* played on it through the same double agents who had first fed the story to German intelligence. And it was because my own pre-war research had been in infra-red that the ruse was a natural one for us to try.

Deceiver and Deceivee

In the foregoing examples of technical deception it may seem that I have given undue attention to episodes in which I myself was concerned. The reason for this defect is that I know of few other examples; little opportunity existed in previous wars. Although we can assume that much technical deception has been practised since 1945, the results are too obscure for philosophical analysis, except for such episodes as the use of Chaff and infra-red decoys in Vietnam, the Falklands, and the Israeli-Arab conflict, particularly the brilliant Israeli use of drones for deception and jamming in the Bekaa Valley in 1982. The Germans in World War II had similar opportunities for technical deception to those we had ourselves, but they lacked the close relations between scientists and serving officers that, thanks to the Lindemann–Tizard generation, we had in Britain. Thus, although a talent for deception was not lacking in Germany it was not applied in the technical field: for this, I was particularly thankful because not only would my own efforts in deception have been more difficult against a practised opponent, but also I might have been hoodwinked in my main task of intelligence.

One of my objects in analysing technical deception at some length has been to underline the concept of channels of intelligence, for technology has opened up a multiplicity of channels by which information may be gained about an opponent's activities and intentions. The easiest of deceptions of all are those in which only a single channel exists through which information can be gained, for it is then necessary only to synthesize false information in this one channel. That is why, for example, a telephone hoax such as persuading a victim to put his telephone into a bucket of water could be so successful, once he was persuaded that the voice instructing him to do so was that of the maintenance engineer in the local telephone exchange. Had the victim had a second channel available – say a television picture – the hoaxer would have to disguise his appearance as well as his voice to simulate that of the engineer. So the more channels of intelligence that are operated in parallel, the more difficult the task of deception in that the deceiver has to provide consistent impressions in all the available channels.

If there is inconsistency between the impressions derived from the several channels, the potential deceivee would do well to suspect a deception. What should he then do, beyond a critical reappraisal of the intelligence picture as he sees it? The reappraisal should include examining afresh the evidence coming in through each channel in turn, and particularly those channels giving conflicting evidence. If possible, the deceivee should attempt to go to a deeper level of information in each of these channels, for example in checking that a radar echo coming back from a supposed target will be very slightly shifted in frequency if the target is moving. Or, on aerial photographs of a supposed site of rocket storage or radar, intended to decoy bombs away from genuine sites, the deception will be unmasked if the photographic interpreter notices that there are insufficient signs of human activity. Or an alert radio intercept operator may notice that counterfeit radio messages purportedly being sent by two different stations are being 'morsed' by a single operator, since no two telegraphists have exactly the same 'fist', and a skilled listener can recognize Morse style almost as easily as handwriting or manner of speech.

The second measure that may be open to the deceivee is to find a further channel by which the deceiver can be observed, and of which he himself may not be aware – just as our V1 bomb deception could have been unmasked by Wachtel's sampling bombs carrying radio transmitters, or a Chaff cloud because it does not give the right signal in the infra-red channel.

While it is easy to analyse the battle between deceiver and deceivee in terms of the creation of new channels of intelligence and the deepening of old ones, and so compile rules to guide both sides in the battle, observance of these rules is only one of the attributes that are necessary to success on either side. For deception is an art as well as a science, and it calls for creative talent in addition to a mastery of the relevant technology. So good deceivers are artists in their own right; and while their products may not receive the financial recognition accorded to works of art, whose high prices were justified by Karl Marx on the grounds that innumerable bad paintings had to be produced for every good one, successful deception can be a priceless factor in military success.

6

Intelligence and Command

The ultimate object of intelligence is to enable action to be optimized. The individual or body which has to decide on action needs information about its opponent as one of the factors likely to be vital in shaping its decision; this information may suggest that the action should be on a larger or smaller scale than would otherwise be taken, or even that a completely different course of action would be better. It therefore follows that an intelligence organization has two tasks: first to ascertain an opponent's dispositions, intentions and potentials, and then to ensure that the relevant knowledge and its inevitable uncertainties are presented to the commanding entity (be it an individual commander or a committee), in the form that it can best assimilate. For me in World War II, for example, this entity might be the Chief of Air Staff, or the head of an RAF Command or, on occasion, the Defence Committee of the War Cabinet, or the Prime Minister himself. In the light of that experience, this chapter will discuss first the relations between a commander and his intelligence organization, and then consider some of the problems of command that arise within the intelligence organization itself.

My personal experience may well not be typical, and in that respect its value may be limited. It was gained in a period in which intelligence was entering into a phase of internal expansion because advances in science and technology were having profound effects on warfare. These had a dual effect on intelligence: far more information than ever before needed to be known about the enemy, and the new channels of intelligence described in the preceding chapters had to be created.

A second special feature of my experience was that at the summit we had Winston Churchill who had a keen appreciation of science and technology, and also an experience of high command in World War I. He, for one, had a sharp memory of the mistakes that had then been made, and a determination to avoid their repetition.[1] Here we may note in passing that while it is a strategic sin to fight the next war on the assumption that it will be exactly like the last, there are always likely to be lessons from the last war from which principles can be drawn that will be worth bearing in mind in the new circumstances of the next.

Joshua

Indeed, principles may well endure, not only from one war to the next but throughout the time of human experience: and the nature of relations between a commander and his intelligence organization involves problems so fundamental as to stretch back into antiquity – certainly as far as Moses (Numbers 13, 2) who sent out twelve spies into the land of Canaan; they were selected men, one from each of the twelve tribes, and he briefed them in detail regarding what he wanted to know. All returned with reports that Canaan was a good land indeed, 'flowing with milk and honey', but ten of them stated that the Canaanites were too big and formidable to be attacked. 'All the people we saw in it,' they said, 'were men of great stature. We were in our own sight as grasshoppers, and so we were in their sight.' Just two, Joshua and Caleb, disagreed – and with emphasis; the Canaanites, they said, could with the aid of the Lord be overcome. For this dangerous advice the mob threatened to stone them: and, although they were saved from this fate by the direct intervention of the Lord, Moses decided to reject their report in favour of the majority, and so abandoned any idea of invading Canaan. For this lack of faith he was punished by losing all chance of living in the Promised Land. And not only he, but all who had sided with him,. 'Forty days you spent exploring the country,' said the Lord, 'and forty years you shall spend – a year for each day paying the penalty of your iniquities.' And he allowed only Joshua and Caleb, who had reported faithfully, to survive to occupy Canaan.

Joshua, of course, was promoted leader; and having been a good spy himself and having seen the problem created by having too many on the same job, when his turn came to attack Jericho he sent just two. Although they created an unfortunate precedent for intelligence by consorting with Rahab the harlot, their accurate report encouraged Joshua to attack, and Jericho was taken.

So Joshua, the faithful spy who recognized faithfulness in others, was rewarded. But what happened to the ten who had made false reports? The Lord smote them and 'They died of the plague because they had made a bad report'.

While it is always gratifying to see good intelligence work rewarded, many of us looking over our own past efforts in intelligence may feel a pang of uneasiness at contemplating the fate of the ten.

'Slanted' Intelligence

The question we have to consider is why they did it, and it is one that Moses himself ought to have considered, for it concerns an inherent pitfall in intelligence judgment. Put yourself in the position of one of the spies. If you report that the Canaanites are vulnerable, the consequent operational decision will be to attack. If the attack is successful, then your intelligence contribution to it, although accurate, may well be overlooked; but if the attack is unsuccessful you will be held to blame for false intelligence. So you are in a 'no-win' situation. But if you report that the Canaanites are invulnerable it hardly matters whether you are right or wrong because the operational decision will be not to attack, and the accuracy of your report will not be tested, and so you win both ways. Perhaps because he did not see through this danger of a self-interested appreciation from his intelligence system, Moses too was barred from the Promised Land.

I was myself aware of a temptation in the same direction in World War II, for example to exaggerate the technical potential of the *Luftwaffe*. For the greater this potential was assessed to be, the greater would be my own standing, in effect as one of the spokesmen for the *Luftwaffe* in British defence circles. Moreover, an even greater temptation, if one was concerned with one's own standing in the eyes of an operational commander, was accurately described by Churchill from what he had seen in World War I. His verdict on the disaster of the Somme was 'Sir Douglas Haig was not at this time well served by his advisers in the Intelligence Department of General Headquarters. The temptation to tell a chief in a great position the things he most likes to hear is the commonest explanation of mistaken policy. Thus the outlook of the leader on whose decisions fateful events depend is usually far more sanguine than the brutal facts admit.'[2]

I am afraid that, human nature being what it is, the same weakness is liable to recur whenever men face the problems of command. Certainly

I saw it myself in World War II, and it was also seen by Professor Freeman Dyson in his time as a young operations officer at RAF Bomber Command. In *Disturbing the Universe* he described how 'All our advice to the commander-in-chief was transmitted to him through bureaucratic channels. The process of filtering through a bureaucratic hierarchy eliminated our sharper criticisms and our more radical suggestions. As a rule the commander-in-chief was told only things that the commander-in-chief wanted to hear.' Clearly the commander-in-chief had not availed himself of the advice of King James I of England to his son, which was to choose counsellors who were 'specially free of that filthy vice of Flattery, the pest of all Princes'.

Independence in Intelligence

There was, moreover, another variety of account that a commander might receive, where the criterion was not what he wanted to hear but what whoever was reporting to him wanted him to hear. Such accounts could fall into two categories, depending on the motive of the reporter. The first of these was entirely reputable even if sometimes misguided, for the teller would be trying to influence the commander in favour of action that the teller believed to be correct. The second category, though, had the much less worthy motive of showing the reporter himself to the commander in an unduly favourable light. Again, this could lead the commander to take too rosy a view not only of the reporter but also of the military situation to be faced. The cases that I myself saw were mainly concerned with electronic countermeasures, where reports going upwards from the countermeasures organization sometimes discounted evidence from intelligence which showed that their countermeasures were not being as successful as the organization claimed. Fortunately, I was able to maintain an independent voice; and from that experience I would stress the need for intelligence to be able to report independently to the highest level of command.

The possession of an independent voice calls for both responsible discrimination and courage from the intelligence officer. My first experience of writing a report for Churchill was immediately after he became Prime Minister in 1940, and I was asked by MI6 to produce a report listing all the novel weapons, however far-fetched, that had been mentioned in the files. The motive was primarily to ensure that whatever new weapons did in fact appear, Churchill could not afterwards reproach the intelligence service for not having warned him. Such an undiscriminating catalogue, however much it might protect the service, would have been of little value to the Prime Minister. This was yet another way in which an intelligence organization might attempt to 'play safe' and in doing so put a commander at a disadvantage.

The fact that Churchill himself had experienced the dangers of coloured appreciations was one of our sources of strength. Although one could on occasion be in danger of encountering his passing wrath when telling him unpleasing truths, he was easily big enough to recognize both that certain problems had to be faced and that it required courage to bring them to his notice. I would make a point here of refuting an assertion recently made in the *Bulletin of the Atomic Scientists* by Barton J. Bernstein that 'Knowing Churchill's intolerance of moral and legal restraints, his military advisers, even if they had been so inclined, would not have reminded him that first use of bacteriological warfare violated the Geneva Protocol and the moral code of war. He did not want such advice.'

It happens that I was present at a key incident in the episode to which this assertion refers. It was the meeting of the War Cabinet's Crossbow Committee on 18 July 1944, when I had surprised Churchill by telling him of my conclusion that the Germans must have built at least a thousand V2 rockets. Angry both with me and with the Germans, he mooted the proposal that we should attempt to deter them by threatening to use poison gas if they launched the rocket. None present supported him: some of us spoke positively against the idea, and he gave way. His advisers were not as spineless as Barton Bernstein believes, and they would not have lasted long with Churchill if they had been.

Hierarchical Attenuation

For all their merits, though, Churchill was quite prepared to go beyond his immediate circle of advisers, and cut through to the level where the detailed work was done. Indeed he would sometimes do it for himself: writing afterwards of the Joint Intelligence Committee's tardiness in June 1941 in divining the German intention to attack Russia, he said that 'I had not been content with this form of collective wisdom, and preferred to see the originals (decrypts, agents' reports, etc.) myself . . . thus forming my own opinions, sometimes at much earlier dates.' This was entirely in keeping with his nature, which was always to get as near 'the sharp end' as possible and appreciate the situation for himself.

He recognized, of course, that in intelligence he could only do this on rare occasions, but always his instinct was to have as few stages as possible between himself and the front line; these stages being manned by men whom he felt he could trust. Thus he used Lindemann to 'decipher the signals from the experts on the far horizons [of science] and explain to me in simple homely terms what the issues were'.[3] In the same spirit Churchill called me in from time to time on matters of scientific intelligence. Again he remembered what he had learnt from the U-boat crisis of 1917 (see above, page 120) about the importance of front-line experience being appreciated at command level, a lesson which had increasing force as science and technology increased the pace in development of new weapons. This became widely realized among commanders by the end of World War II, which showed still further that a successful commander needed to be able to probe with discretion into situations at any level within his command. While a commander must thereby be free to gain information directly from any level, he must avoid the temptation to give orders directly to that level, except in utter emergency, for he would thereby sabotage the authority of all those officers in the chain of command between him and the level concerned. Orders consequent upon information from any level must go down through the chain of command.

Modern commanders, though, for all that they may do to concern themselves as much as Churchill did in crucial matters of intelligence, generally depend, as he himself did for most of the time, on intelligence officers whom they can trust to make the best possible appreciation of the enemy in the relevant field, to understand the commander's problems, and to present the appreciation to him both in good time and in a form that he can readily assimilate.

Intelligence as Watchdog

The intelligence organization must be like a good watchdog, drawing the commander's attention to real threats to his intended course of action but not barking too early to enable a real threat to be distinguished from a false one. Nor should the organization overload the commander with a continuous trickle of reports none of which is firm enough to determine action, but which with others might – when properly appreciated – form part of a meaningful picture. If anything, the trickle may have the opposite effect of dulling the commander's interest and acclimatizing him by slow change to what if freshly viewed might be seen to be a dangerous threat.

It is rarely easy to satisfy all these criteria, as an example from my own experience will show. It concerns the build-up for the V1 campaign of 1944, where we had achieved the remarkable position of having in effect a continuous ringside seat at the German trials in Peenemünde for nine months before the campaign opened. We soon knew almost everything that a commander would need to know to plan his defence. And yet, when the campaign opened, our anti-aircraft gunners thought that we had misled them about the height at which the V1s would fly. In December 1943 we had correctly reported that the height band mainly used in the Peenemünde trials was six to seven thousand feet, although we also mentioned that some trials were flown as low as fifteen hundred feet. As the trials progressed, the height band was gradually brought down, and we duly reported the fact – but without any emphasis because our early reports had already shown that the V1s could fly well at the lower heights. What I did not know was that Air Marshal Hill, who commanded our fighters and guns, had said that if the bombs flew at between two and three thousand feet this would be too high for the low-altitude guns, and yet awkward for the heavier high-altitude guns because of their slower speed of traverse. Had I known of his anxiety, I would have stressed the change in height that was taking place in the trials, and so he would have been better prepared for the event. As it was, I was not in direct contact with him because a special section had been set up on the Air Staff to deal with matters between intelligence and the commands, and so this introduced a degree of attenuation that, as this example shows, should always where possible be avoided.

Detail and Discrimination

It is easy to overload a commander's mind with detail. Some of my operations research colleagues had not realized this when in the early sixties they tried to devise an operations room for a field commander which would present him with displays of all the information they thought he might require. They then arranged for war games in which officers of acknowledged command ability would fight battles from the information available on the displays. The scientists were surprised to find that the best commanders were those who used relatively little of the information provided. What the scientists had in effect done was provide photographic detail, whereas the commander only required key details such as whether a particular bridge or hill was being held, for this would determine the entire situation in that area. The commander acted much more on a pictorial rather than a photographic impression.

Churchill himself understood this; in fact, he put it the other way round, because he had mastered problems of command long before he attempted to master a paintbrush on canvas. In 'Painting as a Pastime' in *Thoughts and Adventures* he wrote:

> In all battles two things are usually required of the Commander-in-Chief: to make a good plan for his army and, secondly, to keep a strong reserve. Both these are also obligatory upon the painter. To make a plan, thorough reconnaissance of the country where the battle is to be fought is needed. Its fields, its mountains, its rivers, its bridges, its trees, its flowers, its atmosphere – all require and repay attentive observation from a special point of view . . . I think this heightened sense of observation of Nature is one of the chief delights that have come to me through trying to paint.

So the intelligence officer's problem is to paint the picture in a style that will best convey its intended content to the commander. Here, of course, he must be punctilious in making the picture as objective as possible, while inevitably emphasizing the points which he himself believes to be important; he must not attempt to achieve emphasis by suppressing justifiable doubts about the validity of any evidence on which he draws. Essentially, though, it will be a *picture* which he presents and not a *photograph* with so much detail that the commander, unless he is exceptional, will be unable to digest it. Also essentially, it will be as coherent a picture as possible and not a jumble of jigsaw pieces individually tipped on to the commander's table from time to time.

Timing

Timing can indeed be important, although not so much between an intelligence officer and his commander, who ought to know one another well enough to be able to exchange ideas and information on an absolutely continuous basis. But if the intelligence officer's reports go to officers whom he knows less well, and particularly if there are more than one of them, he may have to consider the timing of his presentation. I myself encountered this problem, and was on occasion criticized for holding back information; I hope that I never did so when it mattered, and I was quite clear about when it would be justified. In fact, I wrote on 20 November 1942:

> We are sometimes criticized for withholding information, but while no instance has ever been proved, we reserve our right to do so because (1) to spread half-truth is often to precipitate erroneous action by the Air Staff, and (2) the steady and immediate broadcasting of each insignificant and uncollated fact automatically and insidiously acclimatizes the recipients to knowledge of enemy developments, so that they feel no stimulation to action. The presentation of the complete picture of an enemy development is the best way of stimulating the appropriate authority to action. The production of such pictures involves much effort, but it has been justified by results. Although we think that the above policy is the best, it obviously has some defects, which we try to remedy by frequent oral communications to the appropriate bodies.[4]

Positive as that statement was, I should have been grateful to know that I was unwittingly following the practice of Admiral Sir Reginald Hall twenty-five years before, for in *The Eyes of the Navy* his biographer, Admiral James, summarized his gifts for intelligence work. Among them:

> He had a perfect sense of timing. We have seen how skilfully he timed each move after he had read the Zimmermann telegram. He frequently delayed disclosing information until the time was ripe . . .[5]

There is also another sense in which timing can be important: this concerns the frequency with which a routinely developing situation is reviewed. Too frequent reviews may insensitize the reviewer, who will then overlook small changes between one review and the next, and may tire both him and the operational staff to whom he presents his reviews. 'If a man watch too long,' wrote Francis Bacon, 'it is odds he will fall asleep.' There was probably something of this involved in our missing the escape of *Scharnhorst* and *Gneisenau* from Brest in 1942; we had been watching them for so long that our wakefulness was impaired. And, after months of watching for the V1s to be brought up to their launching sites in 1944, we very nearly missed them for the same reason. In the Falklands crisis of 1982 it seemed that the lesson had once again been forgotten, for in the post-mortem the Franks Committee recorded: 'we believe that, in dealing with Argentina and the Falkland Islands it [the Joint Intelligence machinery] was too passive in operation to respond quickly and critically to a rapidly changing situation that demanded urgent attention.'[6]

While there is a danger of something being missed by routine reviews, there is the complementary danger of its not being reported in good time if reviews are too infrequent. Once again there is an art in choosing the best reviewing frequency, which needs to be matched to the nature of the situation being watched.

Short-term vs Long-term

Here a conflict can arise between the interests of long-term and short-term intelligence, where there will almost always be a tendency to concentrate on the short-term. This arises partly because unless a short-term danger is parried, any interest in the long-term could be futile. That is a good reason; what is not so good is the tendency for an intelligence organization to concentrate on the short-term because its topicality will often bring the organization to the notice of senior officers. Neglect of the long-term is all the more tempting because there is an exhilaration about applying short-term intelligence to immediate operations which is good for morale on both sides. But it is almost as dangerous to concentrate entirely on the immediate and thereby prejudice the future by failing to anticipate new developments, as it is to concentrate on the future and ignore the immediate.

The only difference of opinion that I had at Bletchley in the entire war was on this very point. In the exhilaration of providing immediate intelligence to field commanders operating in Africa and Italy, Bletchley tended to jib at my insistence as their scientific adviser that they must give comparable priority of cryptographic effort to those lines of Enigma traffic that might throw light on the development of the new weapons which we believed might be appearing in the year ahead. And on reading Ralph Bennett's *Ultra in the West* I have wondered whether the coming German offensive in the Ardennes might have been detected if Bletchley or some other organization had undertaken longer-term reviews, say fortnightly or monthly, of the information contained in the copious stream of short-term decrypts. As he records, 'So far from conveying little intelligence these signals had a great deal to say about German movements in and near the Ardennes during the weeks preceding 16 December . . . it does seem to point much more convincingly towards a coming attack than it was then held to do.' Partly, perhaps, the fault lay in the numbing of intelligence through acclimatization by slow change that I have earlier stressed. It would certainly seem to point to the need for both long-term and short-term analyses of the import of the decrypts; and since overall effort is limited, a balance has to be struck between the two.

The apportioning of effort, as between long-term and short-term, is one of the internal problems of intelligence, which is also bedevilled by several others. One of these is the fact that input into intelligence is by source, whereas its output is by subject. Each type of source, such as espionage, electronic reconnaissance, cryptography, and photo-reconnaissance, requires a specialist organization to run it, and so does each subject, such as naval, military, air, scientific, economic and political intelligence. Each of the latter may have to compete for the attention of any one of the former. Co-ordination of effort is therefore necessary, and committees are to some degree inevitable.

Committees

Committees have an essential role in smoothing out difficulties of organization, but it is otherwise when an intelligence picture has to be put together. As we have seen, this is something of an art, and no committee has ever created a good work of art. In 1954, after I had spent a year as a member of the Joint Intelligence Committee in London, I recorded that 'too much time and effort was dissipated in the JIC machine. I did my best to make it work despite memories of the comparative ineffectuality of the JIC in war. Even at the best of times it is far from easy to produce a good joint report when there is a reasonable amount of information to draw upon and whose interpretation is relatively unambiguous . . . A joint report is only as effective as common agreement will allow, and – so far as interpreting intelligence evidence goes – common agreement rarely goes far enough . . .'[7] Were it more expert the Committee might realize that 'many of the arguments that arise in its discussions are simply evidence that an adequate amount of information is lacking. In these circumstances, the proper course is to stop arguing and to seek fresh information.'

These comments had no effect at the time but I was interested to read, some thirty years later, that after the Falklands the Franks

Committee recommended changes, making one full-time individual responsible for chairing the JIC. He was to be appointed directly by the Prime Minister, and made a member of the Cabinet Office.

Command in Intelligence

I know nothing of how effective the resulting changes have been, but they should certainly have done good. Implicitly, they recognize that intelligence is a professional pursuit and that just as a military force needs an individual to head it, so does intelligence, which in effect is waging a war the whole time. Just as a military force needs specialized arms, such as armour and infantry, each of which requires an individual to head it, so does intelligence. The relationships of these heads to the individual at the centre, and to the staff below them, generate problems of command inside their own organizations very similar to those we have already discussed as arising between a commander and his intelligence officer.

The head of an intelligence organization, for example, will rarely be able to do much of the detailed intelligence work himself. However he certainly must be ready to sample the working situation at any level in the organization under him with the intention not of meddling but of getting a better appreciation of what is being done, the strength of the evidence which is being revealed, and the potential for improved exploitation. Again, when he thereby finds something that may need action at some subordinate level, he must see that orders for action are properly transmitted down through his internal chain of command and not given by him direct to the level concerned. I do, though, place overwhelming value on his freedom to range at any level in order to learn about what the components of his organization are doing. In World War II, I myself had such freedom partly because I remained a civilian and so could mix at any level in a command structure without embarrassment; but I have certainly known uniformed officers at air chief marshal level who could do it equally well, as could Churchill himself – and they were usually the best commanders.

In an intelligence organization problems of internal command are greater than those in a military one. In part this arises from the nature of the work and the kinds of individual it attracts, many of whom would hardly be amenable to military discipline. The problems are further complicated by the input-by-source, output-by-subject requirement. To take the simplest of examples, my main responsibility in

World War II was for scientific intelligence. For this I had to draw on every conceivable kind of source, such as photographic reconnaissance. But it was clear that there were many other calls on PR besides my own, and that all the operational arrangements connected with sorties – besides the equipment and supply of aircraft and the training of pilots – would have been far beyond my capacity to organize and administer; and it would have been hopelessly extravagant. So all these matters had to be the responsibility of another officer, who would have to fit my requirements in with a host from other subject branches of intelligence. It happened that the arrangement worked outstandingly well, because there was goodwill on both sides from the start. But friction could arise, as it sometimes did in other instances, particularly when two subject branches were bidding for the attention of the same source. It could happen that the head of a source branch might insist that all outside communications with staff in his branch must go through his office. While there could be good reasons for this, it attenuated the rapport between the officers at working level in the source and subject branches. Here I was particularly fortunate because the heads of the source branches were remarkably good in allowing me to talk to their officers directly – for example, photographic pilots had the freedom to come to my office, and I had the freedom to go to their stations, and so they knew directly what I wanted, how I would like the photographs taken, and just what their significance would be. My own personal staff was small, but thanks to this freedom I had something near moral command over staff in most of the source branches.

Here I would comment on the maintenance of morale in an intelligence organization. Again, it has a special problem because of security: the work of many of the staff at working level will never receive popular recognition, nor will they always see the effect of their work on operations. If good work results in success, the credit will tend to fall on those officers who present the results to the forum where they are made known to the operational or political staffs. It is vital that these officers do their utmost to pass on all possible credit to those on whose work the success has depended, and to show them what it has meant in operational or planning decisions. It should always be borne in mind that, as Field Marshal Slim pointed out in *Defeat into Victory*, 'There are in any army, and for that matter any big organization, very large numbers of people whose existence is only remembered when something for which they are responsible has gone wrong.' Whoever heads an intelligence organization must be ever vigilant to offset this failing.

Intelligence and Policy Making

This chapter has been based mainly on my personal experiences in World War II, and it will therefore be salutary to bear in mind more recent experiences gained in wider fields in peace as well as war. In particular, Herbert E. Meyer's *Real World Intelligence* gives a forthright exposition of some of the lessons he drew from his service on the National Intelligence Council in Washington.

Defining intelligence as 'organized information',[8] with an intelligence service fulfilling a function in the making and execution of policy analogous to that of 'on-board ship and aircraft navigation systems', Meyer notes that inside the US intelligence service the emphasis has shifted from the operational to the analytical side. Raw intelligence collected by modern techniques is so prolific that the main problem is to analyse and collate all that comes through the diversity of channels and from it form the intelligence appreciation which will best help the policy makers.

Meyer draws a contrast between the characters of policy makers and intelligence officers: 'A policy maker enjoys power . . . An intelligence officer distrusts power . . . hesitates to make decisions without a total command of all the facts – which, of course, he almost never has.'[9] Following this distinction, Meyer observes that the intelligence officer and the policy maker are always best at odds. While recognizing the element of truth in the contrast, though, I find it difficult to agree with the 'at odds' observation, at least if the term 'policy maker' includes 'commander' in the sense of the present chapter. I myself had sometimes to work with commanders with whom I was at odds, with a few who were apathetic, and others with whom relations were understanding and enthusiastic. And while 'at odds' was certainly more stimulating than apathy it was less stimulating than work with a commander of kindred spirit.

In fact, Meyer suggests the way in which the 'at odds' syndrome can be minimized: 'For intelligence officers the trick is to bring policy makers the bad news they need to know without seeming to attack the entire policy.' That is an art indeed; but the trick should not be attempted by sacrifice of the most vital of all Meyer's instructions: 'Never, never, cook the books!'[10]

A Note on Scale

The effects of scale need to be borne in mind in applying principles, however sound, in command as well as in all other activities. Napoleon, for example, said that in actions between his cavalrymen and the Mamelukes, two of the latter would beat three of the former but a force of one thousand cavalry would beat 1,500 Mamelukes, because on the small scale skilled horsemanship was the paramount factor but on the large scale discipline and order would prevail. Similar considerations hold in intelligence: in World War II, we in Britain were fortunate enough to be operating on a relatively small scale where personal ability in intelligence could be a decisive factor. Today, with large organizations such as CIA, NSA, and GCHQ, the balance between personal ability and administrative skill may well have changed, although both will always be important.

7

Science in World War I

The success in the application of science to warfare in World War II owed much to the foundations laid by the scientists who worked with the armed forces in World War I. They led the way for my generation, and we – their pupils – learned from their experiences. Until recently little tribute has been paid to what they achieved, but much of this now can be found in Guy Hartcup's *The War of Invention*. In the present chapter I add my own tribute, drawing where possible on personal knowledge of those of the principal figures of 1914–18 with whom I came into contact when they were in senior positions in World War II. As we built on their achievements, let us first recall what they in turn had to build on when war broke out in 1914.

Earlier Applications

The earliest uses of science in the waging of war can but dimly be discerned through the haze of legend. As far back as 2400 BC, according to Lord Kelvin, the Chinese Emperor Hoang Ti successfully led his army through a fog by means of a magnetic compass. In 429 BC the Greeks used the choking fumes from burning pitch and sulphur against their enemy at the battle of Plataea, and in 212 BC Archimedes surprised the Roman besiegers of Syracuse with a range of novel weapons, only to die at the hands of a Roman soldier when the city fell. Gunpowder and rockets were invented in China, and came to Europe in the Middle Ages. Balloons, invented in France in 1783, were taken by Napoleon on his Egyptian expedition in 1798; when they became 'war surplus' one was used to explore the upper atmosphere by the French scientist Gay-Lussac, who in 1804 reached the remarkable height of 7,000 metres, a record that stood for more than fifty years. In 1804 William Congreve began to develop rockets as weapons for the British Army: in 1806 they were used to bombard Boulogne, and at the battle of Bladensburg in 1814 during the Anglo-American war they turned the tide in favour of the British, who went on to sack Washington. They were not so successful, though, at the siege of Fort McHenry in Baltimore Harbour a month later, and Americans commemorate their experience with mention of 'the rocket's red glare' in their national anthem.

At sea the torpedo and the submarine were both first used successfully in the American Civil War of 1861–5, which also led to several other technical developments in warfare. One, which was not actually used, was to fill shells with chlorine. A similar proposal had been made at the outbreak of the Crimean War in 1854 by Lyon Playfair who suggested that shells should be filled with 'chloride of cacodyl', a highly poisonous compound, but it was turned down on the argument that this would be as much against the conventions of civilized warfare as would be the poisoning of wells. Playfair also suggested that incendiary shells could be made by filling a brittle case with phosphorus dissolved in carbon bisulphide; but this suggestion, too, was rejected.

Similar measures were considered in the defence of Paris in 1870, when a scientific Commission was set up under the distinguished chemist, Berthelot. One of the minutes in the Commission's Report ran: 'Propositions for the use of phosphorus, sulphuric acid, ammonia, wild animals, poisons and viruses as means of defence were discussed but the Commission dismissed them all either as useless or as too cruel if not contrary to morality and humanity.'[1] In their dire plight the defenders of Paris thus showed restraint as noble as it was exemplary.

Sooner or later, though, such ideas were bound to be exploited as warfare hardened – as they indeed were in World War I to such an extent that it came to be described as a 'chemist's war'. But while chemistry may have predominated, inventions based on discoveries in physics also came into use in ways that foreshadowed their employment in World War II. Above all, the prediction of the existence of radio waves by Clerk Maxwell in 1864 and their experimental confirmation by Heinrich Hertz in 1887, coupled with the discovery of the electron in 1896 by J. J. Thomson, led to the development of signalling by radio so rapidly that in 1899 Marconi operators were already working with the British forces in the South African war.[2]

Research, Pure and Applied

These remarkably rapid developments in radio tend to refute the charge that discoveries in science have to wait twenty years before they are taken up for development. Even more dramatic was the case of X-rays: they were discovered by Wilhelm Röntgen in Würzburg in November 1895 and within a few months they were in use for surgical diagnosis, and portable X-ray sets for the examination of wound fractures were taken to Khartoum in 1897 by surgeons accompanying Kitchener's expedition.

Afterwards, J. J. Thomson asked the telling question, if you were contemplating a benefaction to encourage developments in surgery in 1895, to what use would you have directed it? To better steels for surgical implements, perhaps? Or for better anaesthetics? Or better antiseptics? Perhaps, but you would never have thought of giving it to a professor of physics obscurely working on the conduction of electricity through gases in a small German university. And yet, 'J.J.' remarked, that was where X-rays were discovered, and so provided one of the most classic of all examples of the value of benefits that can unexpectedly come from pure research. It is one of the difficulties of policy in scientific research that such benefits defy the concepts of planning and cannot be quantified in advance, but the world would be poorer if pure research were abandoned. On the other hand, the argument can be too easily exploited by academics who make pretence of working at intellectually difficult problems as a way of explaining why they produce little of interest – a type that conforms to F. M. Cornford's description, 'learning is called sound when no one has ever heard of it; and "sound scholar" is a term of praise applied to one another by learned men who have no reputation outside the University and a rather queer one inside it.'[3] The basic difficulty in planning, as Abraham Flexner pointed out in his study of Oxford and Cambridge, is that 'the same conditions that permit idleness, neglect, or perfunctory performance of duty are necessary to the highest exertions of the human intellect.'[4] As I call to mind the many discussions that I have heard on the distinction between pure and applied research over more than forty years, I increasingly sympathize with the bewilderment of an American colonel who sat on an Anglo-American committee in 1945 to decide what researches should be permitted in post-war Germany. The committee consisted mainly of serving officers and scientists, and the general feeling was that pure research should be allowed but that applied research should be forbidden. The colonel asked what was the difference between pure research and applied research, and others round the table did their best to explain. At last the colonel said that he now understood: 'Let us define pure research as research with no known objective.'

New Technology

Besides discoveries in pure science there were several practical inventions that would affect military technology and tactics, and indeed strategy, in 1914. The advent of the aeroplane would have its impact both on land and at sea, and would result in warfare of its own in the air. But at first it was rejected by both the British Admiralty and the Army; the former, to whom the Wright brothers offered their aeroplane, told them, 'Their Lordships are of the opinion that they could not be of any practical use to the Naval Service,' and two members of the Army Council argued that aeroplanes could have no conceivable military use because they would have to fly at more than forty miles an hour, at which speed a pilot would be unable to see anything.

The Navy, though, was not always so short-sighted, and it showed notable enthusiasm for radio communication. It had also been jolted by Charles Parsons when he raced his *Turbinia* through the lines of warships assembled for the Jubilee Review by their Sovereign in 1897 at Spithead, with no naval ship able to catch him. The Parsons turbine was rapidly adopted by Admiral John Fisher, the First Sea Lord, who became convinced that naval officers needed to know more science. Actually his predecessors of the 1860s were of the same opinion, for they had founded the Royal Naval College at Greenwich in 1873 for this very purpose, but the results were evidently not enough for Fisher. So determined was he that he created the new post of Director of Naval Education in 1903 with a salary of £2,500 a year plus a house to tempt the engineer and physicist Alfred Ewing from his chair in Cambridge at a time when the salary of a superintendent at the National Physics Laboratory was £400. 'Why,' said Fisher, 'it will be our proud boast ever afterwards to be known as Engineer Admirals, all of us!' Under Ewing the colleges at Osborne and Dartmouth were set up and Fisher made a point of interviewing prospective midshipmen himself. Ewing recorded that one boy, who was in danger of being rejected because, in reply to a question on what a vacuum was, he had ventured that it was where the Pope lived, was accepted by Fisher because he knew that a horse got up forelegs first and a cow with its hindlegs.

Despite its alertness in radio, and with all Fisher's support for engineering, the Navy had failed before the war to anticipate that battles would henceforth be fought at long range, following the adoption of defensive armour and the consequent technical advances in guns to penetrate that armour. The earlier concepts of naval actions had been that of exchanges of broadsides at close range, but the higher velocities of guns developed to penetrate broadside armour also gave them greater range, with the additional merit of firing at elevations such that their shells would strike their targets at plunging angles, so that some could penetrate the lightly armoured decks. This advantage, though, could not be exploited until there was an adequate means of predicting where the target would be in relation to the guns when both target and attacker were in motion, and when the shells took ten to twenty seconds to reach the target. So as late as 1900 the maximum practice range for 13.5-inch guns was 1,500 yards, although even the 4.7-inch naval guns in the relief of Ladysmith were firing with effect at 10,000 yards.

A London solicitor, Arthur Pollen, said that the problem of aiming at sea could be solved if accurate gyroscopes and rangefinders could be made, and between 1900 and 1910 he stimulated their development and devised a system to incorporate them. Had the British battleships been fitted with the system at Jutland in 1916, Jellicoe would have been able to continue firing when he gave his much questioned order to turn away from the torpedo attack by the German destroyers while his opponent Scheer retreated out of range, never to be found again. Only after the war was the superiority of Pollen's over the Navy's own system admitted, and its principal features embodied in the new battleships of 1926 – HMS *Nelson* and *Rodney*.

Science in Aid of the Navy

With the scene now set for 1914, let us look at some of the episodes concerning science in the war that followed. In no way is this survey intended to be definitive: my aim is much more to point to attitudes, experiences, and lessons – both serious and humorous – which my generation absorbed from those of our seniors – parents, teachers, military instructors and professors – who had been involved. A more detailed study can be found in Guy Hartcup's *The War of Invention* and there is much about developments in the United States in *The Physicists* by Daniel J. Kevles.

The greatest threat to be faced at sea came from the German U-boats; the heavy losses that these inflicted led the Navy to consider any help that science might be able to provide. The key problem, which even seventy years later is still only partly solved, is to locate a submerged submarine in an ocean of salt water almost impenetrable to light or radio waves. Sound waves, which are much more effectively transmitted by water, offered almost the only hope, and this was obvious from the start. In fact, as William Hackman records in his history of sonar and submarine warfare *Seek & Strike*, Leonardo da Vinci heard the movement of a ship by listening through a tube held under water, and in Ancient China fishermen followed shoals of fish by listening to the noise they made by means of a bamboo stick with its end in the water. The noise of the submarine's engines and propellers could be detected, or pulses of higher frequency sound waves bounced off its hull, the acoustic forerunner of radar now known as SONAR and formerly as ASDIC. Its principal inventors were Langevin in France and Rutherford in Britain, but despite the readiness of scientists to help, they found that naval officers were not always sympathetic to their approach. A minute of a Sub-Committee of the Admiralty's Board for Invention and Research, dated 27 March 1917, ran:

> It was pointed out that in scientific research it was found to be essential that the researcher should have the widest knowledge and personal experience of the difficulties to be solved. Commodore Hall dissented, and expressed the view that the only information necessary to be given was that the enemy submarines were in the sea, and that means were required to detect their presence.

The episode epitomizes a narrow viewpoint fatal to the most effective use of scientific aid; fortunately, the survivors of the 1914–18 generation of scientists such as Tizard and Lindemann were able to foster a broader spirit in 1935–45.

Although the basic invention of sonar had been made, acoustic and electronic technologies were not sufficiently advanced for an effective system to result, and scientists wondered whether alternatives could be devised. A skilled musician and distinguished conductor, Hamilton Harty, was brought in to listen to submarine noises to identify the most promising frequency bands (anticipating by a whole war a similar attempt in America, where the conductor André Kostelanetz was approached for much the same purpose according to his memoirs, *Echoes*, published by Harcourt Brace Jovanovich) and, not for the last time, the aid of the highly developed senses of animals was sought. An alsatian dog, for example, is thought to be about a hundred million times as sensitive as a man to the smell of acetic acid. Fish, too, can be extremely sensitive: salmon can detect the organic 'smell' of not only their own river, but of the particular tributary in which they were hatched. So, could some animal sense be employed to detect U-boats? It was known that seals could be trained to perform tricks – could they have an acute sense of hearing that would enable them to be trained to find U-boats? Trials were made, but were not successful enough for a serious application to develop.

Another approach, so Lord Cherwell (F. A. Lindemann) told me, was to elaborate on the Chinese method of fishing with cormorants. The cormorant is kept captive by a string while it flies around the fisherman's boat until with its keen eyesight it spots a fish and dives on it. A ring round the bird's neck stops it swallowing the fish, which is retrieved along with the bird by the fisherman. According to Lord Cherwell, the idea was to train a cormorant to spot U-boat periscopes by setting out a dummy periscope with a herring attached to it. The bird was first released at short range, and this was increased as the bird became more expert. Also, after a time, the herring was omitted, and the bird would nevertheless optimistically alight on the periscope. Trials were successful, but use in operation a failure: it had not been realized just how keen was the sight of cormorants. They had been trained on British and not on German periscopes, and they could tell the difference between the two, ignoring the latter and alighting only on the former. That, at any rate, was Cherwell's story.

Sound Ranging

While acoustic science was not of great help to the Navy in World War I, it scored successes in support of the Army in locating enemy gun batteries. If an observer could register both the flash and the bang from a gun it was easy to establish its distance from him, knowing that light takes negligible time to travel, but that sound is delayed by approximately one second for every 1,100 feet, relative to the light. So the gun must lie on a circle of appropriate radius from the observation point. Two different observation points thus give two circles which will in general intersect in two points, one of which will lie in friendly and the other in enemy territory; if there is any ambiguity this can be eliminated by observing from a third point. The technique was known as 'flash spotting'.

A more sophisticated technique did not depend on observing the flash but on sound waves alone. If two observers at different stations listen for the report of the gun they will not in general hear it at the same time but at instants differing by an interval which depends on how much nearer the one observation point is to the gun than is the other. The gun must therefore be at some point where its distances from the two points differ by the distance indicated by the difference in times that the sound takes to reach them. This by itself does not define a unique point for the gun, but it does define a curve which is the locus of points whose distances from the two observation points differ by a constant amount. Such a curve has been known from the time of the Ancient Greeks – it is a branch of a hyperbola about the two observation points as foci. The observers can therefore establish a curved line on which the gun must lie. If a third observer also records the time at which he hears the gun, this can define two extra hyperbolae, and the gun must be at the common point of intersection of all three. This seminal principle (first conceived by a French astronomer turned artilleryman, Charles Nordmann, in the autumn of 1914[5]), which applies to radio as well as sound waves, inspired the development in World War II of the GEE and other systems of radio position fixing and, more recently, navigation by transmissions from satellites; it is sometimes designated as 'T.O.A.' (Time of Arrival). In World War I it was known as 'sound ranging', and was developed by a team of physicists under W. L. (later Sir Lawrence) Bragg.

If it was difficult to locate a distant gun, it was sometimes even more difficult for the gunners to locate where their shells were falling. The supreme instance was that of the famous long-range gun that bombarded Paris in 1918 at a range of about seventy miles. A German friend, Carl Bosch, of my research student days told me that he had heard that the gun's own designers were surprised by the range that it attained in trials in Germany. They had fired their shots at twenty-minute intervals and had posted observers in the area in which they were expected to fall. The observers, however, reported nothing, and for several days the disappearance of the shells was a mystery until a meteorologist, who had previously been consulted about the density of air in the upper atmosphere and who therefore knew of the trials, received a report from an area further along the line of fire that three meteorites had fallen at twenty-minute intervals on the day concerned. The unexpected increase in range was due to the air resistance in the upper atmosphere being smaller than the designers had calculated. It was this story, incidentally, that led me to anticipate that the V1 and V2 designers of 1943 would have similar problems in the trials of their missiles, and that they might therefore call for radar assistance – with the results described in *Most Secret War*.[6] Anecdotes can indeed have value beyond mere entertainment.

Chemical Warfare

Whatever help physicists could give the Army, it had a much greater need for help from chemists. This was because on 22 April 1915, the Germans inaugurated chemical warfare with an attack with chlorine gas released from cylinders against the French in the Ypres salient; two days later similar attacks started against the British, my father being among those who watched the yellow-green cloud as it approached during one of these attacks and then wafted back to the German lines as the wind changed.

Thereafter it was a continuous battle with both sides developing gases (the British starting with improvised supplies of chlorine on 25 September 1915, at Loos) and means of protection such as gas-masks and impermeable clothing for defence against such agents as mustard gas, latterly delivered by artillery bombardment in shells. A distinguished Oxford chemist, Harold Hartley, became responsible for gas warfare developments in Britain, and was given the rank of Brigadier General. As with others, he found the return to teaching and research only partly satisfactory after the war, and he continued for some time to wear his uniform in the Balliol–Trinity laboratories – an episode which led one of his research students, Cyril Hinshelwood, later a Nobel Laureate and President of the Royal Society, to write:

> After the war Brigadier General Hartley returned to civil life – partly.

Chemical warfare had been outlawed by the Hague Conventions of 1899 and 1907, and there was widespread indignation when the Germans broke the Convention; but in surveying the war in 1919, Hartley stated that gas proved more humane, in producing fewer permanent casualties for a given military result than conventional warfare by high explosive, a verdict endorsed by other authorities.[7] Reviewing the contribution of British chemists in his Report of 1919, Hartley concluded: 'The true measure of their success can be gauged from the general impression, confirmed by the statements of many German prisoners, both officers and men, that had the enemy foreseen the results of the treacherous use of gas in April 1915, the new weapon would never have been employed.' And, indeed, Hitler, who had himself been gassed, was so deterred throughout World War II.

As a lighter aside on the early days of gas warfare, I recall that at an Oxford University Physical Society dinner in 1931 Professor J. S. E. Townsend told us of an officer whose company was to carry out an attack using cylinders of gas. Knowing that a balloon full of gas is lighter than an empty one, as evidenced by its floating upwards in the air, and also knowing that it needed one platoon to carry the gas cylinders full of gas up to the front line, he thoughtfully detailed two platoons to carry the empty cylinders back.

Air Warfare

Besides new methods of warfare in the age-old media of land and sea, World War I introduced warfare in the air, and this was a medium in which there were so many unknown factors that scientists could be given a liberal, almost free, rein. Moreover, the problems were so challenging that they attracted the attention of many able scientists, who gravitated naturally to the Royal Aircraft Factory (later Establishment) at Farnborough. One of the few Oxford Fellows in physics, I. O. Griffith, the deputy head of the Clarendon Laboratory when I started there in 1930, had volunteered his services at Farnborough and reported to the Superintendent, explaining that he was a physicist. He told us that the Superintendent thereupon picked up his telephone and spoke to one of his deputies: 'I say, I have a fellow from Oxford here. His name is Griffith. Bald as an egg. Says he's something to do with soda water!' The Superintendent, Mervyn O'Gorman, collected a remarkably able group of physicists and mathematicians, and at least one physiologist – E. D. Adrian, later Lord Adrian, Nobel Prizewinner, Nobel Laureate, and Master of Trinity. Other future Nobel Prizewinners were F. W. Aston, of the mass spectrograph, and G. P. Thomson who demonstrated the wave properties of the electron, while the applied mathematician, G. I. Taylor, became a member of the Order of Merit.

Probably the most spectacular of their achievements was Lindemann's, who in 1917 developed the principles of recovering an aircraft from a spin, and who learned to fly in order to prove his theory correct – the drill that he formulated became the standard means of recovery from what had hitherto frequently been a fatal condition. While a few other pilots had successfully recovered from a spin before him, Lindemann was the first to put an aeroplane into a spin intentionally and to have previously worked out the theory of the actions necessary to bring it out again. To get permission to learn to fly, incidentally, he had had to bluff his way through the eyesight test, with one of his eyes almost blind: while chatting to the examining doctor he had memorized the side of the test card that was showing. With his German name, Lindemann was viewed with some distrust by the servicing personnel at Farnborough, who were said to ensure that he could never escape to Germany by seeing that he never had sufficient petrol in his tank. Their suspicions appeared to be confirmed when on one flight he made a forced landing near Dover Castle, and was held by the Army who telephoned Farnborough to say that they had captured a pilot with a bowler hat and all he would say was that his name was Lindemann and he claimed to have come from Farnborough.

Early aircraft had very few instruments, and much of the work at Farnborough went into developing airspeed indicators, compasses, both magnetic and gyro, altimeters, rate-of-climb meters, artificial horizons and bombsights. One of those who worked on instruments was Horace Darwin, the son of Charles Darwin and the founder of the Cambridge Instrument Company. Even before the war he had become interested and had given the newly founded Wilbur Wright Lecture to the Royal Aeronautical Society in 1913 on the design of aircraft instruments. In the lecture he enunciated an important principle of design which he illustrated by the problem of putting a wheel on a wheelbarrow: you can either have the wheel fixed to an axle which rotates in holes in the two shafts of the fork, or you fix the axle to the fork, and let the wheel rotate round it. When the wheelbarrow is new, there is little to choose between the two alternatives; but when it becomes worn, the alternative with the wheel rotating around the axle developed a much greater wobble than the design where the axle rotates in the fork. So, as Horace Darwin pointed out, when you think you have made a good design, try it the other way round – this may work better. Moreover the principle applies far more widely than to engineering design: was man made for the Sabbath or the Sabbath made for man? Was Mae West right to be more interested in the life in her men than in the men in her life?[8]

Another of the main interests at Farnborough, aerodynamics, was a new science in which the seemingly perverse behaviour of airflow sometimes held surprises, such as a dimpled golf ball having a lower air resistance than a smooth one. One of the chief aerodynamicists, H. Glauert, shared with Lindemann the wartime embarrassment of a German name. Unlike Lindemann, though, he was a heavy smoker, filling his evening pipe with a noisome shag, oblivious of the offence he thereby caused to other members of the mess. They thought they would teach him a lesson by mixing in ebonite shavings with the contents of his tobacco pouch: they then expectantly waited for him to light up after dinner. The first puff brought an expression of shocked surprise to his face; the second reduced the shock to bewilderment; the third to tentative approval and then appreciative contentment blind to the ensuing exodus as the fumes emptied the mess.

Lindemann recounted to me another Farnborough incident which concerned one of his colleagues, also an academic in peacetime, who had become exasperated by the delays caused by Civil Service procedure for even small and local purchases. He needed a darkroom lamp, which could have been purchased for about a pound or so, but it would take several weeks for a purchase order to go through. Thinking therefore that it would be quicker to get a lamp made in the workshop, he sketched a design for a case of hexagonal cross-section, with three of the sides being filled with red, orange, and yellow glass panes, each about 6 inches high by 3 inches wide, and movable screens so that any of the panes could be screened off as necessary. He then took the sketch to the workshop, and his troubles began: the workshop would not proceed without proper drawings, which would have to be made from the sketch in the drawing office. So he took the sketch to the drawing office and explained what he wanted: the drawings were made after some delay while others more urgent were completed, and then sent on to the workshop. Several weeks went by and, when no lamp appeared, the frustrated designer engineer telephoned the head of the workshop who said that the work was in hand, but would still take some time to complete, and that he would telephone back when the lamp was ready. Ultimately he telephoned to that effect, and said that he knew the designer was anxious to get the lamp and so he would send it round on a hand-truck instead of waiting for the normal delivery by lorry. The designer asked why he could not get a boy to carry it across, but the workshop man insisted that it would have to come by truck. Two hours later the designer heard men struggling with some heavy article in the corridor outside his office, and opened the door to see the largest darkroom lamp the world has ever known. In the elaborate procedure of going through the drawing office, intended inches had become actual feet; the Farnborough academics learned how hard it is to beat the system – and how easy it is to induce the comic merely by a mismatch of dimensions.[9]

One of the admirable aspects of the band of scientists at Farnborough was that several of them, like Lindemann, learned to fly and so experience aerial problems for themselves. They incurred far less resistance from the serving officers of the Royal Naval Air Service and the Royal Flying Corps than their colleagues supporting the other two services, partly because those serving officers who had taken up flying were by nature progressive and ready to entertain new ideas. Henry Tizard, a chemist, had already joined the Royal Flying Corps and had become a test pilot. Another scientist who started to fly as early as 1914 was the applied mathematician, G. I. Taylor, who described the department at Farnborough to which he was assigned as an 'asylum for theoreticians . . . [which] tackled odd jobs which the engineers did not care about'. Let him tell his own story of one of the projects which he was asked to investigate:

> One job which was assigned to Melvill Jones and myself illustrates the kind of thought which prevailed at that time. The French had been dropping pointed darts called *flechettes* on troops from their planes. It was found that these whirled when dropped, even though they would point into the wind when suspended at their centre of gravity, and we were asked to design one which would fall straight. We pointed out that a bomb which projects its fragments horizontally would have a much better chance of hitting troops than darts coming vertically, but it seemed a matter of prestige that we should have our own dart and that it should be better than the French dart, so we took on the job of designing one. After we had done this we took a few hundred of them in a satchel up a steel ladder inside a disused tall chimney so that we could watch them from above as they fell. They flew quite straight.
>
> Having designed the dart, we were asked whether the terminal velocity in free flight was big enough to damage troops, so we bored out a rifle barrel and shot the darts with reduced charge at a leg of mutton hanging as a ballistic pendulum so that we could find out the impact speed and correlate it with penetration. Finally, we were asked how the darts would spread if a bundle of them were dropped from a plane. To answer this we got a pilot to throw a few hundred over a field from a height of several hundred feet. When this had been done, Melvill Jones and I went over the field and pushed a square of paper over every dart we could find sticking out of the ground. When we had gone over the field in this way and were looking at the distribution, a cavalry officer came up on his horse and asked us what we were doing. When we explained that the darts had been dropped from an airplane, he

> looked at them and seeing a dart piercing each sheet remarked: 'If I had not seen it with my own eyes I would never have believed it possible to make such good shooting from the air.'[10]

After the war, as meteorologist and navigational adviser, G. I. Taylor joined the Handley Page team competing for the *Daily Mail*'s £10,000 prize for the first aerial non-stop crossing of the Atlantic, and he later recalled a conversation with Brown, the navigator of the Vickers aircraft piloted by Alcock. When, with Brown's professed ignorance of navigation, Taylor asked him how he would know where he was if he succeeded in reaching Europe, Brown replied, 'I will come down and if I see people in mantillas I will know it is Spain. If I see people eating frogs I will know it is France and if I see them hitting one another over the head I'll know it's Ireland.'

G. I. Taylor had great respect, as indeed was shared by all his colleagues, for Bertram Hopkinson who held the chair of Mechanism and Applied Mechanics in Cambridge. In 1914 he had been commissioned in the Royal Engineers, and his talents both for research and for leadership led to his being appointed as Deputy Controller of the Technical Department of the newly formed Royal Air Force in 1918. Unfortunately he was killed on 26 August 1918, flying solo in a Bristol fighter; he was succeeded by Tizard, who later wrote of him, '. . . in his position, and with his knowledge and character, he would have had a great influence on Government policy between the wars. I will go so far as to say that the chance of the Second World War breaking out would have been greatly lessened. Certainly we would have been better prepared for it.'[11]

One of the problems tackled by Hopkinson was that of accurate bombing by night. G. I. Taylor recorded that in 1918 Hopkinson thought of a system that entailed shining two searchlights vertically from points about a mile apart on the line to the target. On most nights there would be enough haze to show up the beams and the pilot could line up his plane to fly through them, and thereafter continue on the same compass heading. This would automatically allow for the cross-wind if it could be assumed constant; he could then calculate the flying time to a target from the time it took him to fly the known distance between the beams. The arrangement, which was only intended for short ranges, was set up for a trial against Coblenz from a point in the American sector in France, but the war ended on the very day that the system was to be tried. It was the forerunner of some of the radio-beam systems that materialized in World War II.

Another development which anticipated World War II, and which could have affected it beneficially had it not been forgotten between the wars, was operational research: its conception by Lord Tiverton and others in World War I is described in Chapter 8.

Cryptography

A still greater achievement of World War II, the cryptographic brilliance of Bletchley Park, likewise had its 1914–18 precedent. By August 1914, listening stations belonging to the Navy, the Post Office and the Marconi Company were receiving unintelligible Morse intercepts suspected to be of German origin, and these were handed by the Director of Naval Intelligence on 4 August 1914 to Alfred Ewing, whose appointment as Director of Naval Education we have already noted. (Ewing had been succeeded at Cambridge, incidentally, by Bertram Hopkinson.) The fact that Ewing was an engineer and a physicist was largely incidental, but he had become interested in telegraphic codes through working as a research student in 1874 on the cable to Montevideo. Ewing, though, made no claims to being a cryptographer, and he proceeded to gather around him a group of men and women who might have the necessary background and qualities, some of them from the colleges at Osborne and Dartmouth that he had initiated. They became known as Room OB40 from the number of the room they occupied in the Old Building of the Admiralty.

The story of their achievements belongs more properly to the general history of World War I than to this partial account, but it has been fairly said that one of their decrypts was the most important single decrypt ever made, even including the marvellous work of their successors at Bletchley Park in World War II. This yielded the text of the Zimmermann telegram, the import of which brought America into the war.

Ewing was warmly sensitive to the problems of running a highly secret organization where many of its operators, such as those on the intercept receivers taking down streams of seemingly meaningless letters and figures day after day, could not be told much about the significance of their work. Just as the Germans were led to believe in World War II that British radio intelligence on the positions of the U-boats was obtained solely by direction finding and not mainly by cryptography, so in World War I DF was used as an alibi for cryptographic intelligence. The alibi was all the more piquant because the British Admiralty had itself earlier dismissed direction finding as impracticable because of its inaccuracy. It was only after Round and Franklin of the Marconi Company made technical improvements early in 1915 and their system had been successfully adopted by the Army that the Admiralty took it up.[12]

E. W. B. Gill, a Fellow of Merton College, who taught my generation of undergraduates the theory of radio circuits, could be as scathing about his German opponents as he sometimes was about us, his pupils. Regarding cryptography at field level he wrote: 'Nobody could desire more admirable opponents than the Germans for this class of work. The orderly Teutonic mind was especially suited for devising schemes which any child could unravel.' Gill also described how in Egypt he used the Great Pyramid as a mast to support his aerial for radio interception, and how in Cyprus he encountered a mysterious individual who hovered in the society surrounding his secret Army installations and who, in unwitting anticipation of the identity of the best known of all defence correspondents, carried the nickname of 'Chinchey Pinchey'.

Gill related that when Ludendorff's spring offensive of 1918 appeared to be going so well that Haig issued his famous 'backs-to-the-wall' order, British morale was unexpectedly raised by the tonic effect of a decrypted intercept in which Ludendorff said that his own situation was so desperate that all German troops were to be withdrawn at once from Palestine and Turkey and sent back to the Western Front. This experience conformed to the doctrine that I was later taught in the Officers Training Corps that when things seem at their blackest for you they may look just as bleak to your opponent. For another example, see Lord Slim's *Unofficial History* where he related that in November 1940 he withdrew, against his instinct, from Gallabat in East Africa after capturing it from the Italians because he was advised that his own troops were exhausted: 'My bitterest pill, however, came about ten days after our withdrawal when I saw for the first time some intercepted messages, sent from Mentemme just after our capture of Gallabat, which showed that the enemy was – or thought he was – at his last gasp . . . If only I had followed my hunch!'

The Ludendorff message had gone by landline from Germany to Constantinople, but the German commander to whom it was addressed happened to be away from his headquarters on a ship in the Black Sea, and so it had to be sent on by radio which was intercepted by listening stations in Salonika and England. The episode closely paralleled that in 1941 when the battleship *Bismarck* had evaded our searches in the

Atlantic; by fortunate accident her intention to make for the west coast of France was revealed by an Enigma decrypt which we only obtained because the German Chief of Air Staff, being away from Berlin in Athens, had asked to be informed about her because his son was on board – the information was sent to him by radio.

To balance Gill's scathing verdict on the insecurity of German low-grade ciphers, we must note that the Germans, too, had their cryptographic successes at the same level. Long afterwards, one of their cryptographers told us how easy it was to break the daily ciphers used by the British Army. In training its signallers in England, the Army employed the same cipher as was being used for operational messages in France. To ensure that a practice message would not be mistaken for an operational one, with the subsequent confusion that could result, the instruction was given that any practice message should be prefixed by an animal name which would be enciphered along with the text. All the German cryptographers had to do, therefore, was to try as 'cribs' a succession of names such as bear, tiger, giraffe, at the beginning of messages, and they could then quickly reconstruct the cipher.

Scientific Method

Radio or 'Wireless' was indeed a new field in which new experiences were to be gained under the intense conditions of warfare. E. V. Appleton, who had freshly graduated in physics at Cambridge in 1914, immediately volunteered for active service and, after a short spell as an infantryman with the West Yorkshire Regiment, went to the Royal Engineers as a signals officer. He became interested in the fact that at some times of the twenty-four-hour day he could hear distant radio transmitters which were inaudible at other times: moreover, at night the transmissions though audible might be subject to rapid 'fading'. This puzzle determined that his post-war research would be not on nuclear physics but on radio propagation; he found his explanation in the existence of the already suspected Heaviside ionized layers in the upper regions of the earth's atmosphere, and the changing properties of the layers as they became further ionized in daytime by ultra-violet light from the sun – work for which he was awarded a Nobel Prize.

Appleton, incidentally, became a very good friend to me as a result of our contacts during World War II, when he was head of the Department of Scientific and Industrial Research and I was responsible for scientific intelligence; and he told me a delicious story about his

Nobel Prize. At the Nobel Prize Banquet, with the Crown Prince of Sweden presiding, he was asked to speak on behalf of the Nobel Prizewinners who were being entertained, and it occurred to him that he had an anecdote that would exactly fit the occasion. It was a caricature of the scientific method as enunciated by Francis Bacon, in which the researcher collects a series of observations and then looks for a common factor which would point to the underlying cause that would explain all the observations. Even better, the anecdote concerned a scientist who as a result of the improved public status of science through its wartime achievements was at last earning a salary with which he could begin to enjoy comforts hitherto beyond his means, and which would enable him to mix in society. He decided that he must learn to drink, and he had heard that whisky and soda was a popular tipple. He therefore tried it one evening by himself, only to wake next morning with a headache. In hope of finding a variation that might not have this unpleasant consequence, the following evening he sampled brandy and soda with, alas, the same result. On successive evenings he then experimented with rum and soda, and gin and soda, but the result was always a headache. His systematic analysis at the end of the trials revealed the common factor, and so he gave up drinking soda!

Rarely could an anecdote have been so perfectly matched to an occasion: a caricature of scientific method, a laugh at the naivety of scientists, topicality regarding their rise in status, and all before a distinguished international company of laymen and scientists. Appleton had rightly expected an hilarious reaction. The response, though, was even more thunderous and prolonged than anything that he could possibly have hoped for: could his story have really been all that good? It was only after he sat down that he discovered that the Crown Prince was drinking nothing but soda water because his doctors had told him to refrain from alcohol. Their advice had become well known throughout Sweden, where it was widely rumoured that the Prince had a drinking problem.

The Upper Atmosphere

The existence of the same layers as those producing radio fading had also been suspected by Lindemann on entirely different evidence, although this also involved wartime observations on waves coming from distant sources. These were sound waves from explosions, when sometimes the noise from artillery barrages in France could be heard at some points in England but not at others. Controlled experiments with large explosions after the war showed that typically an explosion could be heard for a radius of about twenty miles; outside this would be a zone of silence, and then perhaps at eighty to a hundred miles the explosion would be heard again; there was then a further zone of silence, followed sometimes by the explosion being heard at upwards of 150 miles. Lindemann and his colleague, G. M. B. Dobson, advanced the explanation that sound waves from the explosion had travelled upwards into a region of the atmosphere where the velocity of sound was greater and this had caused the wave fronts to be bent over so that the sound travelled down to the ground again, striking it at distant points after having travelled high over the heads of observers in the zone of silence. The wave might then be reflected up from the ground to the layer again and deflected downwards once more to be heard in a still more distant zone. This 'skipping' of the sound waves (and there was a rather similar effect for radio waves) was caused by their increased speed in the layer, due to its temperature having been raised by the sun's radiation. Lindemann and Dobson found further evidence for the existence of the layer by measuring the heights at which meteors appeared and disappeared. The layer was at around 100 kilometres' altitude.[13]

Infra-red

Besides such wartime experiences which led to later research, there were ideas advanced in World War I which were not exploitable until long afterwards when the necessary advances in technique had been made. Two of these were again due to Lindemann, of which the first was his suggestion, as early as 1914, to use infra-red radiation to detect ships by their hot funnels; and then in 1915 aircraft by their hot engines. Even at that time infra-red detectors were in principle sufficiently sensitive to detect an aircraft at several miles' range, but their response was so slow that the aircraft would have moved much too far before it was detected. Although both the British and, more significantly, the Germans developed infra-red detection before and during World War II, it did not become of major importance until the advent of the guided missile, for which purpose it had outstanding advantages; and it has since proved a valuable method of surveillance for the launch of ballistic rockets.

Nuclear Energy

Further, Lindemann was prompted in discussions with F. W. Aston in the mess at Farnborough to ponder on the possibility of whether physical means could be devised to separate F. W. Soddy's recently discovered chemically inseparable isotopes. Such methods indeed became important in World War II for the separation of the isotopes of uranium, and some of the basic thinking was to be found in a paper that Aston and Lindemann published in 1919.

Although Soddy's work on nuclear chemistry had no bearing on World War I, he had as early as 1904 drawn the attention of the Corps of Royal Engineers to the huge quantity of energy stored in atoms of radium in his book *Atomic Transmutation*, saying,

> The man who put his hand on the lever by which a parsimonious nature regulated so jealously the output of this store of energy would possess a weapon by which he could destroy the earth if he chose.

In 1915 he gave a remarkably prescient lecture in the remote forum of the Aberdeen Independent Labour Party. Referring to the surprising energy which he had found in fragments of disintegrating nuclei, he said:

> We have obtained evidence, in consequence of these new discoveries, that in the atoms of matter exists a store of energy beyond comparison greater than any other over which we have obtained control . . . The energy is there, but the knowledge of how to liberate it at will and apply it to useful ends is not – not yet . . . It is unlikely, but not impossible, that such a discovery might be made almost at once. A magnificent scientific achievement it would be, but, all the same, I trust it will not be made until it is clearly understood what is involved . . . Imagine, if you can, what the present war would be like if such an explosive had actually been discovered instead of being still in the keeping of the future. Yet it is a discovery that conceivably might be made tomorrow, in time for its development and perfection for the use or destruction, let us say, of the next generation, and which, it is pretty certain, will be made by science sooner or later. Surely it will not need this actual last demonstration to convince the world that it is doomed, if it fools with the achievements of science as it has fooled too long in the past. Physical force, the slave of science, is it to be the master or the servant of man? The cold logic of science shows, without the possibility of escape, that this question if not faced now can have only one miserable end.[14]

Biology and Warfare

While, fortunately, the release of nuclei energy for military purposes only became possible in 1945, another horrible form of warfare did make its debut in World War I. This was biological warfare, and it was introduced by the Germans. Berlin did decline a proposal to infect the rivers of Portugal with cholera to cause human casualties and thus seal the Spanish frontier; but it did approve a proposal to employ anthrax against reindeer sledging British arms through north Norway to the Russians, against Romanian sheep being supplied to Russia, and Argentinian sheep, cattle and mules being supplied to Britain and the Indian Army. Most of these moves were uncovered by the cryptographic efforts of Room OB40, and confirmed by on-the-spot investigations by agents both from Britain and from the neutral countries being attacked. Thanks to their surveillance, the only German success appears to have been 200 mules which were being shipped from the Argentine. The means of infection were ampoules inside sugar cubes, taken to Buenos Aires by U-boat.[15] If this should prove an unhappy precedent, it illustrated the lesson that there are few limits beyond which some nation or other will not go in conceiving – and using – means of causing wholesale pain and destruction if its situation becomes desperate, and if it thinks it can thereby win. It may start a war with high intentions, but these can be degraded by adversity.

The Bitterness of War

The extent to which feelings can be eroded may be illustrated by the deterioration of outlook of even such supposedly objective men as scientists. I was aware, even as a boy, of the bitterness of public feeling as the war progressed, when the shops of decent German bakers were stoned by mobs in the London suburb in which I lived. In the more civilized atmosphere of the musical world, there were attempts in concert programmes to anglicize the names of German composers. Even in the high-minded atmosphere of the Royal Society there was a move to force out the Secretary, Sir Arthur Schuster, because of his German antecedents; fortunately the move found little support, although it was favoured by some eminent men. There was also a move to expel from the Foreign Membership of the Society all enemy aliens, but the war ended before the issue was resolved. The Chemical Society, though, did in 1916 expel the German chemists it had earlier honoured with Honorary Membership.

The bitterness was, of course, not unique to Britain: in America and France, and in Germany, many scientists felt likewise, and the ridiculous extent to which their feelings sometimes rose can be seen from the correspondence between Sir William Ramsay, the discoverer of helium and a Nobel Prizewinner, and his friend in Baltimore, Ira Remsen. Fondly recalling their research student days in Göttingen, where they had found the Germans such a warm and friendly people, Ramsay speculated on how it had come about that they now showed themselves such barbarians. He thought that he had found the answer: a medical colleague had told him that while in Britain the incidence of syphilis was less than half a percent, and in France about 1½ per cent, in Germany it was 85 per cent. 'While syphilitics often keep going and retain energy,' he wrote, 'they appear almost always to have a mental twist; they become abnormal in one way or another. So it comes to this: this is a war against syphilis.'[16] The fact that the circumstances of war could lead such an eminent chemist to such a distorted outlook is worthy of recall by any of us in similar danger.

After the war the bridges of international co-operation had to be rebuilt, and it is a pleasure to record that one of the most effective steps had been taken in 1917 by the Royal Astronomical Society and the Royal Society, when they proposed that there should be a British expedition to Africa and Brazil to photograph the eclipse of the sun on 29 May 1919, to test Einstein's theory of relativity which had concluded that light from a distant star passing near the sun should be deviated by its gravitational pull. The expedition was successful, and the fact that even at the height of the war British scientists were prepared to test the theory of one who was technically an enemy alien, along with the fact that what was being confirmed was one of the major steps in human thought, did much to provide the foundation on which international co-operation in science could be rebuilt.

Losses

While many scientists on both sides had worked on aspects of research and development, some had enlisted as fighting men, and among these were inevitable casualties. On the British side the most conspicuous loss was H. G. J. Moseley, whose work on X-ray spectra had settled the roll-call of the elements in the Periodic Table. Moseley had been in Australia with the British Association when war broke out. On hearing the news he and Henry Tizard, who had also been at the same meeting, at once left for England to volunteer for the Army. They took a ship for San Francisco, and crossed America by train to New York where they arrived just in time to catch the *Lusitania* for Southampton.[17] After Moseley's death in Gallipoli in 1915, Rutherford wrote in *Nature*:

> Scientific men of this country have viewed with mingled feelings of pride and apprehension the enlistment in the new armies of so many of our promising young men of science . . . It is a national tragedy that our military organisation at the start was so inelastic as to be unable, with a few exceptions, to utilise the offers of service of our scientific men except as combatants in the front line. Our regret for the untimely death of Moseley is all the more poignant because we recognise that his services would have been far more useful to his country in one of the numerous fields of scientific enquiry rendered necessary by the war than by exposure to the chances of a Turkish bullet.

The one good to result from Moseley's death was the fact that Britain gave more thought to how it would deploy its scientists in 1939.

There were other losses among men of science, and they were not confined to one side: the *Zeitschrift für Physik* published obituaries of eighteen German physicists who were killed, mainly fighting, during the war. As regards losses in general, an American historian, Dr Harold Deutsch of the US Army War College, has pointed out that the British forces were unique in that for much of the war they consisted entirely of volunteers; conscription was not introduced until March 1916, and so every man who fought in any battle up to and including the Somme in July 1916 was a volunteer. Compared with the other combatants, the British therefore lost proportionately more of their public-spirited men.

The Pre-war Neglect of Science

Moseley's death may well have been a factor in the disquiet that grew among British scientists as the war went on. The shocks of the use of gas, the attacks by U-boats and by Zeppelins, and the manifest pre-war dependence of Britain on some of the products of German industry such as dyes, and magnets for magnetos, all combined to produce the rising feeling of indignation at the neglect of science that was expressed by thirty-six of our most distinguished scientists in a letter published in *The Times* of 2 February 1916. It asked that science be given its proper place in education: of thirty-five leading public schools, thirty-four had classicists as headmasters. Sandhurst was possibly the only military academy which required science neither as an entry qualification nor indeed in the curriculum. The letter was followed by a meeting on 3 May 1916 chaired by Lord Rayleigh in the rooms of the Linnean Society. To their credit several of the classicist headmasters and heads of Oxford and Cambridge colleges, together with the Poet Laureate, Robert Bridges, spoke in support. They deplored the fact that Britain had suffered checks since the war began, 'due directly as well as indirectly to a lack of knowledge on the part of our legislators and officials of what is called "science" or "physical science"'. They also pointed out that 'In the whole history of British Governments there has only been one Cabinet Minister who was a trained professional man of science – the late Lord Playfair.'[18] The Government had already started to act, with the formation of a Committee of the Privy Council for Scientific Research in July 1915, but further pressure was evidently needed. A committee on the machinery of government under Lord Haldane emphasized the importance of research in the formulation of government policy, and recommended extension of activity promoting scientific and industrial research. This was the genesis of the Department of Scientific and Industrial Research which became the main sponsor of research until it was superseded by the Ministry of Science in the late 1950s. The Research Associations date from the same period, as did the University Grants Committee. The first report of the UGC in 1921, incidentally, pronounced carpingly on technology: 'There is nothing in the nature of technology which makes it necessarily unsuited to the methods and spirit of university work.' It would take another fifty years and another war to make the universities concede more.

So Britain ended the war with its administrators and educators more aware of science, if only grudgingly, with its scientists more sensitive to military problems and to the ways of administrators, and with its technology – particularly in aeronautics and electronics – advanced by the spurs of war. Science at least emerged with some credit: but politics, education, religion, the economic and social orders, and the higher military command had all been found wanting – and not only in Britain. How could the leaders of Europe have steered their nations into a war so bitter and terrible when the men in their front trenches had as little hatred as to exchange greetings and comforts in a spontaneous truce at Christmas? Almost the only redeeming memories were the courage and endurance of the common man.

8

Defence and Scientific Method

The preceding chapter pointed to some of the fields in which science came to the aid of the armed services in the 1914–18 war. The instances cited were mainly concerned with developments in weapons and techniques of actual warfare, but science could also provide aid by subjecting past and present military operations to scientific analysis in order that future operations might be carried out more efficiently.

Numbers: Franklin, Kelvin, Huxley, Galton

A light-hearted example from the eighteenth century illustrates one feature of the method. It originated with Benjamin Franklin who, early (3 October 1775) in the War of American Independence, wrote to his friend Joseph Priestley in England expressing in numerical terms the futility of the British effort:

> Britain, at the expense of three millions, has killed 150 Yankees this campaign which is £20,000 a head. And at Bunker's Hill she gained a mile of ground half of which she lost by our taking post on Ploughed Hill. During the same time 60,000 children have been born in America. From these data any mathematical head will easily calculate the time and expense necessary to kill us all, and conquer our whole territory.[1]

Nearly two centuries later, Franklin's countryman, Amrom Katz of the Rand Corporation, was similarly advising his government that to kill each member of the Vietcong it was costing the Americans around fifty times as much as the man would have earned in his entire lifetime. Numerical examples such as this can be especially startling because numbers can so easily be compared by the human mind; and the conversion of observations into numerical form has been one of the principal tools of the scientist's stock in trade. Moreover, the full power of mathematical analysis can then be applied, so much so that in 1883 Lord Kelvin made the celebrated statement:

> In physical science a first essential step in the direction of learning any subject is to find principles of numerical reckoning and methods for practicably measuring some quality connected with it. I often say that when you can measure what you are speaking about, and express it in numbers, you know something about it; but when you cannot measure it, when you cannot express it in numbers, your knowledge is of a meagre and unsatisfactory kind: it may be the beginning of knowledge, but you have scarcely, in your thoughts, advanced to the stage of science, whatever the matter may be.[2]

Kelvin's authority, combined with the manifold successes of measurement in science, created the impression that before any activity could claim to be 'scientific' it must develop its own system of measurement, thus tempting psychologists, for example, to attempt to measure intelligence by an 'Intelligence Quotient', not always with happy results.

Kelvin's viewpoint was exemplified by his near-contemporary, Francis Galton, who tried to put as many observations as possible into numbers – even the boring capacity of lecturers, from his observations at the Royal Geographical Society that in an audience of fifty the number of fidgets per minute averaged about forty-five, dropping to about half this value when the interest of the audience was aroused. He also tried to measure the affinities between his guests by placing devices under their chairs to see which neighbours inclined towards one another as they talked at dinner. Daringly, for a Victorian, he assessed the efficacy of prayer from the longevity of those about whom prayers were regularly offered: the average age at death of eminent members of the clergy (66.42 years) was rather less than that for lawyers (66.51) and doctors (67.04). He therefore concluded, 'Hence the prayers of the clergy for protection against the perils and dangers of the night, for protection during the day, and for recovery from sickness appear to be futile in result.' He carried the analysis to the most prayed-for of all, the sovereign, the aristocracy and the gentry. Of these three classes the sovereigns were shortest lived, indicating if anything that prayer had an adverse effect.

Little could stop Galton measuring, even the exigencies of African exploration: encountering 'a veritable Hottentot Venus' in South West Africa,

> I profess to be a scientific man, and was exceedingly anxious to obtain accurate measurements of her shape; but there was a difficulty in doing this. I did not know a word of Hottentot, and could never therefore have explained to the lady what the object of my footrule could be; and I really dared not ask my worthy missionary host to interpret for me. The object of my admiration stood under a tree, and was turning herself about to all points of the compass, as ladies who wish to be admired usually do. Of a sudden my eye fell upon my sextant; the bright thought struck me, and I took a series of observations upon her figure in every direction, up and down, crossways, diagonally, and so forth, and I registered them carefully upon an outline drawing for fear of any mistake; this being done, I boldly pulled out my measuring tape, and measured the distance from where I was to the place where she stood, and having thus obtained both base and angles, I worked out the results by trigonometry and logarithms.[3]

If such anecdotes portray Galton almost as a caricature of a scientist, we must also remember that he invented the supersonic dog-whistle and he proposed finger-printing as a method of identification. He also gave his name to Galtonism, the common red-green variety of colour-blindness which afflicted him: and if the anecdotes show that on occasion either the measurement or the measurer can be objects of legitimate ridicule, they will be a helpful warning against taking measurement too far, as Kelvin himself was to learn.

He had in the 1860s attempted to assess the age of the earth,[4] by calculating how long it had taken to fall to its present temperature from a molten state, and the age of the sun assuming that its heat was developed as it was struck by particles and bodies falling into it because of its gravitational pull. The calculations suggested that the sun and the earth could not be much older than a few hundred million years. This was much less than the time the geologists believed would have been needed for the evolution of the earth's geological features, and it happened that the President of the Geological Society was the formidable T. H. Huxley who responded to Kelvin's calculations thus:

> This seems to be one of the many cases in which the admitted accuracy of mathematical processes is allowed to throw a wholly inadmissible appearance of authority over the results obtained by them. Mathematics may be compared to a mill of exquisite workmanship, which grinds you stuff of any degree of fineness; but, nevertheless, what you get out depends on what you put in; and as the grandest mill in the world will not extract wheat flour from peascods, so pages of formulas will not get a definite result out of loose data.[5]

In summary Huxley was saying that there must be something wrong, not with Kelvin's calculations but his assumptions. We now know that Huxley was right: the sun's heat is derived from thermonuclear reactions and not from gravitational contraction (although the latter may have supplied the heat necessary to kindle the thermonuclear furnace) while much of the earth's surface heat also comes from a nuclear source unknown to Kelvin, the fission of radioactive elements such as uranium and thorium in the earth's crust.

The Kelvin–Huxley exchange should provide a salutary warning to those who place too much faith in elaborate computation based on unreliable assumptions; but Huxley's point about the impossibility of getting a definite result out of loose data should not be misinterpreted, for modern information processing technology can be amazingly successful in extracting valuable information otherwise hidden in a clutter of disturbances. The weak radar echoes returning to the earth from the surface of Venus, for example, are accompanied by an overwhelming din of electronic noise, but information processing techniques enable the echoes to be sorted from the noise so successfully that some of the surface details of Venus can be revealed in the 'picture' developed from the echoes.

At the same time, the main moral to be drawn from his exchange with Huxley is that Kelvin's doctrine that you can only claim to know something about your subject when you can express it in numbers needs to be reversed: only when you know enough about the subject of your intended measurement should you dare to risk putting it into numbers. Otherwise your insecurely based numbers may lead you to false conclusions.

Viscount Tiverton, 1917

Despite its pitfalls, though, the great part played by measurement in science made it inevitable that sooner or later it would be brought to bear on warfare once scientists became seriously engaged. The problem of hitting an aircraft in flight by guns on the ground, for example, involved a multiplicity of difficult measurements, and in Britain in 1917 this was presented to A. V. Hill, later a Nobel Prizewinner in Medicine (Physiology), whose small but distinguished team began to think not only about how to make the measurements but also how best to operate the guns. Hill claimed that this work was the forerunner of the operational research that became so prominent in the 1939–45 war: in a sense it was, but the claim could also be made at least as effectively not for a scientist but for Viscount Tiverton who, like Pollen in naval gunnery (see above, page 165), was a lawyer.

Tiverton had joined the Royal Naval Air Service, and after a spell of experimental flying he was attached to the British Aviation Commission in Paris. There, in 1917, he submitted papers in strategic bombing, a subject which he had begun to study in 1915. His papers, a true landmark in operational research, were as profound as they were individual, and covered a wide range of factors that could affect the success of a bombing campaign such as was then being considered against the German munition industry from bases in the regions of Ostend or Verdun. He was instructed to assume that 2,000 aircraft could be available. Of these he assumed that 1,000 might be ready for any one operation, and that they could carry nine bombs apiece. He discussed the merits of going by day or by night, and ruled out the latter because even by day navigation was still hardly precise enough. 'Experience has shown', he wrote, 'that it is quite easy for five squadrons to set out to bomb a particular target and for only one of those five ever to reach the objective, while the other four, in the honest belief that they have done so, have bombed four different villages which bear little or no resemblance to the one they desired to attack.'[6] Moreover, weather was often unfavourable: as for attacking the Ruhr from a base at Ostend, at a range of some 200 miles, no more than four or five days a month might be suitable, and he urged the development both of navigational aids and of a meteorological service. One practical detail why he favoured day attacks was that the aircraft were smaller and could therefore be more easily supplied with spares such as wings which would be small enough to go under the French bridges. He also pressed the advantages of concentrating on single targets, to produce the greatest possible damage both to material and to morale, as well as saturating the defences.

Lord Tiverton's first paper was dated 3 September 1917, and he followed with a second paper early in November on the selection of targets. He investigated the vulnerability of nearly a hundred factories manufacturing war materials. For each factory the total area was calculated, and the fraction of this area that was occupied by buildings. Then, assuming that the force of 1,000 bombers was launched against it, and that operational aiming errors would be double those achieved in practice-bombing in England, he calculated the number of bombs that would do effective damage. For the Badische Analin und Soda

Fabrik at Ludwigshafen, which occupied 168 acres, 4,150 of the 9,000 dropped would cause damage, while against the Cassella factory at Frankfurt, occupying 23 acres, only 225 bombs would be effective.

As for the type of factory most vital to the German war effort, Tiverton positively selected chemical plants, especially those making synthetic nitrates, with aero-engine factories of almost equal importance but more difficult to attack because the details of their wartime expansion and their use of sub-contractors were difficult to ascertain. Explosives factories, though equally vital, were thought by Tiverton to be unpromising targets because they had already been designed to minimize the effects of explosions.

Reading even a mere precis of Tiverton's two papers,[7] it is impossible not to be struck by his prescience and comprehension; and had his remarkable work been kept in view during the inter-war years, the bombing fiasco of the first two years of the Second World War could have been avoided. As it was, the lessons which he so brilliantly exemplified had to be learnt by hard experience all over again. We often hear about the dangers of being prepared to fight the last war over again; but Tiverton's is an outstanding example of what could have been learnt for future application by a wise study of past actions.

The Origins of Operational Research

So much was Tiverton's work forgotten that the official publication, *The Origins and Development of Operational Research in the Royal Air Force,* made no mention whatever of it. The concept had to be reinvented completely afresh for World War II, and the official publication credits the inception to Tizard in 1936 sending B. G. Dickins (an Air Ministry Scientific Officer) to the RAF fighter station at Biggin Hill to study how information from the prospective radar chain might best be used to enable fighters to intercept incoming bombers. The actual term 'operational research' appears to have originated somewhat later when A. P. Rowe, then superintendent of the radar research station at Bawdsey, used it to describe the work being done there into assessing the information coming from the original chain of radar stations, and processing it for Fighter Command and its subordinate controllers. At the outbreak of war the work was transferred to Headquarters of the Command and the first Operational Research Station was formed there.

The fact that there was a group of scientists already in place at

Fighter Command in 1939 is evidence of the close relation that had sprung up between the Command and scientists such as Henry Tizard. How had this come about? There was, of course, a legacy from 1914–18, when scientists of Tizard's generation, such as Lindemann, had worked alongside serving officers, as the last chapter recorded. In peacetime, though, the services and the universities tended to revert to their traditional interests and make their own divergent ways into the future. One factor alone brought the two together again: the rise of the Nazi threat, and above all the prospect of *Luftwaffe* attacks on England. The air defence exercises of 1934 had shown how easy it was for bombers to penetrate our defences almost unscathed, once again justifying the Trenchard–Baldwin doctrine that 'the bomber will always get through'.

It is now a matter of history that Lindemann wrote to *The Times* in August 1934 protesting that this was a counsel of despair which should not be accepted, 'until it has definitely been shown that all the resources of science and invention have been exhausted'; that A. P. Rowe in the Air Ministry independently urged the Director of Scientific Research to seek such aid; that the chairmanship of the resulting committee was given not to Lindemann but to his erstwhile friend Tizard; and that at the very first meeting of the committee in January 1935 there was the proposal by Watson-Watt that the vital problem of detecting incoming bombers at long range might be solved by means of the feeble echoes which they would reflect from radio transmitters on the ground. From that moment spectacular progress was made, perhaps the greatest of all examples of Dr Johnson's dictum of September 1777: 'Depend upon it, Sir, when a man knows he is to be hanged in a fortnight, it concentrates his mind wonderfully.'

The result was that within four years we had designed, developed, deployed and manned a chain of radar stations capable of detecting bombers at a hundred-mile range, and a plotting, reporting and control system that would enable defending fighters to be directed to intercept incoming bombers. Moreover, officers of the Royal Air Force had learnt how to use the whole and entirely novel system to such effect that it turned the balance in the Battle of Britain.

Scientists and Serving Officers

How had all this happened? In the previous war scientists had wanted to get to grips with the actual conditions under which their devices would have to be operated, but had encountered resistance such as that of Commodore Hall over the detection of submarines: they should not be encouraged to go to sea, and the only information that they should need 'was that enemy submarines were in the sea, and that means were required to detect their presence' (see above, page 166). Presumably the Commodore did not know of, or disregarded, the pronouncement on a similar problem by Isaac Newton more than two centuries earlier:

> If, instead of sending the observations of able seamen to able mathematicians on land, the land would send able mathematicians to sea, it would signify much more to the improvement of navigation and the safety of men's lives and estates on that element.[8]

One who firmly followed Newton's precept was Bertram Hopkinson (see above, page 174) who held the Chair of Mechanism and Applied Mechanics in Cambridge, and who before he was killed flying in August 1918 had become Controller of Research and Experiments in the newly created Air Ministry. Tizard, who became his deputy, wrote of him in the *RAF Review*:

> His chief legacy to the Royal Air Force was the doctrine that in order to bring science most effectively to bear on the problems of the Service, it was necessary to carry all experimental work, under scientific direction, right through the laboratory and workshops to the final stages of use in the air; and that as the work progressed the close collaboration of scientists and fighting men became more and more necessary.[9]

This was the spirit that Tizard himself so effectively fostered as Chairman of the Committee for the Scientific Survey of Air Defence, and it was put into practice at all levels. At my very junior level we flew with the experimental pilots at such establishments as Farnborough, Martlesham and Boscombe Down, and they were free to come into our laboratories. We would discuss technical and tactical problems together. They would tell us what they would like a device to do; often we would have to tell them that we could not make what they wanted, and offer them the nearest that we thought we could do in order to achieve the objective. We would ask them, if we made that, could they make some use of it, even if it were not what they had originally asked for? Alternatively the initiative might come from our side: we might have an idea of how to make something quite novel – if so, could they think of a way of putting it to use?

It was an exhilarating time, and it resulted in Britain having the defence against day attacks that we saw in such dramatic action in 1940. The outcome was not so much due to a high standard of technology, for German radar, which had been started even earlier than ours, was in some (but not all) technical respects better. Our superiority lay in the operational usefulness of the equipment and in the way in which RAF personnel had learnt to employ it, including the vital reporting links between radar stations and the fighter controllers. Neither our German opponents nor any other of the major air powers had anything comparable: part of the reason, of course, was that we had both the greatest need for air defence, and also the greatest opportunity thanks to our being an island.

'The Great Lesson'

Looking back on the period in 1946, Tizard himself said:

> The first time, I believe, that scientists were ever called in to study the needs of the Services as distinct from their wants, was in 1935, and then only as a last resort. The Air Staff were convinced of the inadequacy of existing methods and equipment to defeat air attack on Great Britain, and a Committee was established for the scientific survey of air defence. I want to emphasise that this committee, although it consisted on paper only of scientists, was in fact from the first a committee of scientists and serving officers, working together.

And

> When I went to Washington in 1940 I found that radar had been invented in America about the same time as it had been invented in England. We were, however, a very long way ahead in its practical applications to war. The reason for this was that scientists and serving officers had combined before the War to study its tactical uses. This is the great lesson of the last war.[10]

Tizard's phrase 'only as a last resort' conveys something of the resistance that he and his colleagues had encountered: in Fighter Command alone had this resistance been melted by the pressing threat of the *Luftwaffe*. For besides Tizard's own 'great lesson of the last war' his further experiences demonstrated yet another. By the end of 1936 his Committee for the Scientific Survey of Air Defence was so manifestly successful that an obvious step appeared to be the creation of a similar

Committee for the Scientific Survey of Air Offence, in the hope that this could do for Bomber Command what its sister was clearly doing for Fighter Command; and to give it every chance of success, its chairman was to be Tizard.

Historians are rarely able to make 'control experiments' in the way that scientists can, where all the conditions can be repeated except for the one whose effect is to be observed, but in this instance the evolution of events unwittingly provided such a control, for the composition of the CSSAO was very similar to that of the CSSAD, and, of course, Tizard was chairman of both. Yet, despite Tizard's leadership, the Offence Committee was a failure in stark contrast to the success that was evident in Defence. In notes that he prepared for his posthumous biographer Tizard wrote:

> It did not meet with such enthusiastic welcome from the Royal Air Force. As a result its influence before the war started was only small.[11]

The welcome would have had to come predominantly from Bomber Command: but the Command, basking in the doctrine that 'the bomber will always get through', believed that it had little need for scientific aid. Even if it might be intercepted by day it believed that by flying in formation its bombers could defend themselves by mutual support; and if that failed it could attack by night, when fighters could not find the bombers, and yet the latter could precisely find their targets by astronavigation and dead reckoning. So the Command saw little need for advanced scientific devices, which were dismissed as 'adventitious aids'.

The difference in attitudes of the two Commands persisted into 1941: at Fighter Command we were immediately welcome, and the Commander-in-Chief would readily see us; at Bomber Command it was more like visiting a gentlemen's country club – we would be courteously heard and entertained but would leave with the impression that what we had said would have little effect. Then two things changed: photographs showed that our bombers were rarely finding their targets (only one-tenth were within five miles of their targets in the Ruhr in June–July 1941[12]), and increasing numbers were being shot down as the Germans brought in radar to guide their nightfighters and guns. *Then* the Command began to take notice of us, and we ended the war on the same close and warm terms with Bomber Command as we had long enjoyed with Fighter Command.

A corollary ought therefore to be added to Tizard's 'great lesson' which, without in any way detracting from its importance, may act as a further guide, or even a consolation in failure, to anyone, scientist or not, seeking to aid some individual or organization: it is only when the intended recipient realizes his need for aid that this can be fully effective, and the aider's first task may be to persuade the recipient of his need.

Complacency

In my own experience there were two other examples which demonstrate the point. The preceding chapter mentioned the reluctance of the Admiralty to adopt Pollen's ideas on gunnery, while in Chapter 5 a similar reluctance to adopt the convoy system was discussed. Again, as World War II approached, the Admiralty was so complacent about the threat to capital ships from bombers that, at a meeting of the Joint Planning Staff, General Ismay, who was present, told Sir John Colville,

> The naval representative, Captain Tom Phillips, RN, held forth on the invulnerability of modern capital ships to air attack. It was an Admiralty theme that infuriated the Air Ministry. It was even more frequently propounded, and was only a few degrees less ridiculous, than that voiced in some War Office quarters that tanks had frequent mechanical failures whereas cavalry horses did not. On this occasion the Air Ministry representative was Air Commodore Arthur Harris. According to Ismay he thumped the table and said, 'Phillips, you make me sick. I can tell you what is going to happen. One day we shall be at war with Japan and you will be sailing across the South China seas in one of your beautiful battleships. Out of a cloud there will come a squadron of Japanese bombers and as your great ship capsizes, you will turn to your navigating officer and say, "That was a whopping great mine we hit".'[13]

In the event, Phillips was to die tragically when his flagship *Prince of Wales* was sunk by Japanese torpedo-bombers in 1941, while Harris's Lancasters were to sink the even more powerful *Tirpitz*. Just as, within the Air Force, the men with the heavy ironware, Bomber Command, were more resistant to change than their Fighter counterparts, so within the three Services the Navy with its battleships was more conservative than the Air Force, and it had in fact largely to follow the Air Force's lead when it began to take radar seriously.

After the war I found a similar contrast between the several components that were absorbed into the Transport Commission when I became chairman of its Research Advisory Council. The railways were the analogue of the Navy: they had been a mainstay of the country for more than a century, they had enormously heavy rolling stock, they had basked in success, they were courteous hosts – so why change their ways? We struggled, almost without success, to get rolling stock made lighter, to get through-breaks adopted on freight trains, and to get the air-brake substituted for the vacuum-brake. The road transport organization was the analogue of the Air Force or, even closer, Fighter Command. It was new, its vehicles were light, and it was ready, even anxious, to try new ideas. Then as road competition to the railways increased, the latter gradually changed.

Operational Research During World War II

A further aspect of Bomber Command's disregard of the need for scientific help in the early years of the war was that until August 1941 it had no operational research section. Actually in September 1939, D. R. Pye, the Director of Scientific Research – impressed by what was happening at Fighter Command – had sent one of his officers to each of Bomber, Coastal, and Balloon Commands; but within a month or two he recalled them all because there were insufficient calls on their services. At the same time he had sent me to intelligence, and now proposed to withdraw me for the same reason: I managed to convince him, however, that while I had little to show in the first three months other than 'debunking' the supposed 'secret weapon' that Hitler did not say he had, I was putting in spadework that sooner or later might produce results. I often used to meet A. E. Woodward Nutt, one of his senior scientific officers, who was secretary to Tizard's committees, and who had proposed me for intelligence. Woodward Nutt told me that despite the apparent failure at Bomber Command he thought that the reports of bomber crews regarding their encounters with the German defences ought to be analysed, and in the absence of anyone being specifically appointed, he would do the job himself. This was the beginning of operational research at Bomber Command; it was taken over by B. G. Dickins when Woodward Nutt had to go as Secretary to the famous Tizard Mission that took the cavity magnetron (described by the American author James Phinney Baxter in *Scientists Against Time* as 'the most valuable cargo ever brought to our shores') to America.

Ultimately, in August 1941 Bomber Command asked the Air Ministry to set up an operational research section there. Shortly before this, Coastal Command also requested an OR section. Thenceforward, all operational research for the Royal Air Force was to be co-ordinated by an Operational Research Centre in the Air Ministry backed by the Ministry's own Operational Research Committee of which I (mainly in my effective capacity as the British OR officer for the *Luftwaffe*) was made an original member. Later, OR sections were formed at Transport, Flying Training, Middle East, 2nd Tactical Air Force, Mediterranean, Allied Expeditionary Air Force, India, and Southeast Asia Commands. Operational research, and with it scientists, now permeated both the heart of the Royal Air Force organization in the Air Ministry and all its extremities in Commands.

The other two Services lagged behind the Air Force, or rather Fighter Command, in recognizing operational research as a specific activity. As with the Air Force, it was the problem of air defence that first brought the Army to call for scientific aid, when General Pile, commanding Anti-Aircraft Command, brought in P.M.S. Blackett (who had been an original member of the Tizard Committee, a midshipman at the 1914 Battle of the Falklands, and a gunnery officer at Jutland, as well as an outstanding Fellow of the Royal Society) to look at the problems of anti-aircraft gunnery where 20,000 shells were being fired for every aircraft brought down.[14] Blackett instituted the Army Operational Research Group in the autumn of 1940; by the end of the Blitz the 'rounds per bird' had fallen to 4,000. AORG went on to undertake widespread work for the Army in all theatres of war, while Blackett left it in March 1941 to inaugurate operational research at Coastal Command – again, the stimulus was a defensive one against the threat from the U-boats, where the opportunities for analysis were twofold in type: (1) how best to search an area with a radar-equipped aircraft and how best to approach a U-boat once it was contacted, and (2) how to design aircraft bombs and depth charges to give the greatest chance of a kill. One investigation that had widespread effects was into how to keep a given number of aircraft in operational condition with the minimum of servicing effort by ground staff.

After nine months with Coastal Command Blackett left its now strong operation research section in January 1942 to introduce the same activity into the Admiralty, where much of his work concerned the optimum size of convoys, and how to defend them with escorts. Thought was also being directed towards the problem of the landings in Normandy, and operational research problems were cropping up at Combined Operations Headquarters, where Lord Louis Mountbatten brought in J. D. Bernal, whose robust approach gave rise to the illuminating episode described above, on page 59.

One of the problems was how best to paralyse the French rail system so as to give maximum hindrance to the movement of German troops and supplies in reaction to the landings. This brought out a problem of conduct that has often beset operational researchers and indeed all experts, scientific or not, in advising on courses of action. The first step for an adviser is to establish the relevant facts, but there are many occasions when these cannot be known well enough to determine a unique course of action. The adviser then has to weigh the various items of evidence and recommend one course of action rather than another: a different adviser might give different weights to the evidence, depending on his personal predilection and past experience, and so recommend a different course of action. How far is either of these advisers justified in pressing his own recommendation?

Conflicts of Experts

The question is all the more testing when the recommendation will 'take us into the arena of power, vested interest, and personality where forces quite different from straightforward intellectual argument were at work'. That description is W. W. Rostow's, and comes from his book *Pre-Invasion Bombing Strategy* describing the Anglo-American controversy of 1944 about which types of rail target should be attacked – bridges or marshalling yards? This was only part of a greater controversy over whether pre-invasion bombing should concentrate on rail targets or on oil plants in Germany as likely to have the greater effect on German mobility, and the controversy was not entirely on national lines, Lord Cherwell for example siding with the predominantly American view that oil would be the better target. The opposing view was expounded by Solly Zuckerman, whose account can be found in his *From Apes to War Lords*, to which Rostow's book gives the other side of the argument. It is some indication of the height of feeling during the controversy that Zuckerman considered that 'the Prof [Cherwell] was not speaking objectively or indeed honestly', and thought this worthy of record.[15] Without raising the question of how far honesty and objectivity pervaded either side, we may take it as one example of the dangers besetting an adviser once he commits himself to a viewpoint that has to make assumptions beyond the available evidence.

For those who believe natural science to be an objective pursuit after truth by inquiry, it may be surprising how emotionally involved men of science may become in their disputations. The bombing controversy before the Normandy landings is but one example. At much the same time I myself was engaged in an equally testy argument about the expected size of the V2 rocket, where British rocket experts thought that it was going to be much bigger, and therefore more destructive, than the conclusion that was emerging from the evidence gained by intelligence. Walt Rostow (later Special Adviser to President Johnson, and himself a major figure in the bombing controversy) was called in as an American umpire to assess the relative strengths of the arguments about the prospective size of the V2. His retrospective comments convey an idea of the intensity with which we held our respective views. 'Although', he wrote, 'I was at that time relatively young [27] I had acquired some experience with both academic and government bureaucratic structure and their capacity for bloodless tribal warfare. But I had never been present at, let alone presided over, a meeting with more emotional tension than that centred on the size of the V2 warhead . . . What emerged was a reasonably solid Intelligence case for a one-ton warhead.'[16]

Whenever anyone, scientist or not, has to advise a course of action when the available evidence leaves some ground for uncertainty, he has to go for the most likely interpretation of the evidence in the light of his own experience. If another expert then comes to a different conclusion in the light of his different experiences, then, in the argument to decide which conclusion is the more probable one, the two experts become adversarial advocates for their respective views. In such circumstances it is tempting for each side to overstate its case in an attempt to win the argument; the yield to this temptation will often be subconscious, but it is sometimes conscious, resulting in the advocate suppressing evidence that conflicts with his conclusion, or 'improving' evidence that may support it.

Arguments between experts often arise, particularly when, despite every effort to put numerical values on all the considerations involved, there are some that defy quantification. For example, in a national health service, analysis may show that some particular course of medical or surgical treatment costs less in region A, owing to greater efficiency or more favourable circumstances, than it does in region B. While everything should be done to reduce the costs for, say, a hip or heart operation, in region B to those in region A, this may not be possible. If not, should patients be exported from B to A? The costs to the health service should be less – but it may result in a patient's relatives being unable to visit him, or able to do so at much inconvenience, and his morale may be impaired. How do you weigh these factors against the savings to the health service? A hard-headed 'efficiency expert' will very probably rate them lower than would a humanitarian, and the two would therefore advise differing courses of action.

The Slanting of Testimony

If such a relatively simple and current question can be so difficult to resolve, it is hardly surprising that intense controversies can arise over decisions concerning what should be done to meet a situation that might arise five or ten years ahead. In the late sixties such a controversy arose in the United States regarding the prospective vulnerability of the American land-based Minuteman ballistic missiles to attack by the Russian SS9 missiles. The conduct of experts on both sides led the Operations Research Society of America to draw up a code of conduct to govern future disputations.[17] This recognized that

> When the analyst participates in an adversary process he is, and should expect to be treated as, an advocate. The rules for an adversary process are different from those of operations research. For the former permit biased or slanted testimony and the latter are directed toward objective evaluation.

The question arising from this recognition is whether 'biased or slanted' testimony can ever be compatible with honour for a man of science. Is he ever justified, for example, in putting his case more strongly than he believes can be fully justified by the evidence? It can sometimes simply be done by presenting the evidence in such a way that it will appear convincing to anyone less experienced than the analyst himself. I myself came very near on two occasions to an ethical borderline in that direction.

The first was in September 1940, when Ultra revealed that near Cherbourg the Germans had an installation they called *Knickebein Dezi* while another Ultra decrypt mentioned 13 centimetres. One interpretation was that the Germans had a new radio-beam system working on a much shorter wavelength than the original beams, and this would give much greater bombing accuracy and would also be very difficult to jam. Although I was not absolutely convinced of the interpretation, I nevertheless drew attention to it with some emphasis because there had been a statement in the Oslo Report of November 1939 that the Germans had radar equipment working on a wavelength of about 50 centimetres and yet, nearly a year later, we still had no effort devoted to intercepting transmissions on such wavelengths. Now, the threat of being bombed by the German use of these wavelengths in their radio-beam transmitters might at last get our own radio experts to make receivers to detect them. The alarm had the necessary effect: fortunately, there were no German beams for bombing on these wavelengths, but the new receivers promptly intercepted German radar transmissions on an 80-centimetre wavelength from the Calais–Boulogne area. Had I not succeeded in raising the alarm on less than positive evidence, the radar transmissions might not have been discovered for another twelve to eighteen months.

My second instance was related to the first. Because we now knew that the Germans were working extensively on short wavelengths they should be well equipped to intercept our own radar transmissions, for which most of the development work was being done near Swanage. German listening receivers stationed near Cherbourg could therefore hear our transmissions from Swanage as easily as we could hear theirs from Cherbourg – with this important difference: whereas the German transmissions were coming from equipment already in operational use, ours would largely be from equipment under experiment and development. If these were intercepted they could enable the Germans to develop countermeasures that would be ready even before our new equipment reached the operational stage.

I had therefore pleaded for our experimental work to be moved from Swanage to some location well away from the limits at which interception by the Germans would be possible. My pleas had no effect: Swanage was a pleasant location, and the experts there did not want to move. Then, on 27/28 February 1942 our parachute forces made their brilliantly successful raid on the German station at Bruneval, near Le Havre, and in the aftermath there was speculation about the possibility of the Germans mounting a retaliatory attack on Swanage. This speculation intensified when it transpired from Ultra that a German parachute unit had moved into the Cherbourg area and news of the movement became known at Swanage. The Superintendent there had been at Bawdsey (where pre-war radar work was concentrated) and at the time of Munich I had personally witnessed his apprehension at the possibility that the *Luftwaffe* might have selected Bawdsey as an immediate target. I therefore arranged to visit Swanage with my colleague Hugh Smith, ostensibly to discuss the German equipment from Bruneval which was now being examined at Swanage; although we studiously refrained from any mention of a parachute threat, we wore tin hats, gas-masks and pistols and gave the impression that we were anxious to get away as soon as possible. The intended inference that we ourselves with our special intelligence knowledge thought that danger was imminent but that we did not wish to cause a panic, appears to have worked, for within a few weeks the whole establishment was abruptly transferred from Swanage to Malvern where, forty years later, it still is.

Given that the move was a wise one, and so justified our ruse, how much further would I have been justified in going in 'slanting' the evidence to produce the desired result? Suppose, for example, we had had positive evidence that the Germans were ignorant of the presence of the radar experimental work at Swanage, and that the parachute unit was intended for an entirely different eventuality, would I have been justified in suppressing this information? Or, even further, in inventing the evidence about the parachute unit had we not genuinely had it from the Ultra?

Such an argument might be held to justify an otherwise dubious action. In the years before 1939, when radar was being developed, it was clear to some of us that it had features that were vulnerable to countermeasures, one of which was developed during the subsequent war as Window or Chaff. I had proposed the idea in 1937, but nothing was done to check whether it would work until 1941 – why had no notice been taken until then? Writing to me in 1962 about this matter, A. P. Rowe, who in 1938 had become Superintendent at Bawdsey, said, 'When I took over from W.W. at Bawdsey, I found that it was "not done" to suggest that the whole affair would not work . . . from no one at no time did I hear a breath of anything like Window.' In defence of that attitude, it could be argued that anything that might indicate that radar was vulnerable might have weakened the Air Staff trust in it and so we might not have had the effective radar chain of 1940. The upshot was that Window was not even tried out experimentally. Now, had the Germans been ahead of us with radar, and had they had Window ready in time for the Battle of Britain, they might have made our radar chain impotent, and we would not have any countermeasures available to deal with Window because our own work on it had been inhibited. Indeed, during the period of which Rowe was writing, this very danger had been foreseen by Lindemann in a memorandum of 8 March 1938, written after I had suggested the idea of Window to him, for Churchill to submit to the Air Defence Research Sub-Committee of the Committee of Imperial Defence:

> It is known that a system similar to the RDF [Radar] was patented in Germany a good many years ago . . . in these circumstances it is to be apprehended that they will adopt some simple counter method, such as has been outlined, with disastrous results if we have failed to take this possibility into account.[18]

The intentional 'slanting' of evidence borders on deception, and so if it is to be justified at all, this must be by results; the deceiver should recognize an obligation to view his deception objectively and be prepared to amend it when he recognizes that it is producing dangerous results.

'Slanting' of course rarely goes as far as intentional deception, at least in men who respect truth, scientific or otherwise; it more often occurs subconsciously. Most of us have probably at some time allowed our personal prejudices to colour our conclusions from the evidence before us. Normally, for example, Lindemann and Tizard would interpret any ambiguity in the evidence in opposing senses in their wartime confrontations, Tizard being naturally inclined to the defensive and Lindemann the offensive, as in the instance of whether the H_2S radar bombing equipment should go primarily to Bomber or to Coastal Command; Tizard wished the latter to have priority to enable us to survive against the U-boats, Lindemann the former so that we should more effectively bomb German towns.

A dangerous result of slanting of interpretation by self-interest that we have also noted is that of telling 'the commander-in-chief only the things that the commander-in-chief would like to hear' in the hope of enhancing the adviser's personal standing in the commander's eyes. Not all advisers are as valiant as Lyon Playfair of whom the Duke of Wellington said, 'Of all the men I ever knew, he had the greatest regard for truth,' and who as a young chemist was sent in 1845 by the Prime Minister, Robert Peel, to investigate and advise upon the potato famine in Ireland. Playfair's frank report that Ireland was doomed to starvation unless the Corn Laws were repealed obviously put Peel in a very difficult position since his own party had been responsible for the laws, but he immediately accepted Playfair's advice with the comment, 'I am indeed sorry that you are compelled to make so unfavourable a report, but the knowledge of the whole truth is one element of security' (Wemyss Reid, *Memoirs and Correspondence of Lyon Playfair*, p. 99, Cassell, 1899). Between them Peel and Playfair, politician and scientist, set a flawless model for all such relations.

In our own time we saw an even closer example in the relation between Churchill and Lindemann, which I sketched in *Most Secret War* and elsewhere.[19] While the relation aroused both criticism and envy, it was the first since that between Peel and Playfair where a Prime Minister placed such importance on scientific advice as to want someone beside him who 'could decipher the signals from the experts on the far horizons of science and technology and explain to me in lucid homely terms what the issues were'.[20] Whatever the defects, the relationship did not in the main depend either on sycophancy on the part of Lindemann or unquestioning favouritism on the part of Churchill. Lindemann, for example, took a stand against Churchill in Cabinet in 1953 over the creation of the Atomic Energy Authority, and won; and Churchill over-ruled Lindemann's denial of the V2 threat in 1943.

'On tap but not on top'

Although he elevated Lindemann to a ministerial post, Churchill had firm views on the role of scientists, as he told Parliament in November 1945, regarding decisions concerning policy:

> On many occasions in the past we have seen attempts to rule the world by experts of one kind and another. There have been theocratic governments, military governments, and aristocratic governments. It is now suggested that we should have scientistic – not scientific – governments. It is the duty of scientists, like all other people, to serve the State and not to rule it because they are scientists. If they want to rule the State they must get elected to Parliament or win distinction in the Upper House and so gain access to some of the various administrations which are formed from time to time.[21]

Exactly ten years later, in the Soviet Union, Andrei Sakharov was proposing a toast at a dinner to celebrate the success of the first Russian thermonuclear explosion, to which his contribution had been large, that 'our handiwork would never explode over cities'. He subsequently recorded that the director of the tests, a high-ranking general, 'felt obliged to respond with a parable. Its gist was that the scientists' job is to improve a weapon; how it is used is none of their business. Actually he anticipated what Khrushchev said several years later, at greater length at a meeting with scientists in the Kremlin.'[22]

This doctrine, that 'scientists should be on tap but not on top', has an unquestionable element of reason, but rigorous application can be dangerous. Fortunately for us in Britain it was widely observed in Nazi Germany, where it inhibited the intimate collaboration between serving officers and scientists that we ourselves enjoyed. For the first three years of the war, for example, I searched in vain for a German Tizard or a Lindemann; and there seemed to be no counterparts to operational research or scientific intelligence as we ourselves had developed them.

In complete contrast, relations between serving officers and scientists in America both followed the British model and extended it with enthusiasm. After the war, the US services not only had their own scientists but also sponsored the setting up of enterprises such as the Rand Corporation to think deeply and widely about their future problems and opportunities. At one stage indeed, I began to wonder whether the 'on tap but not on top' doctrine had been too far reversed. This was in 1960 when I was invited to be a member of a Prime Ministerial delegation to meet a Presidential delegation in the White House to discuss problems of common interest in defence science. One was the optimum size of aircraft-carriers when the Americans had decided on 75,000 tons, but wanted to know why we were going for 45,000 tons, and where they assumed that we had arrived at that lower figure as a result of operational research. We had rather shamedly to tell them that there was no such subtlety behind the British figure – 45,000 tons was the largest ship we could afford.

Another problem concerned the amount of information a tactical Army commander would require in battle, and how this might best be acquired, co-ordinated and presented to him. I sat uneasily throughout the discussions, for I realized that I had insufficient direct experience with the problems, and I thought that this was also true of most of those who spoke. At the final dinner one of the two joint chairmen challenged me, 'R.V., you have been pretty quiet – now tell us what you think.' My reply was, 'Well, if you really want to know, I think that this conference has been a scandal. Before the war we scientists used to complain that the services took their decisions without calling us in. Then came the war with Tizard's "great lesson" that success had been due to scientists and serving officers working together. I thought we had all learned that, and would never forget it. Well, what have we been doing for the last three days? We have been discussing problems of direct operational concern, and yet there has not been a single serving officer present. We are now just as bad as they were!'

There have been other occasions since which have similarly demonstrated how even such a great lesson as Tizard's can be forgotten with the passage of time and the decline of external threat, and yet it is as vital as ever – and not only in the relations between science and the services.

Neither merely on tap nor uniquely on top

The notion that scientists are specially qualified to be on top is as misguided as that which would hold them on tap. The latter implies that scientists would only be called in when the need for their help is realized; and that, as we have seen, may well be too late. But, equally, scientists have to realize that while their experiences qualify them to speak with authority in their own fields, and on occasion to extrapolate from their fundamental concepts – such as extending the conservation of energy to the principle that in the end everything has to be either paid for or worked for – the tides and eddies of human relationships are often beyond the simple experiences of science. With Edmund Burke, scientists and indeed all academics need to appreciate that

> A statesman differs from a professor in a university; the former, the statesman, has a number of circumstances to combine with these general ideas, and to take into his consideration. Circumstances are infinite; are variable and transient; he who does not take them into consideration is not erroneous but stark mad. The statesman, never losing sight of principles, is to be guided by circumstances; and judging contrary to the exigencies of the moment he may ruin his country for ever.[23]

Only when they are aware of this can scientists enter into fully effective partnership with politicians and the services.

Conscience

The concept of partnership entails responsibilities as well as privileges; and responsibilities can entail problems. Taking Churchill's words out of context, 'It is the duty of scientists to serve the State.' These might be a comfort to a man of science helping to build a horrid weapon by salving his conscience with the argument that he is merely performing a duty which the State has imposed on him. This has always been the defence of soldiers carrying out orders with which they disagree; and the question of when they ought to disobey on the grounds of inhumanity is one of the most vexing of all to resolve. The problem for the scientist, though, may go beyond that, because he may face the prospect of initiating a new weapon or technique of warfare and not merely of working on it at someone else's behest.

I myself faced this problem in a minor way in 1936 when I was working at Oxford on infra-red equipment to detect incoming bombers by means of the infra-red radiation from their hot engines. The objective was the purely defensive one of protecting our cities from German attack but part way through the development it occurred to me that, as so often with defensive equipment, it might be applied also to offence. But that might mean that although I had set out simply with the motive of protecting British citizens, I might now be contributing to the killing of German citizens – should I keep the idea to myself, or should I draw the Air Ministry's attention to the possibility? I argued with myself for days. Ultimately, on 10 May 1936 I wrote to the Director of Scientific Research:

> One thing has occurred to me recently, which you may already have thought of, and that is how effective an offensive weapon this type of thing could be. Suppose that it were mounted in a bomber. One could be certain of being over a town, even though all its lights were extinguished. Factories and works should give colossal readings, and are much easier to detect than aircraft. It should be very easy to locate towns in darkness by the behaviour of the galvanometer.

The consideration that decided me to write was this: if the idea had occurred to me it might well occur to a German scientist too, and if he had Nazi sympathies – or perhaps even if he were apolitical – he might propose the idea to the *Luftwaffe*. If the idea were then developed in Germany we could be at a disadvantage. Further, even if we eschewed its employment ourselves on humane grounds, we ought to examine its potential so as to learn what countermeasures we might develop to parry its use against our own towns.

More than fifty years have elapsed since I wrote that letter, but none of many subsequent experiences would have led me to a different conclusion.[24] I can conceive of circumstances in which a humanely minded scientist should refrain from giving an unworthy regime ideas from which it might take inhumane advantage; but fortune never condemned me to such a position. Generally, in a democracy, my inclination would be to air the idea, if only to encourage countermeasures against it or even to lead a government to seek an international ban.

Such a policy still leaves open the question of how far even a normally humane democracy can be trusted so to act. In February 1940, for example, Neville Chamberlain as Prime Minister declared in Parliament, 'Whatever the lengths to which others might go, the Government will never resort to blackguardly attacks on women and children and other civilians for the purpose of mere terrorism.'[25] Stung by the Blitz, though, Britain began to react differently, and the cry arose 'Give it to them back.' By 14 February 1942 the War Cabinet was directing Bomber Command: 'the primary object of your operations should now be focussed on the morale of the civil population and, in particular, of the industrial workers.'[26] That directive is defensible on the grounds that, despite all the civilian casualties it would cause, it could have appeared to be the most humane way of winning the war if other ways would have resulted in still greater casualties, but it showed how far policy could shift in the desperate circumstances of war.

It is therefore to be expected that a scientist should feel a special responsibility when he has contributed to the development of a new weapon, even as innocently as Otto Hahn did when he discovered nuclear fission: after the Hiroshima bomb he contemplated suicide. On the same issue Robert Oppenheimer remorsefully said 'the physicists have known sin!' Nevertheless I think that in general scientists need to take the risk of bringing political leaders into their confidence, and that reciprocally scientists have a special claim to be consulted about the exploitation of their ideas. If, as in the case of nuclear weapons, these ideas offer horrifying prospects, it is better in the long run that national leaders and populations generally should be soberly aware of them.

And as long ago as 1620, at the beginning of the scientific revolution, the answer was given by Francis Bacon (in *Novum Organum*, Book the First, Aphorism CXXIX) to those who might seize on Oppenheimer's cry of remorse as admission that science can itself be evil:

> Lastly, let none be alarmed at the objection of the Arts and Sciences

becoming depraved to malevolent or luxurious purpose and the like, for the same can be said of every worldly Good: Talent, Courage, Strength, Beauty, Riches, Light itself, and the rest. Only let mankind regain their rights over Nature assigned to them by the gift of God, and obtain that power whose exercise will be governed by right Reason and true Religion.

Part Two

9

Some Postscipts to Most Secret War

In some ways I must be grateful to the unknown civil servant who in 1972 did not trouble to ask me whether any damage to official secrecy or to personal relations might ensue before he transferred all my wartime reports from the Ministry of Defence to the Public Record Office. For it was the fact that BBC TV researchers found them there, and in 1976 insisted on their right to use them as the basis for a television series even if I myself declined to take part, that precipitated me into writing *Most Secret War*. Otherwise, although the Ultra secret had been released in 1974, I would not have considered writing until I retired in 1981, at the earliest.

Had there been more time I would have been able to correct inaccuracies and mend gaps in my knowledge, but the earlier-than-intended publication has had the compensations of prompting others to draw such matters to my attention and of bringing me into acquaintance and friendship with many who have thrown further light on wartime episodes. This chapter therefore consists of a sequence of postscripts on those topics in *Most Secret War* where further comment may improve the record.

The Polish Contribution

One such instance concerns the contribution of the Polish cryptographers to the 'breaking' of the Enigma machine, where the credit that I gave them was utterly inadequate. In 1939 I had been billeted at Bletchley with Commander Edward Travis, its deputy head, and he had told me that Bletchley was making headway with the breaking of Enigma because the Poles had presented us with the wheels whose secret internal wiring was the vital feature of the machine, and that somehow the Poles had stolen a set of wheels from the Germans. Such a theft, of course, would have been a tremendous coup of the cloak-

and-dagger variety, but it would not by itself have been a feat to ascribe to cryptography. Various accounts have been given of how the Poles managed to steal the wheels without the Germans realizing they had been lost,[1] as Gordon Welchman, who was the head of the section at Bletchley responsible for the British breaking of Enigma, recorded in his book *The Hut Six Story*.

Welchman himself deserves tremendous credit for his personal part in the breaking of Enigma, which I was unable to mention in *Most Secret War* because of security protocol. In the meantime, his own account has appeared, and it explains in detail how the breaking was achieved. Incidentally, until Welchman's book many German cryptographers refused to believe that the machine had been broken, even though *The Ultra Secret* by F. W. Winterbotham and several others books, as well as official statements, had given much positive evidence. At last, after *The Hut Six Story*, one of the German cryptographers told an American counterpart who had been at Bletchley, 'Now we believe that you really did it!'

As for how the Poles acquired the wheels, Welchman had the same impression as I had gained from Travis: 'as an achievement of pure cryptanalysis it is hard to believe,' he wrote. 'It seems to me that the Poles must have obtained the new five-wheel Enigma by capture or some other nefarious means.' Nevertheless, even as Welchman was writing, much information was coming to light that the Poles had indeed divined the secret wiring inside the wheels by pure cryptography and not by cloak-and-dagger although that, too, thanks to the French, had played a part. Welchman, rightly anxious to give credit where it had previously been overlooked, then wrote a paper for *Intelligence and National Security*[2] which appeared shortly after his death in October 1985. His paper begins:

> Until just before the Second World War a small Polish team of three mathematician-cryptologists, headed by the brilliant Marian Rejewski, had been happily breaking the German military cipher machine, the Enigma, for many years. A small British team under the First World War cryptanalyst, Dilly Knox, was near to success, but was foiled by failure to make a guess which, in retrospect, seems an obvious one. The French cryptanalysts do not appear to have tried, but Captain Gustave Bertrand, involved in French espionage, achieved a coup without which the Polish Breaks and the subsequent British successes might never have been achieved.

The Poles had worked on the problem of decrypting the Enigma machine since early in 1928; they shortly set up a cryptology course in the University of Poznan for mathematics students with a good knowledge of German, and three students from this course were engaged in 1932 to work in the Cipher Bureau in Warsaw, where one of them, Rejewski, was set to work on Enigma. Early in 1933 he made his first breaks; almost his sole aid had been a knowledge of the operating procedure for the Enigma machine and a list of the key settings for the machine for September and October 1932 that had been obtained by Captain Gustave Bertrand of French intelligence from a German cipher employee[3] (Bertrand, incidentally, published his own account, *Enigma, The Greatest Riddle of World War II*, before the Ultra secret was released in Britain).

One almost trivial point that nearly defeated Rejewski was that although the Enigma machine had a keyboard that closely resembled that of a conventional typewriter, with the letters arranged QWERT . . ., the wiring inside the machine connected Q, for example, not to position No. 1 in the pins around the entry to the enciphering unit of the machine but to position No. 17, since Q is the seventeenth letter of the alphabet, W to position No. 23, E to No. 5, and so forth (in the replica machines made by the Poles, they substituted an ABCD keyboard for the QWERT original). When he at last tried this latter arrangement Rejewski found that he was able to deduce the wiring inside the first of the unknown wheels. From that point onwards the Poles were 'in business'. This was January 1933, only four months after Rejewski had set to work; and although German cryptographic security gradually tightened, the Poles were able to keep going, to the extent that by the summer of 1939 they had worked out the connections inside all of the five available wheels (for two new ones had been introduced), any three of which would be used at the same time in a machine (for German Army and Air Force Enigmas – those of the Navy latterly used four). They built copies of the machine and the wheels; and in July 1939, fearing that their country would shortly be over-run, they presented specimens to the British and the French. Our chief Enigma worker of pre-war days, Dilly Knox, met them and discovered that he, too, had nearly succeeded in breaking the machine, but had been foiled by the same QWERT switch to ABCDE that had troubled Rejewski. From then onwards Bletchley made the tremendous progress that *The Hut Six Story* describes.

The full Polish story is to be found in *Enigma* by Wladyslaw

Kozaczuk, and many further references are given in Welchman's 1986 paper. The details of the story are of tremendous interest to cryptographers and the foregoing summary barley scratches the surface. The point that I wish to emphasize here is that the story contains yet another achievement as commanding of admiration as the cryptographic feat, which was itself so great as to be hardly believable, even by the ablest of our experts. It concerns the fate of the Polish cryptographers.

After desperate fighting Warsaw had fallen within a few weeks of the opening of war on 1 September 1939, and the cryptographers had been evacuated south-eastwards after destroying their files on 5 September. On 17 September they crossed into Rumania, where from Bucharest they moved via Italy to Paris which they reached by 29 September. During October they restarted their work as a team at the Château de Vignolles, one of the headquarters of French intelligence, about forty kilometres north of Paris. Before this was over-run by the Germans in May 1940 the team was evacuated to Algeria, but after three months they were recalled to work in Vichy France at Uzès near Avignon. There they set to work yet again: it happens that I saw some of their handiwork.

It came to me through the office of Commander 'Bill' Dunderdale, one of the legendary figures of British intelligence.Travelling widely in Europe, he held that it was a good thing for him to be well known as 'Commander Dunderdale of the British Secret Service' because members of the European public would bring information to his notice when otherwise they would not have known what to do with it. At the beginning of the war he had a lively office in Paris, collecting secret intelligence on Germany. I had quickly come to know him and to respect his talents as an 'operator'. One day, for example, we received from him a first-class technical report on the engines of the new Junkers 88 aircraft; somewhat later there was another on the armament of the Ju88, and then another on the electrical equipment. Although these purported to come from secret agents, they seemed to be too detailed and forthright, and so I challenged him with, 'I don't know how you've done it, Bill, but I think that you must have acquired an operating handbook for the Ju88 and are dressing it up as agents' reports to make it last longer.' He confirmed that this was indeed so, and asked me to keep it to myself, for he could better maintain London's interest in his office by a continuous stream of reports rather than simply sending over the manual.

With the fall of France he came back to London, to liaise with the French and the Poles. Then, mysteriously, reports purportedly coming from spies on German military units occasionally appeared via his office. By that time, however, having had experience myself of having to 'dress up' Bletchley decrypts to make them appear to be reports written by spies, I surmised that Bill's new 'agents' were not spies at all, and that someone with whom he was in contact must have been dressing up decrypts. Once again I challenged him by telephone: 'I don't know who you are in contact with, Bill, but these are no agents' reports. Someone in France must be breaking German codes.' I can still recall his chuckle which was the only enlightenment that he allowed himself to shed.

I realize now that these reports which had so puzzled me had very probably resulted from the work of the Polish team in Vichy France. There were not many of them, and they did not continue for long: Vichy France was occupied by the Germans in November 1942, and the team had to flee once again. Destroying all their material, Rejewski and his colleague, Zygalski, escaped arduously over the Pyrenees to Spain in January 1943; but five others, including Colonel Gwido Langer, the head of the Polish Cipher Bureau, were betrayed just as they, too, had set out for the Pyrenees in March 1943. They were captured by the Gestapo, who sent them to concentration camps where two of them died. Any one of those five men, Langer, Ciezki, Palluth, Fokczynski and Gaca, might have purchased freedom by telling their captors that Enigma had been broken: none did. Their loyalty to their allies matched their brilliance in cryptography: and in them the poignant faith of their national anthem – 'Poland is not yet lost' – found sublime vindication.

André Mathy

In *Most Secret War* I quoted the moving message that reached us in London from an unknown member of the Belgian Resistance in the late summer of 1942. It came at the end of a report on an extensive reconnaissance that he and his comrades had made of the German radio stations in the main nightfighter defence line and it ran (in translation):

> The Germans' interest in them is clearly shown by the extremely strict way in which they guard the approaches which has several times resulted in our being fired at by sentries, fortunately with more zeal

> than accuracy. The Jauche installation is particularly easy to spot and to attack from the air.
>
> As far as our work is concerned, it would be helpful if we knew to what extent you and the British services are interested. We have been working so long in the dark that any reaction from London about our work would be welcome to such obscure workers as ourselves. We hope this will not be resented since, whatever may happen you can rely on our entire devotion and on the sacrifice of our lives.[4]

As I slowly made out the text in the blurred microfilm in which the report was sent, I thought of the arduous circumstances in which it must have been written, and I warmed to the bright personality of the courageous man who wrote it. All that I could find out about him was that he was agent VNAR 2 of Service Marc; there could be no doubt from his poignant call that he and his comrades were ready to die for us, but the few inquiries that I could make after the war threw no light on his identity or what happened to him. In 1983, however, I received a letter from M. Maurice Royaux (who himself had been awarded the MBE for his wartime services) saying that he had read my account of VNAR 2's report in *Most Secret War*, and he could identify VNAR 2 as André Mathy, enclosing a photograph. This gallant man was a doctor, born on 23 August 1912, and an officer in the reserve; he had joined the Resistance on 1 March 1941. Unhappily, he was captured by the Germans on 13 March 1943: we can only speculate on the unspeakable treatment that he would have received as a key member of the Resistance, which ended in his being executed in Germany on 21 June 1944. His surviving comrades remember him as one 'whose value was exceptional' and who was 'very well aware of his heroic and tragic destiny during his dangerous missions'. It is a privilege to join them in saluting his memory.[5]

Most Secret War also reproduced the sketch of the plotting 'Seeburg' table used by German fighter controllers which was one of an exquisite series that had been made by a Brussels jeweller who had bribed a member of the Belgian SS responsible for guarding a fighter control station when the German controllers were off duty. His sketches, drawn *in situ*, took a week of nights to make: some of them are reproduced in Figures 1–4. At the time of writing *Most Secret War* I could not remember the jeweller's surname, but M. Royaux has jogged my memory; he was Willi Badart. M. Badart survived the war and received the King's Medal for Courage, being also recognized by both the Belgian and French Governments. He died on 24 October 1985.

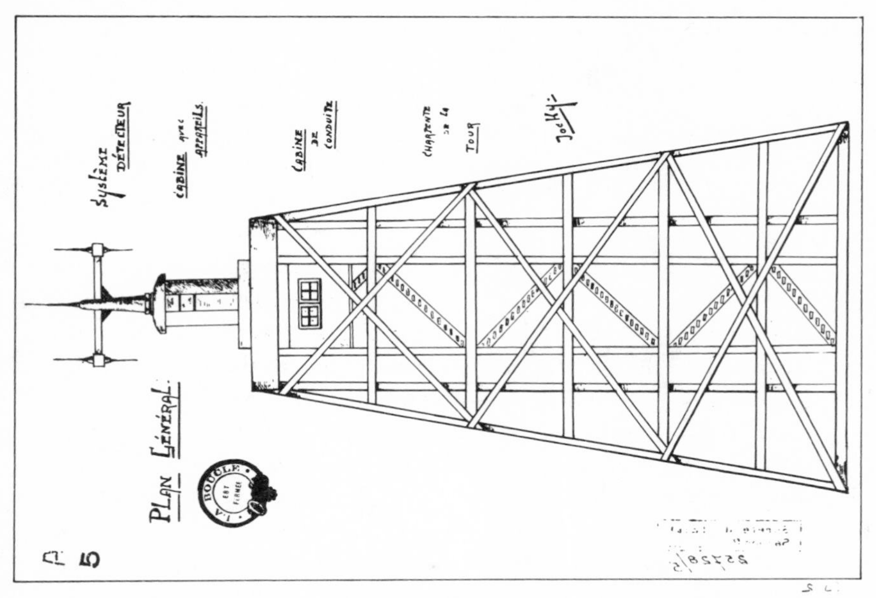

Figure 2

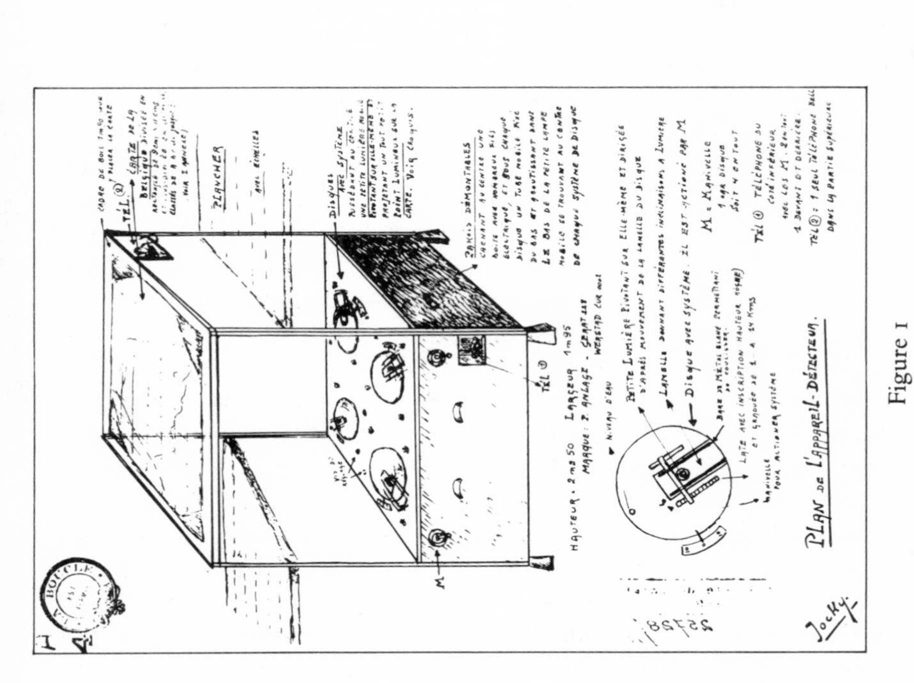

Figure 1

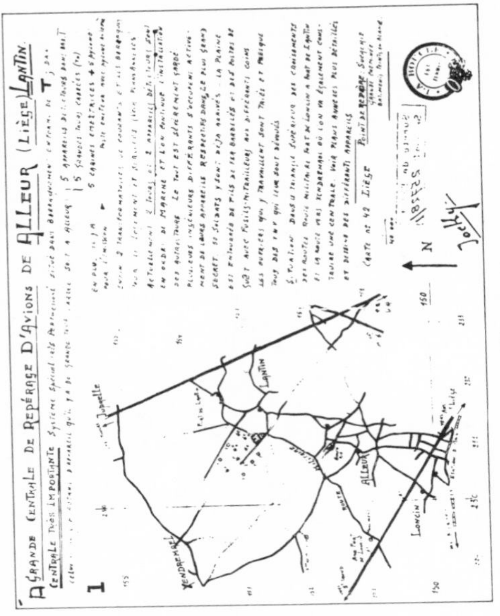

Figure 3

Figures 1–4:
A series of sketches made by a
Belgian agent of the German dayfighter
Y-control station at Lantin near Liege 1943.
These sketches were the best produced
by an agent during the war.

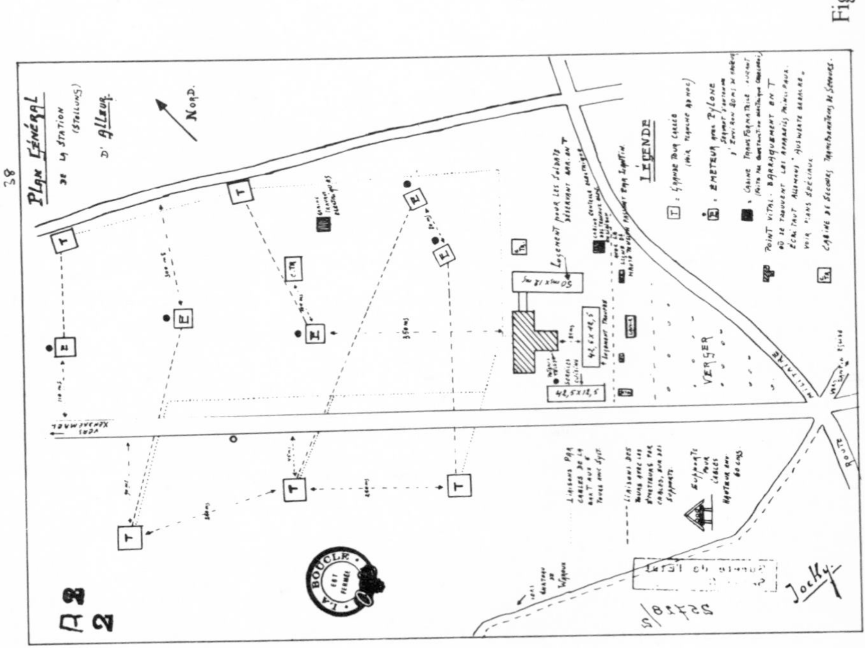

Figure 4

Wizernes

Most Secret War brought me many new contacts with former members of the resistance movements whose reports had filtered through to my office but whose identities were unknown to me. One came about through an invitation that I received in June 1987 from M. Yves le Maner of St Omer, telling me that the big V2 servicing and launching bunker at Wizernes near St Omer was to be opened as a national museum, and that to awaken public awareness two Open Days were being organized for 20 and 21 June 1987. The letter generously continued:

> The prominent role you played at the head of the RAF Information Services throughout the whole of the Second World War, and more particularly in the analysis of the German Secret Weapons, has not been forgotten on the other side of the Channel, in the Nord–Pas de Calais region, which has been so strongly linked in friendship with the British since the First World War conflict.
>
> What is more, the Controlling Authorities in the Nord–Pas de Calais region would be very pleased if you would do us the honour of presiding over the afore mentioned 'Open Days' . . .

Of course I went, helped by the good offices of Mr Winston Ramsey, the editor of *After the Battle* magazine, who ferried me between London and St Omer at very short notice. I had looked at many aerial photographs of Wizernes in 1943 and 1944, but had never been exactly certain of how it was to be used. All we could see was a huge concrete dome being cast over the ground immediately adjacent to the head of a chalk quarry resembling those in our own North Downs (indeed the same ridge extends to the other side of the Channel). There was much activity in the quarry, and it was on such a scale as to suggest that it was part of a large and urgent scheme which, from its siting, was likely to be associated with a forthcoming bombardment of London. This was the only deduction needed to determine our decision to destroy it by bombing, or at least to hinder its completion before the Germans could be driven from France.

Aerial photographs had also revealed several other large constructional sites in northern France, and our decision to bomb applied to them all. It later transpired that Wizernes was originally intended to be a storage site for V2 rockets brought from Germany, and that when serviced and needed they would be transferred to the large site at

Watten some sixteen kilometres to the north; this was to be both a factory for producing liquid oxygen as a fuel for the rockets, and a launching site. Our heavy attacks so damaged Watten while it was in course of construction that the Germans shortly decided that they would concentrate on Wizernes and upgrade it so that it could act not only as a store but also as a liquid oxygen factory and a launching site. The reason for their decision was that at Wizernes they could in effect start by constructing the protective roof on the land at the head of the quarry, and then tunnel under it from the quarry floor to form all the necessary galleries and chambers for servicing and storage. The main feature was, of course, the roof, which was in the form of a cupola of reinforced concrete eighty metres in diameter and five metres thick. It involved pouring a million tons of concrete.

Despite intense bombing the cupola survived almost undamaged; but although it was not itself hit by 10-ton Tallboys, these and other bombs caused so much damage that this made access to the site very difficult and thus heavily retarded the constructional programme. The engineering and construction of the cupola was one of the great feats of concrete technology; and the museum authorities had invited the German engineer responsible, Herr Werner Flos, to take part in the opening ceremony. It appealed to their sense of humour to bring together the man struggling to build the site, and one of those trying to knock it down. We found that he and I were almost exactly the same age, and so he was no more than thirty-two years old when he was in charge not only of this project, but also of constructing all the other huge sites in the V2 programme. Wizernes was the forerunner of the launching sites that have since figured so prominently in the ballistic missile arguments between the superpowers. As for the Open Days, despite initial bad weather, more than 20,000 visitors attended.

Emile Rocourt

Some of the galleries had already been reconditioned, and some interesting exhibits arranged. After the opening ceremony one of those quietly standing in the background approached me and said that he had been in the Resistance and worked with 'Colonel Remy';[6] from his card I saw that he was Emile Rocourt, previously known to me by name but whom I had not previously met. Some of his exploits are described in *L'Espion du Nord* by André-Georges Vasseur. As regards the V-weapons, he was especially responsible for gathering information about

Watten, but he also undertook many other tasks, which included aiding Allied airmen as a section head of the famous escape organization run by 'Pat O'Leary' (Albert-Marie Guérisse, GC).

Both Rocourt and his brother were ultimately captured and condemned to death. His brother was executed at Pilsen, but Emile survived some seventeen interrogations and torture. One of the strange twists of fate was that when he returned to France after all this, he found himself suspected of having turned *collaborateur* because the Germans had not shot him along with his brother. Recognition, though, ultimately came in abundance – Légion d'honneur, Croix de Guerre (both French and Belgian) and the Medal of Freedom (US). He died in November 1987, veritably 'une grande figure de la Résistance'.

Information that did not get through

Sometimes on meeting former members of the Resistance I am driven to recall the lines of Gray's Elegy:

> Full many a gem of purest ray serene,
> The dark unfathom'd caves of ocean bear:
> Full many a flower is born to blush unseen,
> And waste its sweetness on the desert air.

when I am told of reports that for some reason or other did not get through to us, and yet involved much risk and enterprise in their gathering and which could have directed us to German developments to which we were only awakened later. One such example was the work of General J. Pomès-Barrère, who had started in the war as an officer of the Deuxième Bureau, and who after the collapse of France was involved in gathering intelligence in Germany itself. As early as December 1943 he had collected details of the design of the V2-rocket then being made at the RAX Works near Wiener-Neustadt and sent them to his Madrid office for onward transmission to us but the report never arrived in London. Figure 5 shows his sketches of the rocket and its jet design, giving its weight as between 10 and 15 tons; the number and distribution of the eighteen input nozzles are correctly shown, while 'reservoir' on the sketch implied liquid fuel. This was a first-class piece of intelligence which would have saved us a great deal of erroneous speculation had it come through, for we had no comparable information until June 1944 when the trial V2-rocket from Peenemünde went astray and fell in Sweden; Figure 6 shows the rocket

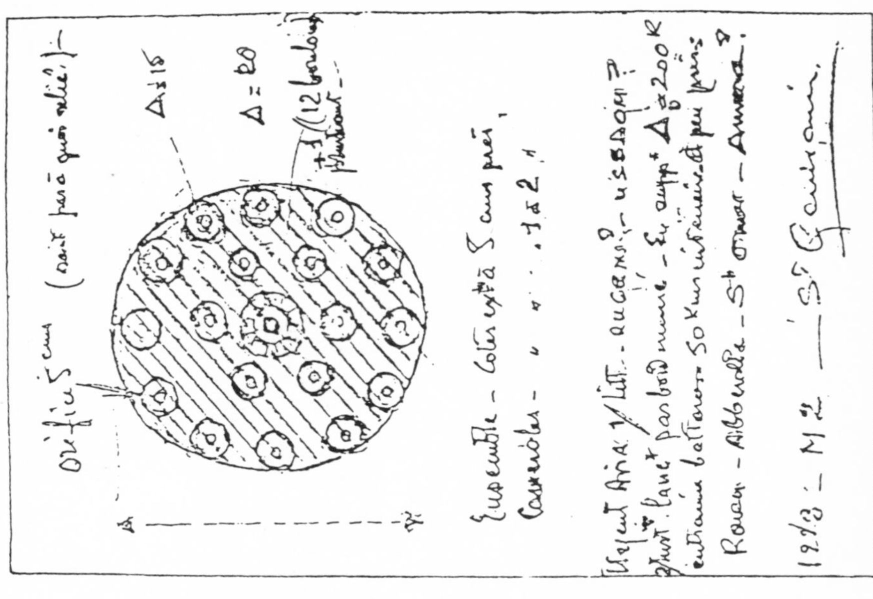

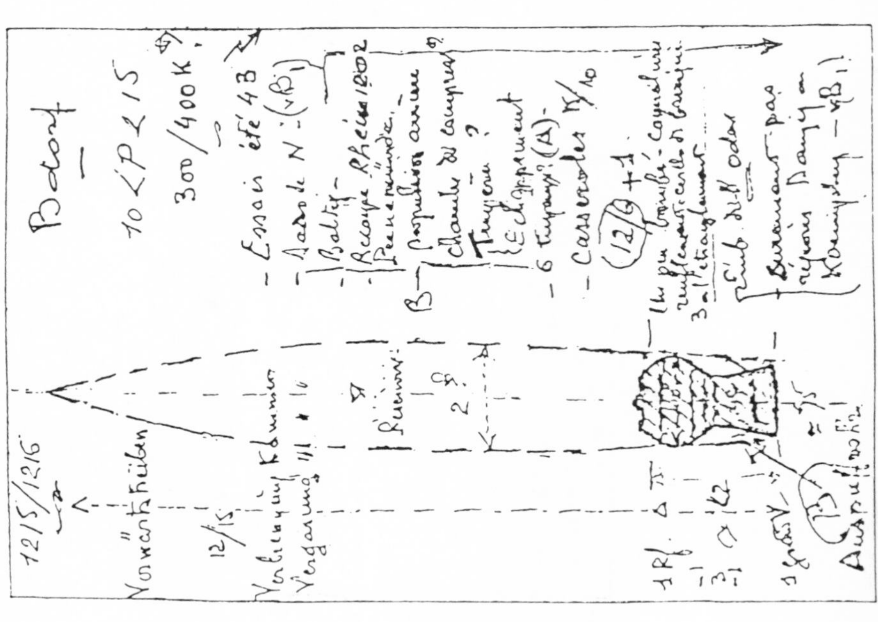

Figure 5 Sketches of the V2 rocket design by General J. Pomès-Barrère, c. December 1943

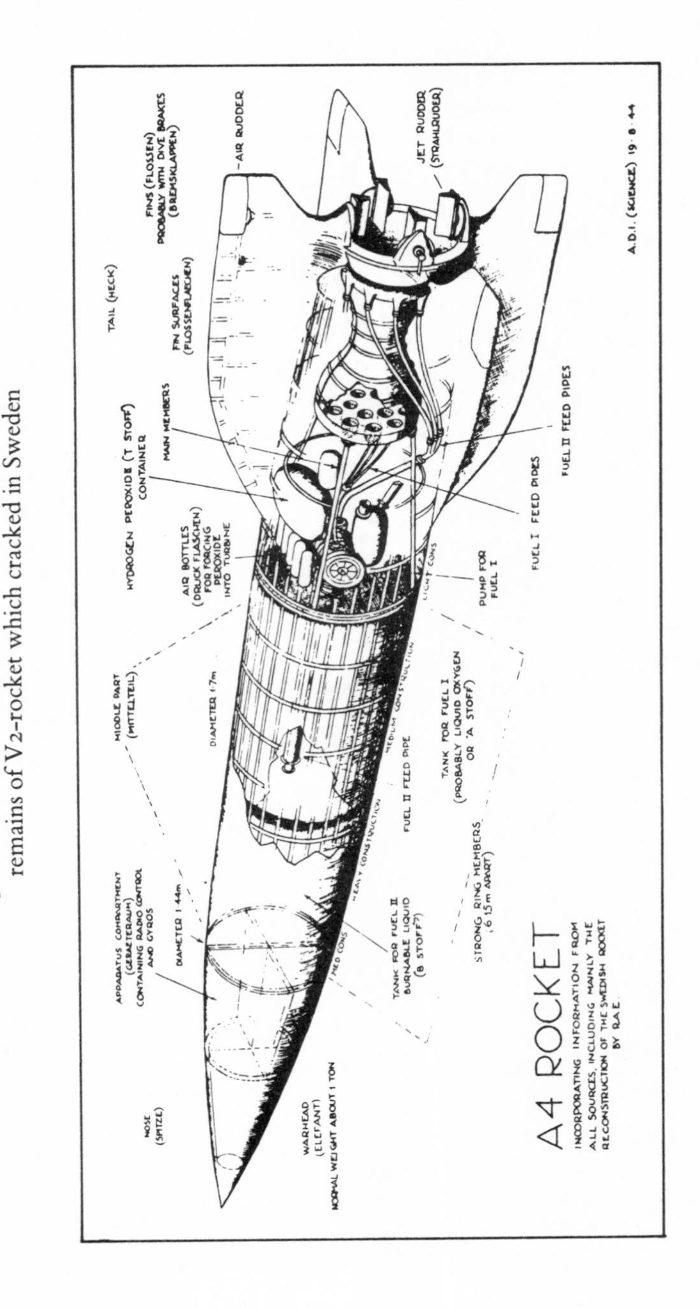

Figure 6 Rocket design reconstructed in June 1944 from remains of V2-rocket which cracked in Sweden

design we reconstructed from the remains and shows how accurate his information was. General Pomès-Barrère told me that he had since tried to locate why his crucial information failed to get through and he could only conclude that (borrowing a phrase from *Most Secret War*) 'once again, it was an example of the hierarchical attenuation of the information.' He surmised that the failure had occurred somewhere in Madrid in the hand-over between French and British officers. The General, who was as courteous as he was brilliant, died in 1986; in the meantime, he had given me six years of treasured friendship.

It is galling to find that such a failure to transmit vital intelligence should have occurred – and not only because of the effect that it might have had on the war, but also, while the men and women of the Resistance were not seeking credit, the fact that such instances in which reports did not get through blinded us from giving the recognition that they so amply deserved. There are doubtless many other instances – I understand, for example, that there were reports from Polish workers at Peenemünde that did not get through – for it was of course inevitable that, under clandestine conditions in war, breakdowns in transmission should occur. Perhaps we should be grateful that so much successfully came through.

The same comments apply to the escape lines for helping Allied personnel out from the Low Countries and France to Spain. I knew at the time that the final stage was an arduous fourteen hour climb over the Pyrenees – but it was only at a Resistance reunion, when I met one of the guides and mentioned the fourteen hours, that I realized that for him this was only half the story. 'Yes,' he said, 'but for us it was then another fourteen hours back' – for he had to return immediately to minimize the chance that the Germans would notice his absence from home.

Peenemünde

Reverting to Peenemünde, the performance of intelligence in locating it as the seat of rocket research has been criticized, notably by Martin Middlebrook in his extensive and thoughtful post-mortem *The Peenemünde Raid*. In it he states, 'British Intelligence was too slow in discovering what was happening at Peenemünde.' Admitting the force of the stricture, we have to ask whether we could have been quicker and whether, in the context of the war, we were too late.

Since we had to start in 1939 with no scientific and very little technical intelligence, and after our secret intelligence had been so blind that it had failed in peacetime to spot the huge *Knickebein* antennae 30 metres high on turntables 100 metres in diameter in open country within a few miles of the German frontier, we had not only to try to bring ourselves mentally abreast of German advances in technology that were new to us, but also to create the organizations by which intelligence might be gained.

Starting as late as we did, with the war already in progress, I saw that in general, as far as new weapons were concerned, we should have to concentrate on detecting them as they reached the stage of trials, where we might pick up clues which would be hard to conceal, and yet which might give us just enough time to devise countermeasures. Anything much more than this would have been unrealistic; if in peacetime we could miss high radio aerials in open country, how in wartime could we hope to get inside weapon research establishments in the heart of Germany? By concentrating on the trials stage we inevitably ran the risk of being too late, but this was a danger that we had to face – once again I am reminded of Churchill's comment to a visiting general in the trenches of 1916, 'Sir, this is a very dangerous war!' Peenemünde in fact exemplified the approach: we *did* find the V2 in the trials stage, and early enough for us to hinder its development and production programme to some effect. In fact, had we known much more about Peenemünde much earlier it is doubtful whether we could have done much more to retard the development of the V2, given the limitations of our bombing accuracy.

Middlebrook, though, points to the fact that even though we might otherwise have known nothing, the Oslo Report of November 1939 should have alerted us, for it included 'brief details of large, long range rockets being tested at Peenemünde, a place easily found on pre-war German maps'. I shall be treating the Oslo Report in some detail in a later chapter, and its full text can be found at Appendix A. Careful reading of the Report will show that, contrary to Middlebrook's précis, it did not associate Peenemünde with large rockets but with a remote-controlled rocket-propelled glider bomb being developed by the German Navy for use against shipping. Moreover, it did not say that Peenemünde was a development establishment, but a testing range; and since the bomb was to be dropped from an aircraft, and there was an airfield at Peenemunde – this had been spotted and photographed by one of the most alert and best of our PR pilots, Flight Lieutenant D. W. Steventon, whilst on a sortie against another objective in May 1942 – it was reasonable, and indeed correct, to associate the range with trials from the airfield. When at last we were able to fly regular reconnaissances over Peenemünde, it was clear that there was much activity outside the confines of the airfield, and this of course was the rocket establishment; but its independence from the airfield was only recognized in 1943 when we had already been alerted by other evidence.

While the Oslo Report had told us that the German Army was developing shells 80 centimetres in diameter with rocket propulsion, it had said that these were intended for use against the Maginot Line, and that the development was 'still in its early stages'. Use against the Maginot Line did not imply a weapon of great range, and in the military situation of 1939, 1940, 1941 or even 1942, it was more important to concentrate our extremely limited intelligence resources against more imminent and more dangerous weapons. That is why, in Middlebrook's words, 'there is no evidence in his own book [i.e. mine, *Most Secret War*] that his department went into top gear until the conversation between two German generals alerted everyone.' Also, incidentally, what the generals alerted us to was not Peenemünde but the earlier establishment at Kummersdorf. In the meantime it was more urgent, up to the end of 1942, to devote most of our effort to containing the nightfighter threat to our bombers and to mastering the U-boats and German radar on the prospective invasion coastline.

A later chapter will show the debts we truly owe to the writer of the Oslo Report.

The Dambusters

One of the pleasures resulting from the publication of *Most Secret War* has been that, in the voluminous correspondence that I received, I have sometimes been able to recognize that two writers had had the common interest of serving together during the war, and as a result I have been able to put old comrades in touch. In one instance this has even happened with two *Luftwaffe* officers, and in another between an RAF pilot and a member of the flak battery who shot him down. In the latter case, the radar operator of the flak battery, an Austrian now domiciled in Australia, wrote in 1986 telling me that his battery had been positioned to defend the V1 (flying bomb) storage depot in the railway tunnel at Rilly-la-Montagne, near Rheims, mentioned in *Most Secret War*. It was attacked by the Lancasters of 617 Squadron with Tallboys in July 1944, and two aircrew (actually he said three, but the

RAF only know of two) baled out after their aircraft had been hit and they were taken prisoner. Could I possibly find out their names and what happened to them after the war? So here was a question coming from an Austrian in New South Wales about an incident of more than forty years before – was there any hope of answering it? In the event, the 617 Squadron records showed that the two survivors were Flying Officer D. Luker and Flight Lieutenant William Reid, VC – and it happened that, only a fortnight or so before, I had met the latter when he presided over a lecture that I gave to the Strathallan Aircraft Society in Auchterarder, Perthshire!

Among my other contacts with 617 Squadron (the Dambusters) has been one with 'Mickey' (Air Marshal Sir Harold) Martin, who joined me in a Royal Institution Christmas Lecture in 1981 to demonstrate the measuring techniques by which the crews flew correctly at the vitally low height and released their bouncing bombs at the right distance from the dam. Each explosion created so much spray and such enormous waves that it took three minutes for the spray to clear and the water to settle down enough for the aircrew to judge their height above it. I knew that after they had released their own bombs Gibson and Martin had flown on either side of each successive aircraft as it made its attack, so as to draw the fire of the defending gunners, but it only dawned on me in the middle of the TV demonstration that if they escorted nine of their comrades, they had been flying up and down, drawing fire, for nearly half an hour. Once again, what a privilege it was to know such men.

The film *The Dambusters* credits the invention of the device by which the aircrew checked that they were flying at the correct height, which depended on their watching two spots of light projected downwards from the aircraft and getting them into coincidence on the water surface, to Guy Gibson's inspiration when he watched the limelights on a performer in a theatre. In fact, the device was conceived at Farnborough, by George Pickard, who had joined me in the early infra-red work at Oxford, and who went to Farnborough when our Oxford effort was closed.

Barnes Wallis

Another link with the Dambusters rose through my increasing contact with Barnes Wallis after the war. I had heard that he was in tears after the Dams raid, when only ten out of nineteen Lancasters returned, and fifty-three aircrew died. Just how deeply it affected him I saw in 1954 when he and I were talking about the loss of the third de Havilland Comet airliner, and speculating on the cause. 'They're going too fast!' he said, referring not to the speed of the aircraft but to the pace of its development. I can still see him standing in the hall of the Athenaeum, his hands clenching so hard that his knuckles were white, and then, 'After the Dams I swore I would never risk another pilot's life again.' Indeed he had thought that flying at speeds approaching the sound barrier would involve so many undetermined factors that it should first be tried on unmanned models. This would, of course, need both remote radio control and telemetry back to base, but he persuaded the Ministry of Supply that it was the right way ahead, and he gained the Ministry's support. Unfortunately he undertook responsibility for the electronic developments, which he had to learn from scratch, and this slowed his progress so much that long before he could make any trials the Americans simply took the risk of using pilots and found that supersonic flight was much less dangerous than had been feared.

Barnes Wallis was a great patriot who saw fast aircraft of long range as a way of holding the British Commonwealth together and, if necessary, of it defending itself. One of his proposals was what he called 'variable geometry' but which subsequently became known 'swing-wing', and he fought a long battle to get it adopted. The resistance did not entirely come from the Government, for F. E. Jones – who had been Deputy Director at Farnborough – told me that the Government had offered to put in 'pound for pound' with Wallis's firm, Vickers, to support the development but the firm had declined. There certainly had been doubts at Farnborough, for when in 1963 I had to conduct the inquiry into the future of air defence one of my first steps was to call for the current official assessment of the merits of variable geometry. As I remember, the opening of the assessment, which came from Farnborough, ran 'variable geometry is no longer a wild idea'. Indeed the Americans were already taking it up in the design of the F111; and the genesis of the Tornado – which uses swing-wing – can be traced back to our deliberations. But when I told Barnes Wallis that officialdom had now capitulated, he told me that he had had too much frustration to be gratified, and his thoughts were now directed towards aircraft that would fly in the high stratosphere at speeds up to Mach 26, reaching Australia in under an hour. Twenty years later, designs such as Hotol are heading along the same line.

'The Fun of the Fair'

Most Secret War appears to have given the unwitting impression that few aspects of World War II were closed books to me, for it has stimulated a widely ranging stream of inquiries ever since. Mostly they have come by post, but one came right 'out of the blue' amid the drams and drums of the Lonach Gathering at Strathdon in Aberdeenshire in August 1987. From the convivial throng I was sought out by George Thomson, the former Scots Guardsman who annually marshals the Lonach Highlanders for their arduous if bibulous march to the Gathering. He had with him a man with a query that they thought I might be able to answer. The man explained that he ran one of the stands in the travelling fair that moves from one Highland gathering to another throughout the summer. He and his fellow standholders belonged to their professional body, the Showmen's Guild, as his father had done before him, and his father had told him that in 1940 the Guild had clubbed together and raised £5,000 for a Spitfire. Could I tell him what had happened to it?

It was a difficult, albeit worthy, question to find the fate of a single aircraft among all the thousands[7] of Spitfires produced and flown in 'the havoc of war' more than forty years ago; but once again Air Commodore Henry Probert of the Air Historical Branch of the Ministry of Defence miraculously gave the answer within a few days. The Showmen's Guild had indeed provided a Spitfire: it was a Mark VB, RAF No. W3764, and it went into service on 17 August 1941 and was flown in succession by Nos. 303, 306 and 310 Squadrons on missions over France before being retired a year later for training duties. Finally, it was 'reduced to produce' on 14 October 1943.

Throughout its flying life it had borne the apt and happy name of 'The Fun of the Fair'; the name fitted not only the Showmen who provided it, but also the pilots who flew it, for Nos. 303, 306 and 310 Squadrons were all Polish and famous for their light-hearted enthusiasm. Earlier in this chapter we recalled the Polish contribution to Enigma: here let us recall the astonishing figure of 139 Polish pilots who scrambled their diverse ways across Europe after their country was overrun, and flew with the Royal Air Force in the Battle of Britain.

Christmas Eve, 1940

In 1940 I myself contributed in a minor way to a Spitfire fund, although less deliberately than did the Showmen's Guild. It happened that on Christmas Eve Bletchley broke Enigma in the afternoon and we read that our opponents in *Kampfgruppe* 100, the German pathfinders, had been instructed that there were to be no operations that night. So this would be the first occasion for three and a half months on which we could look forward to a peaceful night.

We were therefore on the point of putting our papers away when the door of my office opened and Maggie, the wife of my colleague Harold Blyth, came in and asked me where he was. She herself was a cryptographer at Bletchley, and therefore had the freedom of MI6 Headquarters, so we were not unduly surprised to see her. I told her that Harold was somewhere in Headquarters and would doubtless be back before long, if she cared to wait. 'Anyway, Maggie,' I added, 'you can go home and sleep soundly in your bed tonight!' When she asked why, I told her the news from Bletchley that *KGr* 100 would not be coming out. 'In that case, Doc,' she replied, 'to hell with bed! We're going over to The Feathers, and, what's more, you're coming with us!' So on Harold's return we all went to The Feathers, just across Broadway from the office.

Despite the Blitz, the bar was full of Christmas cheer, and before long Maggie said, 'Come on, Doc, play us a few carols on your mouth-organ!' One carol led to another, including *Stille Nacht* which struck me as a peculiarly appropriate tribute to our German opponents who were giving us a quiet night, during which I saw Maggie remove Harold's RAF cap and start to take a collection. Our colleague John Perkins, who was a squadron leader, followed her example, and to my embarrassment they collected fifty-one shillings and sixpence.

The embarrassment was solved by putting the money into the pub's own Spitfire fund, but in addition John Perkins had collected a comment that I still treasure. It came from a Londoner sitting rather morosely at the far end of the bar, his head propped up on his hands. He, of course, did not have the benefit of our privileged knowledge about *KGr* 100, but he was the kind of man who was going to have his usual Christmas drink, *Luftwaffe* or no *Luftwaffe*, and by this time he had had several. Seeing the RAF cap thrust on the bar in front of him he put his hand in his pocket and dropped a half-crown into the cap. In an alcoholic voice he asked the squadron leader, 'Who's the chap who's playing? What does he do?' John replied. 'Oh, I don't know – he's a scientist of some sort.' Whereupon the man again put his hand into his pocket and dropped a second half-crown into the cap with a sad comment, 'They're badly paid, poor buggers!' *In Vino Veritas!*

Harold Jordan

One of the most inspiring passages for an author to write was that in *Most Secret War* which described the electronic reconnaissance flight by a Wellington aircraft of 1474 flight on 2/3 December 1943 to investigate the transmissions of the Liechtenstein radar carried by German nightfighters to detect our bombers.[8] The information due to be gained was crucial for devising countermeasures such as Window and jamming to reduce our losses. The mission was outstandingly dangerous because it involved the reconnaissance aircraft flying in front of a German nightfighter and, more likely than not, in being attacked by it. Moreover, with the fighter's great advantage in speed, if its first attack was unsuccessful it could attack again – and again.

Most Secret War summarized the details of what happened as far as they had filtered through to me: west of Mainz a nightfighter's transmissions were detected by the special radio operator, Pilot Officer Harold Jordan, and the information was signalled back to us in England. Immediately the fighter attacked, and our rear-gunner fired about a thousand rounds until his turret was put out of action and he was hit in the shoulder. Jordan himself was hit in the arm, and then in the jaw and an eye. He continued to listen to the fighter's radar and warn his pilot, Pilot Officer Paulton, as the fighter approached for each attack. Four of the crew of six were badly wounded; the port engine throttle was shot away, the starboard throttle jammed at full power, an aileron and the air-speed indicators were out of action. Yet the Wellington continued to fly. It struggled back to the coast of Kent, where the wireless operator, Flight Sergeant Bigoray, was pushed out on a parachute over land because the captain thought that he might not survive immersion in the sea, and the aircraft was too damaged to risk coming down on land. Bigoray carried with him a report to confirm that the radar transmission was on the frequency that we expected, in case the original radio message had not got through and the rest of the crew should perish in an attempt to come down in the sea. It was typical of the whole crew in this epic mission that just as he was about to be pushed out, and badly wounded though he was, Bigoray was not sure that he had left his transmitting key down in the position to broadcast the distress signal, and struggled back through the aircraft to check.

The *Most Secret War* account led to George Pollock gathering further details and publishing a fuller story in *Reader's Digest* for September 1987, which I warmly recommend. One of the aspects that

I did not know was that all the crew except Jordan, who came from Croydon, were Canadians: Ted Paulton a car worker from Ontario, Bill Barry a printer from Manitoba, Fred Grant an Ontario salesman, Bill Bigoray and Everett Vachon farm workers from Quebec.

Another fact that I did not know was that although *Most Secret War* correctly recorded that surgeons succeeded in saving Jordan's wounded eye, its sight was lost, and in 1945 it had to be removed, as he told me on reading my account. He also told me that the damaged eye was the reason he was wearing his RAF cap at such a jaunty angle in the photograph taken shortly after his recovery. This incredibly modest man wrote to me on 23 January 1980:

> May I express my deep humility in finding my name included in the Dedication[9] in such transcendent company; I accept it as a tribute to all the other airborne special operators who undertook equally onerous tasks. I was deeply disappointed that my injury prevented me from undertaking further flying investigations . . .
>
> In looking to the future I am encouraged by the fact that you, Dr Frank and other members of your war-time staff returned to academic careers which means that the elements that created such a successful team must have imbued hundreds of your students and colleagues over the last thirty years.

Hal Jordan and his wife were then living a quietly retired life in Winchcomb in Gloucestershire, and not long before he died in May 1986 I was proud to introduce him for the hero that he was to the cheering pupils of nearby Rendcomb College when I was giving their Annual Lecture.

Courage

Increasingly, as I look back on such brave exploits as Jordan's I recall some words of Lord Slim on courage:

> It is the lands where Nature is neither too easy nor too cruel, where a man must work hard to live but where his efforts and his enterprise can bring him great rewards, that breed courage and where it becomes a national tradition. And don't run away with the idea that this limits courage to Northern Europe and North America. Believe me – and I've fought both with and against them – some of the bravest races in the world aren't white at all.

Churchill clearly felt the same when he wrote of the huddled bodies of the dervishes after Omdurman: 'These were as brave men as ever walked the Earth – destroyed, not conquered, by machinery.'

Even Jordan's sublime courage has a close parallel on the German side, to judge by Heinz Nowarra's account in *He 111* of the struggle by the wounded crew of an aircraft of *Kampf Geschwader* 26 in December 1939 to nurse their crippled aircraft back to Germany after a reconnaissance of Scapa Flow. And as the war developed such experiences were to recur many times among the aircrews of all the countries involved on either side, compelling to us to admire across national frontiers the tenacity that the human spirit can show so supremely in extremity.

Bir Hacheim and the Alamo

Such an example was set by the Free French defenders of Bir Hacheim in 1942, which led me in *Most Secret War* to recall that we had, through Enigma, read Rommel's signal which reported that he was being held up 'by fanatical resistance at Bir Hacheim'. It conjured up for me the picture of a band of men, led by General Koenig of the Cuirassiers, to whom the honour of France still meant something, with a determination to fight to the last. On reading that passage, Lord Ballantrae (Bernard Fergusson), himself one of our greatest soldiers, wrote correcting me. General Koenig was not a Cuirassier, and he was in command not of a body of devoted Frenchmen but of the Foreign Legion. So this fanatical defence had not been put up by men fighting for the ashes of their fathers and the temples of their gods, but for the honour of the Legion. This runs somewhat against the theory underlying the constitution of the regiments of the British Army, which many of us believe – myself included – draw part of their spirit from their territorial association with the counties, the Lowlands and the Highlands.

One of the legacies of *Most Secret War* is that it has taken me to San Antonio, in Texas, and the site of the Battle of the Alamo. Here again was a small body of men who fought to the last, for Texas. But were they born Texans, fighting for their homes and families? The memorial shrine in the ruins of the Mission, the focus of the battle, in San Antonio, gives the names of all the 188 men who for thirteen days in 1836 fought to the death there: it also tells where they came from. Born Texans were a tiny minority: most of the Americans came from other States – twenty in all. And besides the Americans there were twelve Englishmen, twelve Irishmen, four Scotsmen, one Welshman, two Germans and a Dane! There can rarely have been such a disparate body of men, and yet there were no traitors and no defectors: what, or who, could have created such fantastic spirit? Two of the legendary figures of America, James Bowie and David Crockett, were there, but the credit must above all go to the twenty-five-year-old Commander, Colonel William Barret Travis, who, determined himself to fight to the last, drew a line with his sword across the ground and called for any man who would fight with him to step across to his side of the line. Anyone who wanted to escape should stay on the other side and would be free to leave. Every man stepped across.

Electronic Security Command, USAF

Although the story of the Alamo seems far from both the science and intelligence with which this book is primarily concerned, I could not resist recording the bare facts of Travis and his men, even if I have to leave them to speak for themselves and to provoke thought in students of leadership. But there is a connection between the Alamo and *Most Secret War* in that but for the latter I would not know the former, at least as regards the composition of the Alamo defenders. For it was as a result of reading *Most Secret War* that the Commander, General Doyle Larson, of the Electronic Security Command of the United States Air Force decided that he would like me to talk to his Command about problems of electronic warfare as I saw them as a veteran of events forty years earlier. And although I demurred because I felt that I would have nothing helpful to present-day operators in a field in which such enormous developments had taken place, the General modestly said that I should not worry about modern complications: I had been involved when the fundamental principles of the subject were being formed, and his Command would like to show me what it was doing, and I could advise whether it was consistent with those principles. His headquarters were stationed just outside San Antonio, and that was how I came to read the names on the Alamo Shrine.

It was a marvellous privilege to be made an honorary member of his Command and to join in some of its discussions. Besides the legendary hospitality of Texas, and at a time when there was much criticism both inside and outside the States of the quality of recruits in the aftermath of Vietnam, I particularly appreciated the quality of the sergeants and other ranks in the Command, and the way in which sergeants could enter freely into discussion with colonels at our meetings. This doubtless owed much to the fact that since his Command was so specialized – electronic warfare being its field – General Larson had the right to set his own standards of entry to it.

I saw some of the other USAF Commands, too, since General Lew Allen, the Chief of Air Staff in the Pentagon, had suggested that I should also lecture at the other Commands to help stimulate their interest in electronic warfare. It would unbalance this chapter too much if I were to try to do justice here to the hospitality so generously extended by the Commands and establishments of the United States Air Force and associated organizations such as the Central Intelligence Agency, the National Security Agency, the Pentagon, the Rand Corporation in Santa Monica, the Aerospace Corporation in El Segundo, Research and Development Associates in Los Angeles, the Honeywell Corporation in Minneapolis, E-Systems in Dallas, Lockheed in Austin, Texas, the South Western Research Institute in San Antonio, Hewlett Packard in Palo Alto, the Stanford Research Institute in Menlo Park, IBM in Gaithersburg, the Centre for Strategic and International Studies in Washington, and the Fletcher School of Law and Diplomacy in Boston. I also spent some days at the Naval Postgraduate Academy at Monterey, and the Army War College near Harrisburg.

Here I can only record that the hospitality was always of the warmest and enthusiasm of the highest. I was a singularly fortunate legatee of that immense fund of goodwill and mutual respect that had been built up in the wartime years, when the fact that we had had two years of war experience ahead of the Americans led them quickly to appreciate what they could learn from us; and for what we could then give them they have given us generously in return ever since, especially in electronic and satellite intelligence.

If I select one of the many generous appreciations I received, it is because it epitomized how far American gratitude goes beyond anything that we ourselves might think we deserved. It comes from a letter of October 1980 from the head scientist of the Foreign Technology Division of the US Air Force at Wright Patterson Air Force Base near Dayton, Ohio:

> I truly hope that you sensed the esteem in which you are held by the FTD analysts. You are the model which we have emulated. We in FTD take pride in our belief that we, more than any other intelligence organization, are the true successors to the analytic tradition established by you in the war years. Thanks for the heritage you have provided us.

These are words which I value in grateful contrast to the ambivalence observed by Peter Wright in *Spycatcher*:

> R. V. Jones worked closely with Churchill on scientific intelligence during the war. His contributions were brilliant but he was widely distrusted in Whitehall for his independence. Like so many others, he was never allowed to make the impact in peacetime that he had made in war.

I would merely remark in passing that one unfortunate result of the publication of *Spycatcher* is that, if it was hard enough for scientists to win the confidence of the intelligence services in the first place, it could be even harder now to reassure them of our judgment and discretion.

Improvement of Bombsights

Whether or not Peter Wright's comment adds credence to his reliability as a source, one difference between peace and war is epitomized in Churchill's 'In war you don't have to be polite, you just have to be right'; and when he commanded the sixth battalion of the Royal Scots Fusiliers in the Ploegsteert trenches of 1916, he often told his men, 'War is a game to be played with a smiling face.'[10] As *Most Secret War* recounted, some of us in World War II were even fortunate enough to have our faces lightened by unforced smiles from time to time, and in fact the war would have been much harder to bear without them. But *Most Secret War* omitted one of the most diverting incidents because it involved a laugh at the expense of my friend of Oxford and wartime days, James Tuck, and I had already gone to the limit of discretion – or so I thought – in describing the impact of his 'Mr Deeds' approach on Oxford and Whitehall.

Viewers of the BBC television series on Robert Oppenheimer may recall an early Oppenheimer party at Los Alamos where a solitary Englishman became intoxicated and danced on a table singing bawdy rugby songs, much to the awed embarrassment of his American hosts. That Englishman was Jim Tuck and although we knew that he could get merry on two glasses of sherry – and cooking sherry at that – none of us was aware of the repertoire of non-Gregorian chant to which he gave voice at Oppenheimer's party. When I expressed surprise to Peter Goodchild, the producer of the TV series, both at the episode and at his daring in including it in the programme because Tuck could very understandably object, he told me that in fact Tuck had readily agreed to its inclusion, provided that it was a faithful account.

Sadly, he died of cancer at Los Alamos early in 1981, and it was for me a fortunate spin-off from General Larson's hospitality in San Antonio that I was able to divert from a flight to Los Angeles to see Jim a few weeks before he died, when he was steadily facing death with collected courage. Had I then known of his dispensation to Peter Goodchild to portray the Oppenheimer party episode, I might have asked for a similar dispensation to tell the story that here follows. Now I can only presume the dispensation, but it would surely have been in keeping with his generous nature to give it, and so here it is.

It started one day in the Cabinet Office (then in Richmond Terrace) in 1940 when Professor Lindemann (later Lord Cherwell) as adviser to Mr Churchill conceived a quick and inexpensive way of doubling the strength of Bomber Command. This was to halve the errors in our bombsights, because then we should drop twice as many bombs within destructive range of our targets, which would be just as effective as sending twice as many bombers with their existing bombsights – and surely it must be much cheaper to make better bombsights than to build twice as many bombers and train the extra crews. So the first step would be to look at the design of these sights and consider how it could be improved. Lindemann therefore told Tuck, who was his scientific assistant, to go and spend some time at the Royal Aircraft Establishment at Farnborough with the section responsible for bombsights, to see what might be done.

At the time, Tuck knew very little about either aeroplanes or bombsights. In fact, it was hardly more than a year after I had driven him and Elsie, his wife, around the Oxfordshire countryside and we had happened to pass Brize Norton, where they were as excited as schoolchildren to see an aircraft take off for the first time in their lives, delightedly craning their necks through the sunshine roof of my car as they followed the aircraft on its climb into the distance. Tuck, though, was never daunted by lack of experience, and he set out for Farnborough with all the enthusiasm of a fresh mind.

It is not difficult to imagine the reactions of the bombsight design team at Farnborough to the onslaught by the man from Whitehall. Ingenuously they suggested that he might care to get some direct experience of aiming current bombsights: if so, they could arrange for him to go to Boscombe Down, where a pilot would take him for a flight and let him drop some bombs at a target on a practice range. I do not know whether I myself would have fallen into the trap, but I might have recalled that Lindemann had told me of a very similar episode at Farnborough around 1917, when he and his colleagues had dealt with an unwelcome visitor from Whitehall by taking him up and giving him such a rough flight that he never troubled them again. Tuck's hosts had evidently hit on the same stratagem, for while he was travelling to Boscombe Down they telephoned the pilot and told him that Tuck wished to learn how the bombsight performed under really adverse conditions of turbulence, so would the pilot simulate these conditions by throwing the aircraft 'all over the sky'? The pilot conscientiously did as he was instructed, and Tuck was so airsick that – as he himself told me – he missed the target by 800 yards from a height of 800 feet. Although he henceforth confined his activities to the ground at Farnborough, he showed better mettle than his 1917 predecessor in not immediately retreating back to Whitehall.

The Furled Umbrella

The bombsight team then decided on a further step to 'get him off their backs'; they had noticed that he carried a tightly furled umbrella, a Whitehall habit he had acquired from Lindemann, and they proceeded to fill it with soot. Any prayers that they may have made for rain so that they might witness the subsequent spectacle went unheeded, and Tuck ultimately left for Whitehall accoutred with his charged umbrella.

Still nothing happened, because he rarely used the umbrella in London, since he lived within a mile of the Cabinet Office, and he usually cycled to work. One day, however, when negotiating Parliament Square, he was squeezed off his bicycle by a lorry that took a corner too close, and in the fall he broke his arm. Henceforth for some weeks he had to walk with that arm in a sling and the other carrying the umbrella. Imagination may readily conceive a host of eventualities that might have transpired from such a conquisition: of these, the one which actually happened was precipitated by a downpour one evening as Tuck was leaving the Cabinet Office, and he stood in the doorway trying to unfurl his umbrella and shake it open with his single arm. Now the Office doorway was guarded by two London policemen, one on either side, flanking Tuck as he struggled with the umbrella. Then one of them stepped forward and took the umbrella, saying, 'Excuse me, sir, let me help you with that!' He opened the umbrella above his head and down came the soot all over him. The expression in the policeman's eyes as he blinked through the fuliginous shower with his bewildered look of reproach was, Tuck recalled, like that to be expected of your favourite retriever when it brought you back a domestic hen you had shot in mistake for a pheasant.

His first ruminations regarding the authorship of this blackening deluge focused on me, but his memory was accurate enough for him to conclude that, although I sometimes lunched with him and Elsie in their flat, I could not have had the necessary opportunity and so he must look elsewhere. Correctly, he decided that it must have been someone at Farnborough; but instead of letting the matter drop he paid a further visit to the Establishment, and called all the suspects together for a meeting in the mess, which he proceeded to address. He told them exactly what had happened, concluding with an admonition: 'You really must not do this sort of thing, chaps. It might not have been a bobby under that umbrella – it might have been the Prime Minister himself!' Truthful history must record that it was not shamed repentance but irreverent applause that greeted this awesome prospect.

Jim came to be regarded affectionately as a figure of fun and respectfully as a man of genius wherever he went, not least at Los Alamos, to which he escaped from assisting Lord Cherwell in the Cabinet Office in 1943, and where he subsequently spent most of his career. As Leona Marshall Libby wrote in her description of wartime life at Los Alamos, *The Uranium People*, 'Tuck is famous for causing the largest traffic jam in the history of Los Alamos . . almost everyone in town was late for work. Tuck's amusing adventures happen seemingly effortlessly.' But she also recorded that he was responsible for suggesting the explosive lenses that made the plutonium bomb work: 'These explosive lenses are called Tuck lenses today [1979] even though Tuck has had nothing to do with explosive research for at least 30 years.' Richard Rhodes in his definitive *The Making of the Atomic Bomb* recorded that Tuck's suggestion was by itself vital enough to 'pay the way' of the entire British mission at Los Alamos. After a brief post-war return to Oxford, where he found no fellowship available, he took American citizenship and became head of thermonuclear developments at Los Alamos, where the work received the official code-name of 'Project Sherwood' because of the legendary activities of Friar Tuck.

The Nuclear Prospect in 1939

Among the many debts, both personal and professional, that I owe Jim Tuck is the fact that he gave me my first serious briefing on the possibility of a nuclear bomb. It was on a Saturday evening in June or July 1939 at a bus stop in The High at Oxford. I had just told him that I was about to leave the Admiralty Research Laboratory to start work in scientific intelligence, and was wondering about the new applications of science that I ought to be looking for. 'Reginald,' he said. 'one day there is going to be a BIG BANG!' He went on to tell me about both nuclear fission and the possibility of a chain reaction, along with the fact that it looked as though the Germans might already be working on it, from a current paper in *Die Naturwissenschaften* in which it appeared that the author, Siegfried Flügge, might be trying to warn the world of what was going on. Incidentally, I met Flügge after the war, when he confirmed that this had indeed been his motive.

Just how remote a prospect the bomb seemed at the time can be judged from another of Tuck's stories when a few months later he was taken up to Whitehall by Lindemann as the latter's scientific assistant. By that time, as *Most Secret War*[11] and many other accounts have related, there was intense rivalry between the former friends, Lindemann and Tizard, and Lindemann was proposing to send Tuck as his representative to a demonstration of new weapons at which Tizard was also likely to be present. Lindemann duly briefed Tuck: 'Tizard is sure to pump you as to what I am up to here.' He suggested that Tuck should throw him off the scent with a cock-and-bull story: 'You say that our big line is a uranium bomb. This is just the sort of thing Tizard would expect me to be thinking about. You know enough about it to make a plausible story.' Tuck was inevitably button-holed by Tizard. 'I duly whispered the astonishing secret,' said Tuck, to be met with a snort from Tizard, exclaiming, 'Ha, just what I would expect! It will never be used in this war, if it works at all!'[12]

The Ranks of Tuscany

That incident took place early in the war, probably in the autumn of 1939, and certainly before May 1940 when Lindemann and Tuck moved with Churchill from the Admiralty; it is of interest as showing that Lindemann and Tizard had formed the same opinion on a scientific prospect. This was often the case: their notorious differences were often the result of personal antagonism where the one would tend to take the opposite view to that which he believed to be held by the other. The resultant differences were emphasized by their partisans and above all by Lord (then Sir Charles) Snow in *Science and Government*, whose account was such as to lead *The Times* to ask me to write three 'turnover' articles[13] setting down the facts of the Lindemann–Tizard controversy as best I knew them.

One result was that Charles Snow and I, who had been on friendly terms, did not speak to one another for many years afterwards. I was therefore most pleasantly surprised to read the outstandingly generous terms in which he reviewed *Most Secret War* in the *Financial Times*. I thereupon wrote thanking him, especially in view of our past differences. Part of his reply (dated 20 March 1976) is worth quoting. It ran,

> It was very pleasant to have your letter. I always thought, in our late controversy, that you behaved with great fairness and courtesy. Even if that had not been so, I should have written as I did about your splendid book.

Besides placing this on record as an example of Charles Snow's magnanimity, my purpose here is to point to the long-term value of being fair to enemies and opponents, hard though this may be in the heat of conflict.

I remember what a shock it was in the aftermath of World War I to hear my Latin master – formerly a Major in the Gloucestershires, who also commanded our OTC and who merely used Caesar Book V as a vehicle for imparting higher military wisdom – tell us that the bravest man he had ever seen was a German sergeant who had fallen with four bullets through his heart when trying to cut the wire in front of our trenches. That anyone could be braver than our own soldiers, let alone equal them, threw an entirely new light on life, for we had not yet been introduced to Kipling's Fuzzy-Wuzzy and Gunga Din.

In the same strain was the contemporary tribute on 25 March 1915 from *The Times*'s London correspondent to 'A brave enemy' and 'Brave German Officers' at the Battle of Neuve Chapelle in March 1915 – a battle, incidentally, where our first Battalion of the Grenadier Guards, in which my father fought, lost 16 of its 21 officers and 325 of its men. All could not be wrong in a Britain ready, despite such losses, to acknowledge the bravery of its enemies.

Another World War I tribute, this time from the other side, came from the *Leipziger Neuerste Nachrichten* on the death of Kitchener in May 1916: 'To Great Britain, indeed to the whole British Empire, the loss of Kitchener counts more than that of an army. It is as if our Hindenburg were taken from us . . .' [14]

Churchill's 1942 tribute to Rommel showed even greater spirit, for he had subjected himself to a vote of censure in the House of Commons and he was having to explain why the Eighth Army was faring so badly in Cyrenaica. He afterwards wrote, in *The Hinge of Fate*, 'I could not resist paying my tribute to Rommel', and he quoted from his speech in the censure debate:

> I cannot tell what the position at the present moment is . . . We have a very daring and skilful opponent against us, and, may I say across the havoc of war, a great general.[15]

Churchill also recorded that 'some people had been offended. They could not feel that any virtue should be recognized in an enemy leader. This churlishness is a well-known streak in human nature, but contrary to the spirit in which a war is won, or a lasting peace established.' He had shown that same spirit in his first speech in Parliament, made in February 1901 while the South African war was still in progress. Happening to refer to 'The Boers who are fighting in the field', he added, 'and if I were a Boer, I hope that I should be fighting in the field!'

One of the most moving letters I received after *Most Secret War* was published came from one of my former academic opponents, Sir Malcolm Knox, the Principal of St Andrews University. He was a moral philosopher whose wide experience included having been at one time secretary to Lord Leverhulme and at another tutor to Harold Wilson in Oxford. We had clashed in the fifties, when we found ourselves on opposite sides regarding the place of physics and chemistry in the Scottish school curriculum. I wanted each of these subjects to be of equal weight to, say, French as in the English schools, whereas they were only treated as half-subjects receiving no more time in joint total than a single language subject. I was told that he had said that I would only get physics and chemistry accepted as whole subjects in the schools 'across his dead body'; his opposition, and that of many others, to the change was certainly strong, and it prevailed for some years. However, 'across the havoc of war' we each recognized that we both valued academic standards however hard we might fight for our own viewpoints; and when *Most Secret War* was published he wrote a most generous letter, ending,

> In February I underwent what the surgeons called a 'severe' operation for cancer. I am far from well. I suspect that cancer cells are growing again. But I felt that I had to write this letter to you in gratitude. *Moriturus*, perhaps, *te saluto*.
>
> Malcolm Knox

Coming from one who in all senses was a 'Greats' man this was the classic salute of the dying gladiator. But to none of the Caesars to whom it was by tradition addressed could it have meant half as much as it did to me.

I felt rather the same on receiving three letters from former officers of *Kampfgruppe* 100, the German pathfinders who caused us so much trouble by their accurate bombing in 1940. Each independently wrote to me on reading *Most Secret War*. Hauptmann Wolfgang Metzke, who had flown many trials of the X-apparatus, generously wrote: 'England was fortunate in having you to ferret out the secrets of the *X-Gerät*.' On the morning of my seventieth birthday a plaque arrived on my desk headed by the Viking ship badge by which *KGr* 100 identified its aircraft and inscribed to 'Professor R. V. Jones, the Master of the X-beams, from a former pilot of *KGr* 100'. This was from Albrecht Zetsche, a Leutnant and aircraft captain in 1940, and within the hour there arrived a cable from Oberstleutnant Johann Schaeder, and Oberst Viktor von Lossberg, who had commanded the other pathfinding unit, the Third *Gruppe* of *Kampf Geschwader* 26. They had all spotted my birthday from *Most Secret War* and had decided to mark it in this singularly felicitous way. All I could say was, 'With enemies like these, who needs friends?' The X-beam tribute was particularly generous because I would myself have readily 'given them best', for it took us at least three months to blunt the sharpness of their attack.

Another remarkable German tribute was that paid to the small British parachute force that captured Würzburg radar equipment at Bruneval on 27/28 February 1942 and which later became C Company of the Second Battalion of the Parachute Regiment ('2 Para'). The tribute came in the official German account of the raid:

> The operation of the British commandos was well planned and executed with great daring. During the operation the British displayed great discipline under fire. Although attacked by German soldiers they concentrated entirely on their primary task.[16]

I had the pleasure of reading it to the survivors of the raid and to their successors in 2 Para forty years later at a reunion in Aldershot on 27 February 1982, thoughtfully arranged by the Battalion Commander, who wrote to me,

> As you will know better than I, the fortieth anniversary of the Bruneval Raid falls on 27 February next year. General John Frost has suggested that it would be appropriate if we got all the survivors of the Raid together here in Aldershot on that day, to commemorate it . . .

The signature on the letter, 'H. Jones', did not mean a great deal to me at the time, although I knew that he was a much respected officer. He and his wife were so kind as to have me as their guest, along with Flight Sergeant C. W. H. Cox, the RAF radar technician who had dismantled the German equipment under fire. This date, 27 February, was a Saturday and after a commemorative dinner in the evening we attended a church parade the following morning. None of us could have known as we stood there that within a few weeks the Battalion would be on its way to the Falklands where four of our officer hosts were to die, and 'H' would become, posthumously, a national hero with a Victoria Cross. I am grateful that life has continued to bring me into the company of such men.

There was bravery on the Argentinian side, too, and I wish that someone on our side could have paid something like Churchill's tribute to Rommel to the Argentinian pilots who attacked our ships, for they were brave men. Two American observers were with them shortly after the fighting ended, in the mess of IV Brigada Aerea at Mendoza when a video recording of the BBC documentary programme on the Falklands was being shown to them. The Americans, Jeff Ethell and Michael O'Leary, described in the magazine *Air Progress* the Argentinians' reactions to seeing their comrades being shot down and their own attacks on our ships:

> Then they watched the terrible destruction they wrought not only on ships but on men during the 8 June attack [on the landing ships *Sir Tristram* and *Sir Galahad*]. British rescue helicopters pressed into the black smoke, going completely blind to get their men out of the sea and pushed the liferafts away from the burning ships with the wind of their rotors . . . great cheers went up in this room full of fellow pilots as the helicopter crews disregarded safety to perform their task. As bleeding and limbless men were brought off the rescue helicopters, the war came home and there were not a few sickened men in the room. War is terrible, exacting a nauseating toll on fellow human beings. Without

> exception we heard nothing but respect for the British crews come from their Argentinian counterparts. The hush in that room of military aviators, no different from any we have met in America or Britain, is something we will never forget.

We can only hope, with Churchill, that such mutual respect will in the end lead to peace through compassion.

Churchill College

In *Most Secret War* I described the considerations that led me to return to academic life in 1946. Paramount among them was the belief, much strengthened by war experience, that we needed to bring on more pure and applied scientists in the post-war generation if we were to earn our national living in a rapidly changing world, to defend ourselves when necessary, and to contribute most effectively to the advance of knowledge. Almost immediately on return to university I could see that, however much we in the universities might try to do, much of our effort would be in vain unless students came up to us from the schools who were already well grounded in science and who enjoyed it so much as to want to make it the basis of their working lives. This largely depended on good teaching by enthusiastic schoolteachers who could kindle the interest of pupils. But how were such teachers to be found and attracted into the profession in view of the widening demand for science graduates from government establishments, industry, the universities and from the United States? On 30 June 1950 I wrote to Mr Churchill:

> Ten years ago, it was my duty to warn you about the Beams. Today I wish to emphasise to you another danger to our nation, all the more threatening because it is undramatic. It concerns the shortage of teachers in our public and secondary schools, particularly in science subjects.
>
> I am not the first to raise this matter. Much has been said in the press and at educational conferences, and it is also mentioned in the Ministry of Education's Report for 1949; but I know of nothing that is being done to deal with the problem and indeed I believe that little will be done until such a leader as yourself points the danger in clear, strong terms.
>
> The cause of the trouble is manifold. First, teachers' salaries are inadequate. For example, the man who taught me Physics at Alleyn's School, Dulwich had a good Honours degree at Oxford: he is now Senior Science Master in the same school (which takes some seven

hundred boys) with twenty two years' experience. His present salary is about £750. Had he gone into Industry or Government Service, where salaries are more reasonable, he would by now be getting well over £1,000; and had he instead become a doctor or a dentist, or even an optician, he would be earning far more, and would require less talent.

A second cause of shortage is that we did not train enough scientists before the war and, following the successes of science during the war, of which you are probably more aware than anyone else, there has been an increased demand, both from Government Service and Private Enterprise, for Science graduates. This demand, offering more attractive prospects, has taken the bulk of our graduates; apart from a few self-sacrificing individuals the only ones who have gone into teaching are those who could not find posts in Industry or Government Service.

The effect of the lack of teachers is only gradually being felt, and may not become generally critical for some years because in the meantime the older men are carrying on. But when they go, as they inevitably must, the damage will be starkly apparent, and it may then be too late to mend it. A bad teaching situation propagates rapidly: lack of good teachers means lack of trained students, and thus a lack of good teachers in the next generation. I can say that here in Aberdeen the situation is bad; Oxford and Cambridge may not be hit for some years, but deterioration of this kind often appears first at the periphery of a civilisation.

Looked at objectively, the flow of educated students represents the 'profit' of an educational system, and unless a due proportion of that profit is ploughed back into teaching, the system will perish in intellectual bankruptcy.

Although salaries are an important factor, the trouble is far from being merely a matter of money. The young graduate no longer feels that it is an honourable calling to be a teacher, and he is often apologetic at becoming one. In this of course, he is only reflecting the general attitude that has grown up. The medical profession has both high salaries and glamour; the two often go together. The teaching profession has neither; but many of us have in fact owed more to our teachers than to our doctors or our dentists.

I therefore believe it to be at least as important to raise the general respect for the schoolteacher as it is to raise his salary, and I believe that nothing could do more towards this end than some public statement, at some convenient moment, by you. It is most important that students should become teachers not because they are unfit for anything else, nor because they are attracted by the remuneration (supposing that this were made adequate) but because they feel that teaching is an honourable and responsible profession. In my own opinion, the schoolteacher is in a more vital position in our educational system than the University Professor. He deals with more students, and has a greater hand in their basic education and a greater influence on their choice of careers; and good schools are essential before Universities can flourish.

I trust that I have said enough to draw your interest to the matter, and I hope that it will receive a share of your attention even at a time when many other matters must be troubling you. The danger to our national defence of a decline in our scientific competence will be evident to you – and it is this that is ultimately involved. Apart from national defence, we have also to maintain our place in Western Civilisation and Thought and this place will be in jeopardy if our unsatisfactory school-teaching situation persists.

It will require much effort by many of us to right the situation, but I am confident that no other single act could so effectively direct public thought to the matter, and the Government to action, as a statement by you, if you believe me, on an appropriate occasion. Anything that you feel able to say about the responsibilities of the teacher, and the respect due to him, would do much to restore the dignity of an honourable profession.

If there are any further facts that you would like, I will do my best to find them.

The Conservatives were in Opposition at the time, and Mr Churchill could only reply, on 11 September 1950:

I quite agree that it is most important that science should be well taught in schools and that the future of our defences no less than of our industries depends in the long run upon having a good flow of boys to the universities with a thorough grounding in the fundamental sciences . . . Perhaps it might be possible for me, on a suitable occasion, to say something to this effect. But whether it would do much good is another question. Today other problems, much more urgent and dangerous, must be uppermost in our minds.

However, some of us continued to press, particularly Lord Cherwell and Sir Francis Simon at Oxford; and when I became Director of Scientific Intelligence at the Ministry of Defence in 1952 we were able to produce figures for the Russian production of scientists and engineers. In the meantime, Churchill himself appeared to do very little; but in 1955 he retired as Prime Minister and went on holiday to Messina with Lord Cherwell and his private secretary, Sir John Colville. Of that holiday Sir John later wrote in July 1959:

While in Sicily Sir Winston told me several times how much he regretted that owing to so many other preoccupations he had not, while Prime Minister, devoted more of his energies to procuring an increase in facilities for giving the highest possible technological training. He was sure that for Great Britain, whose future depended on the brains of her inhabitants, this was a vital necessity. It appalled him to think that we, who had contributed more than any other nation by our inventiveness in the past, should now apparently be falling behind in the race. I remember his saying that he believed the United States were too confident of their own power, ingenuity and progress and that they would, before many years had passed, suffer a rude awakening by the discovery that the Russians were ahead of them.

Sir Winston Churchill said he would like to devote his remaining strength and his prestige to awakening the British people to the importance of these matters and to ensuring that steps were taken to remedy our deficiency. As I was about to resign from the Foreign Service, and to go into the City, I offered my services to help Sir Winston in such a campaign and volunteered to seek the financial support of British industry. He said that if I would do so I might make free use of his name and support.[17]

And again, in September 1965, Sir John wrote to me personally:

My recollection is that Sir Winston, during his last months in office, had been oppressed and rather shaken by the accounts which reached him of what the Russians were doing in the way of training technologists. Lord Cherwell had shown him a report written by the scientists who had recently visited Moscow, and I am pretty sure that your name was also mentioned quite a lot in the conversations which took place about the whole matter. If I remember right, Lord Cherwell quoted your views with great emphasis. Lord Cherwell had indeed been urging Sir Winston to take some definite steps about technological education for the previous six months, but there had been many other things to do and Sir Winston was of course by that time getting old. It was therefore during the comparative peace of our fortnight in Sicily that the matter was really discussed at length, and Sir Winston suddenly became enthusiastic to do something! I also in a fit of enthusiasm said that I would be delighted to devote all the time and energy I could spare to raising money for the project we had in mind. It was in fact to build something approaching an MIT in England, and Sir Winston gave me full authority to use his name to see if I could raise the money.

Despite the enormous benefits that might accrue from the creation of a Massachusetts Institute of Technology in Britain, Sir John immediately encountered strong opposition from industrialists, academics, and administrators. One alternative offered was the building of a postgraduate institute attached to Birmingham University and another was the establishment of Churchill postgraduate studentships in technology. Finally, from Mr Carl Gilbert, Chairman of the Gillette Company, came the idea of founding 'a new college at one of the older universities, devoted to technology'.

Now Lord Nuffield had already anticipated the idea by several years in his intention to found Nuffield College at Oxford, to focus its attention on engineering. According to what I heard at the time this prospect alarmed the strong humanist elements in Oxford, headed by the Vice-Chancellor, Lord Lindsay, who sought to palliate the engineering onslaught by persuading Nuffield to broaden his objective. There would be less opposition to the foundation of the new college, he said, if Nuffield could disguise his intentions by replacing specific mention of engineering by some more subtle wording. Engineering was a science but it also made a direct impact on society, and so it might be fairly described as 'social science'. Therefore, if Lord Nuffield would specify social science as the primary interest of his college, there would be much less opposition to its creation. It was only after the college had been founded and staffed not with engineers but with social scientists that Lord Nuffield realized that he had been outwitted – 'bamboozled', as he is said to have described it.[18]

When the question came up of whether Churchill College should be in Oxford or in Cambridge, Lord Cherwell's natural bias in favour of Oxford may have been offset by his knowledge of the Nuffield episode: he agreed that the better prospect would be in Cambridge where support for science and technology was manifestly greater. The new college, Churchill's most tangible memorial, opened with Sir John Cockcroft as its first Master in 1964.

Churchill, Anthrax and Deterrence

Neither chemical nor biological warfare figures prominently in *Most Secret War*. This was partly because, as explained in this chapter (see below, page 254), special arrangements had been made for the relevant intelligence to be handled by Porton, and partly because neither form of warfare was used by either side in World War II. This last fact is, in retrospect, one of the most surprising aspects of the war, for who in 1939, with all its issues of gas-masks and its memories of 1914–18, would have predicted that the war would end without gas being used?

Since *Most Secret War* was published, much has been made both on television and in the Press of a story that Churchill threatened to 'drench the Ruhr' with anthrax. It happens that I myself had a brushing contact with the events that provided the basis of what little truth there was in the story, where two separate issues became confused by writers seeking sensation rather than history. The confusion was unravelled by Dr J. M. Lewis, whose paper in *Encounter*[19] should be consulted for the details.

One strand in the confusion concerns the development of biological warfare agents, in particular anthrax, at Porton where by December 1941 research had shown that cattlecake could be impregnated with anthrax ('agent N') and five million doses fatal to cattle were prepared. Further research showed that anthrax spores could be effectively dispersed from bombs, and on 25 February 1944 Lord Cherwell advised Churchill that six Lancasters carrying loads of anthrax bombs each weighing four pounds could kill everyone living in a square mile – hardly less devastating than an atomic bomb, and causing much longer paralysis of the territory attacked. As with other nasty weapons, the declared purpose of development and production was to have the N-bombs in reserve as a deterrent should the Germans produce something similar, and orders were placed for half a million N-bombs to be made in America.

When the V1 bombardment of London started in June 1944, the British Government was rather slow to tell the Londoners what it was that was harassing them, and to declare the steps it had already taken and without which the bombardment would have been very much worse. Churchill, after nearly five years of war and now criticized for the Government's seemingly inadequate response to the V1, also had in mind the prospective further bombardment by the V2 rockets which experts had said would weigh eighty tons with five- to ten-ton warheads each capable of killing up to four thousand people. As there was no way of stopping a V2 once it was launched, Churchill then, on 6 July 1944, contemplated the possibility of deterring Hitler by threatening to respond with gas – particularly mustard – warfare if rockets were fired against London. He asked the Chiefs of Staff to examine the feasibility of making such a threat; this was the start of the second strand in the tangle in which some would-be historians found themselves.

While the threat feasibility was being examined, there was a meeting of the Crossbow Committee in Churchill's underground war room on 18 July, when he was in the chair, and it fell to me to present the most recent intelligence on the V2. It happened that I now had good evidence that at least a thousand V2s had been made, and Churchill – doubtless thinking of each of the thousand causing up to four thousand deaths – reacted strongly. Besides accusing intelligence of having been 'caught napping' he brought up the proposal of trying deterrence by threatening the Germans with gas warfare, reminding the Chiefs of Staff that he had already raised the question with them. Several of us, led by the Chiefs of Staff, were against the idea, and he seemed grudgingly to subside; but once again, on 25 July, he reminded the Chiefs that he had not yet had the assessment for which he had asked on 6 July. It turned out that on 8 July the Chiefs had referred the matter to the Vice-Chiefs, who did not consider it until 13 July, and who in turn referred it to the Joint Planning Committee with the additional proviso (which appears to have come from the Chiefs of Staff on 8 July) that should we use gas there could be a chance that the Germans might retaliate with bacterial warfare, so this, too, had better be included in the remit. The terms of reference given to the Joint Planning Committee on 16 July then ran:

> The Prime Minister has directed that a comprehensive examination should be undertaken of the military implications of our deciding on an all-out use of gas, principally mustard gas, or any other method of warfare which we have hitherto refrained from using against the Germans, in the following circumstances:
>
> (*a*) As a counter-offensive in the event of the use by the enemy of flying bombs and/or giant rockets developing into a serious threat to our ability to prosecute the war,
>
> or, alternatively,
>
> (*b*) as a means of shortening the war or of bringing to an end a situation in which there was a danger of a stalemate.[20]

So, unknown to Churchill, the Joint Staff's secretariat had added 'or any other method of warfare which we have hitherto refrained from using' which subsequent readers have taken to mean anthrax. Some of them have failed to note that this was not what Churchill himself had asked for, but an extension added at a less exalted level.

The whole matter soon became academic because we were rapidly realizing that the V2 was not nearly such a frightful weapon, nasty enough though it was, and that it would not in the entire campaign drop much more explosive on London than Bomber Command could drop on Berlin in a single night. However, even if the V2 threat had turned out to be much more serious, the mood around the Crossbow table had been heavily against the threatening of gas as a deterrent; and the further question of threatening anthrax warfare had at no time been posed by Churchill. If it had, I believe that the Chiefs of Staff would have been even more firmly against it than they were against gas.

In the discussion Churchill asked me why I thought that the Germans had not themselves resorted to gas warfare. I was able to tell him one positive item of evidence for we had learnt from decrypting Japanese diplomatic signals that Hitler had told the Japanese Ambassador in Berlin that he had some new and very effective gases, but that he was refraining from using them because he thought that we had equally deadly ones. Here he was wrong, because his chemists had discovered nerve gases and ours had not; but the fact that he thought that they had was itself a deterrent, and neither side resorted to gas warfare. The episode is worthy of record both for this precedent of effective deterrence and for righting the account regarding Churchill and anthrax; it also shows his deference, albeit reluctant, to the opinion of the Chiefs of Staff.

The subsequent deliberations of the Chiefs on anthrax and other new weapons have been punctiliously treated in Dr Julian Lewis's *Changing Direction: British Military Planning for Post-war Strategy, 1942–47*, which also reprints his *Encounter* 1982 paper.

Intelligence and Nerve Gases

One of the failures of British intelligence in World War II was our protracted ignorance of the German development of nerve gases. I refrained from telling in *Most Secret War* how this came about, because it occurred in a branch of scientific intelligence for which I was not responsible, and it might have reflected disrepute on others. Further, my motive in telling it then might have been suspected as bias; but it exemplified such an important lesson in intelligence organization, that it is worth telling in the hope that now, ten years later, any suspicion of bias will have faded.

When I was appointed in 1939, I had expected, as the only scientist in intelligence, to watch for developments in chemical warfare. Within a few weeks of my recruitment, however, I learned that the appointment had alarmed the head of a Naval Section, a splendid Royal Naval Captain, and my senior by two ranks, who had hitherto looked after any incoming reports on chemical warfare and who passed them on to the experts at Porton, receiving in return briefings from them about what intelligence should be seeking. Although it was a sideline on his main naval interest, and he knew little science, he cherished this activity almost as a hobby, and he was clearly worried that I was going to try to deprive him of it. So we met, and he assured me that his link with Porton worked well. I had no wish to arouse unnecessary opposition, and I truthfully told him that my own hands were likely to be so full with improving intelligence in fields where none yet existed that I had no intention of disturbing his arrangements, given his assurance that they were working well. We were thenceforth on the best of terms throughout the war, and I saw such reports as came in on chemical warfare, but I made no attempt to interfere or even comment.

Had I realized it, the arrangement for chemical intelligence was to provide in effect a 'control experiment' by which its merits and defects could be compared with my own arrangements where we in scientific intelligence came to regard the experts on our own side as our spies on the laws of nature and the state of current technology, as explained in Chapter 8. The Porton arrangement, by contrast, made the experts at Porton the final authorities on what the Germans were doing, with intelligence being gathered under their instructions.

The upshot was that while we in scientific intelligence detected most of the new German applications of science to warfare, the nerve gases seem not to have been picked up by the Porton arrangement. The reason was that, as I tended to labour in *Most Secret War* regarding the beam radar and rockets, the experts had placed themselves in an incorrect relation to intelligence. In fairness to them, they may have found so little expertise in pre-war intelligence that they were forced to do as much as possible themselves.

Their failure is the more notable because there had been occasional reports of 'nerve gases' in Germany in 1940. On 31 July 1940 I myself noted in a more general monthly report that I sent to the Director of Scientific Research in the Air Ministry,

> There have been several reports, none of which is thought to be reliable, of a gas which is alternatively known as 'sleeping', 'stupefying' or 'paralysing'. These may have originated from 'Nerven gas' which has also been reported twice; this is almost certainly an aberration, indicating the arsenicals.[21]

The foregoing interpretation was that placed on the reports by the experts at Porton, and I was merely reporting it to my Director as a matter of general interest since as far as both of us were concerned we were on the sidelines. The passage shows that nerve gases had been reported, but incorrectly assessed by our own experts in the light of their experience, and this did not extend to the necessary discovery.

Had a competent intelligence officer been responsible he might have queried the experts' discounting of the reports. Although they were too nebulous to be used as a basis for an intelligence warning to the operational staff, and they might have been simply deceptive propaganda, hindsight shows that they contained a vital element of truth and were worth more than a summary dismissal.

Fortunately, the episode did not result in any disaster for our defence, as it might have done, and we were lucky to have this bloodless demonstration of the danger of leaving the guiding and interpretation of intelligence solely to experts in the nearest research field in our own country, however competent they may be.

Youth and Age

In one of our reflective moments during the war I remarked to my colleague, Charles Frank, 'Charles, I wonder what you and I may be doing in the next war!' His response was that we should probably be in senior positions such as Lindemann and Tizard then had, while young men such as we then were would be having all the excitement.

Events have from time to time reminded me of that reply, one of the more recent being the meeting with Werner Flos mentioned above, on page 222. He and I were within a few months of the same age, and in his early thirties he was the leading engineer responsible for the design and construction of the massive concrete V-bunkers. Wernher von Braun was also of exactly the same age, and he was both the inventor and the driving force behind the V2 rocket, with all that it presaged for the exploitation of space. Adolf Galland, too, was our age to within a few months, and by 1944 he was commanding the entire German dayfighter force.

I doubt whether any of us thought much about our youth at the time; it was only when I heard senior scientists who had visited the radar or atomic energy establishments commenting on the fact that they were staffed by very young men that I thought about the matter at all.

The examples of von Braun, Flos and Galland show that the encouragement of youth was by no means a uniquely British characteristic. If anything, despite the precedent of the younger Pitt, the tendency in Britain might have been the other way but for Churchill himself. He had been in Cabinet posts in his early thirties, and he had seen the need for those in high positions to draw on the experiences of the young men 'at the sharp end'. 'It is no use,' he reproved the Chief Whip of the Conservative Party in the 1920s, 'being intolerant of young men.' He himself was always ready to listen to us.

There were two distinct features to the contribution we could make. First there was the 'sharp end' experience such as Churchill and Lloyd George had drawn upon in 1917 by listening to the younger naval officers who were doing the actual fighting in the U-boat war. The second feature came from the fact that youth is the phase during which new ideas are most likely to occur. Writing of the years 1665 and 1666 Isaac Newton, who was born in 1642, reflected, 'In those days I was in the prime of my age for invention, and minded mathematics and philosophy more than at any time since.' Although there are some distinguished exceptions, most of us – albeit on an incomparably humbler plane – find that our experiences accord with Newton's.

As so often, Francis Bacon had seen the ways in which youth could best contribute:

> Young men are fitter to invent than to judge, fitter for execution than for counsel, and fitter for new projects than for settled business.[22]

If such a division could be rigorously obeyed, there would be little conflict between youth and age; but differences in viewpoint there will always be, and they must be resolved as occasion demands. It helps if, as Bacon also saw, men can be found who are 'young in years' but 'old in hours' – 'But that happeneth rarely'. In retrospect, the senior officers of the Royal Air Force were remarkably tolerant of our youth; and we would have to admit that youth was not always right. In particular, in the 'big wing' controversy which contributed to the removal of Sir Hugh Dowding from his post as Commander-in-Chief of Fighter Command, it is hard to sustain the thesis that he was wrong in not supporting the 'big wing' idea advanced by the much younger Douglas Bader, even though it was the latter who had the 'sharp end' experience.

Dowding's policy was to try to intercept German bombers on their way in to their targets. This necessarily meant that they were attacked by the small number of fighters which could be 'scrambled' in time to intercept them. Bader, by contrast, wanted to assemble large formations of fighters for attack. This required time and so the bombers would be primarily attacked on their way home from their targets. Bader could point to the heavy losses that could thus be inflicted on the bombers, as assessed from the fighter pilots' claims by his 'Duxford Wing'. But while these claims were accepted at the time they were wildly in excess of German casualties – part of the excess being doubtless due to more than one fighter attacking the same raider and thus claiming credit for its destruction. On 18 September 1940, for example, the Wing claimed to have destroyed thirty aircraft when the German records showed four, and on 9 September nineteen Dornier 17s when the German records showed none.[23]

The Dowding case is a salutary warning that while youth is often right, especially in the directions indicated by Bacon, it is not necessarily so, as those of us who have fortunately survived to look back on our efforts of fifty years ago would have to admit. But equally we would hope that the youth of any future age will be granted opportunities no less than those which we ourselves enjoyed.

Memory and History

We have seen the limitations in history compiled exclusively from documentary records (see above, page 81), but there are complementary dangers in depending too much on the personal memories of participants in events, enlightening though these may often be. Two examples that I myself encountered may therefore be of some interest, especially since they involved two of the great figures of World War II, Lord Dowding and Sir Henry Tizard.

When Robert Wright's biography of Lord Dowding was published in 1969, some of us could hardly believe Dowding's account of his abrupt dismissal as Commander-in-Chief, Fighter Command, in November 1940:

> I received a sudden phone call at my Headquarters from the Secretary of State for Air. He told me that I was to relinquish my Command immediately.[24]

Among others, Marshal of the Royal Air Force Sir John Slessor and I thought that Sir Archibald Sinclair, the Secretary of State for Air with whom we had both worked, was so naturally courteous that he would never have dismissed a Commander-in-Chief in so curt a fashion, let alone one who had just won such a vital battle in our history. Slessor[25] and I[26] both expressed our doubts in letters to *The Times*, only to be met by an emphatic letter from Lord Dowding himself confirming his biographer's accout:

> He has recorded correctly and exactly the experiences that were mine and the views that are held by me. The actions that were taken by others were far too deeply and, if I may say so, grievously imprinted on my mind for me ever to forget them.[27]

There the matter might have rested, but by coincidence the historian A. J. P. Taylor was currently working on the biography of Lord Beaverbrook, and so came across a letter dated 14 November 1940 from Sinclair to Beaverbrook, describing an interview that Sinclair had had on 13 November with Dowding in the Air Ministry to inform him of the Air Council's decision to move him from Fighter Command. Part of the letter ran:

> I wished to express to him, in no perfunctory way, my appreciation of his great services as Commander-in-Chief of the Fighter Command. Nevertheless, I had come to the conclusion that it was right to make the change which this new project would involve.[28]

Assuming that the Air Council had taken the decision, this is exactly the manner in which we would have expected Sinclair to handle the unhappy situation: Taylor's discovery of the letter put the fact of a personal meeting beyond argument.

The removal of Dowding in the military field had a near parallel with the ousting of Tizard in favour of Lindemann in the scientific field during the same period. Tizard and Lindemann had once been good friends, but had become rivals in the years before 1939; and it was generally assumed that the rivalry had arisen in 1935 over the headship of the scientific effort in support of air defence. I myself, though, had wondered whether the explanation might lie in a failure by Tizard to use his administrative weight in London to promote Lindemann's interest (or so Lindemann might have thought), perhaps when he wanted grants for his laboratory or a seat on one or more committees in London.

After C. P. Snow's *Science and Government* appeared in 1961,[29] *The Times* asked me to set out what I knew of the Lindemann–Tizard relationship.[30] It happened that, with Sir William Farren, I had had to write the biographical memoir of Tizard for the Royal Society, and in the course of it Tizard's son, Professor J. P. M. Tizard, gave me access to his father's unfinished autobiography. I was therefore gratified to find, in Tizard's own words, and at the very point at which the narrative broke off, exactly what I had surmised. Speaking of his relationship with Lindemann he described how, despite his support,

> The Aeronautical Research Council refused to have Lindemann as a member, although he was at the Royal Aircraft Establishment, during the war of 1914/18, and, hence well known to many of the members. I think this may have influenced his subsequent behaviour.[31]

So here it was – or so it seemed. At the same time, however, I was also trying to check a story that throughout the war Lindemann had kept in his safe, as a final 'shot in the locker' in his battle with Tizard, a copy of a report by Tizard turning down the proposal for a jet engine in the early 1930s. I could hardly believe that Tizard would have done so, and could only surmise that – at most – something that he had said could be malevolently misinterpreted.

This turned out to be true. The jet idea had been proposed to the Engine Sub-Committee of the ARC of which Tizard was chairman, and in 1926 the Sub-Committee had cautiously proposed that a test rig should be built at Farnborough before full-scale development should be undertaken. This rig showed enough promise for a further rig to be recommended by the Sub-Committee in 1930, even though doubts had been expressed concerning the ability of current materials to withstand the operating conditions in a jet engine. Little was thereafter done at Farnborough because, it seems, A. A. Griffith, the very distinguished scientist/engineer there who had proposed the development (which was for an axial-flow design and so a forerunner of modern jets in contrast to the radial-flow of Whittle's engine), was discouraged by what he interpreted as merely luke-warm support from the Sub-Committee, and so dropped the work in favour of others of his fertile interests.

All this came to light as a result of my asking the Secretary of the Aeronautical Research Council in 1961, R. O. Gandy, to look into the records. It seemed that we could perhaps have had a jet engine even before one materialized through Whittle's independent efforts, but Tizard's record in the episode was blameless; indeed he appears to have considered that 'there seemed to be no fundamental reason why success should not be achieved, despite discouraging evidence on the part of some of the experts'.[32]

While the record therefore exonerated Tizard in the sense I had expected, Gandy's investigation also produced a shock, as his letter[33] showed:

> As a preliminary, you might wish to note that Prof. Lindemann (as he then was) was a member of the Aeronautical Research Committee continuously for 6 years from April, 1926 to March, 1932, at which date

> he was replaced by Prof. (now Sir) Geoffrey Taylor. I was somewhat puzzled by the statement in one of your recent special articles in *The Times* which appeared to me to give the impression that Lindemann had never been a member of the A.R.C. and that he held Tizard responsible for not having pressed his claims for membership. Mr. Tizard (as he then was) was a member of the Aeronautical Research Committee and Chairman of its Engine Sub-Committee throughout the period when Prof. Lindemann was a member.

So Lindemann had been a member of the Aeronautical Research Committee for six years, and Tizard was also a member throughout the same period; and the minutes showed many meetings when they were present together. Somehow, Tizard's normally excellent memory had for once gone adrift; and, as also with Dowding, death deprived him of any chance to check it.

The common feature of the Dowding and Tizard experiences was that each had been grievously hurt by his treatment. The hurt appears somehow to have blocked the facts, and memory to have subconsciously substituted an alternative account. Without theorizing too far about the subconscious process in either case, I note a tendency for my own memory to 'round-off' the rough corners of experience or even, occasionally, to reverse the chronological order in which two events occurred. Since such reversals could sometimes make one's own past actions appear in a better light, the temptation to do so needs stringent monitoring by reference to impartial records. More generally, though, the subconscious process may have no more questionable an aim than to order past events into a coherent theme which is easily remembered and hence recounted, just as a random series of words or numbers can be more easily recalled if they can be linked into a coherent sequence or pattern. Indeed, the search of science for the laws of nature may be the highest expression of this same human tendency to seek for unities between events.

Part Three

10

The Oslo Report: Its Contribution to Intelligence

Most Secret War related how one evening in November 1939 Fred Winterbotham, the head of the Air section of MI6, came into my office and put a package on my desk saying, 'Here is a present for you!' It had been forwarded to MI6 by the British Legation in Oslo, where it had been received a few days before by our Naval Attaché, Captain Hector Boyes. The package contained several pages of typescript in German, to which the Legation had added its English translation, and a small cardboard box separately wrapped. A glance was enough to tell that the typescript referred to various applications of science to warfare, and this was why Winterbotham was handing it over to me.

I asked him whether he knew how it had come to be sent to us, and he told me that he understood that the anonymous sender had first inquired whether we would like to be informed of new scientific developments in Germany. If so, we should make some minor change in the preamble to our BBC broadcast to Germany such as saying, 'Hullo, hier ist London!' instead of whatever had been the previous opening, and the unknown writer would then send his information. The story sounded odd in that, if he believed he had valuable information, why did he not send it immediately instead of waiting for an indication that we should be interested? I was merely told that the requested change in the broadcast had been duly made and here was the package.

Most Secret War did not give the full text of the original typescript, because it might have contained some clue to the authorship which I myself had not detected, but which might have narrowed the search for the author by someone with unfriendly intentions. I have since found that there is at least one such clue, but in the meantime the full text has been published by the Official Historians in Volume 1 of *British Intelligence in the Second World War* and so there is now no need for further restraint in a critical discussion of the text of the Report and the extent to which it enlightened us about German developments in technology applied to warfare. That is the main purpose of the present chapter, which will also indicate some internal clues in the Report that may point towards the identity of its author.

The Contents of the Oslo Report

The full text of the English translation is reprinted in Appendix A. The translation was dated 4 November 1939, and its items may be summarized:

1. The Ju88 is a two-engined long-range bomber capable of dive-bombing. Production rate probably 5,000 per month.
2. The *Franken* is the first German aircraft-carrier. It is currently being completed in Kiel.
3. Remote-controlled glider bombs with code number FZ21 are being developed at Peenemünde by the German navy, with electric altimeters and rocket propulsion, so that they would skim the surface of the sea and strike the side of a ship.
4. Another pilotless aircraft FZ10 is being developed, to be controlled from a manned aircraft for use against targets such as balloon barrages.
5. Eighty-centimetre calibre rockets are being developed with built-in gyroscopes for use against the Maginot Line. Currently they are prone to fly in uncontrollable curves.
6. Research for the *Luftwaffe* is conducted at Rechlin, which should be a profitable target for bombing.
7. Polish gun emplacements were first blinded with smoke and then the crews overcome by flame-throwers.
8. German radar equipment with 10-microsecond pulses had detected the British air raid on Wilhelmshaven at a range of 120 kilometres. The radar could be jammed once its wavelength has been ascertained by listening for its transmissions. Another form of radar also exists, working on 50-centimetre wavelength.
9. A new radio method of establishing the distance of a friendly bomber from its base has been developed at Rechlin by sending out a continuous modulated transmission on about a 6-metre wavelength which is received by the bomber, and transmitted back to base on a slightly different wavelength. From the phase delay in the modulated signal arriving back at base, the distance of the bomber can be determined. Further technical details were given.
10. Torpedoes both with remote radio control and acoustic homing have been developed. They could be countered by radio or acoustic jamming. Another type of torpedo is designed to pass under a ship and be fired by a magnetic fuse operated by the change of magnetic

field below the ship. This was probably the type that sank the *Royal Oak*. It could be countered by a current-carrying cable suspended around the ship.

11 Mechanical fuses in bombs have been replaced by electrical ones, based on the charging and discharge of capacitances. A proximity fuse is being developed for anti-aircraft shells in which the capacitance formed between two halves of a shell is changed by the proximity of a third body such as an aircraft; the same effect could be used to explode a shell at a predetermined height above the ground. This new kind of fuse has required the development of an electronic trigger tube, a sample of which is enclosed in the accompanying package.

Having read the Report, I decided – rather gingerly – to open the package. It might have been a small bomb set to detonate on opening, but the Report seemed so genuine as to suggest that there was little risk. Inside I found the trigger tube exactly as described, and I immediately took it to my former colleagues at the Admiralty Research Laboratory for them to investigate its performance. This proved to be much better than anything we had available in Britain.

Most Secret War described how even with this evidence of good faith, there was much scepticism in Whitehall regarding the genuineness of the information. In fact, although it was circulated to the service ministries, it was either disregarded or completely forgotten within a short time, except for my own interest and conviction that it was genuine.

Loopholes for Scepticism

There were some improbable items in the Report which offered grounds for scepticism. The alleged rate of production of Ju88s was far in excess of actuality: instead of 5,000 per month, the most optimistic planned production in August 1939 was 300 per month.[1] On the other hand, the statement that the Ju88 was to be capable of dive-bombing was correct, although it had not been reported by any other source, and it was this requirement, added at Udet's insistence, that had delayed the final development of the 'wonderbomber' of which Goering had declared in 1938, 'I want a powerful force of Ju88 bombers in the shortest time possible!' All this suggests that the Oslo writer, in contrast with other matters of which he had direct experience, was reporting what he had been led to believe by exaggerated stories circulating in German technical circles and arising from Goering's enthusiasm and Udet's conception.

Another discrepancy which puzzled me for years was the statement that the first German aircraft-carrier was to be the *Franken* and that she was being fitted out in Kiel. In fact, the first carrier was to be the *Graf Zeppelin*, so what was the origin of the erroneous statement? The puzzle was ultimately solved thanks to the German naval historian, Professor Jürgen Rohwer. The *Franken* was indeed fitting out in Kiel, at the Deutsche Werke, with the yard number 258, but she was a sister to the supply ship *Altmark* from which British prisoners were spectacularly released in Norwegian waters by HMS *Cossack* – 'The Navy's here' – in February 1940. How could a source who was to prove so right in so many of his statements have been so wrong regarding the ship? The answer appears to have been a simple confusion, for at the same time as the *Franken* was fitting out, the *Graf Zeppelin* was also in the same yard, with yard number 252. The writer had presumably heard that the aircraft-carrier was being fitted out, and had either seen or been told that the *Franken* was in the yard and concluded that this was the carrier.

Such doubts and obscurities, though, were minuscule in comparison with the air of authority and technical competence which in general suffused the Report. It was methodically set out, and the author must have almost certainly been an engineer or a physicist with inside knowledge of most of the developments that he was describing, or someone else who was in his confidence and writing at his instruction. Moreover, his knowledge was particularly detailed in electronics and radio propagation. Although his Report was largely discounted in Whitehall as a German 'plant' on the grounds that it was unlikely that any one man in Germany would have had access to so many technical secrets, and that it must therefore be an overdone concoction perpetrated by German intelligence to mislead us, I decided to trust it.

The Phoney War ensued, and there was so little information coming in from the standard sources of intelligence that I could not check any of the items that the Report had described; and when at last intelligence did begin to flow in, leading to the discovery that the Germans had developed the *Knickebein* and X radio-beam systems by which they could bomb targets at night in Britain, it was a development which had not even been hinted at in the Oslo Report. This therefore played no part in my air scientific intelligence report, 'The Crooked Leg', of 30 June 1940, which described the *Knickebein* system and which enabled countermeasures to be developed just in time for the opening of the Blitz in September.

Knickebein

Incidentally 'Crooked Leg' or 'Dog-leg' was a translation of '*Knickebein*', and we have never been sure of why the Germans so named their first beam system. Perhaps they were wise enough to have no reason at all, because secrets have sometimes been given away by code-names which have some hidden connection with the purpose of the equipments to which they refer. One possible connection is that the antennae of some of the *Knickebein* transmitters were carried on cross-beams which were bent after the manner of a lance-corporal's stripe, or a shallow dog-leg. In fact, the historian of German radio and radar developments, Fritz Trenkle, has stated that this was indeed the origin of the code-name,[2] and gives the further information that the angle between the arms of the shallow vee was 165°.

Most Secret War also mentioned that *Knickebein* was the name of a German cocktail: within a month of the book's publication I received a letter from Herr Helmut Drubba, librarian in the Technical University of Hanover, confirming that this was indeed so, and giving the derivation of the name, quoting in particular F. Kluge's *Etymologisches Wörterbuch der deutschen Sprache* and *Der Grosse Brockhaus*,[3] which state that it was a layered drink invented by a student in the University of Jena around 1840, the layers being of different colours and formed by careful pourings of various alcoholic drinks with differing densities. When mixed, the result had a flavour so pleasing that it became popular not only as a drink but also as the flavouring in the filling of chocolate-cream Easter eggs. Because the student–inventor was a cripple with a 'gammy' leg, he had been nicknamed '*Knickebein*' by his fellow students, and the nickname became attached to his invention. In further confirmation Herr Drubba enclosed the foil wrapping of an Easter egg, bearing the legend '*Knickebein*'.

He had also enclosed copies of an entry in a survey of the alcoholic spectrum, entitled *The Dictionary of Drink and Drinking* by O. A. Mendelsohn, and, in writing to thank him for this profound erudition, I expressed the hope that one day he and I might meet and jointly explore some of the other entries in *The Dictionary* in a practical way. His prompt reply began, 'Under separate cover I am sending you some real *Knickebein* chocolate Easter eggs. It has been quite a task still getting them a few days after Easter – in fact they were on sale at a greatly reduced price. Please, accept them with my compliments.' He, too, hoped that we might meet, and I have often since been grateful for both his scholarship and his friendship.

Oslo and the Revival of the Edda

Although the Oslo Report had played no part in alerting us to the existence of *Knickebein*, which might be described as the 'Mark I' model of the German beam-bombing systems or of 'Mark II', the X-beams, it was shortly to prove its value in helping us to discern the underlying principles of 'Mark III' well in advance of this more sophisticated version being used in operations. On 27 June, only six days after we had confirmed the existence and nature of *Knickebein*, Bletchley decrypted an Enigma signal saying that our opponents intended to set up *'Knickebein und Wotan'* installations near Cherbourg and Brest. So, what was Wotan? Presumably, from the context, it was somehow allied with *Knickebein*; could it therefore be another beam system? Was there a clue in its code-name? Was there anything special about Wotan? I telephoned my Bletchley colleague, Professor F. ('Bimbo') Norman. 'He was head of the German gods,' he replied, 'Wait a moment . . . he had only one eye' – and then, shouting triumphantly – 'ONE EYE – ONE BEAM! Can you think of a system that would use only one beam?' It was then that I remembered the Oslo Report – one beam pointing over the target, plus the radio ranging system described in the Report for measuring the distance of a bomber along the beam from the transmitter, would enable the bomber to be told when it was approaching the target, and indeed when to drop its bombs.

I wrote up this deduction in a report of 17 July 1940 under the title of 'The Edda Revived', for besides the mention of Wotan in one Enigma decrypt there had been mention of Freya, the Nordic Venus, in another. From various clues, including the fact that she had a necklace that was guarded by Heimdall, a watchman who could see a hundred miles by day or night, and what the Oslo Report had told us about the existence of German radar, I concluded that Freya was indeed one of the radar equipments which it had mentioned.

Direct quotations from 'The Edda Revived' will indicate my assessment of the Oslo Report in July 1940, and the significance of these items of its information:

> A careful review of the whole report leaves only two possible conclusions: (1) that it was a 'plant' to persuade us that the Germans were as well advanced as ourselves, or (2) that the source was genuinely disaffected from Germany, and wished to tell us all he knew. The general accuracy of the information, the gratuitous presentation of the fuse, and the fact that the source made no effort, as far as is known, to exploit the matter, together with the subsequent course of the war and our recent awakening with Knickebein, weigh heavily in favour of the second conclusion. It seems, then, that the source was reliable, and he was manifestly competent.
>
> The contribution of this source to the present problem may be summarised in the statements that the Germans were bringing into use an RDF system similar to our own, and that they were developing a radio method of distance determination for their own aircraft involving an amplified reflected wave.[4]

This latter contribution was shortly to prove valuable in anticipating the third phase of the 'Battle of the Beams'. The dominant feature of the first phase was the attempt of the main bomber force of the *Luftwaffe* to bomb its targets at night using the *Knickebein* beams; but our jamming made these difficult to use, and Feldmarschall Milch had advised Goering that, without such aids, 'On dark nights only the largest targets can effectively be found; in my view the effect on all other targets is about a fifth of a daylight attack.'[5] He advised that the specialist unit *Kampfgruppe* 100 with its advanced X-beam system should receive priority in personnel and aircraft.

The higher frequencies used in the X-beams required us to build new jammers, and, in the meantime, *KGr* 100 was locating its targets unhindered. The Germans therefore decided on the obvious step of making the *KGr* 100 crews into pathfinders by arranging for them to lead the nightly attack and drop incendiary bombs to raise fires in the target area which could then be seen and bombed by the main force. After a few minor trials, in October 1940, the technique was first used on a major scale in the attack on Coventry on 14/15 November 1940; this marked the beginning of the second phase which lasted until the X-beams could be effectively jammed. Owing to various British misfortunes this was rarely achieved before January 1941.

The Blitz, Phase III

Believing, nevertheless, that sooner or later we would succeed in jamming the X-beams, which with their added sophistication and accuracy could be fairly regarded as 'Mark II' in beam development, we had to contemplate what system the Germans would use in Mark III. Thanks to the Oslo information and the lucky (although erroneous) deduction of a single-beam system from the code-name Wotan, we thought it likely that the next phase would be based on such a system, and we therefore searched for radio transmissions that had the characteristics foreshadowed by the detailed information from Oslo.

As early as October we had learnt from Enigma that there was a system known as 'Y', which we assumed to be a successor to X, and it seemed to be able to mark a target in England from a single station in France, whereas X always required at least two well separated, to give beams that crossed over or near the target. Could Y therefore have a single beam plus the Oslo ranging system? We duly searched the aether, and we heard a new beam being tried, and also transmissions in the waveband and with the modulation almost exactly as described in the Oslo Report. The aircraft involved were not those of *Kampfgruppe* 100, but of the Third *Gruppe* of *Kampf Geschwader* 26 (III *KG* 26). Before they were ready to use the Y-system in serious operations we were ready to deal with it, adapting the television transmitter at Alexandra Palace for the purpose. Moreover, thanks to the timely warning, our countermeasures to Phase III could be more subtle, with the result that at first some of the German crews thought that faults had developed in their receivers rather than that they were being jammed.

Although the Y-system was capable of great accuracy it was so upset by our countermeasures that, as described in *Most Secret War*,[6] the Germans found that they could not rely on III *KGr* 26 to take over from *KGr* 100 now that the latter could be jammed. In general, the only targets that the *Luftwaffe* could attack with confidence from January onwards were London, which was too big to miss, or those in the south which could be approached along a beam over the English Channel where its signals were too strong to be jammed, for example Portsmouth and Plymouth, or were otherwise situated on or near a coast or estuary whose outline could be seen in moonlight, such as Bristol, Cardiff, Liverpool, Glasgow and Belfast. Many of our inland towns therefore have the Oslo Report partly to thank for their respite from bombing in the third phase of the Blitz from January until its end in May 1941; coastal targets still suffered heavily, but there were no more Coventrys.

Guided Bombs

The success that came from trusting the Oslo Report in anticipating the Y-system strengthened our confidence in its genuine nature even further. In commenting in May 1941 on some information that had come from an entirely different source about a project to develop a bomb with a television head which would enable the bomb to be steered to its target – this information was correct but, as we expected, the technical difficulties were too great until after the war – we summarized what we then knew about German developments in remotely controlled missiles, and I referred to the Oslo Report in the following terms:

> it may be noted that the Oslo source who in his single reported date 4-11-39 gave correct early warning of a larger number of experimental German weapons than any other secret source yet known to us, mentioned (in what appears to be his tallest story) remote-controlled rocket-driven gliders . . .[7]

Once again the information was correct – these missiles were being developed by Bloem and Voss under the designation BV143, with instrumentation by the firms of Anschutz, Askania, Patin and Siemens among others. They were six metres in length and wingspan rather than the three metres of the Report, but they had the foreshadowed altimeter to enable them to skim at about two to three metres above the surface. Although the BV143 was discarded in favour of later developments, the basic ideas materialized in other missiles, the BV246 and the HS293; the latter scored successes against British and American ships in the Mediterranean and the Bay of Biscay.

The V-weapons

Regarding the Germans' most spectacular wartime weapon, the long-range rocket, I had to summarize the evidence of its existence on 26 June 1943 in a report to the Defence Committee of the War Cabinet, and once again turned to the Oslo Report. 'The first pointer', I wrote,

> that Peenemünde was the seat of rocket development came from the remarkable Oslo Report of November 1939. This source, who has since proved correct in almost everything that he described, said that wireless controlled rocket gliders were being tried there, for use against ships; their secret number was FZ21 (Ferngesteuerte Zielflugzeug). He also

> said that rocket shells 80 cms. in diameter were being developed for use against the Maginot Line; they were gyrostabilised, but at that time were prone to fly in uncontrollable curves, and so radio remote-control was being considered.

On 25 September 1943, in a further paper for the same committee, when discussing Lord Cherwell's suggestion that the large rocket story was a hoax, I reported:

> The Germans in 1939 could hardly have been contemplating a hoax four years ahead, nor has there been any suspicion of a hoax in any part of the very competent Oslo Report, which has proved a valuable guide in many fields of Scientific Intelligence. It is therefore probable that in 1939 the Germans were developing a large rocket, and experiencing control troubles.

When the V2 (or A4) rocket appeared in 1942 it did indeed have both gyro- and in some cases radio-control; but it was not 80 but 165 centimetres in diameter. The 1939 version, though, was not the A4 but the smaller A5 whose diameter was 77 centimetres, so the Oslo source was correct at the time of writing.

I was reminded again in September 1943 of the Oslo Report when we heard from Enigma of a new weapon, FZG76, later known as the flying bomb. Although we knew that 'FZG' stood for *Flak Ziel Gerät*, the letters FZ had occurred twice in the Oslo letter – FZ10 and FZ21, and I even noted that 10, 21 and 76 could all be expressed as (11n-1) – this turned out to be no more than coincidence. In fact, when I remarked the FZ occurrence many years later to the historian of German radio developments, Fritz Trenkle, he pointed out to me in his letter of 7 October 1982 that, whereas 'FZG' was an official designation, 'The FZ-designations were not official, but internal Siemens designations'.

Finally, in April 1946 I had to summarize my experiences with the various channels of intelligence for a projected official history of air intelligence, and one of these channels was what we termed 'casual sources' of which one type

> is often called into play by a national emergency such as the outbreak of war when someone writes to a Cabinet Minister, Service Chief, or Attaché abroad, giving details of something which they believe to be of importance to national defence. They are sometimes valueless, but in October 1939 [actually November] one of the most brilliant intelligence reports received throughout the war arrived from such a source. He

> (or perhaps she) sent in a letter to our Naval Attaché in Oslo . . . We have never discovered who the source was, but the Oslo Report is a sufficient example to show that casual sources should not be treated flippantly. It was probably the best single report received from any source during the war.

Nearly half a century later, I would still stand by this assessment, although it should not be misinterpreted to imply that no other contribution to scientific intelligence was as great as that contained in the Oslo Report. Overall, of course, the contributions of other sources such as the Enigma decrypts, aerial photographs, and reports from the Resistance, outweighed the Oslo contribution, but these were all made by organizations involving many, sometimes thousands of individuals and operating throughout most of the war. The Oslo Report, we believed, had been written by a single individual who in one great flash had given us a synoptic glimpse of much of what was foreshadowed in German military electronics.

11

In Search of an Author

The direct quotations from my wartime reports in the previous chapter will show how valuable I considered the Oslo Report to be at the time, without any sentimentality or other tinge of hindsight arising from subsequent knowledge of who had written it or his reasons for doing so. Clearly his information of electronic developments was much deeper than that in other fields: he appeared to be a 'professional' working in the region where electronic physics and engineering overlapped, with an easy command both of the necessary mathematics and of the professional literature, to judge by his use of formulae and reference to the *Bell System Technical Journal*. His confusion between the *Franken* and the *Graf Zeppelin*, and the exaggeration of the Ju88 production, suggested that outside electronics his knowledge depended more on hearsay evidence. At the same time the report was admirably set out and impressively concise, and it was obviously the work of a powerful, clear mind.

This much could be deduced about the author at the time. As for what his position then was, we could only guess. With hindsight, the 'FZ' references might have been a clue, but their significance was not then known to us. Naturally, we wondered whether the author had survived the war but, if so, he did not come forward. Our hopes had at one time been excited by a message that came to us seemingly from Germany which referred to a phrase, '*Das Haus steht am Hügel*' ('The house is on the hill'), and suggested that we should insert it in the BBC German broadcast when we required information on technical developments. Could this be the Oslo author trying to re-establish contact? Little, though, seemed to come of it; as far as I can recall we tried putting various questions over the air but these went unanswered, and we assumed that contact had been lost.

Hindsight based on Fritz Trenkle's valuable series of histories of German wartime radio developments might also suggest where to look for the author. He was clearly doing his best to inform us and yet he had said nothing about the beams. These had been developed between Rechlin (which he did mention as a rewarding target without giving any details of the work there) and the firms of Telefunken and Lorenz; it was therefore less than probable that he worked either at Rechlin or in one of these firms. By contrast, he gave valuable details of the Y-ranging system, which was developed between Rechlin and Siemens.

A further pointer to the military/industrial environment in which the author worked may be suggested by his description of the proximity fuse based on change of capacitance, since Fritz Trenkle has recorded, in *Die deutschen Funkenverfahren*,[1] that this was developed under the code-name *Kuhglocke* (cowbell) at the Technische Hochschule in Darmstadt and in the firm of Rheinmetall, which the author specifically mentioned as responsible for the normal electrical bomb fuses.

Another technical detail that might have been a clue to the location of the author was his description of the 'delay line' method of precise distance measurement in the radar system, in which the returning pulse is matched with one that has travelled through a calibrated delay line; but although this was more sophisticated than our own technique it was common to the major radar firms in Germany, and therefore of no help as a clue.

After the war I saw an opportunity to let the author know how valuable his Report had been, and give him the chance to declare himself, if he were still alive. This was on 12 February 1947 when, at Henry Tizard's suggestion, I had to address the Royal United Services Institution on scientific intelligence, where among other aspects I discussed casual sources and in particular the value of the Oslo contribution. But although the story made headline news in papers both in Britain and abroad, no author came forward. It seemed that he was either dead or in some position where he preferred to remain unknown or, perhaps, where such news could not reach him.

The RUSI lecture, though, did reach one of the important figures in the story – Admiral Hector Boyes, who, as a captain, had been the Naval Attaché in Oslo in 1939 who had received the Report and forwarded it to London. In a letter dated 21 February 1947 he wrote:

> I was very much interested to read in *The Times* a résumé of your lecture at the United Services Institution.

> Whilst serving as Naval Attaché Oslo I remember receiving the German letters.
>
> At that period one was inundated with various anonymous correspondence which it was necessary to sift.
>
> On translating the German correspondence there appeared to be matters of interest though one had a certain mistrust, the letters having been posted in Norway.
>
> On arrival home after the evacuation I asked about the correspondence without much result. I forgot about it, having been appointed to Japan. Your lecture shows that the writer was genuine – Is there any chance of his being Norwegian? At one period I was in touch with a Norwegian engineer who had been working in Germany on U- and E-boats.
>
> One thing against it being him is that the letters were written in excellent German.
>
> The glass tube mentioned – as far as I can remember that was sent to shew his reliability.

In reply to my response, he wrote on 2 April 1947:

> I did not mention to you that the German letters arrived and the last one asked if any more information was required; if so to alter the German broadcast, which was done but nothing more came in and so I thought that the informant had been liquidated.

Apart from testifying to the little interest that had been taken in London in the contents of the Oslo Report, the Admiral's statements, admittedly recollections seven years after its reception, show that, (1) it arrived in the form of letters through the post; (2) these had been posted in Norway; (3) there were at least two letters and perhaps, if the Admiral's English was strict, three or more; and (4) the author's native language was probably German. The Admiral's second letter also makes better sense of the otherwise puzzling instruction about altering the preamble to the BBC German broadcast.

Unfortunately the trail then ran cold and I, too, tended to assume that 'the informant had been liquidated'. This, of course, did not stop others from theorizing about his identity, and in this chapter I will outline those speculations that most merit consideration.

False Trails: Kummerow and Rosbaud

It was natural that over the years there would be speculation concerning the identity and motive of the Oslo author. With his letter of 2 April

1947 Admiral Boyes sent me a cutting from a Norwegian newspaper which ascribed the Report to the work of a group with the name of the 'Domino Ring'. The newspaper said that the Ring had had sources in Germany and that its information had been smuggled out of Germany, via Denmark, by two Americans, one of them being an employee of an oil company who stayed at the Hotel Bristol in Oslo in September–October 1939. The cutting also gave a photograph which was claimed to show the oil man outside the hotel. I had to return the cutting to Admiral Boyes but Mr Stein Ulrich, the Deputy Director of the Norwegian Security Service, has traced it to the *Morgenbladet* daily edition for 22 February 1947, and has sent me a copy of the article. The photograph is amply clear enough to show that its subject bears no resemblance to the genuine author of the Oslo Report although, as we shall see, the latter did stay in the Hotel Bristol some weeks later. 'The Domino Ring', too, appears to have been a false trail, for nothing about it has come to notice in Norwegian, German or British records. The Norwegian Security Service has also searched for the Hotel's guest register for the period concerned but this cannot now be found.

It was to be expected that other journalists besides the author of the *Morgenbladet* article would also attempt to solve the Oslo mystery. In 1954 Ian Colvin, the Foreign Editor of the *Sunday Express*, and later Deputy Editor of the *Daily Telegraph*, saw it as a challenge. His investigative powers were formidable, and Churchill had named him in the first volume of his war memoirs as one of his principal pre-war agents for keeping in touch with German affairs. 'He plunged very deeply into German politics,' wrote Churchill in *The Gathering Storm*, 'and established contacts of a most secret character with some of the important German generals, and also with independent men of character and quality in Germany who saw in the Hitler Movement the approaching ruin of their native land.'[2]

After the war Colvin's 'nose' for a story led him to think that there was more than mere fiction behind a novel that had been written by Duff Cooper under the title *Operation Heartbreak* which told of an important deception on German intelligence regarding our strategy in the Mediterranean. The key instrument of deception in this matter was a dead body dressed in the uniform of a major in the Royal Marines, launched from a submarine and carrying bogus documents suggesting that the Allies would next land in Greece or Sardinia rather than Sicily which was their true objective. Since, according to the novel, the body had been recovered and examined by the Spanish and the Germans, and then interred in a local cemetery after it had been washed ashore, Colvin set out to check his hunch that this was true by working his way around the coastal cemeteries in Spain and in due course he found one which did contain a grave which purported to be that of a Royal Marine major.

Colvin wrote up his story in 1951, but was threatened with the Official Secrets Act if he published. In the meantime, the Joint Intelligence Committee decided that the secret could not be kept much longer, and invited Euan Montagu, who as a Naval intelligence officer had been involved in the deception plot, to write a book about it. The book came out as *The Man Who Never Was* and deprived Colvin of all that he might have gained from his own book. As for Duff Cooper, the officer who originated the deception plan – Flight Lieutenant Charles Cholmondley – told me that the author had secured immunity from prosecution for the original disclosure by threatening to go into the witness box and declare that the story had been told to him, with no warning of secrecy, by Churchill himself 'in his cups'.

I therefore had much sympathy for Colvin over his shabby treatment by the intelligence establishment, and if possible I should have liked to help him. But when he approached me in 1954 it happened that I had just myself stumbled across the identity of the Oslo author who, I realized, would at minimum be greatly embarrassed and might well be in danger if he were exposed. And so, although I knew that beyond Colvin's natural curiosity he would like genuinely to have told the story as showing that, in the face of the anti-German feeling that was still prevalent in Britain, there were Germans who had transcended patriotism to help us, I told him nothing.

His curiosity, though, had an unforeseen effect. In pursuing inquiries about Oslo among others around me, he found that my views on how intelligence should be conducted were at variance with current practice in the Ministry of Defence, and as a result he published an article in the *Sunday Express* of 22 August 1954, both stressing the value of the Oslo Report and supporting the views which I held on intelligence organization. I was aware that the article had caused a 'flutter in the dovecotes' of the establishment but was at least grateful that he had backed away from chasing the Oslo source any further.

Just how much of a flutter only came to my notice when three months later I received a letter from him saying,

> I saw Norman [my wartime colleague at Bletchley] the other day and

> he suggested I should write you. I was, and almost always am, anxious in stating a case not to have the opposite effect to that intended.
>
> And I found a tendency in the Ministry of Defence to think that a grumble from you had inspired my article in August on the Oslo report and your movements.
>
> I wrote a letter to my friend, L. J. Cheney, the Press Officer, and made it plain in that what the genealogy of my article was, and how I came on your track. It was circulated and 'read with interest'. I think I should tell you of this, because among certain civil servants there is no crime worse in another than that he 'talked to a journalist'.

I had always hoped that, if the time ever came for me to tell the Oslo story, Colvin would be the journalist to whom I would first give it, partly to compensate for his rotten treatment over *The Man Who Never Was*, and partly in gratitude for his own gentlemanly behaviour. Unfortunately, he died some years ago.

A serious attempt to identify the Oslo source was made in the early sixties by a German journalist, Julius Mader, who sent me several courteous letters on the subject. After an impressive investigation he concluded that the author had been Dr Hans Heinrich Kummerow who had been born in Magdeburg in 1903, and who had graduated from the Berlin Technische Hochschule as a Doctor of Engineering in 1929, and had later been in the Development Office of the Loewe Radio Company. As a student he had developed strong Communist sympathies; and, with his chemist friend Dr Erhard Tohmfor, he so disliked the Nazis and the direction in which they were leading Germany that they both decided to gather all available information about new German military technology. By coincidence Kummerow had been at the Berlin Technische Hochschule at the same time as Wernher von Braun, and so knew something about the latter's enthusiasm for rockets. And Tohmfor's wife worked at the BTH with Professor Volmer whom in 1942 we had tentatively identified as the unwitting source of the key report on V2 development, summarized in *Most Secret War.*[3] According to Mader, the information for Oslo was written out by Kummerow's wife, Inge, and taken to Norway by Tohmfor, who had business contacts there and whose grandparents had been Norwegian.

After Germany attacked Russia, Kummerow joined the collective anti-Nazi resistance movement, and in particular a group headed by Lieutenant Schultze-Boysen of the German Air Staff and Dr Harnack, and whose numerous membership included workers, officials, intellectuals, artists, and even a few *Wehrmacht* officers. The group appears to have been part of the famous Rote Kapelle; it was caught and broken by the Nazis in September 1942. Eighty-one of its members died, including both Hans and Inge Kummerow; Volmer was also said to have been arrested and imprisoned. According to Mader, a short letter from Kummerow to an old friend, Wendel, the superintendent of the Dahlem State Botanic Garden, was smuggled out just before Kummerow's death at Plötzensee:

> My dear friend, this is farewell. I am to die, like so many in this war. But I have always fought against National Socialism and for the military defeat of Germany. Had the actions of my friends been successful, then we should have been spared the many sacrifices that must be made before the war ends.

Some of the details of Mader's account show journalistic licence, where he exceeds any knowledge that he could possibly have had in an effort to add convincing colour. According to him, the Report was delivered to the British Legation in Oslo by a man in a hat with his coat pulled up around his ears, who put it through the bronze letter box, and it consisted of a single page of typescript in a thick white envelope, with our Naval Attaché taking so long to translate it that he called in an interpreter, and examining it for further clues by holding it up against the light. Such obviously excessive licence must throw doubt on accepting other details of Mader's account; but it is to be hoped that the moving text of Kummerow's last letter is genuine. If so, it deserves a place in the brave gallery of last messages from condemned resistance workers the world over. It is no discredit to Kummerow to record that although the speculation that he wrote the Oslo Report is one that was well worth pursuing, it is not borne out by my own knowledge.

Recently, an even more impressive candidate for the authorship of the Oslo Report has been proposed by Arnold Kramish who in his book *The Griffin* concludes that it was written by Paul Rosbaud, who was the science adviser to the great German publishing house of Springer. In the years before 1939 he had become acquainted with many scientists throughout western Europe, for he travelled widely and frequently, both in search of authors and in promoting the firm's publications.

Rosbaud, who had been born in 1896 and brought up as a Catholic, served with distinction in the Austrian Army in the 1914–18 war, after which he became a physics student in Berlin and took a doctorate at the Technische Hochschule. He then moved into the publishing world, where he joined Springer in the early thirties. Alarmed by the rise of the Nazis, concerned by their treatment of his Jewish friends, and holding a deep faith in the international character both of science and of the humanities, he used his many contacts to do all that he could to ease the problems of those whose welfare – and indeed lives – were threatened by the increasingly vicious conduct of the Nazis. And not only those threatened by the Nazis, for in 1935 he also tried to persuade the Russians to allow one of their outstanding physicists, Peter Kapitza, who had been working with Rutherford in Cambridge, to return there after they had trapped him on a visit to Leningrad.

With so many warm contacts in the world of pre-war science and with such frequent opportunities for travel, Rosbaud was a natural courier of messages between scientific friends across national frontiers; and from 1939 onwards some of these messages could provide items of intelligence. Opportunely, he had known and liked a long-serving member of the British intelligence service, from the early thirties; and, remaining in Germany throughout the war, he could maintain a fringing contact with German research laboratories whence from time to time he succeeded in getting information passed to us in London.

Rosbaud's life, particularly as an active agent in wartime Germany with ostensible reasons for visits abroad, is thus a promising subject for a biographer; it has now found one in Arnold Kramish who was at one time a physicist in the American Atomic Energy Commission and at others attached to the Rand Corporation and the London School of Economics. Kramish has assiduously gathered details of Rosbaud's life and has delved into the murky world of intelligence with considerable success. He has discovered much about Rosbaud that I for one did not know, even though I saw the most crucial of Rosbaud's reports that were successfully transmitted to us during the war, and though I came to know him fairly well after the war when he lived in London and he wanted me to be the British editor of the new *Handbuch der Physik*. In the meantime, he had returned to publishing and formed a relationship with Robert Maxwell who was, I believe, indebted to him for the name 'Pergamon'. The relationship terminated unhappily in 1956 after a dispute concerning a text book on optics; one account of this dispute is that given by Joe Haines in his biography of Maxwell.

The clearest of Rosbaud's wartime contributions for which I can personally vouch was his letting us know about the doings and movements of the German nuclear physicists headed by Werner Heisenberg. Rosbaud was intensely alive to the possible release of nuclear energy, for it was he who in early 1939 had 'rushed' into the columns of the journal *Naturwissenschaften* the paper by Hahn and Strassman on the new elements created by bombarding uranium with neutrons which was in effect the discovery of nuclear fission that was to lead to the atomic bomb. Rosbaud's wartime reports were particularly valuable because they helped us correctly to conclude that work in Germany towards the release of nuclear energy at no time reached beyond the research stage; his information thus calmed the fears that might otherwise have beset us. In particular, his reports enabled us to follow the move of Heisenberg and his colleagues from Berlin to southern Germany; and although he did not have access to their work it was clear that this had no association with a large-scale effort such as the production of an atomic bomb would require.

One interesting point that Kramish has recorded is that briefing messages to Rosbaud from London were transmitted by the BBC, and that these would begin with the code phrase '*Das Haus steht am Hügel*'. So that was the explanation of the message which had come into MI6 during the war, and which made us wonder whether the Oslo author was trying to re-establish contact! (See above, page 276.) It is a coincidence that the message should then have made us think about Oslo, and that Kramish should now associate it with Rosbaud whom he contends to be in fact the Oslo author.

As for others of Rosbaud's contributions to scientific intelligence outside the atomic field that Kramish has written about, I cannot speak with confidence, for where he describes events and characters with which I had direct contact I sometimes cannot reconcile his account with my own memories. At times, though, he achieves punctilious accuracy, and this has enabled him to take to task another author, Anthony Cave Brown, who in *Bodyguard of Lies* purported to describe how the Oslo Report was delivered to the British Legation. According to Cave Brown, the Report was found in a parcel 'about three inches thick, the size and shape of a block of legal-sized pads' which was found by the Legation guard half covered by snow on a stone ledge by the porter's lodge in a snowstorm on 4 November 1939. Kramish's check on the meteorological records for Oslo shows that the first snow of the winter did not fall there until 24 November. This suggests that Cave Brown's account should be placed on a par with the famous apparition of the Russian soldiers in Britain in 1914 'with snow on their boots'.

Incidentally, Stewart Menzies when he was head of MI6 told me how he believed the Russian story of 1914 to have originated – and coincidentally it involved Aberdeen, which used to be a main trading port with the Baltic ports. Among the regular imports were eggs, which used to be received in large consignments from Poland and Russia. The ship carrying one such consignment had been delayed, perhaps due to the restrictions on merchant shipping imposed by the war, and the London office of the importers was getting anxious about the non-arrival of the eggs. When they eventually did arrive at Aberdeen the agent there telegraphed the good news to the London office, indicating the magnitude of the consignment and its country of origin in a message which, said Menzies, ran: '50,000 Russians arrived at Aberdeen. Now on train to London.' The merest sight of the telegram by unintended eyes would have been enough to start the rumour, to which popular imagination then readily contributed the snow. That was Menzies's account, to which his official standing gives an authenticity over an alternative theory that the rumour started with the statement of some Scottish soldiers to a bewildered Cockney that they came from Ross-shire.

In place of Cave Brown's patently inaccurate account of how the Oslo Report arrived at the Legation, Kramish therefore gave his own in which he followed Cave Brown to the extent of assuming that the Oslo Report was delivered to the Legation by the hand of an anonymous messenger. There the package was taken to the Naval Attaché who allegedly 'sighed and began to open it'. With such access to the minute detail of the story, it was then little further trouble for Kramish to identify the caller who had brought the package to the Legation: 'it seems indisputable that the mysterious messenger who delivered the report to the British Legation was Odd Hassel.' Hassel was a young Norwegian scientist, later to win a Nobel Prize, with whom Rosbaud was acquainted; Kramish supposes that in the course of a visit to Oslo in early November 1939, Rosbaud asked Hassel to take 'the package' to the Legation.

Two difficulties stand in the way of accepting Kramish's account, even if we refrain from questioning the authenticity of its picturesque and imaginative detail. One of these difficulties was pointed out by Kramish himself, for Rosbaud – in discussing after the war his scientific relationships – noted that his next contact with Hassel after August

1939 was not until the following December. Kramish disposes of this difficulty by supposing that Rosbaud's memory was at fault. Now, whether or not this was so, and putting aside the matter that on some occasion Rosbaud had to ask Hassel to take a package to the Legation, Kramish appears to have overlooked the critical evidence of the Naval Attaché himself in what he wrote to me after my RUSI lecture. At no point did he mention a package but instead referred to 'the letters having been posted in Norway' and 'the letters were in excellent German' and 'the German letters arrived and the last one asked . . .' So the Oslo Report arrived in the form of letters through the post, and there were at least two of them. Kramish appears to have overlooked this evidence, although I myself took care to draw it to his attention.

The fact that Kramish can thus seriously discount a significant detail inevitably casts doubt on his main conclusion that Rosbaud was the author of the Oslo Report. Also against this conclusion may be set the fact that although Rosbaud readily described his relations with the German nuclear physicists to American investigators after the war, he appears not to have claimed to them any connection with the Oslo Report. Nor did he do so to me, although I saw him from time to time after the war, both before and after I gave the RUSI lecture.

Certainly he had the scientific background, the motivation, and the courage to compile such a report as that which came into the Oslo Legation, and he could have created the opportunity. Ultimately, therefore, supposing that he had somehow gained access to the detail of secret military research such as I never saw in any of his other wartime reports, and despite all the flaws in Kramish's presentation, it would be impossible by negative arguments alone to disprove completely his attribution of the Oslo Report to Rosbaud. For that, positive proof is needed that it came from another author; this will emerge later.

Although the Oslo Report was not one of Rosbaud's contributions to our wartime cause, his contributions were considerable and, in nuclear energy at least, approached the crucial. Moreover, they were made with the bravest determination, and I would warmly endorse the tribute paid to him by Samuel Goudsmit in *Alsos*, describing his Alsos Mission to investigate nuclear developments in Germany at the end of the war:

> Rosbaud, an Austrian citizen, is among the few who kept their integrity throughout the Nazi regime and the war. His personality and deep understanding gave him the friendship and confidence of all true

> scientists who came in contact with him and they were many. Everyone knew of his outspoken anti-Nazi feelings and that he tried to keep in contact with Allied colleagues via neutral countries. He was living proof that it was possible to continue unmolested without giving in to the Nazi pressure. He never gave the Nazi salute, never displayed a Nazi flag. There were fortunately a few more among the scientists who acted similarly, notably the physicist Von Laue. These and a few other cases belie the contention that it was absolutely necessary to follow the Nazis in order to be able to live.

It is also worthy of record in the annals of intelligence that Rosbaud's service did not spring solely and negatively from his dislike of the Nazis. Kramish quotes from one of his letters referring to his experience as a prisoner-of-war in 1918:

> My first two days as a prisoner under British guard were the origins of my long-time anglophilia. For the British soldiers, war was over and forgotten. They did not treat us as enemies but as unfortunate losers of the war. They did not fraternize, but they were polite and correct.

Thanks to decent treatment, a former enemy had become a friend.

The Pneumatic Monkey

An unforeseen reward of answering Churchill's call back to the Ministry of Defence in 1952 (see above, page 3) was that it led me to the discovery of the origin of the Oslo Report. This owed nothing to official sources; instead it arose from some prodigious coincidences that befell me in the course of living once again in London and of visiting America. Discursive as the following pages may seem, with their challenge no less to credulity than to patience, they will chart the diverse trails of experience whose ultimate conjunction led me to the Oslo author.

One of the routes started in the Athenaeum club, to which I had just been elected in 1952. In its Ladies' Annexe at 6 Carlton Gardens – a Georgian house, since demolished, which had once been Gladstone's residence – it had half-a-dozen bedrooms which it let members occupy for periods up to twelve months. I was fortunate enough to be offered one; it enabled me to live conveniently near my office in Northumberland Avenue, it relieved me of domestic chores, and it allowed me to spend nearly all my time on the work for which I had been recalled.

On most nights I dined in the club. It was certainly not the quality of the food that was the attraction, for by that criterion the club should have been more aptly called the Sparteum, to judge by the comment of a Sybarite that Athenasus recorded about AD 200: 'It is natural enough for the Spartans to be the bravest of men; for any man in his senses would rather die ten thousand times over than live as miserably as this.'[4] But the Athenaeum was a great club, situated some four hundred yards south of Piccadilly Circus and having been started in 1824 with Humphry Davy as its first chairman and Michael Faraday its first secretary. There is still a granite block so placed outside the club that the Duke of Wellington could mount his horse on departure.

The Duke may well have dined in silence, for this appeared to be the custom of his day, to judge by the observation of the visiting American physicist, Joseph Henry, who, dining several times in 1836, found 'little tables spread in different parts of the room with many occupied by single persons'.[5] Happily, the custom of solitary dining no longer prevailed, for had it done so I might never have learned the identity of the Oslo author. Instead, the nightly conversation could sparkle, thanks largely to the character of one man who dined every night, the late C. K. Ogden, best known for his invention of Basic English.

Had it not been for the fact that Ogden was the most learned man any of us had ever met, he would have been the epitome of a club bore. Always late to bed himself, he would entice you to stay up with him; sensing that you were trying to escape, he would cast some new appetizing morsel of knowledge in your direction which you had no better chance of resisting than a trout could a may-fly. Such was his range that he had reviewed the entire three volumes of the 1923 supplement to the *Encyclopaedia Britannica* single-handed. When he died in 1957 he left a collection of a hundred thousand books and four houses – besides his current residence in Gordon Square, he had others in Cambridge, Brighton and Buxton. He explained to me that as each house became so congested that he could no longer negotiate the stairs for the books that he had stacked on them, he simply bought another house. Primarily concerned with language – when he was not playing billiards, at which he had been university champion in his undergraduate days at Cambridge – he had founded the Orthographical Institute, and written several books of which the most important was *The Meaning of Meaning*, in which he formulated principles for the understanding of the function of language. His work in that field had led him to devise the system of

Basic English with which he claimed that he could express everything that might be needed for the purposes of everyday existence and communication, with a basic vocabulary of no more than 850 words.

This was the achievement of which Ogden was most proud, and he had the 850 words printed on a postage stamp. The notion appealed to Winston Churchill, who set up a wartime Cabinet committee to consider its development; and Churchill himself praised Basic English in a fireside radio broadcast on the post-war world, minuting the Secretary to the Cabinet on 11 July 1943, 'I am very much interested in the question of Basic English. The widespread use of this would be a gain to us far more durable and fruitful than the annexation of great provinces. It would also fit in with my ideas of closer union with the United States by making it even more worthwhile to belong to the English-speaking club.'

Ogden thereupon received official support, ultimately receiving £23,000 to pursue the development by which he hoped, in his own words, to 'debabelize' the world. But he encountered a mixed reception from the students of linguistics, some pointing out that Basic English would often require the use of three words in place of the one in normal use; for example, the substitution of 'an unmarried woman' for 'a virgin' implied a degree of innocence on Ogden's part which might only be ascribed to his own celibacy. So he found his progress frustrated, not least by the civil servants who from 1943 onwards were brought in to administer the government grant that he then received, and he tersely recorded his frustration in his *Who's Who?* entry as '1944–6, bedevilled by officials'. Delighted when I read this, I teased him when we next met into claiming that he could express any idea in Basic English, and then challenged him to express 'bedevilled by officials' half so effectively. Much put out, he went off in an uncharacteristic huff; he returned the next day with several versions such as 'chased by devil men' but he had to agree that none was so expressive as his original.

Apart from that one occasion, I never saw him out of humour, and dinner in his presence was invariably entertaining. Any member of the club who was at a loose end for dinner in London knew that he would find Ogden dining in the Athenaeum, usually with a coterie of other members who likewise enjoyed his company. Prominent among these was Alfred Munnings, the President of the Royal Academy, who was apt to scoff uproariously at the French Impressionists and point to one of his own paintings and challenge, 'Which of 'em could paint a n'orse like that?' The last time that I saw him he was skipping up the steps of the Athenaeum, telling me that he had been taking colchicum to alleviate his gout, with the result that he was excreting 'pure yellow ochre' – an expert opinion if ever there was one.

So we put up with the mediocre food, and with the curious shelving of books in the library that had resulted, as Ogden pointed out, in those on anaesthetics being located immediately next to those on aesthetics, because the claret at dinner was good and the company even better. It was at one such dinner that a clue cropped up about the Oslo author; but since, as Winston Churchill once told me, strict chronology is the secret of good narrative, I must now relate how that dinner came about.

The trail to the dinner of enlightenment started some six thousand miles away in the Sierra Madre near Los Angeles, where I had gone in May 1953 to visit my wartime colleague, Bob Robertson (see above, page 19). Just as I was leaving for the 'Sidewinder' visit Bob's wife, Angela, said that it looked as though I was not going to have any free time for shopping, and she offered to give me the few toys that she had in the house to amuse her grandchildren so that I would not return home empty handed. The toys looked rather trivial, and I myself would never have bought them, but it would have been churlish to reject such kindness and so they went into the bottom of my suitcase. One of them was a little yellow monkey about two and a half inches high, moulded in hollow rubber and with arms and legs of the thin kind of rubber used in toy balloons. The monkey was connected, by a narrow flexible tube about eighteen inches long, to a squeeze bulb; when the bulb was pressed, the extra air forced into the monkey caused the arms and legs to thrust sharply outwards with all the triumph of a victor at sport or, perhaps, of Archimedes in his bath. I felt rather embarrassed at the thought of what a customs officer would think if he went through my case and found such a childish toy, and I even wondered whether I might 'lose' it on the way across America. But this would have broken faith with Angela, and so the monkey stayed with me – and it was to be a vital element in the Oslo denouement.

The pneumatic monkey remained discreetly in my suitcase as I travelled from the Robertsons' to the Naval Ordnance Test Station at China Lake; then on by rail via the Grand Canyon and Chicago to Washington for the Nomination Conference (see above, page 18);

then to Middleburg in Virginia, by legend so replete with millionaires that its sands were panned for gold, where I met Kingman Douglas, former chief USAAF intelligence officer in London during the war, and his wife (who was Fred Astaire's sister, Adele); and finally on to New York. There I was due to catch the *Queen Mary* for the voyage home, and so diverting had been the passage across America that I had completely forgotten about the embarrassing monkey long before I joined ship.

From the height of the Empire State Building it was impressive to watch the *Queen Mary* docking; but on boarding I found that, although good, she was not as taut as the *Mauretania*, on which I had crossed from Southampton. Luggage took several hours to appear in one's cabin, whereas with the *Mauretania* it had only taken a few minutes, and I had the impression that the *Queen* had been rather spoilt by the glamour which attended her and her sister, the *Queen Elizabeth*. As we got under way, the Manhattan skyline disappeared in the evening sunset, and we went below to change for dinner.

As on the *Mauretania*, I was invited to the Staff Captain's table, which had eight covers set. At that first dinner none of us knew who the others were; I was paired with an unattached lady, and we informally exchanged names – the passenger list, which was circulated the following day, showed that she was a viscountess. Our fellow passengers at table were an American surgeon and his wife, and a very pleasant lady from Boston who was bringing her sixteen-year-old daughter on a tour of Europe. One chair was unfilled when we sat down, but it was soon occupied by a man older than the rest of us, rather bulky; the rumpling of his shirt and the skewness of his tie suggested that he had changed for dinner in a hurry. By his speech he seemed to be a north country businessman, probably self-made, with a fair amount of technical knowledge and with no doubt that British was best. He also seemed determined to establish himself as 'the life and soul' of our table and he tried – perhaps subconsciously – to provoke each of the other men at the table into an exchange in which he clearly expected from past experience to come off best. I myself automatically sat back to await his attacks; fortunately every time one of them came it was on ground where I knew rather more than he did, and so he had to retire to try another approach. Clearly, life on the *Queen Mary* was going to be livelier than it had been on the *Mauretania*; but since I was tired after my travels across America, I rather withdrew from the socializing to get on with examining a ponderous Ph.D. thesis that had been sent to await me on the ship.

It transpired that the American women at our table had decided between themselves after the first dinner that I was probably a snobbish London playboy – as they subsequently told me – and they were puzzled to find me in the lounge the following morning absorbed in the Ph.D. thesis. By now we were able to sort one another out with the aid of the passenger list, and the thesis was consistent – if my appearance was not – with my being a professor. Our Lancashire companion appeared to see my title as a direct challenge, and he tried time after time to take my measure: the professor must be cut down to size by the practical man. For practical man he was, as it turned out. A Fellow of all our three principal engineering institutions, he was managing director of an electrical instrument company, always on the lookout for bright ideas that he could turn to commercial advantage. Later I was to come to know and like him well; but for the moment he was constantly trying to spar with me in front of our table companions. They all had money, and he quickly formed them into a syndicate to bet in the daily sweepstake on how many miles the ship would cover in the twenty-four hours. They were laying out a hundred pounds every night, and I was not sorry to remain aloof and enjoy a quiet passage.

The third night out, though, everything changed. Having no commitments I was down for dinner in good time and was in fact first at our table. As I stood waiting in the sumptuous dining room, the Viscountess appeared. It was then that she told me about the betting syndicate, and how after the bets had been made the preceding night our north country companion had invited the others down to his cabin. 'What an extraordinary man!' she said. 'He has a double cabin and has his spare washbasin full of little live turtles he is taking home for his grandchildren. He also has a lot of toys, and I think that you ought to know that he is going to try and make a fool of you tonight. I don't know how it works, but he has a little rubber monkey which moves its arms and legs, and he is going to challenge you to guess how he does it.' As I thanked her for the warning, I remembered Angela's monkey which was still at the bottom of my suitcase. I thought that I might just have time to go back to my cabin and find it, and be back at table before the others sat down. This indeed proved possible and, with pulse beating with anticipation, I returned with the monkey in my pocket.

It was not long before I saw our Lancastrian surreptitiously extract his monkey from his pocket and place it upon his lapel, secreting the tube behind the lapel, with the bulb at the other end back in his pocket. To my delight it was a yellow monkey, the spitting image of the one that I myself had.

It was not long before he started working his monkey, whose arms and legs moved ever more frantically as I contrived to look in every direction except at him. With frustrated determination that I should take notice, he thrust his chest further and further forward, with the result that the diners at neighbouring tables were treated to the incongruous spectacle of this rather bulky sexagenarian in dinner jacket with his ridiculous monkey gesticulating to everybody within sight. Both amusement and disdain could be seen in the bewildered glances that he attracted. At last, he demanded almost angrily, 'Can't you see my monkey?' I replied that I had indeed seen it, but could not see anything remarkable about it. 'Well, then, how does it work?' he asked.

The professor then proceeded to give one explanation after another, each growing more complex as its predecessor was dismissed. Finally, I confessed that I was beaten, only to be shown that it was something far simpler than I could ever have thought of – a simple tube leading to a squeeze bulb at the other end. Everyone at table who had been in the know laughed, except for the Viscountess, who clearly thought that I had let her down despite her forewarning.

I did not see how I could turn the situation to advantage as my tormentor took his monkey from his lapel, showed me how it worked and laid it on the table beside him. Despite the incredible luck of having Angela's monkey, and the timely warning from the Viscountess, I felt that I had failed the occasion; and then the Lord delivered me, for pulling from his pocket another trick the Lancastrian said, 'Well, if you couldn't make out how that one worked, perhaps you can tell us how this one does!' What he then produced was an age-old trick involving a bogus egg in a cup, on to which a cover could be screwed and then unscrewed, with the egg apparently no longer being there. I now saw my salvation. 'Oh, conjuring!' I said. 'I'm not much good at conjuring – I only know one trick!' 'What's that?' he asked. 'Just this,' I replied, and, taking up my table napkin, I palmed my own monkey at the same time and then spread the napkin over his monkey, leaving my monkey beside it under the napkin. 'Now take that up!' I said. 'Why?' he said. 'Have you made my monkey disappear?' 'Just take the napkin up and look!' I replied. After further urging from me he gingerly removed the napkin and found that there were now two identical monkeys where he had left one. There was utter silence at the table, and our Lancastrian's jaw dropped as he contemplated the clone: 'Good God!' he exclaimed. Then, looking intensely at me, he said, 'You and I must meet again!'

That was the end of my quiet trip on the *Queen Mary*. The Viscountess was delighted, and the American women full of admiration. They demanded that I should join them at the party that evening, because, thanks to our Lancastrian's shrewdness, they had won the pool for the day; and a joyous celebration was in prospect. I was elected clerk of the pool for the rest of the voyage.

We parted at Southampton, the Lancastrian having a car to take him home all the way northwards, while I boarded the boat-train to London. He had told me that his name was Cobden Turner, and that he had a flat in Grosvenor House to which he would invite me for lunch. If he were still wondering how the cloning had been done, I was joyously pondering on the improbability that two grown men in dinner jackets at the Staff Captain's table on the *Queen Mary* should each have in his pocket a yellow toy pneumatic monkey complete with connecting tube and squeeze bulb – one bought in New York and the other in California. But ponder as I might, I could not have imagined that a link had been forged with Oslo.

OSLO!

Back at work in London, I resumed dining in the Athenaeum, almost always in the company of C. K. Ogden, and there was often a morsel of entertainment or learning to be picked up from the coterie of other members of like mind who gravitated to his table. One night, for example, the archaeologist, O. G. S. Crawford, came in overflowing with excitement to tell us that he had just heard that a young architect, Michael Ventris, had succeeded in deciphering the ancient Minoan script known as 'Linear B' which had baffled all previous attempts, and that another young archaeologist had discovered a Mycenaean dagger carved on one of the stones at Stonehenge.

One regular diner was Henry Harding, the Dean of Medicine at Westminster Hospital. As relief after a full day as a surgeon in the operating theatre, he would entertain us with stories from his medical past; one such story told of his debut as an expert witness in a law suit, which had occurred when he was a resident casualty officer at the London Hospital, and had to attend a workman who had fallen from a ladder and fractured his skull. Some time afterwards Harding found himself buttonholed by solicitors' representatives acting for the workman, who asked Harding whether he would stand as a witness and affirm that he had examined the casualty and found clinical evidence of a fractured skull. Since this was indeed what he had found, Harding agreed. Then, a few days later, he was buttonholed again, but by a different pair of men who asked him whether the patient had been X-rayed, and whether this had shown evidence of a fracture. When Harding told them that the X-rays had not shown a fracture, they asked him whether he was prepared to attest to this in a court of law. Again, he agreed. When he arrived at the court for the subsequent action he found himself greeted by both sides, until they realized that the one had recruited him as an expert witness for the plaintiff and the other for the defence. Actually, he said, he had simply told the truth – the fracture had shown up on clinical examination but was too fine to appear on an X-radiograph.

The best of Harding's stories, though, concerned his wartime days as a lieutenant colonel in the RAMC when in the autumn of 1940 he had been posted to the Borders where a Polish battalion was stationed. One night a Polish soldier was brought in, still alive but with a knife plunged into his back, piercing his heart. Harding saw that there was little he could do beyond sending for a priest to give the victim absolution before he expired. Clearly, the case was one of murder, and so on the following morning Harding went into the nearby town to inform the procurator fiscal, who listened impassively to his statement. Sensing that the fiscal was unmoved, Harding said, 'Look, man! Aren't you going to do anything about it? In all my experience I have never seen such a clear case of murder. It can't be suicide because he could never have put that knife through his heart from the back.' To which the fiscal replied, 'Now see here, laddie! We've nae had a murder in this town for forty years, and we're nae having one now!'

A less frequent, but equally welcome, diner was Stanley Morison, who had been editor of the *Times Literary Supplement* and of *The History of The Times*. He was pre-eminent as a typographer, and had been responsible for the design of several of the most elegant of modern type-faces, including those used by *The Times*. One rough night in November 1953 he came in looking rather shaken and dishevelled, and explained that he had just come off a very bumpy flight from Paris. 'I was sitting next to a most extraordinary man,' said Morison, 'who started to wonder whether we were going to survive.' So they began to talk about belief in the afterlife and eternity. Morison told his fellow passenger that he was a Roman Catholic, whereupon the other attacked the Catholic faith with all kinds of ingenious arguments which derived from his own matter-of-fact view of the universe based on his experiences as a professional engineer. Morison ruefully said that he had been fully stretched to reply to the arguments, which as he related them developed a character which I thought I recognized. Finally, I asked, 'Did you get the name of the man you were travelling with? Was it by any chance Cobden Turner?' 'Why, yes!' said Morison in a surprise that was shared by the rest of the company. 'Do you know him?' When I said that I did, and Morison said that he would like to meet him again, I replied that I could easily invite Cobden Turner to dinner; and Morison's account had made the others keen to meet him, too. So I saw a happy way of repaying some small fraction of the generous hospitality that I was beginning to enjoy from Cobden (for, as good as his word, he had entertained me several times in Grosvenor House since our parting at Southampton), and at the same time providing a bright evening in the club. I therefore offered to give a dinner for him.

I wrote to Cobden telling him that some of my friends in the Athenaeum would like to meet him, and we agreed that 15 December would be a suitable date. So I booked a table for eight, and let the others know. Then things began to go wrong. Worst of all, Stanley Morison, with whom I hoped to entertain Cobden in an unexpected reunion, had to fall out, as did some of the others, like Alfred Munnings and Thomas Bodkin, the Director of the Barber Art Gallery in Birmingham, who with his mischievous Irish brogue and goatee beard looked like Bernard Shaw and was becoming a television personality.

Having built up Cobden's hopes of good and illustrious company, I was therefore faced with a 'flop' and had at the last moment to look around the club for other members who might fill the vacant places. Fortunately, my wartime colleague and friend 'Bimbo' Norman, the professor of German at King's College, happened to come into the club, and I asked him to help me out. Somehow we managed to find a full company of eight – including of course Ogden – and Bimbo sat down next to Cobden. Happily, the dinner began to go well, so well in fact that I felt that I could sit back and let it run itself. Certainly there was no need to be solicitous about Cobden even though it was his first time in the club, and he was chatting cheerfully to Bimbo, two or three places away from me, while I was conversing with my immediate neighbours.

Suddenly, I heard an excited shout of 'OSLO!' from Bimbo, loud enough to be heard several tables away. I had known Bimbo shout before; it always meant something – as it did that July afternoon in 1940 when we had found that the German Air Force had a new device called Wotan, and I had asked him what he knew about Wotan. Norman had replied, 'He was head of the German gods . . . wait a moment . . . He had only one eye,' and then came the shout, 'ONE EYE, ONE BEAM. Can you think of a system that would only use one beam?' The point of his question was that the other beam system that we had recently discovered, *Knickebein*, used two beams crossed over the target. Thanks to the timely warning in the Oslo Report, I had been immediately able to think of a way in which the ranging system described in the Report could be used in combination with a single beam to locate a target, and this turned out to be absolutely correct.

Now here was Bimbo shouting again! What could it be this time? And why Oslo? Almost shamefaced at the disturbance that he had caused at a polite dinner by his involuntary shout, he quietly said to me, 'You must hear this story afterwards!' As soon as the dinner was over and the others had left, Bimbo and Cobden and I sat down together, and they told me what had happened. Cobden had asked Bimbo what he was professor of and Bimbo had told him that it was German. Cobden, never loathe to 'bat on the other man's wicket', said that he knew Germany well, and had for a long time been going there on business. In fact, he had a very good German friend who had written to him during the war from Oslo, offering to establish a channel of communication with him via a lady they both knew in Denmark. He had reported the offer to the Ministry of Information and had subsequently been visited by two MI5 officers about it but he had heard nothing more. He added that his friend had sent other letters to the Embassy in Oslo. With Cobden Turner being an electrical engineer, presumably his friend might be one also, and with his mention of the Oslo Embassy, the association was too much for Bimbo's self-control – and hence his explosive shout of 'Oslo!'

Well, could Cobden's friend be the writer of the Oslo Report? If so, how had he missed the publicity after my RUSI lecture, or if he had not missed it, why was he still silent? And although Germany was in such chaos in 1947 that my lecture may not have been widely noticed there, why had Cobden in Salford not associated his friend with the writing of the Oslo Report? My lecture had been the subject of a front-page article in the *Daily Telegraph*, for example, which I took to be his regular reading. So, just in case this fantastic coincidence was merely a superbly contrived confidence trick, I decided to proceed carefully. It was a case for Crow's Law: do not think what you want to think until you know what you ought to know. So, as proof, I asked Cobden to get his friend not only to confirm that he had sent the Oslo Report but also to recall, as far as he could, its contents.

The test, which I did not reveal to Cobden, was to see whether his friend would mention any items other than those that I had listed in my lecture – two kinds of radar, large rockets, rocket-driven glider bombs, Peenemünde and the radio range-determining system. His German friend soon answered with a list that included several of these, along with magnetic torpedoes and the electronic discharge tube, which I had also not mentioned. I was convinced.

In fact, more than convinced; I was elated. Every now and again something extraordinary occurs in life for which there is no immediate explanation, and the mystery may rankle in one's mind for years; then suddenly the explanation breaks, almost as though a prodigal son had returned or a lost sheep found ('Rejoice with me . . .'). Beyond elation at the solution of the Oslo mystery I marvelled at the chain of coincidences that had brought it about: the CIA arranging for me to visit Bob Robertson in California; Angela Robertson giving me the ridiculous pneumatic monkey that I would never have bought for myself; sitting at the same table on the *Queen Mary* with Cobden Turner and being forewarned by the Viscountess; guessing that Stanley Morison's companion on the flight from Paris had been Cobden Turner; 'roping in' Bimbo Norman at the last moment for the Athenaeum dinner; and Bimbo being the man at Bletchley most sensitive to Oslo because of Wotan in 1940. Of course, once I had come to know Cobden Turner well, his connection with the Oslo Report might have been revealed in other ways, and so some of the later coincidences might not have been absolutely essential. But as for the coincidence that two grown men, one a managing director and the other a director of intelligence, should each have had in their dinner jackets at the Staff Captain's table on the *Queen Mary* identical little yellow monkeys – well, if there is a Providence the expression on its face must have been that same enigmatic grin of satisfaction that was worn by the monkeys.

Cobden's failure to link his friend with the Oslo Report until the conversation with Bimbo Norman was simply due to his having missed the press accounts of my RUSI lecture; so that, although his friend had told him of his sending letters to our Embassy, he imagined that these had been lost in the bureaucratic machine, just as his offer of a contact with the lady in Denmark appeared to have been.

When I told him my side of the Oslo story, from which it was plain that I should be fascinated to meet the author of the Report, Cobden said that sooner or later there might be an occasion for his friend to come to London, and so we could meet then. By now Cobden had told me who his friend was, and the position that he currently held in post-war Germany. For his own protection I thought it out of the question either for me to meet him in Germany or for him to come to London without some genuinely different reason for visiting the other's country, and so we should wait until an occasion for a visit arose in the natural course of events. Such an occasion did indeed arise about a year later when my wartime opponent General Wolfgang Martini, who had been Director General of Signals in the *Luftwaffe* all through the war, was invited to the Farnborough Air Show in September 1954, as a later section describes.

Cobden Turner

How had it come about that Cobden Turner had a friend in Germany so well disposed towards us that he had sent the Oslo Report? Both during the war and at the time I met him he was the managing director of the Salford Electrical Instrument Company, with some of whose products I was already acquainted. These gave us a warm common ground, for I had admired their quality; the firm made easily the most precise photographic exposure meter and the best photoelectric cells of the iron-selenium type then available in Britain, as I had discovered in the course of my researches in optics. Moreover, from my work in growing crystals I knew that the firm was the principal, and perhaps the only, one in Britain that had mastered the difficult technique of growing artificial rubies and sapphires. So, if it is true that 'by their fruits ye shall know them', then there must be someone pretty good behind a firm that could show excellence in such diverse fields.

The experience had puzzled me because I knew that the firm was a subsidiary of the General Electric Company whose domestic products such as cooking stoves and radio receivers could at best be described in those days as 'dull but reliable'. Meeting Cobden Turner resolved my previous bewilderment; it was he who provided the drive at Salford, and he was a great entrepreneur whose activities were sometimes viewed askance by his staider colleagues in the GEC hierarchy.

I do not know whether all the activities with which he was associated would have stood up to a narrowly ethical scrutiny – at one time he was worried because he had found himself on the fringes of a fraud for which the son of a Cabinet minister received a prison sentence – but they certainly produced results that benefited his firm and his country. He was anxious for some public honour, not for himself he explained to me, but for his wife who had to tolerate his frequent absences in London and abroad. One evening he was lamenting to me his lack of public recognition, and I ventured to speculate whether, despite all his good work, he had overstepped some boundary of reputable conduct in business. As a tentative example, I remarked that he had taken me to tremendous dinners of such bodies as the Worshipful Company of Makers of Playing Cards (of which, incidentally, he was a past master), and that his other guests had been senior admirals, generals, air marshals and civil servants all of whom were in posts where they might be tempted by his hospitality to sway government contracts in his firm's direction. I commented that this might be verging on bribery. 'I would admit that,' he replied, 'but everybody does it. And I'm different from the rest: I invite these people because I really like them – and if they die I take their widows out, too!'

This turned out to be absolutely true, as I myself witnessed. Cobden was one of the most generous-hearted men I have ever encountered, just as he was one of the most astute. Through his flat in Grosvenor House, where they often stayed at his expense, streamed a cavalcade of characters: a gypsy who had been in the Grenadiers in World War I and who, after buying a load of scrap from the Handley Page works at Cricklewood in 1921, had never looked back – he could neither read nor write but loved horses so much that now in his millionaire days he had won the Ascot gold vase; a master of foxhounds who had made a fortune in Middle East oil, and who had in World War I been in the Duke of Westminster's squadron of armoured cars, where the Duke had kitted out all his officers in uniforms of pure silk; an opera tenor of international repute; and a host of senior officials from the field of defence and telecommunications, as well as of impecunious individuals of both sexes whom Cobden was in course of helping.

Cobden regarded every field of human enterprise as open to his talents, whether it was getting tickets at the last minute for a test match at Lord's or a multi-million pound contract from the British Transport Commission for a system for automatically recording the position of every one of the million freight trucks on British railways. New methods of grinding lenses, or a sophisticated automatic system of four-colour printing, or a colour-stereoscope with slides of well-known views for tourists. For all of these I have known him to make bids, and try to have them developed by his staff at Salford who regarded him with exasperated admiration. One evening, after he had me to dinner at the Royal Automobile Club, he said, 'Come along, I have heard that a Swiss consortium is going to make a bid for the Dorchester. If I can get an option on it before them, I could make quite a bit out of the deal.' So we took a taxi to the Dorchester, and I stood as a dazed witness as Cobden walked up to the astonished head porter and announced, 'We've come to buy the place. How much do you think that they would want for it?'

My phenomenal companion had been born on 25 November 1888, the son of Wilberforce Turner, an oil and chemical merchant in Salford. Educated successively at Manchester Grammar School, Salford Royal Technical College, and the Manchester College of Technology, he served an apprenticeship with the General Electric Company, and then joined Ferranti's, where he worked in the test room and was engaged in experimental work. In 1918 he moved to the Salford Electrical Instrument Company as managing director, and so wide were his technical interests that all three major engineering institutions (Civil, Mechanical and Electrical) elected him to their membership.

In his thirty-nine years as managing director, his firm never had a strike, a record which testifies to his relations with workers. Indeed, in the Great Depression of the early thirties he was moved by the daily sight of unemployed men sitting listlessly on chairs on the pavements outside their drab homes, expelled by their wives and with nothing to occupy them. On 12 September 1932 he expressed his thoughts in the *Manchester Guardian*:

SOMETHING TO DO

To the Editor of the Manchester Guardian.

Sir, Your account of the successful scheme carried out by the unemployed in Littleborough prompts me to ask whether the 'Manchester Guardian' will take the lead in endeavouring to do something for the mass of the unemployed in Lancashire and elsewhere.

They are like good ships rotting away for want of use and care, and one wonders, when the pendulum of trade swings back, whether they will be ready physically and mentally to take up their places in industry; and, furthermore, whether employers will not prefer, or as far as possible, to employ younger persons, whose morale has not been depressed by years of inactivity.

The Psalmist of old, who said, 'Man goeth forth to his labour in the morning until the evening,' knew what he was singing about, for there is nothing in the world like an evening return from a day's work well done to ensure a pleasant, leisurely evening and a sound sleep with nerves, body, and brain refreshed. The lack of this, putting aside financial stringency, is perhaps the bitterest feature of the unemployed question.

As one perceives the slackening gait and the uninterested mien of the unemployed, one realises that the weeks and months of having nothing to do are producing their baneful effect upon the minds and bodies of these men.

Yet there is so much social work which could be done, land to be reclaimed, sites to be cleared, that I am sure with a little organisation much good could be done for the men themselves and for the community generally. Even organised games and physical drill in open space, perhaps combined with life under canvas in camps, would be preferable to the tramp, tramp, tramp of the streets and loitering at street corners.

Amongst the unemployed are many educated older men who could organise this work or would give their time to instructing the younger unemployed, to their mutual advantage. Yours, &c.,

H. COBDEN TURNER.

Peel Works, Silk Street, Salford,
September 9.

And of the one critic among the many correspondents who wrote approvingly of his letter, he wrote subsequently to the newspaper:

The one dissentient, 'Unwilling Victim,' appears to be a hard case, and as he has written similarly before I beg you to ask him to disclose his address to you or to me, because such matters as empty stomachs and rotten boots can easily be dealt with, but the other kind of rot is more insidious and more difficult to eradicate. One wishes that more could be done, but it is comforting to know that there is no country (except, perhaps, Russia, about which one cannot be sure) in which the poor and unemployed are so well cared for as here. There are, alas, some starving people, but unfortunately they are not those who shout about it, and one only hears of them after it is too late. The bulk of them, I believe, belong to the late upper middle classes, and the pity is that it is their pride and independence which prevent them from obtaining the relief in food and clothes which can be obtained by everybody.[6]

Further, Cobden never rested on words alone; he put his ideas into practice in a remarkable solo effort to relieve unemployment. He cleared part of his Salford works to make an area for an improvised gymnasium to which he tempted unemployed men by offering coffee and biscuits – but only if they had taken part in the daily physical exercises. Besides improving their health, he aimed to re-accustom them to the routine of going out to some form of occupation every day, and to get them out of the way of their harassed wives at home. As many as five hundred men joined his scheme, and he aroused their interest so much that they organized jumble sales and house-to-house collections to buy better equipment for the gymnasium. The work was then taken over by the Salford Council of Social Service, and a Physical Training Committee was set up with Cobden as its chairman. Such were the demands on the gymnasium that it was extended to the greater space afforded by the drill hall of the Eighth Battalion of the famous ('Six VCs before breakfast' at Gallipoli) Lancashire Fusiliers.

That was but the beginning of Cobden's contribution. An active Conservative, he happened to be talking to his MP in the House of Commons when he heard a bystander complain that he could not get men for a new works that he was setting up near Rugby. Having 'butted in' to ask the speaker whether he was serious, Cobden promptly offered to find him all the men he needed. A subsequent letter from the speaker, a Mr Reddish of the Rugby Portland Cement Company, expressed an initial requirement for fifty labourers and twelve joiners, whom Cobden promptly recruited from his gymnasium. He first sent them off on a week's holiday in the country and then despatched them in a hired bus to Rugby, along with one of his PT instructors to look after their welfare. Finding that there was further work in the area, and having acquired a hostel, he then sent a second batch of men which he organized in groups of ten, and provided every group with a bicycle. Each group was to draw lots for the first use of the bicycle, which the winner was to have as long as he cycled around the Rugby area to find a job; when successful, he was to bring the cycle back to the group, who would then draw lots for the next man to have it.

Soon he moved as many as two hundred men to find jobs around Rugby, either by cycling safari or at the Cement Company itself, and then in 1938 the Company sent for another two hundred men. So Cobden had single-handedly rescued four hundred men from unemployment, and given many others back their self-respect, before the rearmament programme of the late thirties made work more generally available.

Even all this, though, was merely 'the tip of the iceberg' concerning Cobden's social activities which included governorships of health and welfare charities and of the Salford Royal Hospital, for which he was also chairman of appeals. His sixteen years (from 1937 to 1953) on the Salford City Council had been enlivened, he told me, by the utterances of one of his fellow councillors, a socialist alderman. Despite their opposing politics Cobden had much affection for the alderman, who was a man of little education but who was anxious to bring the benefits to others of the education that he himself had missed. In his own efforts to improve his command of the English language the alderman had become something of a malaprop, with such happy results as to lead him to oppose a proposal before the Council that Salford's Memorial to the Dead of World War II should be an avenue of trees in a local park in these words: 'I beg to oppose this proposal, Mr Chairman. I think that our memorial should be something practical. What good will an avenue of trees do for us? The only good they will do will be to our posteriors!' 'In which case, Mr Chairman,' said one of his Conservative colleagues, 'we must make them birch trees!'

A further delectable situation arose when the alderman had to represent Salford City Council at a joint meeting of the education committees of Salford, Manchester, and another metropolis, to frame a joint representation to the Ministry of Education for the disbursement of a substantial grant with which the Ministry intended to boost education in post-war Britain. Lady Simon of Wythenshawe, as chairman of the Manchester committee, was in the chair at the joint meeting, and joint agreement was for once easy in that all three committees were keen to get as much money as possible from the Ministry into the Manchester area. Seizing on the joint readiness, Lady Simon said something like, 'Well, it is clear that we are all agreed, and so I think that we should strike while the iron is hot. I suggest that our secretary should prepare a draft over the weekend and get it to us so that we can meet again towards the end of next week to finalize it. Can we fix next Thursday afternoon?' This presented the alderman with a problem; he kept a public house, and nearly all his time went either on his duties as landlord or on his work on the Council. The one period of the week that he kept sacrosanct from these was the few hours on Thursday afternoon between the mid-day and evening sessions when his pub was closed. His practice of reserving these hours off-duty he called 'taking liberties'. Lady Simon was thus astonished to hear his immediate reaction to her proposal. 'It's naw good, Madam Chairman, ah can't coum. You see, Thursday afternoon is the one afternoon of the week when ah teak liberties – with mah wife!'

Cobden's generosity was open-handed, and not to his own countrymen alone. Finding a Jewish woman in Vienna who, with her young daughter, had been disowned by her Nazi husband, Cobden smuggled the girl out of Austria in 1938 to live with his family in Manchester; she stayed with them for nine years, and after the war she was reunited with her mother, who had escaped by a different route. Previously, Cobden had also taken a Spanish boy into his family to save him from the Spanish Civil War. In all such acts he was marvellously supported by his wife, Bessie, who must have often wondered what the next surprise would be; her kindness, like his, was inexhaustible.

Cobden also somehow found time for professional as well as social welfare, serving as chairman of committees of the Institution of Electrical Engineers as well as on the Council of the Engineering Industries Association; and his catholicity extended to the Zoological Society of London, where when I first met him he was in a hard-fought conflict with its new council regarding the Society's policy. The trouble had started over a member of the staff (I think that his name was George Cansdale) who had achieved great public popularity on television programmes as 'The Zoo Man'. His success had aroused the jealousy of some other members of the Society's staff, and – according to Cobden – he had therefore been 'organized out'. Cobden, who could never stand aside if he thought an injustice was being done, took up the Zoo Man's case.

The subsequent row developed into a full-blown battle over policy: was the Society to be a popular one, with only the slightest academic standards required for its Fellowship, or was it to attempt to be primarily a learned society? The council opted for the latter, while a large group, among which Cobden was prominent, wanted it to continue on its previous *laissez-faire* lines. The group held that the council had acted contrary to the Society's rules in bringing in a new constitution, and took the council to court. So good was the group's case that they won; but the council appealed, and the appeal went against the group. Its members were promptly expelled from the Society in what to a bystander such as myself seemed a singularly ungenerous gesture.

All such outside interests, with their successes and defeats, were of course peripheral to Cobden's main concern for the prosperity of his own firm; and in addition to the outstanding products that I had encountered before our first meeting on the *Queen Mary* there were many others. The firm, by the time that he was retired in 1956, had expanded to 3,000 employees from the 79 when he took over in 1918, and it was among the pioneers in producing magnetic tape recorders, and it manufactured its own iron-oxide power used in the tapes. When synthetic quartz crystals were required for stabilizing the radio transmitters employed in military communications, and supplies from abroad were in danger of being cut off during the war, Salford mastered the technique of growing them. Similarly, when the supply of artificial rubies for making jewelled bearings for chronometers, compasses, meters and aircraft instruments was menaced by the imminence of war, Cobden negotiated with the Swiss inventor for the rights and the know-how to make rubies and sapphires by his method. So Salford became the main, and in some respects the only, source of jewelled bearings for the many components of military instrumentation for the British forces throughout World War II. The firm also manufactured complete systems such as gyro-gunsights and heavier equipment including predictors and stabilized platforms for anti-aircraft guns.

As I came to know Cobden Turner I was increasingly reminded of Matthew Boulton, the great eighteenth century industrialist, entrepreneur and silversmith, whose robust vision regarding the potential of the steam engine supported James Watt throughout the latter's morose struggles to make his engine work. Boulton's vision and enthusiasm – 'I would erect all the conveniences necessary for the completion of engines, and from which manufactory we would serve the world with engines of all sizes . . . It would not be worth my while to make for three counties only, but I find it very well worth my while to make for all the world' – reflected Cobden Turner's attitude exactly. I can easily imagine him giving the same advice to Watt as did Boulton: 'I cannot help recommending it to you to pray morning and evening, after the manner of your countrymen (the Scotch Prayer "The Lord grant us a gude conceit of ourselves") for you want nothing but a good opinion and confidence in yourself and good health.' And I can certainly imagine him emulating the patriotism of Boulton who, at his own expense, struck a medal of Nelson after Trafalgar with the 'England expects . . .' signal on the reverse, and presented one to every man in the British Fleet who had fought in the battle. In fact, at the end of the war Cobden Turner did have a medal of Churchill struck, which he distributed to those whom he thought deserving; it was typical that he should have commissioned the medal from an impoverished refugee sculptor, to whom he knew that the work would mean much.

The Proximity Fuse

Of all the devices and inventions developed at Salford, the one that gave Cobden Turner the greatest satisfaction was the radio proximity fuse. It was used with brilliant success in anti-aircraft shells, particularly against the German flying bombs in the V-weapons campaign of 1944, and against the kamikazes in the Pacific. This same invention, though, was also the source of his greatest exasperation, for he thought that he and his Salford team never received the recompense that they deserved. In particular he thought that they ought to have received a share of the prodigious royalties that should have been available in the United States, where the weapon was ultimately developed. But, as so often happens, other organizations and individuals were also involved in inventing and developing the idea of a proximity fuse, and subsequent claims for credit inevitably overlapped.

The notion of a fuse that would fire in the proximity of an aircraft without directly hitting it was not entirely new. P. M. S. Blackett had proposed to the Tizard Committee around 1937 that a bomb dropped by a fighter flying above a formation of bombers so as to fall through the formation could be triggered to explode by a photoelectric eye in the bomb which would 'see' the shadow of any bomber that it happened to pass. Other ideas were to fire a rocket with photoelectric controls to guide it up from the ground along a searchlight beam, and to monitor the distance of the rocket up the beam by radar until it reached the same range as that of its aircraft target, when a radio signal would be sent from the ground to a receiver in the rocket which would command it to explode. The main point of all such devices was to ensure that an explosion should be made sufficiently close to the target to ensure that it would be lethally struck by some of the fragments. An absolutely direct hit would not then be necessary, and so the chance of destroying the target would be very much increased. This had, of course, always been the object of anti-aircraft shells, but hitherto they had been fused by a timing mechanism to explode when they reached the assumed range of their target; the problem was that the errors in timing and in range measurement were such that the huge majority of shells exploded either too soon or too late and left the target unscathed, even if they had been aimed well.

Cobden Turner happened to take a small team from his Salford works to Germany in the summer of 1939 to visit the central laboratories of Siemens and Halske. Although they were on more mundane business, they picked up a hint that the Germans were trying to make a proximity fuse for anti-aircraft shells. The hint almost certainly referred to the capacitative type fuse that was described in the Oslo Report (see above, page 333) but all that the Salford team gathered was that some undisclosed sort of proximity fuse was being attempted. On the train on the way home from Berlin they tried to guess what the Germans were doing; but if the capacitative idea occurred to them they rightly rejected it as unpromising. In the course of their discussion they evolved the notion of a fuse that would depend on a tiny radio transmitter in the shell that would send out waves that would be reflected from any nearby object back to the shell and thus cause a detectable interference in the transmitting circuit itself; this interference, indicating the presence of the object, could be made to operate the fuse. The Salford circuit, as it was subsequently developed, was particularly clever in that it needed only a single valve (tube); moreover, it could be set to operate only on an object whose distance from the shell was changing very rapidly, as would happen when the shell was approaching an aircraft.

When Cobden and his companions returned to Salford they decided to evaluate the feasibility of the idea, and in July 1939 they told the Air Ministry what they were doing. As a private venture they tried various alternative arrangements, and by May 1940 had made so much progress that they were able to demonstrate a successful fuse to officials of the Ministry of Supply. The demonstration, and others that followed, involved dropping proximity-fused bombs from high structures such as the high-level bridge over the Manchester Ship Canal at Warburton and the Menai Tubular Bridge. Further tests were made by flying a Blenheim bomber over a fuse on the ground at Tatton Park, Knutsford, while efforts were being made to develop electronic components that would withstand firing in an anti-aircraft shell. That much is clear from Salford's own account which Cobden Turner gave me years later, and from the conclusions of the post-war Royal Commission on Awards to Inventors.

At this point the account becomes complicated, for unknown to the Salford team there was another led by W. A. S. Butement working on a similar problem at the Air Defence Experimental Establishment at Christchurch. The work of this second team has been described by Guy Hartcup in *The Challege of War*. As early as 1931 Butement had, with P. E. Pollard, proposed a radar system for use at sea and now, in 1940, he was working with E. S. Shire, first on photoelectric fuses for rockets and shells, and then on systems for fusing these missiles by radio means – either a signal from the ground when radar showed the missile to be at the same range as the target aircraft, or alternatively by direct reception of the radio wave reflected to the shell by the aircraft under radio illumination from the ground. Early in May 1940 it occurred to Butement and Shire, who were now joined by A. F. C. Thompson (who had been my exact contemporary in physics at Oxford), that it might be possible to put the radio transmitter into the shell itself, and they thereby arrived independently at a scheme very similar to that of the Salford team. Owing either to the need for secrecy or to interdepartmental rivalry – ADEE worked under the War Office, Salford under the Air Ministry and Ministry of Aircraft Production – each team remained largely in ignorance of what the other was doing throughout the war, and hence for a long time believed themselves to be solely responsible for the invention. Both teams were awarded patents.

By September 1940, when the Tizard mission took some key British inventions to America, both teams had been able to give promising demonstrations; and one member of the mission, John Cockcroft, probably knew both of the Butement scheme, since he was head of ADEE, and of the Salford scheme, since he had attended a demonstration at Salford on 2 June 1940. So, besides the famous centimetric magnetron, the promise of a radio proximity fuse for bombs and shells was one of the most vital of the items that the Tizard mission had to offer. Some accounts have said that they took an actual specimen of the fuse; but the secretary of the mission, A. E. Woodward-Nutt, wrote me in February 1979, 'I . . . can confirm that samples of them [proximity fuses] were *not* taken to the USA by the Tizard Mission, although we did take samples of other devices . . . As I expect you know, Tizard made a great point of spending the first two weeks in telling the Americans about our developments without asking them questions about theirs, in a series of informal meetings. I have a note of the first of these [on proximity fuses] at the War Department on Sept. 17th

[1940] which was attended by Profs. Cockcroft and Fowler, Colonel Wallace, the Army Rep. on the Mission, and Brigadier Lindemann from the British Embassy.' Two days later, according to Guy Hartcup, Cockcroft and Fowler had an informal meeting with the prospective leader of the American effort on proximity fuses, Merle Tuve, at his home, and lent him plans of the British fuse.

The early demonstrations of a successful fuse fitted to a projectile in flight had involved rockets and bombs; but it was much more difficult to make the idea work in an anti-aircraft shell where the near-instantaneous acceleration of the shell up the gun barrel required every component of the fuse to be strong enough to survive forces tens of thousands of times greater than that of gravity. Moreover, each component had to be miniaturized to fit into a shell no more than 3.7 inches in diameter. The most obviously delicate item was the radio valve, which had to be no bigger than the eraser and its metal mount on the end of a lead pencil and, although weighing no more than a tenth of an ounce, it had to withstand a stress equivalent to the weight of a 160-pound woman standing on it with her stiletto heel. This graphic description comes from *The Deadly Fuze* by Professor Ralph B. Baldwin, who from 1942 worked on the development of the fuse in America, and who has given an excellent account of the American effort. Many problems had to be overcome, not least the manufacture of miniature batteries that would function reliably at a moment's notice after being dormant for a long period in the shell. At the peak, both tubes and batteries were being made at rates of a hundred thousand or more per day, a triumph of American production engineering that we could not possibly have emulated in Britain. At the same time Professor Baldwin generously acknowledged:

> The early work in England greatly aided the American effort in its initial phases and great encouragement and help was given to the Americans throughout the war. That the British were able to accomplish so much with the much lesser resources they could commit to this work during their beleaguered days is a tremendous tribute to a gallant people.

The Americans shot down their first demonstration target – a small aircraft statically suspended from a balloon – on 13 April 1942, and their first target drone on 12 August. The shells were then produced in quantity, and especially for the US Navy in the Pacific, and in anticipation of the V1 campaign against London. On 9 January 1943, the efficiency of the proximity fuse was demonstrated for the first time in operations when the American cruiser *Helene* shot down a Japanese bomber. Out of their huge production, the Americans had supplied us with three-quarters of a million shells for our land-based A.A. batteries – and nearly another million for our Navy. All told, over twenty million fuses were produced. They were dramatically successful in the latter stage of the V1 campaign against London, where in the last week of the bombardment A.A. batteries shot down 79 per cent of the bombs that they engaged while, in the last day, they destroyed sixty-eight out of less than ninety that reached the English coast. Proximity-fused shells that burst into shrapnel at a predetermined height above the ground greatly increased the effectiveness of artillery fire against troops – even if they were in foxholes or open trenches – and light equipment and communications. They helped to halt the German breakthrough in the Ardennes, and in the conquest of Okinawa, Iwo Jima, and other Pacific islands.

Figures for the quantitative improvement in anti-aircraft gunnery uniquely due to the proximity fuse are difficult to obtain, although the success against the flying bombs contrasts spectacularly with the ineffectiveness of heavy A.A. fire in 1940, where the rounds fired per aircraft claimed as destroyed ranged from 300 against seen targets to 2,500 against unseen ones.[7] In the meantime, radar and predictors had much improved, and the flying bombs were flying straight and level, and all these factors made the A.A. problem easier. However, Baldwin in *The Deadly Fuze*[8] gives evidence from US Navy experience against Japanese aircraft in the Pacific which permits a reasonable comparison between guns firing proximity-fused shells and those with shells with conventional time fuses, but presumably with the same radar and predictors. In 1943, the proximity-fused shells were three times as effective in bringing down aircraft, and by 1945 this figure had risen to six. In more vivid terms, without the proximity fuse we should have needed six times as many guns, six times as many men and six times the manufacturing and support facilities, to bring down the same number of flying bombs, and there would have been six times as much shrapnel to harass our long-suffering people.

The radio proximity fuse thus proved to be one of the outstanding inventions of World War II, and the question subsequently arose of the reward that should be paid to the inventors. Nothing had come back to Salford, for example, in the profits to be gained from manufacture, for the fuse had been manufactured in the United States. Also, nothing came back by way of royalties because the design had been handed by the British Government to its American counterpart free of charge as an item of Lease-Lend in reverse. The same was true of the alternative design of Butement, Shire and Thompson.

Such inequity was one of the reasons why the Government set up the Royal Commission on Rewards to Inventors, who were accordingly invited to submit claims. The Salford team duly applied, and it appears that the Commission also took into account the work of Butement and Shire. The Commission decided that the Salford team was solely responsible for the proximity fuse as fitted to bombs and that the disclosure of the idea to the United States in 1940 led to the development for shells. As for the relative contributions of the two teams the Commission awarded Salford £11,500 and the ADEE team £3,000. It also awarded a team at the Royal Aircraft Establishment, of which Andrew Stratton was a member, £3,500 for improving the design and making safety devices for the Salford fuse. In a letter to me in 1979, Stratton explained that his contribution was to eliminate a diode from the Salford design, which facilitated its incorporation in A.A. shells. He also noted that the original Salford proposal antedated that from ADEE by a few days, 'but this was not a significant factor in the arguments' laid before the Royal Commission.

A question was then raised about the adequacy of the rewards. The Government had handed over the designs to the Americans without consulting the wishes of the inventors – who would of course have agreed, but would have hoped that the Government would then have later compensated them with some reasonable fraction of what the inventors would have earned had they been dealing directly with the American Government. Even at a mere one per cent royalty, the amount coming back to the inventors in Britain might have totalled over £1,000,000, instead of the less than £20,000 awarded by the Royal Commission. And as for honours, the Salford team received none, either British or American, although Stratton deservedly received the American Medal of Freedom with Bronze Palm.

The awards bitterly disappointed Cobden Turner. The Royal Commission had recognized the priority of the Salford contribution but he had confidently expected a much larger award. It rankled to the end of his life.

Although the development of the proximity fuse described in this chapter may have seemed a diversion from the Oslo story, it was in fact connected. The Salford team had conceived the principle of the fuse because of the hint that they had picked up while visiting Berlin in 1939. The hint had been given to Cobden Turner himself by his German friend who, as it turned out, was to write the Oslo Report a few months later in which he mentioned that the Germans were working on a proximity fuse, with the further information that it depended on the change of capacitance between two halves of the shell resulting from the nearby presence of another body. So, even before he wrote the Oslo Report, its author had provided the stimulus that led the Salford team to develop the radar proximity fuse. Ironically, if he had told them that the Germans were working on the capacitative principle they might have dismissed the whole idea as hopeless. Instead, merely believing that the Germans were working on some new form of fuse based on proximity, and that the Germans would not have started on the work unless its principle showed promise, they invented the radar fuse thinking that this might be what the Germans were trying.

The importance of the hint and the subsequent work at Salford is beyond question. It is true that sooner or later the proximity fuse could have been developed without them, for, as we have seen, it also resulted from the independent work of Butement and Shire. A similar point, though, could be made about many of the inventions of the war, including radar, the jet engine and the hollow charge; and the priority of the Salford work in the case of the proximity fuse was recognized by the Royal Commission.

Munich, 1955

Sooner or later, I hoped, there would be an opportunity to meet the author of the Oslo Report, perhaps while I was visiting Germany on other matters, to learn what had moved him to write it. From time to time I had been called over to Germany to advise the Control Commission on the renaissance of German science and I had even been invited by General Wolfgang Martini, the wartime head of signals and radar in the *Luftwaffe*, to meet him and his former officers and associates from industry at a conference in April 1953 to survey German wartime developments in radar. He was then head of an organization known as the *Ausschuss für Funkortung* (Radar Committee) which had been set up in Düsseldorf. It had fallen to me, when he was a prisoner-of-war in England in 1945, to interrogate him; we had both found the experience memorable, and he later wrote to me, 'Your visits, dear Professor, and the intellectual conversations that we had, were each time a ray of light in what for an old soldier were extremely hard and troubled times. It is unlikely that I shall visit England in the foreseeable future. It would therefore give me all the more pleasure to receive a visit from you when you are next in Germany.'

The 1953 conference was in Frankfurt; and besides General Martini I met another former opponent, General Josef Kammhuber, who had been commander-in-chief of the German nightfighters. He, like Martini, was an honest man, and it was a pleasure to meet them again on more equal terms than those of our previous encounters as interrogator and prisoners. One of Martini's happy touches was to request Colonel Victor von Lossberg to look after me; the Colonel was one of the *Luftwaffe*'s most distinguished younger officers, and we had been direct opponents in 1940 and 1941, when he commanded the III *Gruppe* of *Kampf Geschwader* 26, which had bombed us using the Y-ranging system foreshadowed in the Oslo Report. Since the war he had been working as a watchmaker in Garmisch Partenkirchen.

Field Marshal Kesselring was also there, having just been released from prison after completing his sentence for war crimes. In 1940 he had commanded *Luftflotte* 2, which had made most of the air attacks on Britain both in the Battle of Britain and in the Blitz, and he was reported to have flown himself in the attack on Coventry on 14/15 November. Later he was Supreme Commander of all German Forces in Italy, and finally of all those fighting in western Europe. He arrived some time after the conference had started, and was given a thunderous reception by his former officers. Later I was among a half dozen whom Martini invited to dine with him and Kesselring, who ruefully greeted me with, 'I understand that you caused me some trouble in 1940!' On my return to London, I wrote an account of the conference for the Ministry of Defence, and the Minister, Field Marshal Lord Alexander, sent for me and told me how much he envied me as a civilian free to talk to the Germans, which he was not. He had always admired them as very good soldiers, and would have liked to have met Kesselring in particular, who had been his opposing commander in Italy.

A year later my friend and wartime colleague in the Battle of the Beams, Rowley Scott-Farnie, who was now Managing Director of International Aeradio, telephoned me to say that his friends in the Decca firm were inviting General Martini across to the Air Show at Farnborough, and that he would like to see me again. So we all met on

Westminster pier to go on a trip down river on Decca's launch for a demonstration of the accuracy of the Decca navigator, which proceeded to plot our course faithfully as we followed the meanderings of the Thames as it flows around the Isle of dogs like a giant anaconda. Decca had arranged a dinner for us on our return in the St Stephen's Tavern in Westminster, unknowingly invoking a happy reminiscence for Rowley and me, for this was the very hostelry to which he and I repaired on 22 June 1940 to celebrate the discovery of the *Knickebein* beams. Even Martini appreciated the coincidence.

At dinner he told me that he was arranging another conference, this time in Munich, for June 1955, and that he would like me to be guest of honour. I naturally told Cobden Turner, from whom I already knew that his friend of the Oslo Report was now living in Munich; and with his usual generosity he offered not only to introduce us but also to take Vera and me there in his car and arrange our hotel accommodation. Some weeks before our trip he told me that the Oslo author would also be attending the conference and actually reading a paper, and so we would at last meet.

The Frankfurt conference had seemed big, with its audience of some six hundred; but Munich was to be enormous. While Frankfurt had been entirely German but for four of us, including Watson-Watt, Munich would have an attendance of about sixteen hundred, which included twenty-eight former generals, two admirals and thirty-nine professors, with many delegates from abroad. With such a widely drawn audience I accepted General Martini's suggestion that my theme for the *Festvortrag* (Keynote address) should be 'Natural and Artificial Disturbances to Radar'. Although I knew that the Germans were not credited in England with a great sense of humour, I decided to tackle the subject with a light touch, and draw on a lecture that I had first given to the forestry students at Aberdeen on the theory of practical joking. I thought this was worth risking, for my pre-war German friend, Carl Bosch, had been an exquisite practical joker[9] – and had not one of the best jokers of all time been the Captain of Kopenick? In that spirit, even Goering could laugh at himself. As for the relation between disturbances to radar and practical joking, this is best explained by reference to the text of the lecture, which is reprinted here in Appendix B.

Cobden arranged for his patient and imperturbable amanuensis, Jerry Wadsworth, to pick up Vera and me in London, and to drive us in an Alvis to Munich via an air ferry to Le Touquet, staying for one night in Bouillon, on the river Semois, and a second in Strasbourg, and then through Freiburg and the Black Forest to Munich. Our reception there was enthusiastic from the start, where I met several of the generals at dinner including both Kammhuber and Adolf Galland, who had been commander-in-chief of the dayfighters. I can recall him recounting his exchange with Goering in 1940 when he was asked by the Reichsmarschall during the Battle of Britain what his most urgent requirement was, and he had replied, 'Spitfires!'

Everything went well, including the *Festvortrag*. Instead of Colonel von Lossberg, who was now in *Luftwaffe* intelligence, this time I had Captain Giessler of the German Navy to look after me. He told me that some of Martini's staff were concerned as to how well my theme would go down, but he himself was confident. He had been navigating officer on the *Scharnhorst* when she and *Gneisenau* and *Prinz Eugen* had made the dash up the Channel in February 1942 and he had appreciated the incidental compliment in my text about the way the Germans had jammed our radar. At one point, he told me, they had struck a mine and were actually stationary for half an hour; but, fortunately for them, no British aircraft had spotted them.

Vera and I were being treated so well in Munich that Cobden Turner, who had managed to 'gatecrash' the lectures, was concerned that I might be carried away by the warmth of hospitality. 'I'm taking you out to Dachau this afternoon,' he said grimly, and so off we went. Even ten years after the war, when it had been cleaned up and turned into a memorial, it was a sobering experience, with its ghastly chambers, execution stances and crematoria. Cobden took us for tea to a bright open air restaurant only a mile or two away to recover our spirits; there in the warm Bavarian countryside it was hard to believe that anything as awful as Dachau could have ever existed.

We were back in Munich in time to rejoin the conference for a convivial evening in one of the great beer halls – I cannot remember whether it was the Hofbräu or the Loewenbräu. I was placed at the table which held the most senior generals – Martini, Kammhuber and Galland among them, along with Marini's great friend General Egon Doerstling, whom I had met at Frankfurt, and who explained to me that he was as much a philosophical historian as he was an airman, and whose wartime post had been as Head of Technical Supplies in the German Air Ministry. I recalled from Frankfurt how surprised I had been by his objectivity; when discussing with me some aspects of wartime strategy he had volunteered an opinion that Churchill had been right in wanting to thrust northwards from Italy and to attack Germany from the south. 'Destroy Germany!' said Doerstling, tapping the table at each word. 'ABSOLUTELY CORRECT MILITARY DECISION!' I had never expected to hear a German general talk with such detachment.

With the flowing beer things were going very well indeed, and we were pledging eternal friendship and the hope that Britain and Germany would never fight one another again. At that point I said, 'This is all very well – but I went to Dachau this afternoon: what are you going to do to stop anything like that happening again?' The conviviality was sharply halted and the table hushed as General Doerstling said, 'Professor Jones, you do ask the most direct questions!' This was followed by Martini saying, 'We did not know about the concentration camps. To think that one man could have misled us all so much!' There was a general endorsement of this statement and then a silence, broken pensively by Doerstling: 'It is quite true that most of us did not know about the camps. But it's no use our trying to deny that they exist, because they are there. We cannot understand how they happened – but, because we do not understand, I do not see how we can guarantee that they will not happen again!' Here was the honestly bewildered realism of a humane soldier, whose words I have recalled many times in the years since. For me, in those days, I would have thought it impossible for such inhumanity ever to happen in Britain, that there was something in our national character which would have forbidden it; but now I am not so sure. So, let us never forget the exemplary depth of sadistic immorality to which a great nation could sink, even though it consisted of human beings much like ourselves and among them Luther, Goethe, Beethoven and Einstein. Along with Doerstling's words I recall some of Churchill's: 'Everyone is not a Pastor Niemöller or a martyr . . . I thank God that in this island home of ours we have never been put to the test which many of the peoples of Europe have had to undergo.'

The radar conference itself had been held in the hall of the Deutsches Museum, the greatest museum of science and technology in the world. To illustrate mining techniques, for example, a shaft had actually been sunk under the museum, while to demonstrate the development of the pianoforte a guide took us from one instrument to another, a typical introduction being for him to say, 'Now, Mozart would have composed for such an instrument as this.' He would then proceed to play a fragment from Mozart on a contemporary instrument of Mozart's day. The Museum had been damaged in the war but, as everywhere in western Germany, it had been vigorously repaired. Fortunately, among its surviving treasures was the apparatus by which in the 1880s Heinrich Hertz had discovered the existence and properties of the radio waves which were the basis of the electronic warfare that had occasioned our conference, as well as of the many benefits that have come from their use in communication, navigation, and entertainment. Another of the surviving treasures was the pair of Magdeburg hemispheres in which in 1654 Otto von Guericke created a vacuum, with the result that, thanks to the external atmospheric air pressure, two teams of eight horses could not pull them apart. They are only fifty-one centimetres (twenty inches) in diameter, but it would require a force of two tons weight to separate them when evacuated.

All around Munich there was the noise of pneumatic drills, and the other familiar sounds and sights of energetic clearance and reconstruction. When I had first visited Germany in 1945 I found a state of near paralysis; by 1949 there were signs of recovery. So much so that the German landladies of my officers and men in Obernkirchen were beginning to provide them with extra comforts by way of food. Now, in 1955, recovery was in full spate. This led me to ask General Doerstling and others how it had come about. While some said that the recovery had dated from the 1948 reform of the currency, the answer that I received every time was that it was the result of a completely general feeling that Germany must work for its recovery, just as we in Britain had felt after Dunkirk. Some of the more thoughtful, like Doerstling, were at the same time worried by their countrymen's preoccupation with work to the exclusion of nearly everything else, pointing out that unless a man thinks about the objective which he is being asked to work for, he will be too readily duped into working without question towards such ends as the Nazis had.

Pondering on the resurgence of the German industries, I recalled some words spoken by Adolf Hitler on 10 December 1940: 'When this war is ended Germany will set to work in earnest. A great "Awake!" will sound throughout the country. Then the new German nation will stop manufacturing cannon and will embark on the new work of reconstruction for the millions. Then we shall show the world for the first time who is the real master – Capitalism or work? Out of this work will grow the great German Reich of which great poets have dreamed.'[10] Although not in the way he expected, Hitler's words seemed to be coming true.

I was so impressed by the spirit in Germany, all the more because of the contrast with what was happening in Britain, that when some months later the BBC invited me to give a talk on a scientific subject, I accepted on condition that they allowed me to give an additional talk on the state of Britain. It was broadcast in April 1956 as *The German Challenge to Britain*, and it is reproduced here as Appendix C.

The Munich conference was largely concerned with the development of radar on both sides in World War II, but it also surveyed the developments that had since occurred. One of these was radio-astronomy, for which much of the stimulus had been the wartime discovery that our anti-aircraft gunlaying radar was being unexpectedly jammed whenever the radar 'looked' in the direction of the sun. This led physicists and astronomers at last to take notice of the discovery by Karl Jansky of the Bell Telephone Laboratories in 1931 that radio 'noise' was being emitted by heavenly bodies in the Milky Way, for the sun itself was a star typical of myriads in the Milky Way; if the sun was emitting radio waves, so could they. Indeed, one of the papers at Munich was on '*Die Sonne als Objekt der Radioastronomie*' ('The Sun as a Radioastronomical Object'). It was given by Professor Hans Ferdinand Mayer, of the famous electrical firm of Siemens & Halske; before and during the war he had been head of its Central Laboratories, and he now directed all the research in the firm's new laboratories in Munich. In the turmoil of the immediate post-war years he had held a research post from 1946 to 1950 in Cornell University in Ithaca, New York, and it was there that he had done the work that he now described at Munich. The chairman of the conference pointed him out to me with some amusement, describing him as having done something which led to his being put into a concentration camp during the war. I asked what his offence had been, but the chairman appeared not to know. I hope that I, too, appeared not to know – for I was already aware that not only had Professor Mayer been in concentration camps but that it was he who had been the friend of Cobden Turner who had told him about the proximity fuse and had sent us the Oslo Report.

We were formally introduced to each other in the course of the conference, but we showed no more mutual interest than courtesy between strangers would dictate – 'acting the indifferent', as James Clerk Maxwell once put it. I knew that Cobden Turner had arranged to take Vera and me to Professor Mayer's flat one evening, for he lived in Munich, and so after all the years of wondering about the authorship of the Oslo Report there would at last be the occasion to get know the man who wrote it, and why he had done it.

'The Oslo Person'

Hans Ferdinand Mayer, who ever afterwards signed[11] his letters to me 'The Oslo Person', was born on 23 October 1895 in Pforzheim and completed his school education there in 1914. Immediately on leaving school he joined the German Army, in September 1914, as a volunteer and went to the French front, only to be severely wounded in the leg on his first day in action. After a long convalescence, and no longer fit for active service, he took up the study of physics and mathematics at the Technische Hochschule at Karlsruhe, and went on to Heidelberg and became research assistant to the Nobel Prizewinner Philipp Lenard, both noted for his discoveries in electronic physics and notorious for refusing to accept any physical ideas of Jewish origin, including Einstein's theory of relativity. Mayer's own doctoral thesis was on the interaction of slow electrons with molecules; completed in 1920, it was awarded a distinction. In 1922 he joined Siemens and had been with the firm ever since, except for his four years as professor of signals technique at Cornell. His work resulted in eighty-two patents, and forty-seven papers in science and technology; these achievements were later recognized by the award of the prestigious Gauss-Weber medal of the University of Göttingen in 1968. His contributions to electronics before 1939 were well known internationally, with four citations on different topics in Terman's classic *Radio Engineers Handbook* of 1943. They were characterized by a masterly knowledge of 'state of the art' electronic devices and great ingenuity in their application to achieve new systems – for example a radio receiver that would automatically change its band-width to produce the optimum response for a given strength of signal.

At least as early as 1924 Hans Mayer became involved as a technical expert in negotiations between his firm and others abroad which might wish to secure licences to manufacture some of the products developed by Siemens. Among these firms was the General Electric Company in England, and one class of products concerned included loading coils and repeaters for telephone lines and cables. The Englishman in the GEC organization who had recognized the quality of the

Siemens components, and therefore wished to negotiate a licence to manufacture them in his own firm, was Cobden Turner. Over the years his acquaintance with Hans Mayer was strengthened by their meeting, as representatives of their two countries, on the Comité Consultatif des Communications Téléphoniques à Grandes Distances. Acquaintance grew into so warm a friendship that in 1939 Cobden Turner became godfather to Hans Mayer's second son.

In the meantime, Hans Mayer had become increasingly disturbed by what was happening in Germany. What then transpired is best told by the account he sent to me on 18 July 1967. It was based on a rough draft by Cobden Turner which Hans Mayer corrected and expanded, and it may be read here exactly as I received it from him:

> It is of course well known, that by this time Hitler had established himself as a Dictator and a great power, having annexed Austria and overcome the resistance of Czeckoslavia. He also had proclaimed the Germans to be the 'Master Race', superior to all other nations, which should work for the 'masters' as 'slaves'. He had also deprived the Jews of their citicenship, confining them to the status of 'subjects'.
>
> Although many of my colleages liked such ideas and became members of the Nazi Party, I never believed in such nonsense and never joined any Party Organisation. In the course of time, I became more and more opposed to the Nazi regime. In this I found in Mr. Cobden Turner a very willing ally.
>
> But he was an ally not only in thoughts, but also in deeds. In fall 1938, when I was in London, I told him the sad case of a young schoolgirl – Martyl Karweik – who lived near me, and whose father was a prominent Nazi. He had disowned her and her mother, who was a Jewess. The mother had received an order of expulsion, but was not allowed to take Martyl with her, because the daughter was half-*arian*, and the father did not want Martyl because she was half-*jewish*. This meant eventualy confinement to a forced-labor camp, a place of no return.
>
> Mr. Cobden Turner was visibly affected by this case. Not long afterwards he came to Berlin, went to the British Consul and obtained a British passport and visa for Martyl. In England she was installed as a member of the Turner household and styed there for 8 years. When war was over, in 1946, he sent Martyl to here mother, who lived then in New-York, and Marthyl became married with a parson. – No question, that Mr. Cobden Turner had saved the life of Martyl.
>
> In 1939 it became obvious, that a war was imminent. At that time I was in charge of one of the largest industrial research-and development organisations in the communication and electronic field. By then, our capacity had to be switched over from civil work to military work,

especially to new and secret weapons which requeired communications and electronics techniques. In this field we worked together with the Army, Navy and Airforce, and there was hardly any secret weapon, conceived at that time, which was not known to me. Some of these deadly weapons were already field-tested, and large-scale manufactoring had started. This meant – sooner or later – war!

Middle of 1939 – on his way from Vienna back to London – Mr. Cobden paid me a visit, the last before the war. I told him, that in my opinion a war was imminent, and that – should England be involved – this country would be in great danger, due to new and formidable secret weapons. Of course he was very inquisitive, but at that time I refused to tell him any details. But I promised to provide him with information in case a war between Germany and England would actually break out. For I considered Mr. Cobden Turner to be the right person, who had the ability and the connections to channel this information to the proper authorities in England. A beast like Hiteler should not win the war!

When we said Good-bye, I gave him a small, but very strong magnet, which was incidently part of a proximity fuse. After the war, he told me, that he had soon found out the purpose of this magnet, and that he had put his assistants on the work and produced a proximity fuse, which was patented and used to great effect by the British Forces and United States Forces during the war.

A few months later, on September 1, at 4:30 A.M., World War II started with the German attack on Poland. As a consequence, England declared a state of war with Germany on September 3, 1939. Now, in case Germany would attack England with secret weapons which were known to me, it would be my turn to inform Mr. Cobden Turner. The first such case, which came to my knowledge, was the torpedoing of the *Royal Ark* at Scapa Flow on October 14, 1939. But it was quite impossible to inform Mr. Cobden Turner directly. I therefore mailed a letter to the US-Embassy in Berlin (Oct. 20, 1939) disclosing the secret of the torpedo used (magnetic type) and disclosing countermeasures (degaussing). I also requested that the British Naval Authorities should be informed.

By good fortune I had the possibility to arrange a business trip to Oslo, Norway, on October 29–November 4, 1939. Here, on an old type-writer, borrowed from the hotel porter, I wrote the socalled 'Oslo Report', which incidently consisted of 2 different letters, written on Wednesday, November 1, and Thursday, November 2. These letters were mailed to the Britisch Embassy in Oslo. The address was easily found in the Oslo Telephone Index.

At first, I had intended to mail the report to Mr. Cobden Turner. But on second thought, I feared the report could be lost on its way from Norway to England. – Nevertheless I wrote a special letter to Mr. Cobden Turner from Oslo, pointing out the possibility of establishing a 'contact' in Denmark. For obvious reasons I signed this letter not with my name, but with 'Martyl', thus [not] disclosing the writers proper name.

In order to be sure, that the Oslo Report had reached the right quarters in England, I asked at the end of the second letter for the BBC to change their announcement 'Hello, this ist London calling' into 'Hello, Hello, this is London calling'. This should take place on Monday, November 20, 1939, at the beginning of the 8 o'clock evening news. – This happened as requested.

Looking back to those times, I would say today, that in all probability the 'Oslo Report' would not have been written if I had not known Mr. Cobden Turner so well. For he was my ally, and thus I felt as an ally of England, willing to oppose Hiter's tyranny and to help secure a free and better world.

The Oslo Person

The text of the letter is almost entirely self-explanatory. Besides showing how the writing of the Oslo Report was motivated by the friendship with Cobden Turner that had deepened with the latter's action in rescuing Martyl Karweik, it confirms his statement that Hans Mayer had written to him from Oslo in November 1939 and had signed as 'Martyl' confident that Cobden Turner alone would recognize its origin. The letter in fact reached him, and it was indeed his mention of it at the Athenaeum dinner that had caused Bimbo Norman to explode, and thus to our learning at last the identity of the Oslo author. Cobden Turner duly reported his receipt of the letter to the Ministry of Information because of the prospect it offered of a continuing line through the contact in Denmark; but although he was subsequently visited by two security officers neither he nor Hans Mayer heard anything more.

Hans Mayer's account of the modification that he suggested to the BBC news broadcast to let him know that the Oslo Report had itself been received makes much better sense than what I had been told at the time (see above, page 265). I was also told that the particular news broadcast was in German; but Hans Mayer gives the impression that it was in English, the exceptional but inconspicuous repetition of 'Hello' being all that would be necessary to tell him that his Report had been received.

In Oslo, he stayed at the Hotel Bristol, and it was from the head porter there that he borrowed the typewriter, presumably to avoid the clue to his identity through handwriting should the letters be intercepted. Again, he sent his information in two separate letters rather than one, which would have been more conspicuous for its bulk; another advantage was that he could immediately clear himself of the first day's typescript rather than keep it overnight. The statement that the report came in two letters through the post agrees with that of Admiral Boyes, who received them (see above, page 277), and gives the lie to those other accounts claiming a different authorship and speaking of a single bulky package whether delivered by post or by hand of a furtive messenger. It is perhaps curious that the Hotel Bristol was mentioned in the newspaper article of 1947 (see above, page 278) which claimed that the author of the Oslo Report had stayed there, but this was probably no more than coincidence since the hotel was the popular one for international visitors.

Hans Mayer also gave me the independent evidence of his passport which confirmed the details of his visit to Oslo. These show that he left Germany on Sunday 29 October, travelling on the ferry from Sassnitz to Trelleborg, and arrived in Oslo on 30 October. He arrived back in Berlin airport on 4 November, having flown from Kastrup. In his own notes:

> Left Germany on *Sunday* 29.10.39 via Sassnitz
> *Monday* 30.10 Arrival Oslo. Bristol Hotel
> *Tuesday* 31.10 Technical discussions with Dir. Rynning-Toennessen, P.T.T.Oslo on new Open Wire Carrier Systems
> *Wednesday* 1.11 First O.L.
> *Thursday* 2.11 Second O.L. Left Oslo by night train
> *Friday* 3.11 Technical discussions with Dir. Niels Holmblad, P.T.T. Kopenhagen
> *Saturday* 4.11 Return to Berlin.

Everything in Hans Mayer's account rings true, including not only the fact of the two letters and details in them which he was able to describe and which I had been careful not to tell either him or Cobden Turner, but also the latter's characteristic generosity in taking Martyl Karweik into his own family. Moreover, the fact that Mayer was in the Siemens organization explains the use of the 'FZ' designation of missiles (see above, page 274) in the Oslo Report, which unwittingly pointed to the firm. So we now knew who had written the Oslo Report, why he wrote it, and how he found his opportunity.

There were still more than five years of war to follow. For the first three Hans Mayer remained free, listening whenever he could to BBC broadcasts, and especially those by Churchill, with a radio receiver that he kept in his attic. Torn as he was between his basic loyalty to Germany and the belief that only if Britain survived could his country be released from Nazi domination, he considered emigrating with his wife and three children to America, and in October 1940 applied to the American consular division. Following the inevitable prohibition by the Nazi government, he arranged a visit to Zurich in November 1941 in the hope of approaching the American Embassy in Switzerland; but he was evidently being watched, for just as he was about to enter the Embassy he found a hand on his shoulder and the voice of a German agent telling him not to proceed if he did not want to endanger his family. Either on that visit or a subsequent one he posted a letter to the British Embassy in Berne giving details of the application of the Würzburg radar for the control of nightfighters, and the development of homing torpedoes. Whether or not the letter ultimately reached us in London I cannot recall; if it did, it would not have stood out as spectacularly as the Oslo letters, which had arrived at a time when we knew almost nothing about German developments, and so it may have escaped special notice.

He returned to Berlin, where he continued his clandestine listening to BBC broadcasts. This, of course, was dangerous and in August 1943 'I had the misfortune to repeat something I had heard with the result that the maid in the house next door informed the Gestapo and I was taken into custody'. He was arrested at his desk in Siemens; although a search revealed no further evidence against him he was confined in the concentration camp at Dachau. His faithful wife, a lady of admirable calm and dignity, approached his old professor, Philipp Lenard, who with his railing against the Jews was in excellent standing with the Nazis. Writing to tell her that he was interceding with Himmler he advised, 'Your husband must change his mind. It will not harm him if he thinks as I do. Misfortune is the soap God is washing us with. We cry like little children, when they are being washed.'

It may have been a result of Lenard's intercession, or simply of the fact that by 1943 Germany was short of good scientists and engineers in the electronics field, that Hans Mayer was accorded special status in Dachau. Prisoners in concentration camps with suitable qualifications were being formed into units to undertake programmes of work on scientific and technical problems, and in return were offered better treatment than that given to other inmates. The scientific/technical unit at Dachau was known as the '*Wetterstelle*' (Weather station) and among the problems given it was a study of the British bombing aid known to us as 'H_2S' and to the Germans as the 'Rotterdam *Gerät*'. Hans Mayer became head of the unit and was granted the privileges of unshaven hair and civilian clothes. For administration and discipline the unit was supervised by the SS, while for its technical work it was ultimately responsible to the Chief of High Frequency Research in Germany, the radiophysicist Abraham Esau.

Despite all its horrors, Dachau was one of the less severe of the concentration camps; but this was not true of Gross-Rosen, the camp to which the *Wetterstelle* was for some reason next moved. In all Mayer was in four further camps before the war ended. In these he survived, as he told Cobden Turner, by emulating the example of a mouse, which survives by being so unobtrusive that it escapes notice. So, to minimize the risk of being chosen for exemplary punishment by the guards when they were selecting victims out of a squad, you should aim to be somewhere in the middle and not in the front or rear ranks or on the flanks, and to be as inconspicuous as possible.

As Germany gradually disintegrated in the last stages of the war, and the prisoners were moved from one concentration camp to another in the face of the Allied armies, Hans Mayer still retained the advantage of being a useful technician, with the few consequent privileges that were left. These included a degree of freedom in moving about the camp, and he ultimately found an opportunity to escape simply by walking out. He then found his way across wooded country for some days until, exhausted and hungry, he broke cover in a forest clearing within sight of a cottage. There, in its garden, he could see a great wooden replica of the Nazi emblem of an eagle carrying a swastika in its talons. Perhaps it had been carved by a proud forester in honour of his son serving with the German forces. But now the great emblem was being hacked to bits in a frenzied attack by a woman wielding an axe. She was the mother, and had just received the bitter news that her son had been killed; her grief and disillusion, so mordantly expressed, must have been shared by many throughout Germany. Hans Mayer could at least be sure that she would have no sympathy left for the Nazis, and so he asked her for food and shelter; then, with the war ending, he made his way through the turmoil and debris to find his family.

As order gradually emerged under the Allied Military Government, he obtained recognition from the authorities in both Baden and Berlin who certified that he had 'been interned for the sake of his antifascist activity in the camps of Sachsenhausen, Dachau, Gross-Rosen, Mauthausen and Buchenwald from August 1943 to May 1945' (Baden) and 'as a victim of Fascism' (Berlin). With these clearances and with his high professional reputation he was able to take up the offer of work in America, first for the US Air Force at its main research and development base, Wright Field near Dayton, Ohio. Working behind closed gates, though, was a disturbing reminder of his wartime incarceration, and he was therefore glad in 1947 to accept a professorship at Cornell University and work in the new field of radioastronomy through the painful years of post-war reorganization. Thus being preoccupied in America, he heard nothing of the publicity concerning his Oslo Report following my lecture in London in 1947, and it was only when Cobden Turner told him in 1954 of meeting me that he at last learned how helpful the Report had been.

No Glitter of Trinkets

Now that the origin of the Oslo Report was no longer a mystery, I wondered what might be done to demonstrate the appreciation of the British Government to the two men involved. As the officer who had made the greatest use of the information that their friendship had provided, I had of course thanked both of them personally; but they deserved much more. In the case of Hans Mayer this would be difficult: he had a high position in post-war Germany, and any public recognition could have been an embarrassment. Whether or not any financial reward would have been appropriate, he would not have wished for it, and his circumstances were good enough for him not to need it. There was, though, always the possibility that if a neo-Nazi atmosphere were to develop in Germany, his position – and even his life – might be threatened. I did, therefore, discuss this possibility with Sir John Sinclair, the current head of MI6, to whom I had told the story of how the Oslo Report came to be written, and he gave me the verbal assurance that if such an eventuality developed, funds would be made available to support Mayer and his family in a safe country. That was as far as I could reasonably take the matter.

Cobden Turner, of course, was a British citizen and therefore eligible for public recognition, which he well deserved, even apart from his connection with the Oslo story. Once I was certain of the facts, I wrote on 15 September 1954 to Winston Churchill, to whom I had mentioned the Oslo Report in some of my own wartime papers. Part of my letter ran:

> By a series of accidents I have recently discovered how the report came

> to be written, and who wrote it. I believe that you might find the story no less interesting than that of 'Knickebein'. Arising from the 'Oslo Report' there is the matter of some form of recognition for the men who were instrumental in its coming to us, and I would like to discuss this with you.

Subsequently, on 24 February 1955, I saw Sir Winston alone in the Cabinet Room in Downing Street and told him the whole story. He seemed tired and pensive, but he asked me to let him have a letter giving details of Cobden Turner's services on which he could act, and I set these out in a letter on 1 March.

Unhappily, he retired as Prime Minister a few weeks later (on 6 April) and I could only hope that he had submitted Cobden Turner's name for consideration. When four Honours Lists passed, I wondered whether my letter had been overlooked in the rapid changes in the Premiership (Harold Macmillan had succeeded Anthony Eden on 13 January 1957), and so I considered trying again. My old chief as Secretary of State for Air during the war, Sir Archibald Sinclair – now Lord Thurso – was a member of the Political Honours Scrutiny Committee, and so I consulted him. He was most helpful, for besides putting on record a summary of Cobden Turner's many public services, I had been able to confide to him the details of the Oslo story, and he wrote to me on 24 May 1957, saying:

> I have seen the claim submitted by you to Sir Winston Churchill and it seems to me that the 'orthodox' grounds are – if not definitely better or definitely worse, which is not for me to judge – definitely comparable to those which are reviewed biannually by the Political Honours Scrutiny Committee, of which I am a member; but that in addition, Mr Cobden Turner has this outstanding, if belated, claim for an award.

He also told me that he himself had already written to the Prime Minister, Harold Macmillan, and received the reply:

> I find that Professor Jones has already, on several occasions, approached this office on behalf of Mr Cobden Turner. In February 1955 he saw Sir Winston Churchill, and subsequently sent full details of Mr Cobden Turner's career and services, together with a lengthy memorandum. As a result, Mr Turner's claims were duly considered but were not found sufficiently strong to prevail over other candidates. I can certainly arrange for one of my staff to see Professor Jones if he has anything new to say. But I doubt whether it is worth while if it is only a question of repeating the story that we have already.

Lord Thurso was good enough to press the Prime Minister further, and so it was arranged that I should see one of his secretaries, with Lord Thurso's enthusiastic support: 'I hope we are in time. The first of June is coming – but is not gone! With all good wishes for the success of your recommendation – I shall look eagerly for Mr Cobden Turner's name!'

The Birthday Honours List, though, was out long before the Prime Minister's secretary and I could meet. In the meantime, I collected further support from the Admiralty, the Foreign Office and the Ministry of Supply (on whose list of recommendations Cobden Turner's name, it transpired, had been submitted several times independently of my efforts). On 24 October I met the Prime Minister's secretary in Downing Street; in anticipation of our meeting he had been good enough to check whether there was some 'black mark' against Cobden because he, too, was surprised that nothing had come of the earlier recommendations, and he was able to assure me that no black mark had ever been recorded.

However, Cobden Turner's name did not appear in the next Honour's List, or on any of its successors. Someone else must have pursued the matter at least as far as I had done, for I have a copy of a letter from one of the Downing Street staff in December 1964 which ran:

> I have been asked by the Prime Minister to advise you that he is in complete sympathy and agreement with the views expressed yesterday on Mr Cobden Turner.
>
> It should be appreciated that it is now too late to include him in the forthcoming list, however. The Prime Minister will give the matter his active consideration and one can anticipate Mr Turner's name being included on the Birthday List, when the recommendations are made.
>
> I am sure you will be glad to hear this.

Still Cobden Turner's name did not appear; and in 1969 yet another approach was made, this time by a former Chancellor of the Exchequer who wrote to me, 'I certainly hope that something can be done in the next Honours List.' Unfortunately, his approach proved just as fruitless as all the others; and Cobden Turner died in June 1970, deeply disappointed. To him civil honours would have meant more than the glitter of trinkets that they entitle their recipient to wear on formal occasions; they would have represented the gratitude of the country that in so many ways he had served with so much panache and such great loyalty.

I am not in a position to theorize effectively on why every attempt at achieving recognition failed, except for one comment made by Harold Macmillan which Lord Thurso passed on to me. It was to the effect that it was too late in 1955 to award an honour for services performed during the war – that phase of life was now closed. But surely the passage of time could never wipe out a debt of gratitude. Quite possibly Cobden Turner might have had a better chance of recognition if all his services had been performed for a single ministry, instead of being spread over several, none of which would have recommended him with the same enthusiasm as his overall contribution justified. I had always felt that, with respect to the honours that I saw awarded during the war, both to others and to myself, three conditions were necessary for an honour to be granted; (1) the opportunity to perform the service, (2) performing it with some distinction, and (3) having someone to witness the performance who survived long enough to bring it to the notice of the authorities in a convincingly eloquent manner. The last of these conditions was no less essential than the second. From the unfortunate case of Cobden Turner I would add a fourth condition: ensuring that there is a witness who can report before gratitude has grown cold. Otherwise, the merchant of light will forever be obscured by a bureaucratic bushel.

So the two principal figures in the Oslo story, Hans Ferdinand Mayer and Harry Cobden Turner, passed away unhonoured, albeit with the deep gratitude of those few of us who were privileged to know their story.

Epilogue

The provenance of such a package of valuable information as was contained in the Oslo Report may raise questions in the mind of the morally inclined reader, as it may well have done in the mind of Hans Mayer, himself. When is an action justified that might in other circumstances be classed as treachery? And what are the circumstances under which we can say with Edith Cavell that 'patriotism is not enough'?

It is one thing for a man to sell his country for immediate personal gain, and something very close to this to tempt or blackmail him into doing so: but it can be another if, through loyalty to some higher concept such as truth or humanity, a man feels that his country's, or the world's, long term interests will be better served by his acting to frustrate the intentions of his country's current leaders or even those of the majority of its people. This is not to denigrate the sublime quality of patriotism in its highest forms; but while disagreeing with Samuel Johnson's dictum that it is the last refuge of a scoundrel, we can recognize that it is but the first step (albeit an essential one – it is doubtful whether a man devoid of patriotism is likely to proceed higher) on the ladder of altruism ascending from the interests of oneself to those of one's country and on to those of mankind the world over. But if we do grant that there can be a higher loyalty than that owed immediately to one's own country, can we distinguish between Hans Mayer and, for example, Kim Philby?

Both were men of intelligence and courage; each acted from idealistic motives, one for us and the other – as it happened – against us. At least I am sure that Mayer did, and I am prepared to assume that Philby also did, distasteful though I feel his conduct to be. Both acted to change their worlds using what they saw as the best means to their ends, no doubt subconsciously acting on Burke's dictum, that all that is necessary for the triumph of evil is that good men should do nothing.

Philby appears to have acted cold-bloodedly from a naively academic assessment of the relative merits of communism and capitalism, an assessment which he professed to hold to the end of his life despite all the evidence to be seen in Russia that communism is at least as vulnerable as capitalism to exploitation by human greed and ambition. Philby might argue today that the Gorbachev reforms give the hope that his faith in Russia is being justified – but could he claim that his actions helped them to come about? Mayer, by contrast, acted from direct experience of a shockingly vicious regime and from a warm affection and respect for Cobden Turner as a representative Englishman. Philby's objective was the world triumph of a system that permitted the Stalin purges and, almost certainly, the massacre of the Polish officer corps and intellectuals at Katyn. Mayer's was the defeat of the Nazi masters of the concentration camps by helping the country of his friend to resist them, and thereby to restore his own country to the decencies of civilization. Far from treachery, his action was that of a patriot loyal to the longer-term interests both of his country and of the great European family that encompasses both Germany and Britain.

A final point: in recent years we in Britain have been shocked by a sequence of security scandals which may well have given the impression that all intelligence is 'dirty' and that any who work in it must, at best, be devious. There is some truth in both impressions; gentlemanly behaviour can put any who practise it in intelligence at a disadvantage, for too often 'the children of this world are in their generation wiser than the children of light'. But sometimes, happily, things work the other way; with all the wartime defects in MI6 that resulted from the implicit internal assumption that all its members would act in mutual good faith, which Philby so ably exploited, that same ethos resulted in such an upright and distinguished man as the great nuclear physicist, Niels Bohr, telling me that he was happy to co-operate with the British Secret Service because he found that it was run by a gentleman.

On a similar theme, Arnold Kramish has recorded that Paul Rosbaud's readiness to work for us during the war owed something to the decency of the treatment he had experienced as a prisoner-of-war in the hands of the British after the Austrian surrender in Italy in 1918 (see above, page 282). While Paul Rosbaud did not write the Oslo Report, he had much in common with Hans Mayer, even to this feeling for Britain. In both cases that feeling had its origin in decent and generous conduct by Englishmen; integrity can count for as much in intelligence as it does in all other human activities.

Appendix A

The Oslo Report

1 Ju88 Programme

The Ju88 is a twin-engined long-range bomber and has the advantage that it can also be used as a dive-bomber. Several thousands, probably 5,000, are produced per month. Up to April 1940, 25–30,000 bombers have been produced of this type alone.

2 Franken

The first German aircraft-carrier is lying in Kiel Harbour. It is expected to be ready by April 1940 and is called the *Franken*.

3 Remote-controlled gliders

The German Navy have developed remote-controlled gliders, that is, small aircraft of about three metres span and three metres long. They carry a large explosive charge. They are not powered by an engine and are launched at great height from an aircraft. They contain:

(a) an electric altimeter (like the one described in the *Bell System Technical Journal*, January 1939, page 222). This causes the glider to descend to about three metres above the water. It then continues to fly horizontally, actuated by rocket propulsion.

(b) A remote control by means of ultra-short waves in the form of telegraph signals, through which the control members are regulated to the right or left or kept straight, for example, from a ship or an aircraft.

The glider is said to be directed against the side of an enemy ship where the explosive charge is then dropped or exploded under the water.

The secret code number is FZ21 (*Ferngesteuerte Zielflugszeug*). The experimental establishment is Peenemünde, at the mouth of the Peene, near Wolgast, in the vicinity of Greifswald.

4 Autopilot

Under the secret code number FZ10 an autopilot (remote-controlled aircraft) is being developed. This is to be controlled from a manned aircraft and is to be used, for example, for destroying balloon barrages.

5 Remote-controlled projectiles

The Army Ordnance Office (HWA) is the development centre for the Army. This establishment is engaged on the development of projectiles of eighty-centimetre calibre. Rocket propulsion is employed and the stabilization is brought about by an installed gyro. The difficulties in the rocket propulsion are due to the fact that the projectile does not fly straight but in uncontrollable curves. It is therefore equipped with a wireless remote control by means of which the burning of the ignition charge of the rocket is controlled.

This development is still in the initial stages and the eighty-centimetre shells are to be used later against the Maginot Line.

6 Rechlin

This is a small place on the Mueritzsee, north of Berlin. The Laboratories and Development Establishments for the *Luftwaffe* are here; hence they are promising targets for bomber attacks.

7 Methods of attack on pill-boxes [*Bunkers*]

Experience in the Polish Campaign has shown that direct attack against pill-boxes cannot succeed. The Polish pill-box positions were therefore completely smoked out by gas shells, the smoke hanging in a heavy pall until it penetrated deeper and deeper into the pill-box positions. The Polish crews were thus compelled to withdraw from the pill-boxes. Immediately behind the smoke screen, there followed the German flame-throwers which took up position in front of the pill-boxes. The latter were powerless against the flame-throwers and the crews either perished or gave themselves up.

8 Aircraft warning device

In the attack by English airmen on Wilhelmshaven at the beginning of September, the English aircraft were already picked up at a distance of 120 kilometres from the coast. Along the entire German coast there are short-wave transmitters with an output of 20 kilowatts, these sending out very short pulses of a duration of 10^{-5} seconds. These pulses are reflected from the aircraft. In the vicinity of the transmitter is a wireless receiver which is tuned to the same wavelength. There, after a certain interval, the wave reflected from the aircraft is received and it is registered by a cathode-ray tube. From the interval between the transmitted pulse and the reflected pulse, the distance of the aircraft can be ascertained. As the transmitted pulse is much stronger than the reflected pulse, the receiver is blocked during the transmitted pulse. The transmitted pulse is marked on the cathode-ray tube by a local signal.

In conjunction with the Ju88 programme, these transmitters are being installed everywhere in Germany.

Countermeasures: By means of special receivers, which can pick up pulses of a duration of 10^{-5} to 10^{-6} seconds, the wavelengths of the pulses transmitted in Germany must be determined and interfering pulses on the same wavelength sent out. These receivers can be installed on land, so can the transmitters, as the method is very sensitive.

Whilst this method has been installed on a large scale, another method operating on fifty-centimetre waves is being worked on. (See Figure 1.) [Missing.] The transmitter T sends out short pulses which are powerfully directed by means of an electric concave reflector. The receiver R is immediately adjacent the transmitter and also has a directional antenna. It receives the reflected pulses. T and R are connected via an artificial line on which the transmission time is steadily variable. This artificial line is for the following purpose: the receiver is ordinarily blocked and cannot receive pulses. The pulse which is sent out by wireless from T, also passes over the artificial line and makes the receiver operative for a very short time. When the transmission time of the artificial line is equal to the time of transit of the reflected wireless pulse, the latter can be registered on a cathode-ray tube from the receiver. By using this method the distance of an aircraft can be measured very accurately; but it is very insensitive to interference as the receiver is only opened for a very short time.

9 Aircraft distance-measuring instrument

When pilots fly over an enemy territory for attack it is important for them to know how far they have flown from the starting point. The following method is being developed in Rechlin for this purpose:

At the starting station there is a wireless transmitter (six-metre wavelength) which is modulated with a low frequency f. The aircraft which is at the distance a, receives the six-metre wave and after demodulation, obtains the low frequency f. With this low frequency it modulates its own transmitter, which has a somewhat different wavelength. The thus modulated wave of the aircraft is received at the starting station and demodulated. The low frequency f thus obtained is compared with the local frequency f. Both differ by the phase angle,

$$\frac{4\pi\ \mathrm{f.a.,}}{\mathrm{c}}$$

where a is the distance of the aircraft and c the speed of light. By measuring the phase it is thus possible to compute the distance of the aircraft and to give the aircraft its position. In order that the measurement is free from ambiguity the phase angle must be equal to 2π (or remain under 2π. For example, a low frequency of say 150 cycles is chosen, then the phase angle equals 2π for exactly 1000 km). With such a low frequency the degree of accuracy is however only very rough. Therefore at the same time a second higher frequency is sent out; for example, 1,500 cycles per second and the phase angle of this is compared. Thus 150 cycles per second is a coarse measurement and 1,500 cycles a fine measurement.

10 Torpedoes

The German Navy has two new kinds of torpedoes.

(a) Supposing convoys are to be attacked from a distance of ten kilometres. These torpedoes have a wireless receiver which can receive three signals. By means of these signals, the ship which has fired the torpedo, or the aircraft launching same, is able to direct the torpedo to the left or to the right or keep it straight on its course. Use is made of long waves which penetrate well into the water, say of the order of three kilometres. These are modulated with short audio-frequency signals which bring about the control of the torpedoes. In this way the torpedo can be directed very close to the convoy. Now, in order actually to hit the ship, there are two acoustic receivers (microphones) on the head of the torpedo which constitute a directional receiver. By means of this receiver the course of the torpedo is so controlled that it automatically turns towards the acoustic source of sound. Thus, once the torpedo has been directed towards the ship to within a few hundred metres, it turns towards the ship by itself, since the latter generates noise due to the running of its engines. Countermeasures may however be taken relatively easily by acoustic and wireless interfering signals.

(b) The second kind of torpedo is probably the one which sank the *Royal Oak*. These do not strike the hull of the ship but explode underneath the ship's bottom. The fuse is released through magnetic means and is based upon the following principle (see Figure 2) [Missing]. The vertical component of the magnetic earth field is everywhere approximately the same, so that at A and B there is a weaker field and at C a more powerful field. A torpedo coming from the left therefore runs first in the normal field then in the weaker field and so on. In the head of the torpedo a coil rotates about a horizontal axis after the manner of an earth inductor. At the terminals of this coil there arises a direct voltage which is proportional to the vertical component of the magnetic earth field. In series with this voltage there runs a counter-voltage of equal magnitude, so that no current can flow as long as the torpedo is in the normal earth field. If however the torpedo arrives at A, the earth field is smaller there and the voltage at the rotating coil drops. The two opposite voltages are no longer of equal magnitude and a current flows thereby actuating a relay which releases the fuse. The delay is so chosen that the explosion takes place just under the ship's bottom.

Possibly protection against these torpedoes may be afforded by stretching out a cable along the ship and spaced from the hull as far as possible. If a suitably chosen direct current is sent through this cable, a magnetic field is also produced and the dangerous point A shifted far outside the ship. The torpedo will then explode prematurely. Perhaps it is also possible by using suitably chosen compensation coils to compensate the distortion of the magnetic field due to the iron mass of the ship.

11 Electric fuses for aircraft bombs and artillery shells
In Germany mechanical fuses are being abandoned and electric fuses used instead. All fuses for aircraft bombs are already electric. Figure 1 [Missing] shows the principle. When the bomb leaves the aircraft, the condenser xx C_1 is charged from a 150 volt battery through a sliding contact. This charges the condenser C_2 through the resistance R. C_2 is only charged when the bomb is at a safe distance from the aircraft. When the bomb strikes, a mechanical contact K closes and the condenser discharges through the fusing coil Z. The advantage is that the bomb is never live when it is within the aircraft so that the aircraft can always safely land with the bombs.

Figure 2 [Missing] shows an electric time fuse. It operates on the same principle but the mechanical contact is replaced by a glow discharge lamp which lights up after a certain time. This time can be adjusted through the values of the condensers and resistances.

The latest development employs glow discharge lamps with a grid (see Figure 3) [Missing]. If the battery voltage is so chosen that it is somewhat below the ignition voltage and if the grid is insulated, then the lamp can be brought to ignition by changing the component capacities C_{12} and C_{23}. A very slight change in the capacities is sufficient. Figure 4 [Missing] shows the basic principle applied to a shell. The head K of the shell is insulated and is connected to the grid of the discharge lamp. When the shell passes an aircraft for instance, the capacities are slightly altered and the lamp ignites thereby exploding the shell. The fuse can also be so adjusted that all shells explode at a certain distance above the ground, say at three metres.

A lamp fitted with a grid is enclosed herewith: it is an improved type in which the grid consists of a ring.

Release fuses for bombs are designated by No. 25. Production is said to have been 25,000 in October 1939 and will be increased to 100,000 by April 1940.

These fuses are being produced at Sömmerda in Thuringia on the Sangershausen–Erfurt Railway. The name of the firm is Rheinmetall.

Appendix B

The Munich Keynote Address, 1 June 1955

In the course of my duties in 1945, almost ten years ago to this day, it fell to me to meet General Martini and to talk to him about our experiences on opposite sides in the war which had just ended. This meeting proved most unexpectedly pleasant for me, and I hope that the General will take my presence here today as a tribute to the warm feeling which my colleagues and I developed towards him. He has asked me, on behalf of the *Ausschuss für Funkortung*, to talk to you about Natural and Artificial Disturbances to Radar, and I feel both extremely honoured and glad to be here in fulfilment of his request.

I want first to speak of two great physicists, one British and the other German, because on their work is founded everything of which we shall be thinking at this conference: James Clerk Maxwell and Heinrich Hertz. As you know, Maxwell's imaginative conclusions from the simply observed phenomena of elementary electricity and magnetism led him to predict in 1861 that a new kind of wave should exist – a wave in the electromagnetic field. Hertz, by some brilliant experiments, showed in 1887 that Maxwell's prediction was correct. They were both scientists of the greatest stature, and it is particularly fitting from the point of view of this conference that each should have come from one of our countries. I know more, personally, of Maxwell than of Hertz, since Maxwell at one time held the Chair of Natural Philosophy at Aberdeen, and there is one characteristic of Maxwell's to which I should like to draw your attention because, in a perhaps unexpected way, it is connected with the subject of my talk. This was his fondness for practical joking.

Let us consider the essential elements of a practical joke. The final object of such a joke is the contrivance of a humorous situation. It is not easy to define what a humorous situation is – and indeed the joker's idea of such a situation may be very different from his victim's – but it usually has an element of incongruity about it. The small boy laughs, for example, when he sees an old gentleman step on a banana skin because old gentlemen usually carry themselves with dignity, and the old gentleman who slips is generating an incongruity with normal dignified behaviour. It may then become the small boy's idea of a joke to make old gentlemen slip down (and there certainly is a record of Maxwell at the age of six making the maid fall down with a tray of tea), but as the boy's taste in jokes develops he contrives ones that are less crudely practical and which may ultimately become almost 'theoretical'. In these more refined jokes the final situation may be reached only after a relatively long procedure in which a false model of reality is carefully built up in the mind of the victim by supplying him with false information, so that when ultimately he takes what seems reasonable action in his false world, he is sharply brought back to reality by general ridicule at the incongruity of his action.

It is not difficult, for example, to persuade some people to do such incongruous things as putting their telephones into buckets of water. The lead-up process consists of creating in the victim's mind the impression that something is wrong with his telephone by making it ring, and then not speaking when he answers. After this has been done for some minutes, the joker telephones the victim again and pretends to be an engineer with the information that one of the victim's friends has been trying to telephone him and has found that he can get no reply. The engineer then asks the victim's help in diagnosing the fault, with the incentive that if it is a simple fault it may be possible to put it right quickly from the exchange. The victim usually agrees, and it is then not too difficult to persuade him, in the course of looking for a leak to earth, to fetch a bucket of water to act as an earth and, after a few further manoeuvres, to lower the telephone gently into it.

I remember one of my German physicist friends who as a research student found that he worked in a laboratory from which he could see into the apartments of a newspaper correspondent. He telephoned the newspaperman, pretending to be his own professor and saying that he had just succeeded in making a television attachment to an ordinary telephone which enabled the user to see the man to whom he was speaking at the other end of the telephone. Naturally the newspaperman was incredulous, and the 'professor' then offered to give a demonstration by telling the newspaperman to do anything he liked in his room, and then to come back to the telephone, when the 'professor' would tell him what he had done. By the time the newspaperman had performed a few simple contortions such as standing on his head, and was correctly told by my friend, who of course was watching all the time through the window, the victim was completely convinced. He thereupon wrote an enthusiastic article which appeared in his paper the next day, much to the astonishment of my friend's professor.

You will note how the newspaperman had been led to build up a false picture of reality from the information which he received over the telephone. Such jokes are relatively easy to play because the victim has only one channel of information, the telephone, over which he receives his data. It becomes much more difficult when he can use two parallel channels, as for example, both sight and sound, since a false model of reality has then to be built up in both these media. This, incidentally, is also the reason why early radar was relatively vulnerable to deception; it depended on information of a highly limited kind, the radio echo, which was not too difficult to counterfeit.

Even more complicated jokes may be played, where two or more victims are induced to construct complementary and false models of reality. One of the simplest of this type is, for example, to introduce two men, and to warn each of them beforehand that the other is a very pleasant fellow, but has been under a mental strain which makes him very angry if anyone contradicts him. It is therefore advisable to humour him by agreeing with everything he says. Your two friends usually thereafter spend an evening going to great trouble to agree with one another, and go home each delighted that he has handled the other so well.

Now all this may seem a long way from the subject of my lecture, but in fact it is very near to the techniques of producing artificial disturbances to radar. The object of these disturbances is to induce the observers and controllers in the opposing radar system to build up a false model of the military situation, and hence to take incorrect action to deal with it. This may be done in two ways: the first is to persuade your opponent that you are not where you are, and the second – which is slightly different – is that you are where you are not. This may sound remotely philosophical, but it works out fairly simply in practice, as I shall now show.

You may persuade your opponent that you are not where you are by setting up jamming transmitters so that his radar sets become unusable, and he is therefore denied information about your whereabouts.

As regards the use of pure jamming to upset the opposing radar, one of the best examples was that achieved by the *Luftnachrichten* in February 1942, when they jammed such a large proportion of the British radar on the Channel coast that we failed to detect the passage of the *Scharnhorst* and *Gneisnau* until too late. We much admired the way in which this jamming operation was planned and executed.

Another way in which you may persuade your opponent that you are not where you are is by coating your aircraft or ship with a non-reflecting coating, so that the opponent cannot detect you. Germany almost certainly led in this technique during the war, in applying it to U-boats.

You may persuade your opponent that you are where you are not by giving him false indications of your presence. We in Britain developed Window (*Staniolstreifen* or *Düppel*) for this purpose, and we did in fact so use it in simulating a convoy which was to appear to land east of Le Havre when we came back to France in June 1944. The 'convoy' was synthesized by dropping packets of Window from circling aircraft which maintained a net rate of advance appropriate to a naval convoy, and we believe it to have been successful in adding to the deception that we were going to land a large force in the Pas de Calais. We used Window to make comparatively small forces of aircraft look like large ones, and hence to mislead the opposing controllers into concentrating their main defence against the diversion while our main attack went elsewhere. We also used Window as a thickly-sown cloud to hide individual aircraft in it, by providing so many echoes from the sky that the true aircraft echoes could not be distinguished among the false ones. This technique was analogous to the use of a smoke screen, and therefore belongs to the earlier philosophical category.

A technique which belongs to the later category was that which we developed in 1942, and which we called 'Moonshine'. In this device a single aircraft would receive the opponent's pulses, and amplify and distort them in such a manner that when they were received back on the radar screen they made the target look not like one aircraft but like a heavy raid. This was a difficult technique, and it required a separate receiver for each radar station that might look at the aircraft, but we believed that we had a little success with it in the English Channel.

Most of these well-tried ideas depended on a consideration of what evidence it is that a radar operator sees which leads him to deduce that a target has entered the field of view of his station. This is usually a deflection of the time-base of his cathode-ray observing tube, and anything which causes such a disturbance may be considered at first sight as a disturbance to radar. But as the war progressed, both sides realized that, on deeper thought, a false disturbance might be distinguished from an echo from a true target in several ways. The first was the variation in echoing power with frequency; Window, for example, depended for its success on resonance to a particular frequency, and if a Window cloud was surveyed by a radar station on a different frequency, the strength of the echoes would be much less. The second was the fact that 'Window' packets drifted with the wind, and the Doppler effect of frequency shift of the echo would be much less than for an aircraft with its higher speed. This possibility was first exploited by the German Air Force, and resulted in '*Würzlaus*'.

Now, from such possibilities there arises a fundamental question to science. When one contemplates the increasing difficulty of making a perfect model of, say, a bomber flying through the opposing defences, one sees the fundamental impossibility of making a perfect model of anything. To deal, for example, with *Würzlaus*, it would be necessary to make the tinfoil strips into tiny gliders flying at aircraft speeds. And then to deal with the difficulty of frequency response, it would ultimately be necessary to make these gliders into one big glider as large as the bomber itself. Very rapidly you come to the conclusion that the only perfect model of a bomber against an omniscient defence is another bomber – and then it is not quite perfect because you then have two bombers instead of one!

I would note in passing that this illustration of the thesis that no model can be perfect made me see far more clearly than I did before the war the nature of the difficulty in which physics sometimes finds itself. In physics we have largely progressed by inventing a succession of models of real phenomena, and when we can predict a real event from a study of a model we think that we have 'understood' the phenomenon to which it refers. Thus, many of the properties of light may be simulated by a model of wave-motion, and yet other properties may best be simulated by assuming that light consists of a stream of particles. This became a celebrated paradox in physics, but there really is no paradox: both waves and particles are only *models* of the behaviour of light – neither model can be perfect, and since there can be no perfect model we ought not to be too surprised if we can find two equally imperfect models, each of which is partly valid.

Returning to the field of practical operations, however, there is often no time for the opponent to make the crucial observations which would distinguish between real and false, and in the stress of working in difficult or dangerous situations, even very good observers can be deceived into believing imperfect deceptions.

In talking so much of artificial disturbances to radar I do not want to imply that they are of more importance than disturbances arising from natural causes. They have, of course, much value in warfare, but in peace natural disturbances become of first importance, and are indeed of much greater scientific interest. These natural disturbances can be of many kinds including 'noise' generated inside the radar receiver itself, echoes reflected from undesired obstacles, variations in radio propagation velocities, and noise coming from external sources.

As regards the noise generated inside the receiver one finds that for a given band-width there is an inescapable minimum which arises from the thermal agitation of the electrons in the aerial and the early circuits of the receiver. The amplitude of this minimum noise is proportional to the square-root of the absolute temperature of the receiving system. This is not a phenomenon peculiar to radar, but is general to all systems involving physical observations. Therefore, although it is very important and although in several instances our observing systems are already at this natural limit imposed by noise, I shall say nothing more about it in this talk except for the fact that in every physicist's mind its magnitude is linked with the name of the great German physicist, Boltzmann, whose constant enters into every theoretical expression for the noise magnitude.

A form of disturbance which is much more peculiar to radar is the reflection of echoes from unintended targets, which may be of many kinds. Probably the first to be noticed were the 'permanent echoes' arising from geographical features, which could in some circumstances be so numerous as to be almost as effective as a Window cloud in obscuring the true target. In such cases, apparatus (MTI – Moving Target Indicator) resembling *Würzlaus* in that it discriminates such echoes by their lack of Doppler shift, is proving most valuable.

MTI, however, is not of so much use against echoes from unintended targets which appear to be moving, and such objects as flights of geese or even clouds of insects can give appreciable echoes which may alarm the radar observers. In the winter of 1939 one of our radar stations in Norfolk several times alerted our fighters on the basis of echoes which we ultimately realized were due to formations of wild fowl. Variations in refractive index of the atmosphere may make even fixed echoes appear to move; this phenomenon is thought to explain what were first reported as 'flying saucers' near Washington airport in 1952.

During the war, rain was found to give appreciable echoes on centimetric radar, and this phenomenon has been turned to meteorological advantage. It is at its best in detecting heavy precipitation such as occurs in warm fronts, thunderclouds and hurricanes. Aircraft suitably equipped can thus avoid dangerous thunderclouds, and hurricanes can be plotted. These are instances where something that was originally a nuisance has been turned into a benefit.

Some of the most spectacular echoes have come from observations with comparatively long waves (10–30 Mc/s). Here the Radio Research Station at

Slough – the birthplace of British radar – has detected echoes scattered back from as far away as Singapore, nearly 10,000 kilometres distant. These echoes can hardly be classed as disturbances to radar, but they show the power of radar technique.

Echoes arise also from meteors, and studies of these echoes have revealed the presence of daytime meteor streams and have provided much evidence about meteor velocities. Aurorae reflect radio waves, and thus give rise to echoes, whose magnitude can lead to an estimate of the intensity of ionization in the aurorae. Radar echoes from the moon add to our knowledge of the ionosphere, since both outgoing and returning waves have to pass through it. And of course, this survey would be seriously incomplete if I did not mention the classic work of Appleton and his followers on the echoes from the ionosphere, which was in many ways the start of radar science.

The most fascinating of all disturbances to radar arises, however, not from false echoes but from direct jamming. It was first observed by the American engineer Jansky in 1931, when he attempted to make his radio receiver as perfectly noise-free as possible. He found, however, that there was a residual noise which appeared to be coming from such an improbable source as the Milky Way. Few scientists took much notice of Jansky's careful work before the 1939 war, but during that war there were of course many radar sets in action and many skilled observers operating them. It was then gradually established, as an undeniable matter of experience, that radar sets could be jammed when looking at the sun. Since the sun is a fairly typical star, it was a logical step to build larger aerials to look at the more distant stars. From this the new science of radioastronomy has sprung, which has shown that there are many sources of radio noise among the stars. We can only receive this noise at wavelengths between 1 centimetre and 50 metres, because shorter wavelengths are absorbed by molecular vibrations in the earth's atmosphere, while longer wavelengths are intercepted by the Heaviside layer. Despite this limitation, radioastronomy is adding observations of intense interest to the facts already established by visual and photographic astronomy.

Perhaps the most spectacular result of radioastronomy so far is the detection of the radiation on about 21-centimetre wavelength from interstellar hydrogen which was predicted by the Dutch scientist, Van de Hulst. It has been observed that the wavelength of this radiation is slightly different when it comes from different parts of the sky, and the results agree very well with the hypothesis that the differences are due to the Doppler effect acting on radiation coming from different parts of our galaxy. Radioastronomy has thus provided strong evidence that we do indeed live inside one of the spiral galaxies such as we see in all the remoter parts of space.

The great new possibilities revealed by radioastronomy have resulted in vigorous efforts to intercept the radiations from celestial bodies. In Great Britain we have two principal schools – that at Cambridge under Ryle, and that at Manchester under Lovell. Near Manchester, there is being constructed an enormous paraboloid like a Giant, Giant Würzburg of about 90 metres diameter. I remember that during the war we were so impressed by the size of the Giant Würzburgs that we used to indicate their positions on our battle maps by gold-headed pins – we would have had to go to diamonds had we found a paraboloid like that at Manchester! Instruments such as this one, and others now being contemplated at Cambridge, will have enormous collecting power; in the detection of remote celestial bodies, they may well be able to outrange even the great 200-inch telescope on Mount Palomar.

In concluding this address I would remind you that radar owed its tremendous development to the stimulus of a devastating war in which it ultimately became as important to neutralize your opponent's radar as it was to develop your own. I hope that I have shown you that behind all this was a fair measure of philosophy. The attempts to defeat radar had something of the elements of a practical joke about them, but our satisfaction when they were successful was tempered by the fact that we realized they were but minor facets of what Sir Winston Churchill has called 'The Unnecessary War'. One of the few beneficial legacies of that war has been radar, with all that it means in safety in air and marine navigation. Even some of the irritating sources of interference, like rain echoes and cosmic noise, have been turned from disadvantages into aids to safety and knowledge, thus reminding us, like X-rays and penicillin, of the wisdom of Pasteur's saying: 'Chance favours the trained observer.'

I would mention one further legacy of the war. One cannot fight a worthy opponent without developing a respect for him, and such a respect may ultimately be the foremost basis of friendship. I think that we on both sides of the radio war did develop such a mutual respect. Moreover, in the fields of science and technology where all of us are striving towards the same goals, respect for one another's achievements is a feeling that forces itself through all barriers of race, nationality, and creed. Let us hope that conferences like this one may help to foster this respect between our two countries, and indeed all others. And while at present it may seem a naive hope, let us look forward to the time when the danger of war recedes not through the negative fear of the hydrogen bomb but through the positive respect of one nation for another.

Appendix C

Listener Article, 19 April 1956

The German Challenge to Britain

R. V. JONES on western Germany's recovery in science, technology, and morale

From time to time it has been my duty to see whether foreign countries represent a technical or scientific threat to Britain in war. I was concerned, for example, with the German radio beams of 1940, and with the V1 and V2 campaigns of 1944. I now spend most of my time in a university, but I still cannot help keeping watch for threats to this country, and I feel that I must tell you of the two main dangers that I see facing us now. They do not involve a war in the military sense at all, for I am assuming that there is a stalemate in open warfare which will divert the struggle into more peaceful channels. From our point of view, there are going to be two main factors in this struggle: our technical and scientific achievement, and the spirit of our people.

Acute Need for Scientists

I shall not say much about the need for more scientists and technologists. You have only to look at the appointments columns of the newspapers to see how acutely the need is already felt. I will say only this: if I had any success as an intelligence officer in the war it was because I was seeking out the technical achievements of the Germans. Once we were able to find these in a particular field, say radar, we were immediately able to understand all the associated aspects of defence – for example, the German nightfighters and their control – because the technical basis was the key to the whole superstructure of air operations. Even more is this true of the economic and military strength of a nation today, as technology plays a larger and larger part. One nation above all others has realized this: Russia. From Lenin onwards, the masters of the Russian people have understood the value of science and technology, and they have pressed ahead with vast training schemes which are now bearing fruit. In a recent talk on the Third Programe Sir Francis Simon spoke admirably about the Soviet bid for technological leadership,[1] and of the way in which we ought to meet it. He pointed out that more science students are now coming out of Soviet schools of higher education than out of the whole of the schools in the non-communist countries, and that in a few years' time this will give Russia a commanding advantage unless we vastly improve our own position.

With their rising scientific potential, the Russians are able to offer a generous degree of technical aid to less advanced countries. This new tactic enables them to win these countries to their side by sending in technicians who can be far more effective ambassadors than professional diplomats, for technology finds far fewer international barriers than do political creeds – or even religious beliefs.

So we have much to think about in what the Russians have achieved. Let us admit that there is nothing unfair about it; they may have been wiser than we were in encouraging science thirty years ago. At the same time, we must not overlook other countries, and in particular we must pay attention to the rise of western Germany. As with Russia, her progress is due in part to a more lively appreciation of the importance of the scientist and the engineer. A report on *German Research Today*, by Hermann von Müller, describes the part the German scientists are playing:

> Behind their seemingly almost fanatical zest for work there lies not merely a real enthusiasm, but also the force of circumstance. Science and learning . . . particularly in Germany . . . have become cardinal factors in the struggle for existence of millions of people.

This is also brought out in a recent report[2] written by the British Scientific Attaché in Bonn, Mr K. H. Lauder. Here is one paragraph from his report:

> In western Germany there is a very close association between industry and academic science. Industry pays great respect to the academic scientist. Scientists are widely represented in the direction of industry, and larger firms often employ panels of scientists to advise them.

The report states that in western Germany the Government and industry spend between them more than £100,000,000 a year on research; when we remember that this covers neither defence nor atomic work it is, as the report says, 'a considerable sum'. I commend the report for careful reading. It gives a picture of a most vigorous recovery in German science and technology. Let me quote the concluding paragraph:

> Progress in technology, upon which the economic strength and consequently the political effectiveness of any country depends in the world today, rests upon the scientific research effort which the country is prepared to undertake and for which it is prepared to pay. This is clearly appreciated in western Germany on all sides, political, economic, and technological. As a result, western Germany has reached a stage where, starting from widespread destruction and chaos, it has, in a brief space of ten years, regained a position amongst the world's leaders in the scientific and technological fields. It is an impressive achievement.

The extent of German achievement is even more obvious in other fields.

Starting from virtual bankruptcy in 1948, and with its industry largely in ruins, western Germany now holds dollar reserves greater not only than those of this country but of the whole sterling bloc. According to the British Economic Survey of 1956, German-manufactured exports increased by eighteen per cent between 1954 and 1955; ours increased by only seven. Western Germany has outstripped us in steel production, and she is capturing our shipping orders. Anybody who visits Germany must immediately be struck by the enthusiastic sense of purpose that is evident at all levels, from worker to director.

Sense of Purpose

This brings me to my second point. Science and technology are not the only thing in life, indeed it might be very dangerous if they were. We must do more to develop them, and in this direction the concern of our Government over technical education is to be welcomed, and it is to be hoped that the expansion will be executed vigorously; but I believe, even speaking as a scientist, that there is something to do that is even more urgent. I have said that the Germans have an intense sense of purpose. We once had a sense of purpose – after Dunkirk: what a stimulation it was to be in Britain then. 'After 1945' seems to have had the same effect on the Germans as 1940 had on us. When I was in Germany recently, at the invitation of some of my wartime opponents among the German generals, I asked them whether there had been any inspired leadership to bring their country so far in its recovery. They told me that it was no single leadership that had done it. Every individual German had of his own accord set to work after 1945 to put his country back among the leaders. The Germans are now reaping their reward.

But what about us? I can think, and probably you can think too, of a gloomy list of signs ever since the war that all is not well with us. Not many pieces of new equipment come into my laboratory which work properly without our having to overhaul them first. Railway engines grew so dirty that the Chief Inspector of Accidents recorded that the dirt was no longer a negligible factor in rail safety, since it was no longer possible to see whether an engine was mechanically sound or not. Two years ago, the shooting at Bisley went wrong because the marksmen were supplied with inferior ammunition. A signalman leaves his box forty minutes early. A trawler drifts to destruction because she is wasting time outside harbour to qualify for a subsidy, while her master and crew are below playing cards. Cracks in aircraft panels are botched by drilling holes – a strange practice for a product which was nearly Britain's best advertisement. Last year I watched several of the May parades on the Horseguards in London. The dressing was so bad that I found myself, as the son of an old King's Company man, unconsciously swearing out loud as the companies passed. I was brought to my senses by an old guardsman beside me growling 'You're quite right'. This, a demonstration of the precision on which we pride ourselves!

I do not want to make too much of these examples. They just happen to be ones of which I know personally, and they may be no worse than the average of the country as a whole. You probably know of plenty of others. There is one explanation common to them all: someone had not enough pride in his job. I want, therefore, to say something about 'pride in the job', because this is where we face a particular threat from Germany, and, unless we recover our pride, all our achievements in science and technology will be wasted. It is obvious that in a whole variety of products the German version is better engineered and more carefully made than its British counterpart. The world is realizing this and is therefore turning to Germany; even we ourselves are buying German products in preference to our own, because the Germans are putting in that extra care and effort which we used proudly to claim were the characteristics of British workmanship.

True Pride and False Pride

In talking about pride in the job, let me say that there is true pride and false pride, and that I am not proposing that we should become fastidious. The first consideration about any job is that it should be matched to its purpose. It is, in fact, quite possible to do a job too well. Hitler, for example, criticized Russian tanks when they were shown to him because the outside surfaces were left rough. On the other hand, one of his more discerning experts pointed out that where they had to be well machined they were well machined; external finish was comparatively unimportant. It is also possible to have undue pride in, say, individual craftsmanship, and to extol it in comparison with machine-made articles. However much we admire such craftsmanship – and I appreciate it intensely – we must realize what effort it takes, and ask whether it is worthwhile. I think that we used to have a misplaced pride in the job on this account, so that, for example, our English clockmakers, who were the best in the world, clung too long to their handmade products and lost the world market to the automatically produced watches of Switzerland.

Having admitted the danger of misplaced pride, I think that most of us would rather be associated with men who do their jobs too well rather than not well enough. Over and above the immediate purpose of the job itself there is the additional consideration of beauty in the product, and the satisfaction of turning out a job that we are certain will be up to its purpose.

Certainly in Britain today, feeling has swung too far the other way, if indeed there is any conscious feeling at all. What has gone wrong? We were tired after the war. Markets, with Germany and Japan knocked out, were easy, and any product, almost however shoddy, would sell. Threats of strike brought, and continue to bring, more pay without any rise in standard of work. Since 1946 we have paid ourselves eighty per cent more money for producing only twenty per cent more articles, while the quality of the articles has in general remained indifferent. The average British worker now produces less than three-quarters of what he did even in 1948 for every £1 of wages that he is paid. By way of contrast, official German figures obtained for me by Mr Lauder in Bonn show that the German worker has in the same period nearly doubled his output for every Reichsmark of wages that he receives.

At last, the Government is taking a lead in making these facts more generally realized, and there is a good deal of discussion about what ought to be done. I believe, though, that it has been insufficiently emphasized that no political measures can be effective unless each one of us is working at full efficiency, and that this will only happen when each one of us has a due pride in his job. I would put this as one of the foremost factors in our survival among the leaders of the world; it may not be a popular doctrine because it involves both working harder and taking more trouble.

I do not suggest that we should get so obsessed about how we do our immediate jobs that we should forget why we are doing them. That was an aspect of pre-war Germany that lent itself to the possibilities of abuse, such as the Nazis inflicted upon western Europe with their concentration camps, while the diligent German worker was paying so much attention to his own job that he had no time to think what his leaders were getting him to work for. In Britain we are, I hope, a long way from that danger, but the simple fact remains that if the individual German or Russian or American or Japanese does a better job than the individual Briton, then we are not going to sell enough abroad to earn our food. Our efforts at foreign policy will come to nothing if our home effort is not soundly based. The two main props in that base are our ability to invent and our capacity to work. The former we can stimulate by more technical education; the latter must be aroused by leadership.

Satisfaction in Doing a Good Job

So far, I have spoken of mere survival. Beyond that, however, there is the satisfaction, open to all of us, that can alone be obtained from doing a good job. Is not at least part of our industrial discontent due to the fact that so many men have lost that satisfaction? We must call for better work, and support this call by a drive to reduce the drudgery that many still experience. This is where automatic machinery can really help: by reducing drudgery it will give more chance to more men to do jobs they can take pride in.

Despite everything that has happened since the war, I have sufficient faith in our countrymen to believe that they would respond to a call for a better job if it were properly put. After all, we did it after Dunkirk, and we did it a good many times before that. Are we to prove unworthy of our rude forefathers who with few tools, and from their poor homes, went to work every day for centuries to build our great cathedrals? I had the privilege of knowing the chief tester of Rolls-Royce cars. If he found a fault he used to go into the workshop and say to the workman responsible: 'You can't do that sort of thing – this car is England'. Recalling that remark, I do not want to represent that the picture is blacker than it really is. There are fortunately many people who have not let their standards go: you need only have seen some of the recent drill displays by the Sandhurst cadets to appreciate that. At this moment, too, we hold the land, water, and air speed records. In fact, there are plenty of signs that our old powers are still latent, maintained by the devotion of an enthusiastic minority who have refused to submit to the general lethargy, and who may ultimately rank in our history alongside the 'gallant few' of 1940. The present emergency is more insidious, but it is no less acute on that account.

I am sure that we can pull up, if everyone is made to see that the danger that faces us is just as real as any other form of national disaster. In this matter, those of us who are concerned with young people in schools and universities, or who head firms, are in a most responsible position. By our example, we must show those who look to us for leadership that 'the job' ought not to be a thing of which you do a minimum for a maximum of pay, but one of your main ways of finding personal fulfilment. It is also the way to give our country the chance of once again setting an example to the world.

Third Programme

Notes and References

Chapter 1 (pages 7–34).

1 R. V. Jones, *Most Secret War* (subsequently referred to as *MSW*), pp. 492–522, Hamish Hamilton, 1978, Coronet Books, 1979. Also published in the US as *The Wizard War*, Coward, McCann and Geoghegan, 1978.
2 Alexander Keith, *A Thousand Years of Aberdeen*, p. 67, Aberdeen University Press, 1972. Keith also records (pp. 52–3) that as late as the fifteenth century the losers in local feuds were apt to be boiled in a cauldron by their victorious opponents who then partook of the resulting soup. 'Sodden and suppit in broo [broth]' was the technical term for this grisly fate.
3 *Some Aspects of the Directorate of Scientific Intelligence, Ministry of Defence 1952–54*, 1 June 1954.
4 See below, page 58, for a rather similar problem arising between the Central Intelligence Agency and the National Security Agency in Washington.
5 *MSW*, pp. 205–6, 306–9 and 472–83.
6 Peter Wright and Paul Greengrass, *Spycatcher*, p. 25, Heinemann Australia, 1987.
7 *MSW*, pp. 216–17.
8 Andrei Sakharov, *My Country and the World*, p. 73, Vintage Books, 1975.
9 Hansard, 1 March 1955.
10 Francis Bacon, *Of Delayes* in *Essays*, p. 90, Oxford University Press, 1937.
11 Cmnd. 8787, 1983.
12 W. S. Churchill, 'Painting as a Pastime', in *Thoughts and Adventures*, pp. 236–7, Odhams Reprint, 1947.
13 Letter to the Author, 21 June 1979.

Chapter 2 (pages 35–56).

1 Wright and Greengrass, *op. cit.*, pp. 72–3.
2 *ibid.*, pp. 110–13.
3 *MSW*, pp. 262–3, 317 and 496–7.
4 Wright and Greengrass, *op. cit.*, p. 45.
5 William Colby, *Honorable Men*, p. 417, Simon & Schuster, 1978.
6 Parliament Paper, Cmnd. 6144, 1912.
7 J. M. Langley, *Fight Another Day*, p. 202, Collins, 1974.
8 This is an example of the difficulty facing an historian aiming to write a comprehensive account.
9 Air Ministry Weekly Intelligence Summary, No. 261, August 1944.

10 Barbara Tuchman, *August 1914*, pp. 173, 248 and 307, Papermac, 1980.
11 *MSW*, p. 354.
12 Admiral Stansfield Turner, *Secrecy and Democracy*, p. 175, Sidgwick & Jackson, 1986.
13 Thomas Powers, *The Man Who Kept the Secrets*, p. 312, Simon & Schuster, 1979.
14 *ibid.*, p. 266.
15 See Christopher Andrew, *Secret Service*, Heinemann, 1985; p. 690 in Sceptre edition.
16 Powers, *op. cit.*, p. 155.
17 Stansfield Turner, *op. cit.*, p. 86.
18 *ibid.*, p. 205.
19 *ibid.*, p. 178.
20 William Colby, *op. cit.*, p. 334.
21 *The Times*, 'Parliamentary Report', November 1988.
22 Stansfield Turner, *op. cit.*, pp. 97–8, 219.
23 *ibid.*, p. 264 and p. 270.
24 See *ibid.*, p. 276.
25 *ibid.*, p. 168.
26 Robert Woodward, *Veil: The Secret Wars of the CIA 1981–7*, Simon & Schuster, 1987.
27 *ibid.*, p. 227.

Chapter 3 (pages 57–84).

1 Stansfield Turner, *op. cit.*, p. 225.
2 David Hooper, *Official Secrets*, p. 154, Secker & Warburg, 1987.
3 *University of Edinburgh Journal*, vol. 22, pp. 50–5; and privately reprinted by W. James in *Hotch-Potch*, 1968.
4 Letter from Mr D. J. Wills to the Author, 1978.
5 *The New English Bible*, Job, Ch. 31, vv. 35–7. In the King James version, the opening lines read: 'behold, my desire is, that the Almighty would answer me, and that mine adversary had written a book.'
6 *Guardian*, 15 October 1986.
7 vol. 1, no. 2, pp. 277–80.
8 Lord Wavell, *Generals and Generalship*, University of Chicago Press, 1941.
9 William Colby, *op. cit.*, p. 334.
10 Stansfield Turner, *op. cit.*, pp. 154–5.
11 1927, vol. 206, col. 1848.
12 Chapman Pincher, *Inside Story*, pp. 148–50, Sidgwick & Jackson, 1978.
13 Stansfield Turner, *op. cit.*, p. 144.
14 Thomas Powers, *op. cit.*, p. 262.
15 Franks Committee Report, Cmnd. 8787, 1983.
16 Hansard, 12 November 1936.
17 *Science*, vol. 239, 1988, pp. 556–7.
18 David Irving, *Churchill's War*, p. 89, Veritas, 1987.
19 Samuel Eliot Morison, *The Two-Ocean War*, pp. 154–6, Little, Brown, 1963.

20 *MSW*, p. 423.
21 Cmnd. 408.
22 Radcliffe Report, 1976, para. 3.
23 Hooper, *op. cit.*, p. 200.
24 Report: Cmnd. 6386, 1976, paras. 69 and 66.
25 *ibid.*, para. 93.
26 *ibid.*, para. 100.
27 Hansard, 21 December 1988.
28 *ibid.*
29 *ibid.*
30 H. A. Grant, *English Historians*, p. xxv, Blackie (there is no publication date in the book).

Chapter 4 (pages 85–106).

1 *MSW*, pp. 370–2.
2 Dr Stefan Dedijer has drawn my attention to a World War I operator who analysed the combination of new channels with the old in his organization. He was Max Ronge, the last head of military intelligence in the Austrian Empire. He published his analysis in a book, *Kriegs- und Industrie-Spionage*, Vienna, 1930.
3 *MSW*, pp. 102–4, 228–30 and 457–8.
4 W. J. Baker, *A History of the Marconi Company*, pp. 50–1, Methuen, 1970.
5 See Alfred Price, *The History of US Electronic Warfare*, Association of Old Crows, 1984.
6 Excellent references are papers by Admiral B. Scholfield and Professor J. Rohwer in *Die Funkaufklärung und ihre Rolle im 2 Weltkrieg*, ed. J. Rohwer and E. Jäckel, Motorbuch Verlag, 1979; and of course the volumes of *British Intelligence in the Second World War*, HMSO, 1979–88.
7 *MSW*, pp. 335–6, 359–60 and 413–15.
8 William E. Burrows, *Deep Black*, pp. 178–80, Random House, 1986.
9 Stansfield Turner, *op. cit.*, p. 207.
10 Even astrological intelligence may not be beyond the pale. On 18 October 1940 the Chiefs of Staff in London heard the view of an astrologer on Hitler's horoscope regarding the date on which he might invade Britain; this was deemed relevant because of Hitler's known interest in astrology – but the Vice Chief of Naval Staff is suspected of sarcasm when he suggested that the Naval Intelligence Division should set up an astrological section. See F. H. Hinsley, *British Intelligence in the Second World War*, vol. 1, p. 187.
11 A statement by Hamid Algar, a scholar of English origin who became a Muslim, working at the University of California. Reported by Nicholas Wade, in *Science*, vol. 208, 1979, pp. 1281–3.
12 Stansfield Turner, *op. cit.*, p. 92.
13 *ibid.*, p. 197.
14 *ibid.*, p. 207 and p. 60.
15 *ibid.*, p. 229–36.
16 *ibid.*, p. 95.

17 The branch of German military intelligence evaluating information about the armies of the Western Allies.

Chapter 5 (pages 107–45).

1 See H. W. Parker, *Snakes*, Robert Holt, 1963.
2 See C. Munn, *Nature*, 1985, 319, p. 143.
3 See G. W. Pietsch and D. B. Geobecker, *Science*, 201, 1978, pp. 369–70.
4 See J. E. Lloyd, *Science*, 187, 1975, pp. 452–3.
5 See Randy Thornhill, *Science*, 205, 1979, pp. 412–14.
6 *Science*, 237, 1987, pp. 650–2.
7 See Herbert Goldhamer, *Reality and Belief in Military Affairs*, Rand Corporation, 1977.
8 *Plutarch's Lives*, trans. A. H. Clough.
9 David Pritchard, *The Radar War*, p. 69, Patrick Stephens, 1989.
10 Thucydides II, 59.
11 Thucydides V, 9.
12 *The Art of War*, trans. Samuel B. Griffith, Clarendon Press, 1963.
13 Livy XXI and *XXII.*
14 *Leviathan*, ch. 13.
15 F. W. Hamilton, *History of the Grenadier Guards*, vol. II, p. 48, John Murray, 1874.
16 William Casey, *Where and How the War was Fought*, p. 101, Morrow, 1976.
17 *ibid.*, p. 329.
18 Carl Berger, *Broadsides and Bayonets*, p. 211, University of Pennsylvania Press, 1961.
19 Quoted in Allen Dulles, *The Craft of Intelligence*, p. 15, Weidenfeld & Nicolson, 1963.
20 John Lord, *Duty, Honour, Empire*, p. 332, Hutchinson, 1971.
21 Arthur Marder, *From Dreadnought to Scapa Flow*, p. 116, Oxford University Press, 1969.
22 *ibid.*, p. 150.
23 *Microcosmographica Academica*, Introduction to 2nd edn. by F. M. Cornford, Bowes & Bowes, 1922.
24 Z. A. B. Zemen, *Nazi Propaganda*, Oxford University Press, 1973.
25 See C. Cruickshank, *Deception in World War II*, p. 19, Oxford University Press, 1979.
26 See David Hunt, *Intelligence and National Security*, vol. 3, 1988, pp. 190–4.
27 Michael Handel, 'Strategic and Operational Deception in the Second World War', *Intelligence and National Security*, vol. 2, no. 3, 1987, p. 42.
28 *ibid.*, pp. 1–90.
29 D. M. Glantz, *Intelligence and National Security*, vol. 22, 1987, p. 222.
30 D. D. Langford, *War in 2080*, p. 6, Morrow, 1979.
31 i.e. $1/8 \times 4 = 1/2$.
32 *MSW*, pp. 126–78, 203–14, 250–3 and 396–9.
33 *MSW*, pp. 39–40 and 287–305.
34 ASI Report no. 10, 10 January 1942.

35 Besides the account in *Most Secret War*, further information can be found in Alfred Price's *Instruments of Darkness*, Kimber, 1967.
36 *MSW*, pp. 400–12.
37 *MSW*, pp. 420–4.
38 Alfred Price, *Instruments of Darkness*, pp. 102–3, Macdonald, 1977.
39 *British Intelligence in the Second World War*, vol. 3, Part 1, p. 516.

Chapter 6 (pages 146–160).

1 In addition, he habitually took the keenest interest in intelligence: 'it was under his inspirational leadership and in the finest hour of his long career that the previously fragmented British intelligence services achieved at last that degree of co-ordination which turned them into an intelligence community. And it was Churchill also who was the moving force in making the Anglo-American intelligence alliance which has remained ever since the most special part of the "special relationship".' (Christopher Andrew in *Intelligence and National Security*, 'Churchill and Intelligence', vol. 3, no. 3, July 1988, pp. 181–93 – the entire number of 298 pages, edited by Michael I. Handel, consists of papers on the subject of leaders and intelligence.)
2 W. S. Churchill, *The World Crisis*, abridged edition, p. 653, Macmillan, 1941.
3 W. S. Churchill, *The Grand Alliance*, p. 319, Cassell, 1960.
4 Minute to the Assistant Chief of Air Staff (Intelligence), 20 November 1942.
5 W. James, *The Eyes of the Navy*, p. 203, Methuen, 1955.
6 Falkland Islands Review, HMSO, 1983, Cmnd. 8787, p. 318.
7 *Some Aspects of the Directorate of Scientific Intelligence*, Ministry of Defence, 1952–4.
8 Herbert E. Meyer, *Real World Intelligence*, p. 7, Weidenfeld & Nicolson, 1987.
9 *ibid.*, p. 85.
10 *ibid.*, p. 80.

Chapter 7 (pages 161–84).

1 M. Crosland, *Social Studies of Science*, vol. 6, pp. 185–241, 1976.
2 See above, p. 90, in chapter 4.
3 F. M. Cornford, *Microcosmographica Academica*, Bowes & Bowes, 1908.
4 In *Universities: American, English, German*, Oxford University Press, 1930.
5 According to Guy Hartcup, *The War of Invention*, p. 69. Bralley's, 1988.
6 *MSW*, pp. 335–6 and 359–69.
7 H. Hartley, *Chemical Warfare* in British Association Report, pp. 393–402, 1919.
8 See 'The "Other Way Round" Principle' in R. V. Jones, *Instruments and Experiences*, Wiley, 1988.
9 See 'The Theory of Practical Joking' in *A Physics Anthology*, Institute of Physics, 1960.
10 *Nature*, vol. 233, 1971, pp. 527–9.

11 R. W. Clark, *Tizard*, pp. 46–7, Methuen, 1965.
12 See E. W. B. Gill, *War, Wireless and Wangles*, Blackwell, 1934.
13 Dobson, easily the best lecturer of my undergraduate days, went on to associate the warm layer with ozone, and in 1957 discovered the 'hole' in the ozone layer over Antarctica.
14 F. W. Soddy, *Science and Life*, p. 36, Murray, 1920.
15 See W. R. Hall and A. J. Peaslee, *Three Wars with Germany*, Putnam, 1944.
16 L. Badash, *Notes and Records of the Royal Society*, vol. 34, 1979, pp. 91–121.
17 See J. L. Heilbron, *H. G. J. Moseley*, California University Press, 1974.
18 Committee on the Neglect of Science: Report of Conference at Burlington House, 3 May 1916.

Chapter 8 (pages 185–209).

1 Benjamin Franklin, *Works*, vol. 7, ed. J. Bigelow, p. 85, Putnam, 1904.
2 Lord Kelvin, *Popular Lectures and Addresses*, vol. 1, p. 73, Macmillan, 1889.
3 F. Galton, *Tropical South Africa*, p. 54, John Murray, 1953.
4 *Proc. Roy. Soc., Edinburgh*, vol. 5, 1966, pp. 512–13.
5 *Quarterly Journal of the Geological Society*, vol. 25, 1869, pp. 38–53.
6 In *The Origins of Strategic Bombing*, Neville Jones, Kimber, date unknown.
7 *ibid.*
8 Letter to Nathaniel Hawes, 25 May 1964.
9 R. W. Clark, *op. cit.*, p. 37.
10 H. T. Tizard, *Journal of the United Services Institution*, vol. 41, 1946, pp. 333–43.
11 H. T. Tizard, Posthumous Note to his biographer.
12 *The Strategic Bombing Offensive against Germany*, HMSO, vol. 1, 1961.
13 John Colville, *The Churchillians*, p. 140, Weidenfeld & Nicolson, 1981.
14 See A. C. B. Lovell, *Biographical Memoirs of Fellows of the Royal Society*, vol. 21, 1975, p. 57.
15 Solly Zuckerman, *From Apes to War Lords*, p. 251, Hamish Hamilton, 1978.
16 F. I. Ordway and M. R. Sharp, *The Rocket Team*, p. 170, Heinemann, 1979.
17 *Minerva*, vol. 10, 1972, p. 115.
18 Alfred Price, *Instruments of Darkness*, pp. 113–14.
19 R. V. Jones, *Biographical Memoirs of Fellows of the Royal Society*, 'Winston Leonard Spencer Churchill', vol. 12, pp. 34–105, 1966; and *Notes and Records of the Royal Society*, 'Lindemann beyond the Laboratory', vol. 41, pp. 191–210, 1987.
20 W. S. Churchill, *The Finest Hour*, p. 382, Cassell, 1949.
21 Hansard, 7 November 1945.
22 Andrei Sakharov, *My Country and the World*, p. 73, Vintage Books, 1975.
23 Quoted by G. S. Graham in *The British Empire*, Thames and Hudson, 1970.
24 Such issues were discussed at length by R. W. Reid, in *Tongues of Conscience*, Constable, 1969.
25 Hansard, February 1940.
26 *The Strategic Air Offensive Against Germany 1939–45*, vol. IV, 1961, p. 144.

Chapter 9 (page 213–61).

1 For example, see William Stevenson, *A Man Called Intrepid*, Macmillan, 1976.
2 Vol. 1, no. 1, 1986, pp. 71–110.
3 In P. Paillole's *Notre Espion chez Hitler* (Lafont, 1985) the employee is identified as Hans Thilo Schmidt of the *Chiffrierstelle*, the German cipher centre. Colonel Paillole was in French counter-espionage, and its chief from 1940 to 1944. His is a fascinating account.
4 *MSW*, p. 269.
5 In December 1988, former agent VNAR 223 in the same network, Mme de Heusch-van den Bosch, wrote giving me additional details: André Mathy's close colleague, agent VNAR 1, Armand Delsemme, survived the war and is now a Distinguished Professor of Astronomy at the University of Toledo, Ohio.
6 Gilbert Renault, the famous Resistance leader whose contribution to the Bruneval raid is mentioned in *MSW*, pp. 236–7.
7 20,400 Spitfires were built (see Alfred Price, *The Spitfire Story*, Arms and Armour Press, 1982).
8 *MSW*, p. 426.
9 Of *MSW*.
10 A. D. Gibb, writing as 'Captain X', *With Winston Churchill at the Front*, Gowans and Gray, 1924.
11 *MSW*, pp. 12–19, 34–36 and 108–9.
12 R. W. Clark, *op. cit.*, pp. 212.
13 6, 7 and 8 April 1961.
14 See Trevor Royal, *The Kitchener Enigma*, p. 378, Michael Joseph, 1985.
15 W. S. Churchill, *The Hinge of Fate*, p. 59, Cassell, 1951.
16 German Document TSD/FOS/X.378/51 Cabinet Office.
17 John Colville, 'A brief account of the origin of the scheme which ultimately led to the establishment of Churchill College, Cambridge', July 1959.
18 See Maurice Bowr's *Memories*, Weidenfeld & Nicolson, pp. 342–3, 1966.
19 February 1982.
20 Julian Lewis, *Changing Direction*, pp. 388–405, Sherwood Press, 1988.
21 *Air Scientific Intelligence Monthly Report*, 31 July 1940.
22 Essay No. 42, *Of Youth and Age*.
23 See Francis K. Mason, *Battle Over Britain*, pp. 374 and 400, McWhirter Twins, 1969.
24 Robert Wright, *Dowding and the Battle of Britain*, p. 241, Macdonald, 1969.
25 *The Times*, 14 February 1970.
26 *ibid.*, 20 February 1970.
27 *ibid.*, 19 February 1970.
28 *ibid.*, 22 February 1970.
29 C. P. Snow, *Science and Government*, Harvard University Press, 1960.
30 *The Times*, 6, 7 & 8 April 1961.
31 H. T. Tizard, Autobiography (unpublished)
32 R. O. Gandy, Letter to the Author, 18 April 1961.
33 *ibid.*

Chapter 10 (pages 265–275).

1 See D. Irving, *The Rise and Fall of the Luftwaffe*, p. 76, Weidenfeld & Nicolson, 1973.
2 See Fritz Trenkle, *Die deutschen Funk-Navigations und Funk-Führungs-verfahren bis 1945*, p. 66, Motorbuch Verlag, 1979.
3 Vol. 10, 1931.
4 Air Scientific Intelligence Report no. 7, 'The Edda Revived', 17 July 1940.
5 See D. Irving, *op. cit.*, p. 110.
6 *MSW*, pp. 172–8.
7 Air Scientific Intelligence Report no. 11, 'The Photoelectrically Steered Bomb in Germany', 13 May 1941.

Chapter 11 (pages 276–332).

1 See Fritz Trenkle, *Die deutschen Funkenverfahren bis 1945*, p. 187, Telefunken, 1982.
2 p. 64.
3 p. 332.
4 *The Deipmosophistai*, quoted in *The Frank Muir Book*, Heinemann, 1976.
5 *The Papers of Joseph Henry*, vol. 3, p. 245, Smithsonian Institute Press, 1979.
6 *Guardian*, 21 September 1932.
7 Collier, *The Defence of the United Kingdom*, HMSO, 1957.
8 See R. B. Baldwin, *The Deadly Fuze*, p. 245, Jane's, 1980.
9 See *MSW*, pp. 22–6.
10 Alan Bullock, *Hitler, A Study in Tyranny*, p. 581, Odhams, 1952.
11 More generally he signed as 'Hans F. Mayer' or 'H. F. Mayer' to distinguish himself from others with the same Christian name and surname, and in radio circles he was appropriately nicknamed 'H.F.'.

Appendix C (page 345–50).

1 Printed in the *Listener*, 19 January 1956.
2 *Science and Technology in Western Germany. A brief review*, HMSO.

A further note on *Chapter 2*, pages 43–4.
M. Pierre Julitte has commented on the text:

One only of the members of my team is still alive – my childhood friend Philippe – and it is most unfortunate that the others will never have known for certain that they did not risk their lives in vain.

May I, just the same, in respectful friendship, object to the importance which you allot to the sacrifice to which we were exposing ourselves. In the initial French edition of my book, there is a paragraph which its translator merely skipped and which enlightens this point. It says that, as a matter of fact, our lives were already threatened to such an extent by the ordinary camp routine that our chances to survive were very few. They were somewhat like those of winning of a sweepstake ticket. And who would not buy the house of one's dreams if it were possible to pay for it with such a ticket instead of actual money?

In a more psychological way would I say that once a fear is mastered, courage is no longer needed to face the threat of torture and death.

BIBLIOGRAPHY

General

A valuable bibliography of world-wide works on many aspects of intelligence, security, deception and disinformation is *Intelligence and Espionage: An Analytical Bibliography* (Westview Press, Boulder, Colorado, 1983) by George C. Constanides. *Intelligence and National Security*, which appears quarterly and is published by Frank Cass, is an excellent source of papers on intelligence matters. Reviews of current literature can be found in *Foreign Intelligence Literary Scene*, which is a bi-monthly newsletter/news review, published by the National Intelligence Study Center in Washington.

In 1974 the Royal Society held a discussion meeting on *The Organisation and Development of Science in the United Kingdom* and the papers presented by eleven authors who had been involved in science and defence, particularly in World War II, were published in the Society's *Proceedings* A, vol. 342, 1975, pp. 439–580. A bibliography was appended in pp. 581–6 of the same volume.

After the Battle magazine contains much retrospective information concerning the Second World War. Its publishers also produce comprehensive studies such as *The Blitz Then and Now*, vol. 1, 1987.

Minerva is a quarterly journal containing authoritative articles on science, education and policy.

An international bibliography of some 1,500 items on intelligence and security in commerce and industry is available from the Department of Business Administration (Dr S. Dedijer) in the University of Lund, Post Box 5136, Lund 220 05, Sweden.

Intelligence

W. Agrell and B. Huldt, *Clio Goes Spying*, Scandinavian University Books, 1983.

C. M. Andrew, *Secret Service*, Heinemann, 1985.

W. J. Casey, *Where and How the War was Fought*, Morrow, 1976.

W. J. Casey, *The Secret War Against Hitler*, Simon & Schuster, 1989.

R. S. Cline, *Secrets, Spies, and Scholars*, Acropolis Books, 1976.

W. R. Corson and R. Crowley, *The New KGB*, Morrow, 1986.

A. Dulles, *The Craft of Intelligence*, Weidenfeld & Nicolson, 1963.

M. I. Handel (ed.), *Leaders and Intelligence*, Frank Cass, 1989.

H. Hinsley, E. E. Thomas, C. A. G. Simkins, C. F. G. Ransom, *British Intelligence in the Second World War*, vols. 1, 2 and 3, Part 1, vol. 3 Part 2, HMSO, 1981–8.
W. James, *The Eyes of the Navy*, Methuen, 1955.
D. Kahn, *Hitler's Spies*, Hodder & Stoughton, 1978.
A. Kramish, *The Griffin*, Houghton Mifflin, 1986.
D. McLachlan, *Room 39*, Weidenfeld & Nicolson, 1968.
B. Newman, *Spy and Counterspy*, Robert Hale, 1970.
R. L. Pfalzgraff, U. Ra'anan, W. H. Miberg, *Intelligence Policy and National Security*, Archon Books, 1981.
T. Powers, *The Man who kept the Secrets*, Simon & Schuster, 1979.
Stansfield Turner, *Secrecy and Democracy*, Houghton Mifflin, 1985.
R. Varner and W. Collier, *A Matter of Risk*, Random House, 1978.
Nigel West, *MI6*, Weidenfeld & Nicolson, 1983.
Nigel West, *Unreliable Witness*, Weidenfeld & Nicolson, 1984.

Intelligence Technology

C. Babington Smith, *Evidence in Camera*, Chatto & Windus, 1957.
D. Ball, *Pine Gap*, Allen & Unwin, 1988.
Andrew J. Brookes, *Photo Reconnaissance*, Ian Allan, 1975.
W. E. Burrows, *Deep Black*, Random House, 1986.
W. Gunston, *Spy Planes*, Salamander Books, 1983.
W. V. Kennedy (ed.), *The Intelligence War*, Salamander Books, 1987.

Cryptography

J. Bamford, *The Puzzle Palace*, Sidgwick & Jackson, 1983.
P. Beesly, *Very Special Intelligence*, Sphere, 1978.
P. Beesly, *Room 40*, Hamish Hamilton, 1982.
R. Bennett, *Ultra in the West*, Hutchinson, 1979.
G. Bertrand, *Enigma*, Plon, 1973.
A. Clayton, *The Enemy is Listening*, Hutchinson, 1980.
W. R. Hall & A. J. Peaslee, *Three Wars against Germany*, Putnam, 1944.
A. Hodges, *Alan Turing: Enigma*, Burnett Books, 1983.
D. Kahn, *The Codebreakers*, Weidenfeld & Nicolson, 1966.
W. Kozaczuk, *Enigma*, Arms and Armour, 1984.
R. Lewin, *Ultra Goes to War*, Hutchinson, 1978.
R. Lewin, *The Other Ultra*, Hutchinson, 1982.
J. Rohwer and E. Jäckel, *Die Funkaufklärung und ihre Rolle im 2 Weltkrieg*, Motorbuch Verlag, 1983.
B. Tuchman, *The Zimmermann Telegram*, Constable, 1959.
G. Welchman, *The Hut Six Story*, Allen Lane, 1982.
N. West, *GCHQ*, Weidenfeld & Nicolson, 1986.
F. W. Winterbotham, *The Ultra Secret*, Weidenfeld & Nicolson, 1974.
H. Yardley, *The American Black Chamber*, Faber & Faber, 1931.

Security
Andrew Boyle, *The Climate of Treason*, 2nd edn., Hutchinson, 1979.
H. Chapman Pincher, *Inside Story*, Sidgwick & Jackson, 1981.
H. Chapman Pincher, *Too Secret Too Long*, Sidgwick & Jackson, 1984.
H. Chapman Pincher, *Traitors*, Sidgwick & Jackson, 1987.
H. Chapman Pincher, *The Spycatcher Affair*, Sidgwick & Jackson, 1988.
P. and L. Gillman, *'Collar the Lot!'*, Quartet, 1980.
D. Hooper, *Official Secrets*, Secker & Warburg, 1987.
C. Ponting, *The Right to Know*, Sphere, 1985.
N. West, *MI5: British Security Service Operations 1909–1945*, Bodley Head, 1981.
N. West, *A Matter of Trust: MI5: 1945–1972*, Hodder & Stoughton, 1983.
P. Wright and P. Greengrass, *Spycatcher*, Heinemann Australia, 1987.

Deception and Surprise
J. Barton Bowyer, *Cheating*, St Martin's Press, 1980.
R. K. Betts, *Surprise Attack*, Brookings Institution, 1982.
A. Cave Brown, *Bodyguard of Lies*, W. H. Allen, 1956.
H. J. Giskes, *London Calling North Pole*, Kimber 1953.
H. Goldhamer, *Reality and Belief in Military Affairs*, Rand Corporation, 1979.
M. I. Handel, *Perception, Deception and Surprise: Yom Kippur War*, Jerusalem Papers, 1976.
M. I. Handel (ed.), *Strategic and Operational Deception in the Second World War*, Frank Cass, 1987.
E. H. Jones, *The Road to Endor*, John Lane, The Bodley Head, reprinted by White Lion, 1973.
A. Klein, *Grand Deception*, Ballantyne, 1955.
A. M. Ludwig, *The Importance of Lying*, Charles C. Thomas.
J. C. Masterman, *The Double-Cross System*, Yale University Press, 1972.
M. Mihalka, *German Strategic Deception in the 1930s*, Rand Corporation, 1980.
Ewen Montagu, *The Man Who Never Was*, Evans, 1953.
N. Moss, *The Pleasures of Deception*, Chatto & Windus, 1977.
D. Mure, *Practice to Deceive*, Kimber, 1977.
G. W. Prange, *At Dawn We Slept*, Michael Joseph, 1982.
B. Whaley, *Codeword Barbarossa*, MIT Press, 1973.
D. Wheatley, *The Deception Planners*, Hutchinson, 1980.
R. Wohlstetter, *Pearl Harbor: Warning and Decision*, Stanford University Press, 1962.

Electronic Warfare
G. Aders, *History of the German Nightfighter Force, 1917–1945*, Jane's, 1979.
R. B. Baldwin, *The Deadly Fuze*, Jane's, 1980.
U. Balke, *Kampfgeschwader 100 'Wiking'*, Motorbuch, 1981.
E. G. Bowen, *Radar Days*, Adam Hilger, 1987.
B. Johnson, *The Secret War*, BBC Publications, 1978.
A. Price, *Aircraft Versus Submarine*, Kimber, 1973.
A. Price, *Instruments of Darkness*, 2nd edn., Macdonald & Jane's, 1977.

A. Price, *The History of U.S. Electronic Warfare*, The Association of Old Crows, 1984.
D. Pritchard, *The Radar War*, Patrick Stephens, 1989.
P. Townsend, *Duel in the Dark*, Harrap, 1986.
M. Streetley, *Confound & Destroy*, Jane's, 1978.
S. S. Swords, *Technical History of the Beginnings of Radar*, Peter Peregrinus, 1986.
F. Trenkle, *Die deutschen Funkpeil- und Horch-Verfahren bis 1945*, Telefunken, 1981.
F. Trenkle, *Die deutschen Funkstörverfahren bis 1945*, Telefunken, 1981.
F. Trenkle, *Die deutschen Funkenverfahren bis 1945*, Telefunken, 1982.
F. Trenkle, *Die deutschen Funkmessverfahren bis 1945*, Hüthig, 1988.
F. Trenkle, *Die deutschen Funkführungsverfahren bis 1945*, Hüthig, 1988.
K. Wakefield, *The First Pathfinders*, Kimber, 1981.

V-Weapons
Tom Bower, *The Paperclip Conspiracy*, Michael Joseph, 1987.
B. Collier, *The Defence of the United Kingdom*, HMSO, 1957.
B. Collier, *Hidden Weapons*, Hamish Hamilton, 1982.
W. Dornberger, *V2*, Hurst and Blackett, 1954.
R. Hautefeuille, *Constructionns Spéciales*, Jean-Bernard, 1985.
W. Hellmold, *Die V1*, Bechtle, 1988.
H. D. Hölsken, *Die V-Waffen*, Deutsche Verlags-Anstalt, 1984.
D. Irving, *The Mare's Nest*, Kimber, 1964.
E. Klee and Otto Merk, *The Birth of the Missile*, Harrap, 1965.
N. Longmate, *Hitler's Rockets*, Hutchinson, 1985.
F. I. Ordway and M. R. Sharpe, *The Rocket Team*, Heinemann, 1979.
R. A. Young, *The Flying Bomb*, Ian Allan, 1978.

Atomic Weapons
L. Badash, J. O. Hirschfelder and H. T. Broda, *Reminiscences of Los Alamos 1943–1945*, Reidel, 1980.
L. Giovannitti and F. Freed, *The Decision to Drop the Bomb*, Methuen, 1967.
P. Goodchild, *J. Robert Oppenheimer*, BBC, 1980.
S. Goudsmit, *Alsos*, 2nd edn., Tomash, 1983.
M. Gowing, *Britain and Atomic Energy 1939–1945*, Macmillan, 1964.
F. Groueff, *The Manhattan Project*, Collins, 1967.
L. R. Groves, *Now It Can Be Told*, Andre Deutsch, 1963.
L. M. Libby, *The Uranium People*, Scribner's, 1979.
R. Peierls, *Bird of Passage*, Princeton University Press, 1985.
P. Pringle and J. Spigelman, *The Nuclear Barons*, Michael Joseph, 1982.

Operations
C. Bekker, *The Luftwaffe War Diaries*, Macdonald, 1966.
B. Collier, *The Defence of the United Kingdom*, HMSO, 1957.
P. Cremer, *U333*, The Bodley Head, 1984.

A. Galland, *The First and the Last*, Methuen, 1955.
W. Hackmann, *Seek & Strike*, HMSO, 1984.
M. Hastings, *Bomber Command*, Michael Joseph, 1979.
D. Irving, *The Rise and Fall of the Luftwaffe*, Weidenfeld & Nicolson, 1973.
W. E. Jones, *Bomber Intelligence*, Midland Counties Publications, 1983.
J. Lasserre (ed.), *La Bataille d'Angleterre*, *Icare* nos. 93 (1980), 95 (1981), 95 (1982).
A. Marder, *From the Dreadnought to Scapa Flow*, vol. 4, Oxford University Press, 1969.
F. K. Mason, *Battle over Britain*, McWhirter Twins, 1969.
W. Murray, *Luftwaffe*, Allen & Unwin, 1985.
J. Panton, *'Air Force Spoken Here'*, Adler & Adler, 1986.
A. Price, *Aircraft Versus Submarine*, Jane's, 1980.
W. Slim, *Defeat into Victory*, Cassell, 1956.
W. Slim, *Unofficial History*, Cassell, 1959.
P. Townsend, *Duel in the Dark*, Harrap, 1986.
R. Wright, *Dowding and the Battle of Britain*, The Military Book Society, 1969; Macdonald, 1969.
P. Wykeham, *Fighter Command*, Putnam, 1960.

Resistance and Escape
U. Béon, *La Planète Dora*, Editions du Seuil, 1989.
M. R. D. Foot, *Resistance*, Eyre Methuen, 1976.
M. R. D. Foot, *Six Faces of Courage*, Eyre Methuen, 1978.
M. R. D. Foot, *S.O.E.*, BBC Publications, 1984.
M. R. D. Foot and J. M. Langley, *MI9*, The Bodley Head, 1979.
M. M. Foucade, *L'Arch de Noé*, 2nd edn., Plon, 1982.
J. Garlinski, *Poland, SOE and the Allies*, Allen & Unwin, 1969.
J. Garlinski, *Fighting Auschwitz*, Friedmann, 1975.
P. Julitte, *Block 26*, Doubleday, 1971.
J. M. Langley, *Fight Another Day*, Collins, 1974.
J. Michel, *Dora*, Weidenfeld and Nicolson, 1979.
A. Neave, *Saturday at MI9*, Hodder & Stoughton, 1969.
A-G. Vasseur, *L'Espion du Nord*, Dilane, 1978.

Scientific Advice and Operational Research
Air Ministry, *Operational Research in the RAF*, HMSO, 1963.
J. P. Baxter, *Scientists against Time*, Little, Brown, 1946.
R. W. Clark, *The Rise of the Boffins*, Phoenix House, 1962.
F. J. Dyson, *Disturbing the Universe*, Harper & Row, 1979.
R. Feynman, *'What Do You Care What Other People Think?'*, Unwin Hyman, 1989.
R. Gilpin and C. Wright (ed.), *Scientists and National Policy Making*, Columbia University Press, 1964.
A. Goldhamer, *The Adviser*, Elsevier North-Holland, 1978.
D. G. Kevles, *The Physicist*, Vintage Books, 1979.
Gerald Pawle, *The Secret War*, Harrap, 1956.

W. W. Rostow, *Pre-Invasion Bombing Strategy*, University of Texas Press, 1981.
C. H. Waddington, *Operational Research in World War II*, Elek, 1973.
J. B. Wiesner, *Where Science and Politics Meet*, McGraw-Hill, 1965.
S. Zuckerman, *From Apes to Warlords*, Hamish Hamilton, 1978.

Government

C. Barnett, *The Audit of War*, Macmillan, 1986.
J. Colville, *The Churchillians*, Weidenfeld & Nicolson, 1981.
J. Colville, *The Fringes of Power*, Hodder & Stoughton, 1985.
M. Gilbert, *Winston S. Churchill*, vols. 3–8, Heinemann, 1971–88.
P. Hennessy, *Whitehall*, Secker & Warburg, 1989.
J. Pujol and N. West, *Operation Garbo*, Random House, 1988.
S. Roskill, *Hankey: Man of Secrets*, vols. 1, 2 and 3, Collins, 1970–4.
W. L. Shirer, *The Rise and Fall of the Third Reich*, Secker & Warburg, 1960.
A. Speer, *Inside the Third Reich*, Macmillan, 1970.

Command

J. Keegan, *The Mask of Command*, Jonathan Cape, 1987.

Credits

The author and publishers are grateful to the following for permission to quote extracts from previously published works: Martin Secker & Warburg (*Official Secrets* by David Hooper); Sidgwick & Jackson and Houghton Mifflin Co in the US (*Secrecy and Democracy* by Admiral Stansfield Turner); Cassell PLC and Houghton Mifflin Co in the US (*The Hinge of Fate* and *The Gathering Storm* both by W. S. Churchill); William Heinemann Ltd (*The Rocket Team* by F. I. Orway and M. R. Sharpe); Heinemann Australia (*Spycatcher* by Peter Wright); Harper & Row Inc. (*Distributing the Universe* by Freeman Dyson); Methuen London (*Tizard* by R. W. Clark and *The Eyes of the Navy* by Admiral Sir William James); Alfred A. Knopf Inc. (*My Country and the World* by Andrei D. Sakharov); John Murray (Publishers) Ltd (*Science and Life* by F. W. Soddy); Weidenfeld & Nicolson Ltd (*The Churchillians* by John Colville); *The Listener*; the Controller of Her Majesty's Stationery Office; Oxford University Press (*Nazi Propaganda* (1973) by Z. A. B. Zemen); Macdonald Ltd (*Dowding and the Battle of Britain* by Robert Wright); the Royal Society; *University of Edinburgh Journal*; and Frank Cass & Co. Ltd (two articles in *Intelligence and National Security*).

Index